DEMOCRATIC REFORM AND THE POSITION OF WOMEN IN TRANSITIONAL ECONOMIES

WIDER

Studies in Development Economics embody the output of the
research programmes of the World Institute for
Development Economics Research (WIDER), which was
established by the United Nations University as its first
research and training centre in 1984 and started work in
Helsinki in 1985. The principal purpose of the Institute is
to help identify and meet the need for policy-oriented
socio-economic research on pressing global and
development problems, as well as common domestic
problems and their interrelationships.

Democratic Reform and the Position of Women in Transitional Economies

Edited by

Valentine M. Moghadam

CLARENDON PRESS · OXFORD
1993

Oxford University Press, Walton Street, Oxford OX2 6DP
Oxford New York Toronto
Delhi Bombay Calcutta Madras Karachi
Kuala Lumpur Singapore Hong Kong Tokyo
Nairobi Dar es Salaam Cape Town
Melbourne Auckland Madrid
and associated companies in
Berlin Ibadan

Oxford is a trade mark of Oxford University Press

Published in the United States
by Oxford University Press Inc., New York

WIDER: World Institute for Development Economics Research (WIDER)—The
United Nations University, Annankatu 42c, 00100 Helsinki, Finland

British Library Cataloguing in Publication Data
Data available

Library of Congress Cataloging in Publication Data
Democratic reform and the position of women in transitional economies /
edited by Valentine M. Moghadam.
Includes bibliographical references.
1. Women—Europe, Eastern—Congresses.   2. Women—Former Soviet republics—
Congresses.   3. Europe, Eastern—Economic policy—1989-—Congresses.   4. Former
Soviet republics—Economic policy—Congresses.   5. Europe, Eastern—Politics and
government—1989-—Congresses.   6. Former Soviet republics—Politics and
government—Congresses.   I. Moghadam, Valentine M., 1952–
HQ1590.7.D46   1994   93–37552
305.42'0947—dc20
ISBN 0–19–828820–4

1 3 5 7 9 10 8 6 4 2

Typeset by J&L Composition Ltd, Filey, North Yorkshire

Printed in Great Britain
on acid-free paper by
Biddles Ltd, Guildford and King's Lynn

FOREWORD

The subject-matter dealt with in this book explores the implications of political and economic reform in the former state socialist countries with its main focus on gender-related issues. The chapters encapsulate the discussions and findings of a research conference that took place at WIDER in September 1991, organized by the book's editor, WIDER Senior Researcher Val Moghadam. The questions pursued in those discussions covered a range of issues affecting the socio-economic and political status of women as a result of the ongoing process of reform in the former communist countries. The transition from a centrally planned system to a market-determined economy involves a painful adjustment process, especially in the short and medium terms. Before the reform process began, the centrally planned economies were notable for the relatively favourable position held by women in the matter of employment. Not only is the adjustment process resulting in substantial unemployment among the unskilled and semi-skilled of the working population—with the result that a larger proportion of women in the labour force are being deprived of their earnings in the short run—but highly educated women seem to be losing jobs as well.

This book critically reviews the process of economic reform and democratization in country-specific situations and highlights the consequent plight of women and other vulnerable sections of the population. Several chapters address the issue of women, employment, and social policies in Hungary, Bulgaria, East Germany, the Czech and Slovak Republics, Poland, and Russia; while others deal with the question of women and politics. One chapter compares and contrasts economic reform in the former state socialist countries with structural adjustment in developing countries.

Now that the process is well under way and is an irreversible fact, can the rigours of its impact be mitigated through remedial measures? Can the provision of a general safety net, to take care of the situation arising out of the transitional unemployment, adequately meet the problems faced by the more vulnerable sections of the labour force and particularly women? What would be the international resource transfer implications of such policies? Will the dismantling of the old quota system guaranteeing a certain proportion of political representation to women lead to a decline in female participation in the process of governance in countries like the former Soviet Union? The research reported here seeks to answer these and other related questions in terms of the national, regional, and global contexts.

The study of economic reform in the former communist countries of Eastern Europe and the former Soviet Union constituted a theme of a comprehensive WIDER-sponsored project on the transformation of centrally

planned economies. This project focused on three main macroeconomic
subject areas: stabilization; restructuring and liberalization of economic
activity; and the resolution of external debt problems. By highlighting the
social costs involved and their gender dimension, this book will complement
the larger project and will contribute to the ongoing debate on policies of
economic liberalization and reform.

LAL JAYAWARDENA
Director of WIDER 1985–93

CONTENTS

LIST OF CONTRIBUTORS   ix

Introduction: Gender Dynamics of Economic and Political Change:
Efficiency, Equality, and Women   1
Valentine M. Moghadam

PART I: DEMOCRATIZATION AND WOMEN IN CENTRAL AND EASTERN EUROPE

1. Women and the Politics of Transition in Central and Eastern
   Europe   29
   Sharon L. Wolchik

2. Democratization and Women's Movements in Central and
   Eastern Europe: Concepts of Women's Rights   48
   Barbara Einhorn

3. Women in East Germany: From State Socialism to Capitalist
   Welfare State   75
   Marilyn Rueschemeyer

4. The Transition to Democracy in Bulgaria: Challenges and
   Risks for Women   92
   Dobrinka Kostova

5. Educational Attainment, the Status of Women, and the Private
   School Movement in Poland   110
   Ireneusz Białecki and Barbara Heyns

PART II: PERESTROIKA AND WOMEN IN THE SOVIET UNION

6. Gender and Restructuring: The Impact of Perestroika and its
   Aftermath on Soviet Women   137
   Gail Warshofsky Lapidus

7. Changes in Gender Discourses and Policies in the Former
   Soviet Union   162
   Anastasia Posadskaya

8. Glasnost and 'the Woman Question' in the Mirror of Public
   Opinion: Attitudes towards Women, Work, and the Family   180
   Valentina Bodrova

9. Comparative Study of Women's Work Satisfaction and Work
   Commitment: Research Findings from Estonia, Moscow, and
   Scandinavia   197
   Kaisa Kauppinen-Toropainen

PART III: ECONOMIC REFORM AND WOMEN'S EMPLOYMENT

10. Women's Economic Status in the Restructuring of Eastern
    Europe   217
    Monica Fong and Gillian Paull

11. The Changing Economic Status of Women in the Period of
    Transition to a Market Economy System: The Case of the
    Czech and Slovak Republics after 1989   248
    Liba Paukert

12. Economic Reform and Women: A General Framework with
    Specific Reference to Hungary   280
    Gordon Weil

13. Gender Aspects of Dismantling the Command Economy in
    Eastern Europe: The Case of Poland   302
    Maria Ciechocinska

14. Bringing The Third World In: A Comparative Analysis
    of Gender and Restructuring   327
    Valentine M. Moghadam

Afterword   353
Lynn Turgeon

Index   359

LIST OF CONTRIBUTORS

IRENEUSZ BIAŁECKI Institute of Philosophy and Sociology, Institute of Sociology, Warsaw.

VALENTINA BODROVA Population, Women and Family Programmes, Russian Centre for Public Opinion Research, Moscow.

MARIA CIECHOCINSKA Institute of Geography and Spatial Organization, Polish Academy of Sciences, Warsaw.

BARBARA EINHORN School of European Studies, University of Sussex.

MONICA FONG WID Regional Coordinator, World Bank, Washington DC.

BARBARA HEYNS Department of Sociology, New York University, and Institute of Philosophy and Sociology, Warsaw.

KAISA KAUPPINEN-TOROPAINEN Institute of Occupational Health, Helsinki.

DOBRINKA KOSTOVA Institute of Sociology, Bulgarian Academy of Sciences, Sofia.

GAIL LAPIDUS Berkeley–Stanford Program in Soviet Studies, University of California at Berkeley.

VALENTINE MOGHADAM Senior Research Fellow, WIDER, Helsinki.

LIBA PAUKERT Employment and Development Department, International Labour Office, Geneva.

GILLIAN PAULL Department of Economics, Princeton University, Princeton, New Jersey.

ANASTASIA POSADSKAYA Moscow Centre for Gender Studies, Russian Academy of Sciences, Moscow.

MARILYN RUESCHEMEYER Department of Sociology, Brown University, Providence, Rhode Island.

GORDON WEIL Department of Economics, Wheaton College, Norton, Massachusetts.

SHARON WOLCHIK Department of Political Science, Center for Soviet and East European Studies, George Washington University, Washington, DC.

Introduction:

Gender Dynamics of Economic and Political Change: Efficiency, Equality, and Women

Valentine M. Moghadam

Beginning in the late 1980s, perestroika in the Soviet Union and economic reform in Eastern Europe were widely analysed in terms of the profound economic and political changes they heralded for the system of state socialism. Although the wide-ranging discussions and prolific literature drew attention to interesting aspects of the problem, one category of analysis was missing from all the accounts, even those that focused on the likely social consequences of the reforms: gender. This despite the fact that two decades of feminist scholarship and women-in-development (WID) research have revealed the unique impact on women's roles and status of economic development, economic crisis, social breakdown, state formation, and juridical reorganization. Because men and women are situated differentially within systems of production and reproduction, it is necessary to examine the gender dynamics of economic and political changes. In particular, it is important to examine emerging discourses, policies, laws, and institutions pertaining to women, work, and the family.

In addition to the theoretical lacunae, there has been a neglect of a comparative perspective, with the result that certain outcomes of privatization and democratization which are regarded as 'unexpected consequences' in fact could have been predicted. In particular, the Third World experience with structural adjustment offered significant clues as to the possible social, gender, and national developmental consequences of the prescribed economic reforms in Eastern Europe. Moreover, a study of previous revolutions that have resulted in a distinctly disadvantaged position for women, such as those of Algeria and Iran, is relevant to at least one case in Eastern Europe.[1] For example, in comparing Algeria, Iran, and Poland, one finds that in all cases 'revolution' was tied up with questions of cultural and religious identity; the new leadership sought to design policy that was completely different from the policy and approach of the previous leadership; the family attachment of women was exalted; and reproductive rights of women were denied.

Such was the rationale for the UNU/WIDER conference on 'Gender and Restructuring; Perestroika, the 1989 Revolutions, and Women', which was

---

[1] The comparison of developing countries and the former state socialist countries is the subject of Ch. 14. On women and revolutions, see Moghadam (1993).

held in Helsinki on 2–3 September 1991. The conference sought to fill the
gap in existing knowledge and policy formulation by focusing on the gender
dynamics of the transition to a market economy in the former state socialist
societies.

When the conference was being organized, marketization seemed to be
weakening the position of the 'vulnerable social groups'. These groups vary
depending upon the type of society and economy, but generally they include
migrants, rural and women workers, informal urban workers, those who
frequently change jobs, the disabled, and pensioners.[2] If one compares lists
of vulnerable groups across countries, 'women' and 'women workers' are a
common feature. This is one reason for state involvement under capitalism
—to alleviate the negative effects of the market and to provide welfare and
security for citizens. In the former state socialist countries, a distinctive
feature of the female labour force—apart from its high level of educational
attainment and its high rate of salaried labour force participation—was that
women workers benefited from an array of social policies intended to allow
them to combine jobs and motherhood. It was therefore plausible to posit
that, from a market point of view, this would render women 'expensive
labour' rather than 'cheap labour', and that women workers would be
especially vulnerable to redundancy during restructuring. It also appears that
previous forms of female disadvantage—their exclusion from élite politics,
their lower income share, their double burden of productive and reproductive
work—are not so much being replaced as being intensified by the reforms
and the new policies.

This book examines the impact of economic and political changes on the
women of Central and Eastern Europe and the former Soviet Union. It looks
at and compares their roles during the state socialist era and in the post-
socialist transition in order to explain why women are among the principal
losers in the restructuring process, and offers suggestions as to how a
diminution of the status of women may be avoided.

GENDER: A SOURCE OF INEQUALITY AND A DIMENSION OF SOCIAL CHANGE

The concept of gender refers to a social relationship between men and women
predicated on the notion of difference, historically translated into inequality,
and reinforced by law, custom, and socialization. Many feminists and WID
experts implicitly or explicitly adhere to the production–reproduction scheme,
whereby the ideology of gender prescribes different roles for men and women
in production and reproduction—with women almost always attached to the

[2] See Standing (1987).

latter and tolerated or manipulated in the former. The result is that women are seen to have strong family attachment and a weak attachment to the labour force. Across the disciplines, gender analysis has informed studies of state formation, war-making, industrialization, historiography, labour markets, and contemporary 'fundamentalism'.[3] Not all of the disciplines have integrated the concept of gender in their analytic frameworks and research agendas; economics, for example, is less inclined to a systematic treatment of gender than is, say, sociology. For this reason, the study of restructuring and economic reform has tended to ignore the gender dimension.[4]

Gender ideologies and broad social changes are interactive and affect each other. If gender, like class, informs legal systems and is embedded in the operations of the world market, the state, accumulation and social conflict, then gender ideologies and structures are themselves subject to change. Changes in gender relations and the status of women, including laws about women and the family, frequently follow economic and political change, including economic development, state policies, and social or political movements. The world market, the nation-state, systems of production and distribution, and capital–labour relations impact upon gender and the status of women.

States or governments can intervene to encourage or discourage women's participation as workers in transnational corporations or in public sectors. Laws about women and the family have served to reinforce rigid gender roles, restrict women's mobility, and deny women the personal autonomy that men enjoy. In various times and places, women have been *legally* barred from certain types of work; executed for adultery; required to assume 'modest' attire; placed under special restrictions concerning their political behaviour; permitted to attend only inferior, gender-segregated schools; barred from establishing their own residences; denied the opportunity to gain credit or even to control their own income (Chafetz 1990: 69). Some revolutionary political processes have tended to affect women more positively. Despite the many forms of gender inequality that have existed under state socialism, the Bolshevik Revolution in Russia and socialist-inspired revolutions in the Third World have generally enhanced and encouraged women's role in production and public life (see Kruks *et al.* 1989). But in many other political movements, especially those inspired by religious values or right-wing nationalism, women's role in reproduction tends to be emphasized and indeed legislated by the new élites or states (see Moghadam, in press).

---

[3] See e.g. the essays in Hess and Ferree (1987). See also Moghadam (in press).

[4] See e.g. Kornai (1990); Blanchard *et al.* (1991); Collins and Rodrik (1991). An especially good collection on democratization is Szoboszlai (1991). However, like the volumes on economic reform, it does not consider gender as a dimension of social reality requiring attention or analysis.

The 1989 'revolutions' in Eastern Europe, and what Tatyana Zaslavskaya (1990) has called 'the second Russian revolution', evince a conservative cultural component, inasmuch as new discourses have emerged which emphasize women's reproductive roles and responsibility for children and the family unit. During the 1989 revolutions women's role was absolutely crucial, but it was a supporting role and women were not visible as spokespersons or high-profile members of the dissident organizations. In Poland during the Solidarity era women were largely couriers, involved in underground publishing and in sustaining the networks that were crucial to hiding underground Solidarity members. This was an important role, but one that lent itself to a reinforcement of the image of the traditional Polish mother. In the current transition in Central and Eastern Europe, although women were strongly present in the political groups and the street demonstrations that led to the downfall of the Communist parties, women's rights are everywhere being eroded, and women are being urged to restore their 'natural functions' as mothers. At the same time, the discourse of domesticity may be encouraged by the new economic facts of life. In a manner reminiscent of the liberal discourse of the Enlightenment and the French Revolution, women's family attachment is seen as natural, while women's labour force attachment during the era of state socialist construction is regarded as unnatural. Although the stress on individual rights has been justifiably acclaimed, the new 'rights' talk includes the right to choose to stay at home and the right to choose full-time motherhood. The resurgence of patriarchal discourses is a striking feature of the present transition in the former Soviet Union and in Central and Eastern Europe.

An anti-abortion movement has also emerged in some of the former communist countries (see e.g. Newman 1991: 16; Bunting 1990: 11). It may be true that abortion was practised as a form of contraception rather than as a last resort, and that abortion methods were painful and sometimes primitive. But these are probably not the principal reasons for the turn against abortion. Male legislators, motivated either by religious values or by conservative secular values which associate women with the domestic sphere, the reproduction of human life, and family, have initiated the parliamentary bills against abortion. Another explanation is that during periods of political change ideologies are constructed in direct opposition to the ideology of the anterior regime. Policies are enacted which are intended to be as different as possible from the policies of the previous regime. This is as true of Poland in 1989 as it was of Iran in 1979.[5]

[5] The similarities between Poland and Iran are especially pronounced in the anti-abortion crusade and the role of the culturally conservative religious leadership in attempts to legislate a pro-natalist policy and female domesticity. Conversely, in Romania the new leadership is quite liberal on abortion, in a marked departure from the Ceaucescu policy. Nikki Keddie notes that an important but understudied aspect of ideology is the question, 'Who is the Enemy?' against

If gender, like class, is a source of inequality, if men and women are differentially situated in the spheres of production and reproduction, and if economic and political change has gender dynamics, how exactly have democratization and the transition to the market economy affected women in Central and Eastern Europe and the former Soviet Union? The sections below draw from the chapters in this book and from discussions held at the UNU/WIDER conference in Helsinki, September 1991.

POLITICAL PARTICIPATION, DEMOCRATIZATION, AND WOMEN

Socialists and feminists have always argued that women's rights can be seen as a measure of the level of democracy and social achievement. Thus, any evaluation of the democratization process must consider the level of women's rights and what is happening to women's rights, as do several of the chapters in this volume (especially Wolchik, Einhorn, Rueschemeyer, Posadskaya, and Kostova). Although women have shared in the general cultural liberation brought in by the reforms, the balance-sheet has been at best uneven. One of the striking features of the transition is what the feminist Slavenka Drakulić and the sociologist Sonja Licht, both from the former Yugoslavia, call 'democratization with a male face'. The elimination of quotas guaranteeing a certain percentage of seats to women representatives (usually around 30 per cent under state socialism) has resulted in a greatly diminished female political presence.

Sharon Wolchik's chapter (Chapter 1) addresses the following questions. What role did women play in the collapse of communism? How have they been participating in the transition to democracy and market? How do we explain the patterns and levels of involvement that we see in both of these areas? What is the outlook for the future? She finds that, although women were involved in the protests in Czechoslovakia, Romania, and the former German Democratic Republic, very few emerged as leaders of those organizations—such as Solidarity, the Civic Forum, and Public against Violence—that led the revolutions, and those that were involved played mainly supportive roles. The role of women in dissident groups was variable; they were not so active in Poland and Hungary but were more active in the other countries in the dissident formations before 1989, such as Charter 77. Still, it came as a surprise that there were so few women members of the

whom a given ideology is chiefly directed, and she cites the work of Claude Cahen in this regard; see Keddie (1988). The participation of women in dissident politics but their absence from political structures following regime changes in Central and Eastern Europe has parallels in Algeria after independence and Iran after the revolution. Women were integral to the opposition movements but subsequently found themselves completely sidestepped in power positions or parliamentary representation.

governments or leaders of the new political parties or newly revitalized political parties in the region. Women's representation to the national parliaments decreased throughout the region. How do we explain women's exclusion from the exercise of political power? And what accounts for the resurgence of patriarchal statements emphasizing women's domestic and maternal roles?

Wolchik thinks that a large part of the answer lies in the communist period, with its uneven change in women's roles. Most dramatic were increases in women's educational access and their employment levels. But what did not change was the division of labour within the family. The 'double burden' assumed by women proved too onerous. (Indeed, Einhorn in Chapter 2 mentions a 'triple burden', which also included participation in mobilizing activities, political meetings for party members, trade union activities, voting, and so on.) Wolchik also feels that patriarchal attitudes were fostered in Central and Eastern Europe in the late communist period, when the need to take measures to increase the birth rate led many of these governments to adopt pro-natalist policies.

At the conference in Helsinki, Wolchik described an episode in the June 1990 parliamentary elections in Czechoslovakia, which is revealing of the new climate. In one of the televised debates, all the candidates from the major parties that were represented agreed that women with young children should have the opportunity to stay at home until their children reached 3 years of age. One candidate in fact took the position that all women with children under the age of 10 should be forced to stay out of the labour force. It is now possible to make such arguments.

Barbara Einhorn's chapter on gender and political change (Chapter 2) begins by noting that there has been an understandable but misguided 'total rejection of the past'. She argues that it is very important, both for women in Central and Eastern Europe and for outside analysts, not to eradicate what went before but to evaluate it very carefully. Einhorn examines the legacy of state socialism with regard to women's rights, including the theoretical framework and its limitations, the legislation itself, and the contradictions between legally enshrined rights and the everyday reality for women. Her chapter also examines the role of ideology in reinforcing the importance of the family and the private sphere as women's prime area of responsibility; this is contrasted with a feminist attempt in the West to break down the public–private boundary in relation to implementing women's rights. She then considers the role of reproductive rights, questions about women's autonomy, and the current attacks on abortion rights. Finally, she compares and contrasts the state socialist official women's organizations and the newly formed grass-roots women's groups. Despite their positive role in the earlier stages of state socialism, the official women's organizations later became paper organizations and it is in the latter years that they became discredited.

Like Wolchik, Einhorn is concerned about the drop in women's representation in formal political structures in the first democratic governments. In the state socialist system, a certain level of female participation in formal political structures was guaranteed by quotas. Einhorn notes that, when the Independent Women's Association was formed in the former GDR, it demanded quotas. But this was ignored. The current relative lack of female representation in the parliaments and governments in Central and Eastern Europe is a handicap when it comes to articulating, defending, and promoting women's rights on the political agenda. Most of the political parties and politicians of the current transition period do not think that women's rights are important (including the women politicians), and most of the parties do not have a policy for women. Einhorn notes several times that the very rights that women enjoyed under state socialism are now operating against their interests. For example, the right to paid sick leave to look after children is being used as a reason to dismiss women first as unreliable workers.

Marilyn Rueschemeyer's chapter (Chapter 3) stresses the loss of social benefits and the high unemployment facing women in the former German Democratic Republic. In the communist era, women's complaints in the GDR revolved around what is now a familiar theme: the difficulties of integrating work and family life, even with the expansion of day-care centres in the 1960s and housing availability in the 1970s and 1980s. But state socialist supports made it possible for women to say that there is life without the family, and thus a considerable number of women in the GDR chose not to marry. It is important to reiterate the fact that under state socialism few women were in the highest leadership positions, although a third of all middle-level positions were held by women in industry, in the university, and in politics. The new local governments do not have the financial resources to pay for many of the social benefits, the cultural facilities, and the supports that women enjoyed before.

Women in Eastern Germany have been seriously affected by high unemployment, resulting from unification and privatization. GDR women were strongly represented in light industry, textiles, and clothing, and also in electronics, chemistry, and plastics. These are the industries that have been adversely affected by unification, unlike the male-dominated fields of construction and transportation, which are receiving support. Better educated women often filled administrative positions, many of which were related to the central economy and are likely to be decimated. Women were also involved in cultural institutions and publishing houses, many of which have now closed down. It is likely that training quotas for young women will no longer apply. Anticipation of difficulties with day-care and concern about the primary wage-earner provide employers with good excuses to turn women applicants down and choose men instead. The preference for hiring men is combined with the expectation that women will take care of the family matters. This attention also reinforces the traditional notions of the gender division of labour.

How are women responding to the loss of benefits and the new emphasis on domesticity? Einhorn reports that in the immediate post-communist period there was a kind of complacency, whereby women took for granted the rights they previously enjoyed, and at the same time a passivity in the face of the withdrawal of many of these rights. These new 'facts of life' are being accepted because of an apparent rejection of the over-politicization of everyday life under state socialism, as well as pervasive disillusionment and cynicism. Rueschemeyer finds that unskilled women workers, unenthusiastic about their work, responded positively to the new sentiments; factors that made it difficult to combine work and family commitments—location of day-care centres and work-places, access to markets, and attitudes of the men they lived with—made domesticity more attractive. However, many other women recognized that individual women's lives were affected by their participation in work, and that the work-place, especially for the more skilled occupations, did empower women by giving them confidence and independence, as well as providing financial resources and a community outside the home. Polls suggest that, even if women do want to reduce their work hours, most would not consider leaving the work-place altogether. Only 3 per cent described 'housewife' as a desired occupation.

Similar results are reported by Dobrinka Kostova and Liba Paukert. Kostova (Chapter 4) relates that, in many enterprises where lay-offs of fully half the female work-force were expected, a lot of women had thought that other enterprises would hire them immediately, and so they left before the actual lay-off. They did not realize that, according to the compensation law, no compensation is forthcoming if the employer does not initiate the lay-off. Thus, in 1991 some 40 per cent of the women did not receive any compensation, even though they were unemployed.

To summarize and conclude this section, why have women become invisible in the new political structures of democratic Central and Eastern Europe? Is part of the explanation to be found in the type of political activities in which women were engaged during communism, which may have been more 'formal' than 'real' political participation? Einhorn and Rueschemeyer point out that, at least with respect to the former GDR, women's political participation was more 'real' but tended to be at a local government level. Dobrinka Kostova of Bulgaria stressed that women's participation 'was not real at all' during communism, and that 'women's participation now in our countries is invisible'.

It may very well be that politial change is biased against women in that the male–female time budget is so different. Dorothy Rosenberg, who was in the GDR between November 1989 and September 1990, noted that women had to go home at some point in the evening and could not stay until three in the morning to plan and talk about politics. After all, someone has to look after the children and take family responsibilities—and it is invariably the mother rather than the father. These are among the gender dynamics—and gender biases—of politics.

ECONOMIC REFORM AND WOMEN'S EMPLOYMENT

Throughout Central and Eastern Europe, the transition to a market economy has caused much unemployment in a region where full employment was a central tenet of socialist doctrine. 'Shock therapy' was applied in 1990 in Poland, with rather disastrous consequences—unemployment surged and output fell. The end of subsidies and price controls in Russia has resulted in severe hardships for citizens. As in developing countries undergoing IMF-prescribed stabilization and structural adjustment, restructuring in the former state socialist countries entails austerity measures and belt-tightening.

A striking feature of nearly all countries undergoing 'economic reform' is that most of the newly unemployed are female. The chapter by Monica Fong and Gillian Paull (Chapter 10) outlines the various effects of the labour market on women from a perspective of supply and demand of labour. They note that throughout Eastern Europe unemployment has emerged in substantial numbers or risen from previous low levels across the region. In proportion to their labour force participation, women are over-represented among the unemployed, and in most countries they constitute more than half of the unemployed. Available evidence on re-employment possibilities in Hungary and Poland suggest that women are likely to remain unemployed for longer periods than men. If this pattern continues, the share of women among the unemployed can be expected to increase substantially in the future, as new unemployed are added to the pool of unemployed women and most remain there. For this reason, Fong and Paull stress the need for strategic intervention—'proactive measures'—to protect women and indeed to increase efficiency.

Fairly extensive maternity and child-care leaves, return rights to employment after such leaves, and company provision for crèches and kindergartens have facilitated the employment of women with small children in most East European countries. In Hungary, mothers worked on the average 50 per cent of the standard working hours as a result of their legal concessions and leave taken for children's illnesses. The direct cost of such provisions to the company in terms of expenditure, as well as the indirect costs of, say, keeping employment open during child-care leaves or work lost to care for sick children, were of minor significance to a state socialist enterprise. In post-reform conditions, however, such costs can no longer be borne by profit-maximizing enterprises, which will contract for the cheapest qualified labour.

For women, the development of a government-run social insurance system is therefore one of the priorities on the reform agenda.

This need is vividly illustrated in the chapter on Poland by Maria Ciechocinska (Chapter 13). She underscores a correlation between the large number of child-care institutions and the low numbers of mothers on child-care leaves; conversely, cities and towns in Poland with the lowest number of child-care institutions had the highest percentages of women workers on child-care leaves. Thus, one can easily predict a situation in which greater numbers and larger percentages of women will become 'domesticated' as child-care institutions are either closed down or become prohibitively expensive as privatization proceeds. This is a major reason why, as Ciechocinska puts it, women 'are paying a higher price for the transformations now taking place'. The difficulties are also of a generational type, for older women are becoming redundant in the years leading up to retirement. Those who are regarded as having the loosest attachment to the labour force are the most vulnerable. And it is invariably women, no matter what their stage in the life-course.

The transition to a market economy has not only gender and class implications but also generational implications, which have not been properly appreciated. One is that in Eastern Europe we are seeing a backlash against child care by the first generation who were themselves in child care, as Barbara Einhorn suggests, and as Valentina Bodrova also mentions in Chapter 8. A second implication is that, where there was inadequate and uneven distribution of child-care facilities, such as in Poland and the Soviet Union, the grandmother had a central role; she will now be made redundant if the mother comes home to look after the children. Dobrinka Kostova's chapter (Chapter 4) discusses the negative demographic trends in terms of the falling, negative birth rate and emigration, but she also mentions pension rights. Under state socialism, women had the right to retire earlier and could enjoy 20 years of retirement in relative comfort. But now, in the transition to the market economy, they could become poverty-stricken. Moreover, the right to paid sick leave is another reason why women are the first to be made redundant as 'unreliable workers'. Rights to maternity leave militate against a woman's re-employment, for it means that the employers prefer men in newly privatized enterprises or in state enterprises that are struggling to become profitable. Once again, this illustrates the fact that the rights that women enjoyed under state socialism are now operating to their disadvantage.

At the conference in Helsinki, Monica Fong made an interesting rhetorical point. Throughout Eastern Europe (with the exception of Poland and Romania, where fertility is slightly above replacement), women have fewer than two children per head. If they finish their education when they are 20 and work until they are 60 (assuming that retirement age will increase in the years to come), they have approximately 40 years in the labour force.

With fewer than two children, usually fairly closely spaced, one would expect perhaps ten years maximum that they would devote to family and to child care, or 25 per cent of their adult working lives. Why is it then that childbirth and child care affect all women's working lives over a period of 40 years? The answer must be sought in ideology, and in particular gender ideology.

Kostova reports that in Bulgaria it was not the norm for grandmothers to look after children because the kindergarten facilities were more than adequate; they were very cheap, they operated for the whole day, and, according to Kostova, they were beneficial to the child developmentally. With rising female unemployment and the end of state-subsidized kindergartens, many women will have to remove their children from the kindergartens. This may mean the return of the grandmother. Kostova mentions another possibility—the return to a patriarchal situation in which women stay at home and become economically dependent on their husbands.

Gordon Weil's chapter provides a conceptual model for the analysis of women's well-being (Chapter 12). He argues that it is composed of two elements; productive activities and reproductive activities. What determines productive success are safe, secure, sufficient, and satisfying income-earning opportunities. Those are determined by three basic factors: gender relations, economic conditions, and economic policy. In the case of Eastern Europe, economic policy has consisted of 'economic reform', or the transition from central planning to a market economy. He then focuses on Hungary, which has had the longest period of economic reform.

Like other state socialist countries, Hungary had impressive levels of female educational attainment, with tertiary education of women exceeding that of men. But men and women tended to enter different fields of study: women tended to study liberal arts, health, economics, and business, while men took up sciences and engineering. Another investment in human capital was through vocational training and adult education. Although women were not absent from vocational schooling, it tended to be male-dominated. Men studied to be machine operators and vehicle mechanics, and women studied textiles, fashion, restaurants, and so on. Hungary had very high labour force participation rates for both men and women, undoubtedly a result of the communist period. In 1988 some 82 per cent of women between the ages 15 and 55 were employed. As a result of educational and vocational tracking, women were more prevalent in non-manual, white-collar occupations than in manual blue-collar occupations, while three-quarters of men went into blue-collar activities and only about a quarter into white-collar jobs. This is the major source of the wage gap. Wages in heavy industries, where men predominate, have been higher, because heavy industry has been the focus of investment and development and the 'industrial proletariat' is a high-status class. Heavy industry was prioritized by all of the state socialist countries, and jobs in mining and the steel industry were highly remunerated; but these were dominated by men. The earnings differential can also be explained by the fact that women retire earlier from the labour force and that the average age is younger and the average tenure shorter.

In recent years Hungary has joined the International Monetary Fund (IMF) and submitted to a stabilization and adjustment programme to control inflation and restore fiscal balances. Trade and price liberalization were elements of economic reform. Weil then addresses the question of the impact of these macroeconomic aspects of the reform on women. Although unemployment will affect all workers, cultural perceptions that lead women to be the last hired and first fired will certainly mean that they will be particularly hard hit. In Hungary, the elimination of subsidies to mining and energy will hurt men more than women, as these were male-dominated sectors. On the other hand, fiscal entrenchment attempts to restore fiscal balance will certainly hurt women, who are in the service sectors that are dependent on government spending, such as education, health, libraries, and so on.

How does reform affect women in their reproductive roles? Although women's labour-force participation rates grew during the communist period, their reproductive duties did not shrink. Compared with many Western countries, Hungary offered considerable support for women in their reproductive activities. This included a large transfer payment system for child support, a twenty-four-week maternity leave, a birth allowance, mother's wages, and family support. The result was that almost 90 per cent of new mothers stayed at home. Another support for women in their reproductive activities is the institutional support—crèches, kindergartens, and day care. This differs philosophically from maternity supports, and it remains to be seen how continuing marketization will affect the network of institutional supports.

Weil foresees a deteriorating situation for women, although he is more sanguine about the long-term prospects. As new opportunities arise, women need to take advantage of them. But to do so they need a voice in the public sphere, in community organizations, and in trade unions.

Liba Paukert of the International Labour Office (ILO) explains that her organization has extended its technical co-operation activities in the countries of Central and Eastern Europe quite considerably since 1989 (Chapter 11). Technical co-operation was developed in many different fields, such as labour legislation, tripartism, employment services, social security, and labour market policies. In Czechoslovakia, a project on 'Women in the Labour Market: Plan of Action during the Transition to a Market System' was launched in 1990 and was among the first ILO technical co-operation projects implemented in that country. The project had four parts. First was a survey on women in the labour market, showing women's labour market attachment, their knowledge of how to cope under market economy conditions, and their willingness and likelihood to start a small private business. The second part of the project consisted of an action through the media, explaining to the public, and particularly to women, how to cope under the new conditions, what to do in case of loss of employment, and how to contact the project's offices for consultancy services and small business training. The third part consisted of training courses on the running of a small business, carried out through a network of training centres located in most districts of the country. Finally, consultancy services were organized in the two capitals, Prague and Bratislava. The project ran until the end of 1992.

Paukert found many misconceptions about women in the labour market during the transition. There was a widespread sense of complacency. In reality, women's unemployment was greater than men's, it had grown faster, it was higher in every region of the country with the exception of eastern Slovakia, and the widening of the gap between male and female unemployment seemed likely to continue. Women had been losing jobs in favour of men even in some formerly 'female' branches. Another cause for concern was the lower integration of women in small business activities. Small business has started largely on a part-time basis. It has developed from the mostly illegal or only partly legal moonlighting activities before the change of system, which have since become part-time jobs, and women tended to be excluded from that sphere because of the well-known double-burden problem. At present, the small private business sector still employs noticeably fewer women than men, mainly because of women's relative lack of access to credit and to business premises. Additional obstacles are the long hours required in the private sector and, arguably, women's unwillingness to tackle the excessive bureaucracy of the transition period.

In spite of some labour discouragement which appeared with the growing unemployment, most women still have a strong labour attachment. In response to a survey question, 'If your husband's or partner's income increased significantly, would you consider staying at home and leaving the labour market?' only 28 per cent of women said 'yes'.

In the future, the main shift in the occupational structure should be towards services. Apart from small business, employment should grow in banking, insurance, commercial services and tourism. Training will be required in these branches and should be developed rapidly. In this respect, useful lessons could be drawn from the ILO project's training scheme, especially concerning the form of training courses, the level of curricula, and the time schedule best suited to the needs of Czech and Slovak women under the conditions of economic transition.

EDUCATION–EMPLOYMENT LINKAGES

All the chapters note the high levels of female employment and educational attainment in the state socialist era. In addition to regular schools and universities, there was widespread vocational training and adult education. The result is one of the most educated work-forces in the world, with high female shares not only in medicine and law, but also in architecture and economics. The tables in Chapter 10 by Monica Fong and Gillian Paull, particularly Table 2, which presents the percentage of females in higher education by subject, illustrate the very well-known fact that women in the former communist countries are well represented in the sciences, maths, and medicine. Indeed, in Albania, Poland, and Yugoslavia, women's share in the natural sciences and mathematics was about 61–62 per cent. A major accomplishment of the communist regime was the expansion of both labour-force participation and women's roles in economy and society, although gender inequality existed in various ways. The jobs and roles that were filled by women throughout this period were not necessarily those of the highest prestige or power, but women were substantially more likely to move into professional roles as a result of their access to higher education.

The educational benefits that accrued to women under communism is the focus of the chapter on Poland by Ireneusz Białecki and Barbara Heyns (Chapter 5). They began their research by asking the following question: when educational systems expand, do they provide greater opportunity to low-income and low-status groups? In every European and Western country study the answer has been no. Expanding education does give more educational opportunities to everyone, but the ordering and the relative priorities of those do not really change. Low-income youths are more likely to get more education, but they are still behind and in the same proportionate level to the middle class and élites. Even though a kind of logic for expanding educational systems has been to provide greater opportunity, the very best evidence suggests that they do not equalize opportunities at all. Białecki and Heyns pose the same question for state socialist societies: to what extent did expanding education change the probabilities and the likelihood of obtaining higher education, any education, or some level of education?

Looking at forty years' experience with different cohorts and different patterns of attainment in Poland, these authors find that the relationship between parental status and the educational status of children is unchanged, and is as unequal at the end of the system as it was at the beginning. But they also discover interesting gender dynamics. Despite an ideological and structural commitment to increase educational opportunities for the proletariat and for the peasantry, the state socialist education system had a dramatic effect on gender differences. In Poland, the *lyceum*, which was the traditional and remained the best route to higher education, became increasingly feminized. In the 1980s women comprised 70–80 per cent of students in the *lyceum*.

In the developed West, women have become an integral part of the university community, at least since the 1960s, and gender-balanced higher education is becoming increasingly the norm. However, equal access to higher education was attained in Eastern Europe and the Soviet Union at a much earlier period and much more quickly. The educational attainment of women expanded throughout the communist countries much more directly and much more quickly than did that of men. Moreover, this occurred in Eastern Europe and the Soviet Union without a feminist movement. For the Polish case, Białecki and Heyns explain this as an unintended consequence of policies directly involved in expanding vocational and technical schools as opposed to supporting the kind of education that leads into the university and other élite programmes.

Under state socialism, the humanistic, non-vocational, and ultimately non-technical kinds and branches of education became feminized—as did the non-technical professional and administrative positions. The rewards or the returns to this education were not necessarily greater, however, because industrial occupations were more highly remunerated. In the West, in contrast, these positions were highly paid, well rewarded, and also recruited from the educated strata; but they remain dominated by males.

How will the transition from a command economy to a market economy affect both the market position of women in general and the position of the professionals in those fields that have become feminized? Heyns and Białecki explain that in education, as in most fields, the whole process of transition has meant fundamentally questioning all aspects of state policy before the transition, including intentions and outcomes. The new discourse stresses markets, greater choice, and the 'decolonization' and 'democratization' of education, and its separation from state control. It should be noted that in June 1991 the Polish government was unable to pay teachers in the state sector. Ironically, in the West we have come to expect state-provided education, and to regard education as a fundamental aspect of social provision for the next generation.

Given that state socialist societies tended to rationalize the link between schooling and employment, interesting questions arise about how markets affect these linkages as well as the system of provision of education that is rather unique. The transition to a market economy will almost certainly change the educational and training patterns that prevailed for the children (mainly sons) of the labouring class. About half of the vocational programmes were actually run by and organized through state enterprises. They constituted a kind of an apprenticeship which led directly to a job within the firm. These programmes are rapidly being abandoned. State enterprises no longer want to subsidize vocational education, for it is costly even though it provided a kind of low-cost labour pool to enterprises. Hence vocational programmes of all sorts, which were largely male and attached to state firms, are being abandoned. This loosens the ties between education and jobs, making it more like the United States, but in particular it affects young males. Vocational schools in the television industry, in food processing, in textiles, and especially in heavy industry have closed. The first programmes eliminated were those in heavy industry, which were disproportionately male. This may increasingly put pressure on secondary education and on the *lyceum* to become more male-oriented.

If the vocational schools are to be phased out, this may prove to have been another ill-considered aspect of restructuring. It will surely undermine the competitiveness of Polish skilled labour and Poland's industrial products and services, compared with, for example, France and Germany, which continue to invest in their vocational training systems.[6]

In 1991 there were 47 new international business schools in Warsaw, with programmes offering education, retooling, marketing, accounting, business, English, and courses in capital accumulation for the budding entrepreneur. Among the applicants were large numbers of women with administrative and managerial backgrounds in state firms, and with degrees in economics and business. But the new schools prefer men, and their directors will say as much. Białecki and Heyns report that a number of the new schools have discovered that the best way to obtain the preferred 60–70 per cent male composition is to limit the programmes to high-level managers in current state firms. If this gender bias is not checked, it seems likely that such programmes will become increasingly male.

Given that Polish women dominated in business, accountancy, foreign languages, and computer skills, one would expect that they would be at an advantage in a market economy. But according to Białecki, now that business and accounting are profit-making and central to the new market economy, these jobs will become predominantly male. In other words, men will move into previously feminized professions as they become lucrative. Dobrinka Kostova expects the same to happen in Bulgaria. This raises an interesting question regarding medicine, formerly highly feminized but not paid as highly as manual work: will men come to dominate the field as medicine becomes more 'Western'—that is, a high-status and high-income profession?

It appears that many women with higher education now accept jobs that do not require university education at all. Kaisa Kauppinen-Toropainen (Chapter 9) wondered why it was that so many women with such a high degree of education in fields that appear to be needed are not being transferred into the new jobs. The answer seems to be gender bias. Women's qualifications are not being accepted, and women themselves accept less qualified positions out of the need simply to earn money and survive. Women are taking jobs for which they are completely overqualified. This may have occurred in the past as well, presumably in the interest of combining jobs

---

[6] A recent newspaper article describes the contemporary debate on vocational training in unified Germany. See Tomforde (1992: 12).

and domestic life. But if women are ready to work even as cleaners in order to earn a living, as Kostova says is the case in Bulgaria, then this is specific to the transition to the market economy.

Overqualification for jobs during the transition period may also be true for men, but for women the transition, including any period of unemployment, could be far more dangerous to their career path or seniority. We have experience in the West, especially in the United States, that when a woman steps out of her career path and accepts a lower-level position—or takes time off for domestic responsibilities—it is very difficult for her to be reaccepted at the previous position.

As Kaisa Kauppinen-Toropainen notes, mathematics and the sciences 'were not male-labelled' as they have been in the West, where women's so-called 'maths anxiety' has been a psychological barrier to women's entry into technical and scientific fields. Consequently, these fields lack a 'female viewpoint' in the West. She wonders if Westernization will result in a reduced movement of women towards mathematics and the sciences.

THE CASE OF THE FORMER SOVIET UNION

The chapters by Anastasia Posadskaya, Valentina Bodrova, Gail Lapidus, and Kaisa Kauppinen-Toropainen all discuss the contradictions of gender under communism and during the transition. Gail Lapidus (Chapter 6) looks at the historical legacy in terms of factors that have influenced women's roles in the former Soviet Union—including the Marxist-Leninist theory of the family, the economic organization of society, political factors such as the Stalinist legacy, the impact of industrialization, and changes in politics—and their influence on patterns of women's employment. She examines the interrelationship or what she calls interdependency of women's work and family roles, emphasizing some of the contradictions in women's situation. Women's work roles are influenced by their family roles—or, as she puts it, women's family roles intrude into the workplace and are accommodated by it. The policies that were adopted under Brezhnev would most certainly fall into the patriarchal conceptions as discussed by Posadskaya (Chapter 7). Attempts to improve women's situation were based quite clearly on the notion that women's primary role was domestic and maternal, that those roles needed to be accommodated, and that it was women's job to do the juggling and the accommodating.

In Kaisa Kauppinen-Toropainen's comparative study of work commitment and work satisfaction (Chapter 9), women engineers in Estonia and Moscow reported few cases of sexual harassment (as opposed to the experiences of American women engineers interviewed in the Detroit area), perhaps because cross-gender interaction in such professional fields is more common in the

former Soviet Union. Indeed, fully 58 per cent of all engineers in the former
USSR were female, compared with 3 per cent in the United States, 7 per
cent in Finland, and 8 per cent in Sweden. But women engineers reported
significantly less job satisfaction than those surveyed in Scandinavia and in
Detroit. On the other hand, most women medical doctors in Moscow were
satisfied with their work—even though Kauppinen-Toropainen found that
they earned 25 per cent less than their male colleagues.

Posadskaya develops a framework within which she discusses past and
present discourses and policies on women and on gender. She calls these
discourses the patriarchal and the egalitarian. The patriarchal discourse is
gaining ground in a context of unemployment and immiseration in the former
Soviet Union, including the end of state-sponsored crêches. And in this
context, women are not regarded as relevant recruits in the modernized and
privatized sectors of the economy. Unemployment figures for 1991 revealed
that women with higher or secondary technical education are the majority of
those losing their jobs. Some 55–75 per cent of those applying to the new
job centres are women. Women now form the majority of the unemployed;
the enterprises use their new economic independence to close down their
own pre-school facilities for children, and the emerging labour market is dual
and unfavourable to women. Moreover, the whole concept of employment
and of labour is changing.

Posadskaya concludes on a sad note: perestroika and its successor,
marketization, have become a masculine project of restructuring. The
women's perspective is excluded from policy-making and women do not
participate in the process of power or resource distribution. The public and
private spheres are being defined as men's and women's realms, respectively,
and the institution of the family is used as a tool for excluding women.
Can this be called democracy? 'Democracy is not democracy without the
recognition of gender', says Posadskaya.

The chapter by Valentina Bodrova (Chapter 8) reports the results of several
public opinion polls undertaken by her institute in Moscow in 1989 and 1990.
The surveys on attitudes toward women, work, and family do not reveal any
pattern of distribution by age group, by educational attainment level, or by
any of the factors that we tend to associate with those attitudes when we look
at what we call conservative or reactionary or patriarchal attitudes in the
West. We tend to assume that younger groups will be more progressive on
the women question, and there is much evidence to show that in younger
marriages or younger partnerships men do seem to be assuming more
domestic responsibility. But this does not seem to be the case in the former
Soviet Union. Gender prejudices seem to be extremely strong there. This is
surprising, given the years of state socialism which has concentrated on the
emancipation of women. It appears that changes at the level of the economic
base and changes at the level of culture or ideology need not always

correspond.[7] Why this is so would be the subject of another theoretical and empirical exercise. For the moment, the relevant lesson is the need to distinguish analytically between emancipation in the public sphere and emancipation in the private sphere, and to make child care and domestic work more gender-equitable. If the double burden on Soviet women was intolerable, surely the solution is not to remove them from the sphere of production and relegate them to the sphere of reproduction; the feminist and egalitarian approach mentioned by Posadskaya, and apparently endorsed by at least some members of Soviet society, as reported by Bodrova, is the more just and arguably more efficient solution.

The British sociologist David Lane is the author of many studies on the former Soviet Union, focusing on the stratification system and employment structure.[8] At the conference in Helsinki he served as discussant but also spoke briefly on the social consequences of perestroika and marketization in the former Soviet Union. According to Lane, perestroika is a wager on the strong; it is based on market policy and the monetarization of relationships. This will lead to generally greater social differentiation and greater differentials; in theory, what the market will pay will be an important determinant of returns, particularly monetarized returns. None the less the market is itself shaped by other institutional factors. There is no perfect market; for in all societies, to some extent or other, market forces are shaped or restrained through other institutions in the society, including the state and the uneven forces of civil society.

Restructuring in the former Soviet Union has brought about a greater exchange of labour for money, greater monetarization of the labour market, and the growth of inflation. According to the World Bank, inflation in the former Soviet Union in 1991 was in the 150–170 per cent range; in early 1992 it was over 200 per cent. Clearly, inflation will be rapid and high. Both of these tendencies—the greater monetarization of labour services and inflation—will affect those workers who sell their labour, who are in the worst market position. A valid generalization is that the worse the market position, the greater will be the decline in purchasing power of those groups compared with other groups. These two policies will lead at one end to unemployment and poverty. This is due partly to a social infrastructure lacking social security, social insurance programmes, or a supporting ideology for the development of social security. At the other end, there will develop the idea of social differentiation and the fact of social inequality, as people who are able to sell their services or activities or goods on the market acquire higher incomes or profits. The growth of a business class will certainly follow, and

---

[7] To paraphrase Marx in the *Eighteenth Brumaire*, the traditions of the dead generations weigh heavily on the minds of the living.

[8] Among Lane's books are *Soviet Labour and the Ethic of Communism* (1987), *Labour and Employment in the USSR* (1986), and *Soviet Society under Perestroika* (1992).

already one can find articles on the rise of the numbers of millionaires in Moscow. In Poland and some of the other East European societies, there are now far greater differentials through the market than existed before. Although there is much publicity given to the privileges of the *nomenklatura*, the privileges that one can get through the market and through private capital in the West are far greater than any member of the *nomenklatura* ever enjoyed.

In this context of monetarization and marketization, what kinds of groups will have a stronger market position? Who will be the winners and losers? The Soviet so-called intelligentsia believes that it is in a much stronger market position than other groups of the population, and it is probably right. The term 'intelligentsia' is ambiguous, but certainly there are groups within the intelligentsia that in the West are called the professional classes and that have a stronger market position. They are in a better position to sell their labour, they are much more flexible, they are better educated, they know the market, they know what opportunities are available; they have the cultural capital, including connections and networks in addition to knowledge, and the possibilities of raising capital to put themselves in a strong position with regard to the market. For example, a greater professionalization of goods and services will follow, which will be entirely new to the former Soviet Union. Those groups can take advantage of monetarization and marketization to establish themselves in the market economy and the new occupational hierarchy.

As for the workers and the peasantry, they are disadvantaged because of a lack of real unionization. Of course, to some extent the Communist Party represented the interests of these particular groups, certainly under Brezhnev. But with the party dismantled, an important voice for manual labour has been lost in so far as the official trade unions have not been very effective, and do not have a great deal of support. The present 'free unions' are rather poorly organized, do not have a great deal of support, and have very little political clout. Lane concludes that the working class and the peasantry, and within them women, will pay the disproportionate cost of the move to marketization.

What of social mobility? Will the system be more open? Will we witness a democratic pluralism in the democratic evolution, a democratic mobility? Lane doubts this. What is most likely is that groups that are already advantaged by virtue of their relationship to the administrative system will capitalize on this and will move on to the similar market positions. This has already been observed in Eastern European countries where those who had leading positions in the state have been able to undertake similar activities in the market system. If these people are in their fifties, their children are in a good position to benefit. Another possibility is that those people who are at the lower levels of the administrative system, and people who have been working in the shadow economy, may benefit from marketization. Clearly there will be a shift from public employment to private employment, and this will create a distortion in the labour market in so far as the financial restrictions, such as increasing inflation and the greater involvement of the World Bank, will certainly lead to reductions in public expenditure and this will affect greatly people who are employees in the public sector.

Was the original intent of perestroika privatization and greater marketization? Lane feels that the groups that were in the old cabinet of ministers, that is to say the centre of the state bureaucracy, intended to move not towards the privatization of capital and the development of individual small enterprises, but rather towards public corporations on the model of the British Motor Corporation, Renault, British Railways, British Coal, and so on. Rapid privatization was the 'radical' alternative espoused by Yeltsin and his associates in the 'democratic' movement. This may explain why the West had been rather reluctant to support Gorbachev; he was seen as not enough of a free marketeer but rather an advocate of a less radical transformation of the Soviet state socialist system. The decline of Gorbachev and rise of Yeltsin has resulted in the destruction of the previous system, although at the time of writing (1992) a new system has not yet taken root. The explicit goal is the development of a thoroughly privatized socio-economic system with the selling off of national assets and encouragement of foreign investment.

In conclusion, the people in the traditional state sectors—the health, education, and welfare areas—will fare worse and those people who are in the new private enterprise sector will do better. One can foresee greater differentiation of the population, with the growth of a rich business class at one end and, at the other, the growth of poverty on a scale that has been unknown in the Soviet Union up to now.

WHAT IS TO BE DONE?

David Lane's assessment of marketization in the former Soviet Union, and the evidence in the chapters of this book, confirm our initial hypothesis that working women would be most adversely affected by the dismantling of state socialist institutions and the transition to a market economy. Cultural constructions of gender that assign to women responsibility for child care, shopping for food, preparation of meals, mending of clothes, and the myriad other tasks associated with domestic labour result in a structurally disadvantaged position for women, especially in labour markets, the occupational structure, and the career ladder. Women's reproductive capacities have also historically rendered them vulnerable to the manipulations of demographers and social engineers, who at various times discourage or encourage natalism. In the context of economic difficulties arising from the transition to a market economy, and in the context of rising nationalism and xenophobia,

women's maternal and reproductive roles are being exalted. This is a most
pernicious situation for women.

It is clear that strategic interventions are necessary to ensure both fairness
for women and proper utilization of female human resources. Interventions
are needed in two areas in particular: the labour market and the political
system. In the labour market, efforts are needed to protect low-income
working mothers, single mothers, and single women without family support.
For the unemployed and the most vulnerable groups a social safety net is
requisite. Social policies are needed to help women more easily combine
motherhood and jobs; if this necessitates a re-adoption of communist-era
policies on child care and maternity leave, so be it. Indeed, many of the
chapters in this book make a strong case against throwing the baby out with
the bathwater, as it were. The past should not be rejected wholesale, because
it provides a basis for conceptualizing equity and empowerment for women.
It also paves the way for serious consideration of more enlightened policies,
whereby men are encouraged to share domestic responsibilities, including
child-rearing and paternal leave.

Some commentators have suggested that a family wage policy may be an
appropriate and feasible alternative to the full employment of all family
members. Given that women are being encouraged, or coerced, to return to
the domestic sphere in the former Soviet Union, a family wage may at the
very least prevent the impoverishment of families. As it would be far too
onerous for business firms to provide a family wage given the objective of
capital accumulation during the transition, then perhaps the state should be
the provider, or should subsidize firms towards provision of a family wage.

But a principled objection can be raised in this regard. Will not the family
wage strengthen the traditional relationship in the household? Why should
it devolve upon women to carry out household tasks—which as we know are
not especially creative or enriching, especially when done for years on end?
Let us not forget, too, that some of the advocates of the patriarchal approach
that Posadskaya discusses in her chapter are in favour of the family wage and
wages for housework. It should also be noted that polls show that most
women in the former state socialist countries continue to see their labour-
force participation as part of their identity.

In the area of politics, at a time when so many European parties have
adopted a system of quotas to ensure proper female representation and
participation, it behooves the democratic leaders of the Central and Eastern
European countries to rethink their rejection of the communist-era quotas
that guaranteed a certain percentage of party nominations or parliamentary
seats to women members.

This—and previous points—raises the question of the role of the state
and of the public sector. Among the Western capitalist countries there are
important differences in the provision of social policies and supports to

various groups in the labour market. The United States offers relatively poor support for women in the economy, compared with Western Europe and of course Scandinavia. The Nordic model of the mixed economy, with a strong welfare state, egalitarian discourses, and high levels of female employment and political participation, is far more woman-friendly than other existing politico-economic models. Indeed, a feminist slogan in Scandinavian countries is 'The welfare state is a girl's best friend'. Within the United States, it is interesting to note that it is the public sector and not the private sector that is most conducive to female advancement. Data from the US Labor Department show that in private enterprise women make up about 6 per cent of the top business executives; but in state and local government they held 31 per cent of high-level state and local government jobs nationwide in 1990 and about 20 per cent of cabinet-level state posts. The so-called 'glass ceiling', blocking the advancement of women and minorities, is more firmly in place in the private sector than in the public sector, where affirmative action goals are enforced. It is clear that the *laissez-faire* mantra of the past few years has been unrealistic and irresponsible. The state will most certainly have to play a role, especially in the provision of a social safety net as well as of social policies specifically designed for women workers. This should include anti-discrimination legislation to protect women and minorities in the private sector.

The transition will continue to be an inordinately difficult one for many citizens, male and female, especially in the former Soviet Union. The ILO reports that unemployment will probably continue at very high levels—over 15 per cent—'for a long time' (*ILO Information*, December 1991: 2). In the Central and Eastern European (CEE) countries, but not in the former Soviet Union, it is now much easier to shop, to get repairs done, to carry out quotidien tasks which in the past were so onerous and time-consuming, and were invariably done by women. But in both the CEE and the former Soviet Union, high prices render many goods and services out of the reach of many citizens. This is, literally and symbolically, the price that people are paying for the market system. Ordinary working people and the newly unemployed, as opposed to the *nouveau riche* and the intelligentsia who are able to travel or work abroad, may discover that the emerging system does not favour them. How they will respond politically is beyond the scope of this book. But both social justice considerations and political pragmatism should enter into the new leaderships' deliberations.

It is hoped that this book will serve a twofold purpose. It is meant as a theoretical exercise—an elaboration of the gender dynamics of economic restructuring and political change and of the gender-specific impact of marketization and democratization. As mentioned above, mainstream economists and political scientists have dominated the discussions of economic reform and of transitions to democracy. The authors in this volume are informed by feminist and WID concepts in addition to their own disciplinary frameworks, and thus draw out the gender and class dimensions of restructuring that are otherwise occluded in standard accounts. The book is also intended for use at the policy level, to draw attention to rising gender inequalities with a view towards influencing the direction of change. The market point of view should be reconciled with the social justice point of view, to ensure a proper balance between equity and efficiency.

ORGANIZATION OF THE BOOK

I have divided the book into three parts. Part I examines democratization and women in Central and Eastern Europe, with chapters by Wolchik, Einhorn, Rueschemeyer, Kostova, and Białecki and Heyns. The focus of Part II is the former Soviet Union, with chapters by Lapidus, Posadskaya, Bodrova, and Kauppinen-Toropainen. Part III examines economic reform and women's employment, with chapters by Fong and Paull, Paukert, Weil, Ciechocinska, and Moghadam. The book closes with an Afterword by Lynn Turgeon, who is unusual among economists for his attention to gender, the result, no doubt, of his long standing interest in social policies of communist countries.

REFERENCES

BLANCHARD, O., DORNBUSCH, R., KRUGMAN, P., LAYARD, R., and SUMMERS, L. (1991), *Economic Reform in Eastern Europe*. Cambridge, Mass.: MIT Press.

BUNTING, M. (1990), 'A Crusade Goes East', *Guardian*, 21 September.

CHAFETZ, J. S. (1990), *Gender Equity: An Integrated Theory of Stability and Change*. Newbury Park, Calif.: Sage.

COLLINS, M., and RODRIK, D. (1991), *Eastern Europe and the Soviet Union in the World Economy*. Washington, DC: Institute for International Economics.

HESS, B., and FERREE, M. M. (eds.) (1987), *Analyzing Gender*. Newbury Park, Calif.: Sage.

KEDDIE, N. (1988), 'Ideology, Society and the State in Post-Colonial Muslim Societies', in F. Halliday and H. Alavi (eds.), *State and Ideology in the Middle East and Pakistan*. New York: Monthly Review Press, 9–30.

KORNAI, J. (1990), *The Road to a Free Economy*. New York: W. W. Norton.

KRUKS, S., RAPP, R., and YOUNG, M. (eds.) (1989), *Promissory Notes: Women in the Transition to Socialism*. New York: Monthly Review Press.

LANE, D. (1986), *Labour and Employment in the USSR*. New York University Press.

—— (1987), *Soviet Labour and the Ethic of Communism: Full Employment and the Labour Process in the USSR*. Brighton: Wheatsheaf Books.

—— (1992), *Soviet Society under Perestroika*. London: Routledge (first published 1990).

MOGHADAM, V. M. (1993), *Modernizing Women: Gender and Social Change in the Middle East*. Boulder, Colo.: Lynne Rienner.

—— (ed.) (in press), *Identity Politics and Women: Cultural Reassertions and Feminisms in International Perspective*. Boulder, Colo.: Westview Press.

NEWMAN, K. (1991), 'Eastern Europe: Update on Reproductive Rights', *Ms.*, July/August.

STANDING, G. (1987), 'Vulnerable Groups in Urban Labour Processes', Labour Market Analysis and Employment Planning Working Paper no. 13. Geneva: ILO.

SZOBOSZLAI, G. (ed.) (1991), *Democracy and Political Transformation: Theories and East–Central European Realities*. Budapest: Hungarian Political Science Association.

TOMFORDE, A. (1992), 'Germany Redefines Vocational Training', *International Herald Tribune*, 11 February.

ZASLAVSKAYA, T. (1990), *The Second Socialist Revolution: An Alternative Socialist Revolution*. London: I. B. Tauris.

PART I

DEMOCRATIZATION AND WOMEN IN CENTRAL AND EASTERN EUROPE

1

Women and the Politics of Transition in Central and Eastern Europe

Sharon L. Wolchik

Women's political attitudes and roles in Central and Eastern Europe have been influenced in profound ways by the processes of political and economic change that are unfolding in the region. However, as in other areas of life, women's relationships to the new political systems also continue to bear the imprint of approximately forty years of communist rule.

This chapter analyses the impact of the rapid collapse of communist rule and the effort to recreate market economies, to create or recreate political democracies, and to reorient the external relations that followed the dramatic events of 1989 and 1990 on women's political attitudes and activities. I first examine women's roles in bringing about the collapse of communist systems and their involvement in the new political orders that have emerged to replace one-party rule. I then turn to explanations for the patterns observed. Finally, I draw on studies of women's roles in transitions in other contexts and on my own assessment of current political developments in the region to evaluate likely future trends in women's political engagement. As with other efforts to examine political developments in the region, there are obvious difficulties in analysing women's roles in states that are still very much in flux. However, it is possible to come to some tentative conclusions based on trends to date.

WOMEN AND THE COLLAPSE OF COMMUNIST RULE

Women's direct roles in bringing about the downfall of communist systems in Central and Eastern Europe differed according to the way in which those governments fell. In Hungary and Poland, in which the end of one-party rule took place as the result of a more prolonged process of negotiation between reformist factions of the communist parties and members of the opposition, women's roles were insignificant. Given their exclusion from positions of power within the Communist Party, few women were represented in official positions. Although they had been active in Solidarity in Poland and in the smaller dissident movement that developed in Hungary in the last decades of communist rule, they did not hold leadership positions in those movements and so were not found among dissident representatives at the round-table discussions that led to the end of communist rule in these countries. However, in Poland and Hungary, as elsewhere in the communist world, women contributed indirectly to undermining the legitimacy and support of the communist system, in some cases by their participation in dissent, and more frequently by fostering values and attitudes in the home that contradicted those promulgated by the communist leadership. In those countries such as Czechoslovakia, the former GDR, and Romania, in which mass demonstrations were instrumental in bringing down the old regime, women participated in massive numbers along with men.

Despite the role that women played, either directly or indirectly, in undermining the old systems, the political marginalization of women that characterized the communist period has continued to a large degree in post-communist Central and Eastern Europe. The end of the Communist Party's monopoly of political power, the elimination of censorship, and the repluralization of politics and policy-making have created new opportunities for women as well as for men to express their political views, articulate their interests, and organize with others who share similar political perspectives. Women as well as men thus may now use a much broader variety of tools to make their preferences known to political leaders and to urge action on their own behalf.

As demonstrated by the very high turnout rates for the elections of 1990 and 1991, which reached 96 per cent in the former GDR and 95 per cent in Czechoslovakia, many Central and Eastern European women were eager to make use of the opportunity to support political change by voting in elections that, with the exception of those in Romania and Albania, were widely judged to be free and fair by outside observers. Many also appear to have joined the numerous interest groups and voluntary associations that have sprung up in all of these countries. Certain women have also begun to use their new opportunities to be active politically—to organize independent women's groups or to pressure political leaders to take action on issues of concern to them.

However, most women have continued to play a very limited role in political life in the post-communist period. Evident in the small numbers of women who emerged as leaders in the mass movements, such as Civic Forum and Public against Violence in Czechoslovakia, the Hungarian Democratic Forum, and the National Salvation Front in Romania, that led the process of change or emerged as negotiations with the government continued, this trend is also reflected in the relatively small numbers of women who were selected as leaders of the newly formed or recreated political parties throughout the region. It is also evident in the fact that there are very few women in the national governments formed immediately after the fall of communist systems and legitimated (with the Romanian exception) by free elections, or in the legislative élites elected in the 1990 and 1991 elections.

The end of the communist parties' manipulation of the political recruitment process, and the change in the function of government bodies from largely symbolic organs whose chief function was to approve decisions already made by the communist parties to actual policy-making groups, have been accompanied by a decrease in women's representation in these bodies. The results of the 1990 elections in Czechoslovakia, Hungary, and Bulgaria are typical. In Czechoslovakia women accounted for approximately 12 per cent of the candidates in the parliamentary elections held in June 1990; they constituted approximately 6 per cent of those elected to the state-wide legislature ('Kandidatní listina OF' 1990; Čermaková and Navarová 1990). Women's proportion of candidates ranged from 4.5 to 16.7 per cent in the March 1990 elections in Hungary; 28 women in all were elected, a total of 7.25 per cent of all parliamentary seats (Elections 1990; Barany 1990: 30). In Bulgaria, women made up 14 per cent of the candidates in the Bulgarian Socialist Party, the successor to the Bulgarian Communist Party, in the June 1990 elections, and 7 per cent of the candidates of the Union of Democratic Forces, an umbrella organization of 16 opposition groups; 8 per cent of the legislators chosen in those elections were women (Radio Free Europe 1990).

In all three countries, women comprised a higher proportion of candidates of the Communist Party or its successor than of other parties. In a pattern common in other contexts (see Putnam 1976), women's representation in leading positions in these parties has also increased, now that the power and role of the parties themselves have decreased.

The proportions of women among national-level legislators in these countries, which are similar to those found in the rest of the countries in the region, are significantly lower than they were during the communist period. There are also fewer women than in the communist period who hold leadership positions in the legislatures or ministerial positions.

The decline in the level of women's representation among national political leaders in these countries does not represent as much of a setback for women as it might seem on first sight. Many of the women who were members of the largely symbolic governmental élites during the communist period had social backgrounds and career experiences that were markedly different from those of their male colleagues, and very little power or influence. A disproportionate share of women deputies were ordinary workers or agricultural workers, for example. Most other women deputies were drawn from occupations such as medicine, education, culture, and light industry, in which women predominated in the labour force. Most male deputies, by way of contrast, were party or state officials. The previous careers of women in the party élites also differed from that of their male counterparts. The fact that most women (as well as men) who achieved these positions were dependent on the Communist Party for support, and the official distrust of feminist initiatives during the communist period, also meant that women leaders were unlikely to act as advocates for women's interests (Jancar 1978;

Wolchik 1979: 583–603; Wolchik 1981a: 445–76; 1981b: 252–77; 1981c: 123–42).

Women candidates and leaders in the post-communist period, by way of contrast, have social backgrounds and educational levels that are closer to those of their male counterparts. Although, as during the communist period, many women candidates and leaders have careers in those areas of the work-force in which women predominate, the concentration of women deputies among those who were ordinary workers or agricultural workers, which prevailed during the communist period, has ended.

However, women's continued exclusion from the exercise of political power in the governments that have replaced communist rule in the region has implications for women's situation and gender equality that go beyond the small numbers of women involved. The limited number of women who were chosen as or presented themselves as candidates and the smaller proportion who were elected appear to reflect broader views concerning proper roles for women.

These views are an important part of the explanation of the patterns of women's involvement in politics in the region, for the legacy of élite policies towards women and the pattern of changes in gender roles that occurred during the communist period continue to shape women's relationship with the public sphere. The political systems that have emerged as part of the transition to post-communist rule also have an impact on the political perceptions and activities of women in these countries.

THE LEGACY OF THE COMMUNIST PERIOD

The end of communist rule has been followed by a widespread reaction to the pattern of gender role change encouraged by the regime's policies over the last four decades in Central and Eastern Europe (Wolchik 1990a; 1992; Čermaková and Režková 1990: 449–55; Čermaková and Navarová 1990; Navarová 1990; Šiklová 1990). In contrast to the situation in other Western countries, in which feminist movements and agitation by women themselves put the goal of gender equality on the political agenda, in Central and Eastern Europe the goal of women's equality was not chosen voluntarily by the population, but rather was adopted by political leaders and imposed from above. Official sponsorship of women's equality and other policies, including those designed to promote rapid industrialization, did lead to certain changes in women's situation. Thus, women's educational levels increased and large numbers of women entered the labour force. Sizeable inequalities remain in both areas, however. Because women's mass entry into the work-force was not accompanied by either a sufficient expansion of paid services or a redistribution of duties within the home, the changes in roles that occurred during the communist period in fact merely added new burdens to those that most women already bore (see Jancar 1978; Scott 1974; Heitlinger 1979; Mežnarić 1985; Woodward 1985; Kulcsár 1985; Wolchik 1989: 45–65; 1991*b*; 1992*a*, and 1992*b*).

Faced with the state's appropriation of the goal of equality, and forced to live daily with the contradictions that the uneven pattern of change in gender roles brought for women and their families, many citizens in these countries appear to have rejected the goal of gender equality itself. Others continue to support it in broad terms, but see it as something that can be pursued only in the future, once the more pressing problems of society are resolved.

These attitudes, which are evident in the mass media and in the speeches of political leaders and specialists, as well as in casual conversations with Central and Eastern Europeans, are most often expressed in terms of women's economic role. Thus, there is widespread agreement that current levels of women's employment are too high. Many citizens also appear to feel that women should be able to choose whether to be in the labour force or stay at home. (See Wolchik 1992 for further discussion.)

Similar attitudes have been expressed in regard to women's political roles. Many of the former dissidents and other political leaders of these countries appear to see politics as not quite an appropriate area of activity for women. The notions that politics is too dirty for women, that women have more important things to do, that women do not generally interest themselves in political affairs, and that, while, of course, women should have the opportunity to participate in politics, men must lead now, because there are so many difficult and important issues to deal with, appear to be widespread among present political leaders in many of these societies.

Such attitudes also appear to be held by many women. The results of one of the few studies of women's political attitudes conducted in Czechoslovakia, for example, document widespread lack of interest in most political issues on the part of women. In 1990, Marie Čermaková and Hana Navarová of the Institute of Sociology of the Czechoslovak Academy of Sciences analysed women's political attitudes based on a case study of 263 women, a survey of 1,600 readers of *Vlasta*, the major women's magazine, and a content analysis of letters sent to *Vlasta* by readers. The authors found that an absolute majority of the women studied were not involved in the activities of any political party, civic association, or interest group. Most of those who were active participated in the activities of, first, the Civic Forum, and, second, the Communist Party (Čermaková and Navarová 1990: 2). Most women supported the move to democracy and, with more reservations, efforts to recreate a market economy. However, many feared that the economic reforms would bring about a decline in the standard of living, increased prices, inflation, and other negative effects.

The authors found that public issues fell into two basic categories for women. The first included issues related to the family, the rights of women in society, care of elderly and ill citizens, the environment, education, the peace movement, and culture. The second, which interested most women far less, included economics, the development of citizens' initiatives, internal and external politics, entrepreneurial activity, the nationality issue, church affairs, and religion. Women were most interested in issues related to the family and to the defence of women's rights. However, the authors note that at the same time most women reject the idea of feminism or the development of a feminist movement in Czechoslovakia. In their words, 'Feminism has for Czech women a negative connotation' (Čermaková and Navarová 1990: 210). From the results of their studies, Čermaková and Navarová conclude that a decline in women's willingness to vote, as well as in their levels of support for the current government, is likely to occur as the result of the impact of the economic reforms on women's situation. The portrait of women's political attitudes that emerges from this study, then, reinforces the more impressionistic evidence available from the mass media and conversations with women activists and citizens. For many women, politics remains something outside the realm of their ordinary activities in the new circumstances, as in the old, although for different reasons.

The results of many of the numerous public opinion polls conducted in the region present a similar picture. In Czechoslovakia, for example, the analyses of public opinion on issues related to the transition by the Association for Independent Social Analysis and the Institute for Public Opinion Research throughout 1990 and 1991 found relatively few consistent differences in the attitudes of men and women towards the movement towards democracy, individual political leaders, or the general principles of economic reform. However, women were more pessimistic about the future, in terms of their views concerning the likely impact of the economic reforms on the living standard, and also were less likely than men to indicate that they planned to become entrepreneurs (Boguszak *et al.* 1990*a*, 1990*b*).

To some extent, these attitudes are similar to those that had emerged during the late communist period, when concern over the low birth rates that prevailed in many of these countries led communist leaders to re-emphasize the importance of women's maternal roles. The pro-natalist policies adopted at that time were accompanied in many cases by a change in the model of the ideal socialist woman and by a shift in the emphasis of propaganda campaigns aimed at women (Heitlinger 1979: ch. 17; Wolchik 1981*d*: 135–50; 1981*c*). In those countries such as Poland and Hungary, and briefly in Czechoslovakia in the late 1960s, in which the political élites attempted economic reform, economic officials and managers contributed to these perspectives by arguing that the labour force participation of women with small children did not make economic sense and should be discouraged (Heitlinger 1979; Scott 1974; Wolchik 1981*d*: 135–50; 1981*c*; 1989: 45–65).

The economic and political crises that prevailed in most of these countries for the last decades of communist rule reinforced these tendencies. Preoccupied with declining economic performance and, in many cases, growing political difficulties, political leaders gave very little attention to issues related to gender equality. Many dissidents as well as the broader public welcomed the re-emphasis of women's maternal roles. As Siemienska has argued in the case of Poland, economic and political crisis increased the economic importance of the family and reinforced its role as a place of refuge (Siemienska 1986: 5–36; Wolchik 1989: 45–65; Jancar 1985: 168–85). In this context, there was in many respects a coincidence of interest in the perspectives of the leadership, which emphasized women's maternal roles primarily to increase the birth rate, and the population, which, in retreating from the public realm, sought to return to more traditional roles within the family. (See also Wolchik 1989: 45–65; Jancar 1985: 168–85.)

The elimination of censorship that followed the end of the Communist Party's monopoly of power in Central and Eastern Europe has allowed these attitudes, which previously had to be couched in appropriate Marxist-Leninist terminology, to be voiced openly. It has also allowed groups that support a return to more traditional roles for women, such as the Catholic Church and conservative political groups, to organize and play a greater role in political life.

The organization of political life during the communist period has also had an impact on women's levels of political interest and involvement in the post-communist period. The effort to mobilize women by means of official women's organizations, and the willingness of the leaders of those organizations to follow the party line in most cases, have further fuelled the backlash against women's political involvement. In the last decades of communist rule, the leaders of these organizations were able to discuss problematic aspects of women's situation more openly than during the Stalinist period in many countries in the region. None the less, most women appear to have seen the official women's groups as out of touch with the concerns of ordinary women, and their leaders as objects of private, if not public, ridicule. For many women, including many of the dissident women now engaged in politics, the activities of these functionaries have helped to discredit the idea of women politicians. In an interview in Prague on 16 March 1990, Daša Havlová, a former dissident who emerged as one of the main opponents of Václav Klaus in the struggle for control of the Civic Forum in Czechoslovakia but who none the less denied that she was involved in politics, said that she found 'the idea of women politicians is funny somehow', for example.

The forced mobilization of women that occurred during communist rule also has had an impact. Although the presumed primacy of women's domestic roles allowed them, in many cases, to be less active in politics than men in comparable positions (see Wolchik 1989: 45–65), most women nevertheless had to go through the motions of being politically involved to one extent or another. Now that they are no longer forced to participate in the symbolic political activities such as manipulated elections and officially orchestrated demonstrations that served largely to affirm support for the regime, many women evidently prefer to focus on other areas of life. As the results of the Czech study discussed above illustrate, many women define politics as something out of their areas of competence or interest.

There are also hints that women tend to favour non-partisan politics more than men. For example, the authors of the Czech study note that many women were attracted to the Civic Forum by its seemingly non-political orientation (Čermaková and Navarová 1990). The widespread support of women in the former GDR for the New Forum is further evidence of this tendency. These trends suggest that the difference in the styles of women in opposition during the communist period discussed by Barbara Jancar may have broader application. Noting the tendency for women strikers in Poland during the year when Solidarity was formed to prefer non-hierarchical organizational forms and spontaneous protests, she suggested that there was a distinctly female style of dissent in that country (Jancar 1985: 168–85).

THE IMPACT OF THE TRANSITION ON WOMEN'S POLITICAL ROLES

Part of the explanation for women's limited roles in the exercise of political power, or even interest in political affairs, in the early post-communist period is to be found in the impact of forty years of communist rule on women's roles and their widespread rejection of the pattern of change imposed from above. But in addition, there are a number of structural elements of the current political situation that bear examination.

One of the most obvious of these is the fact that the political systems are still in flux. With the exception of Romania, most of the countries in the area that are no longer communist have held free and fair elections to legitimate the new governments formed soon after the end of communist rule. However, the contours of the current political spectrum vary from country to country, as does the extent to which new political leaders have succeeded in changing the way the old institutions operate or in creating new institutions appropriate to democratic political life (Zubek 1991; Wolchik 1991b; Tökés 1990: 44–65; Schopflin 1991a; Comisso 1991; Di Palma 1990; Kovacs 1991; Tamas 1991; Deacon and Szalai 1990). None the less, in all cases—including Czechoslovakia, Hungary, and Poland, the three countries widely thought at the outset of the post-communist period to have the best chances of making a successful transition to democracy—the situation is still very fluid. As was demonstrated by the surprisingly good showing of a virtually unknown

Polish *émigré* in the presidential elections in Poland in 1990 and the fragmentation of the vote in the November 1991 legislative elections, as well as the decrease in support for Civic Forum and Public against Violence between the June 1990 parliamentary and the November 1990 local elections in what was then Czechoslovakia, the political preferences and attitudes of ordinary citizens continue to be volatile.

Another feature of the political situation common to all of the countries of the region is the absence of a firm party system. The good showing of newly created umbrella organizations, such as those that led the revolutions or developed from the earlier opposition and other citizen's movements in the 1990 elections, suggested that a new politics of social movements, based on the rejection not only of one-party rule but of party rule itself, might predominate. The continuation of such a politics of social movements, or non-partisanship, might have been beneficial to women, for it might have, as in the early days of the post-communist period, created space for non-traditional issues to enter the political arena. A form of politics based on non-hierarchical, non-traditional organizations might also have created greater opportunities for a redefinition of politics to include more of the issues of greater concern to women.

In 1991, interest in joining political parties continued to be low throughout the region, but the non-partisan politics of the early post-communist period itself was being called into question. In Poland, where Solidarity enjoyed a position unique in the region in the early months of the post-communist era, the presidential elections brought several of the underlying divisions of the organization into the open. The results of the November 1991 legislative elections, in which none of the competing parties received more than 12 per cent of the vote, reflect the results of the further fragmentation of Solidarity. Civic Forum, the non-partisan group formed in Czechoslovakia in the early days after the brutal beating of student demonstrators in November 1989 that galvanized the nation, was clearly the dominant political force in the Czech lands in 1990, although it faced a Communist Party that continued to have greater support than those in most other countries in which one-party rule had been successfully challenged. By early 1991 internal divisions between the supporters of Finance Minister Václav Klaus, architect of Czechoslovakia's plan to move rapidly to recreate a market economy, and many former dissidents (including some who had supported the reforms of 1968) who wanted the state to bear more of the burden of the transition resulted in a split of the Forum into three groups: Klaus's Civic Democratic Party, the smaller Civic Movement, and the Civic Democratic Alliance. Public opinion polls in 1991 showed very limited support for the Civic Movement, the heir to the non-partisan tradition of Civic Forum. The split also meant that the Communist Party was the single strongest political force in the Federal Assembly for several months, until it too split. Internal divisions also led to the break-up of Public against Violence, the political force that led the revolution in Slovakia (Wolchik 1991*a*). In Hungary, the divisions within the former opposition took institutional form before the 1990 elections and continue to be reflected in the country's political life. Similar divisions among the opposition in Bulgaria were among the factors responsible for the two-staged process by which communist rule ended in that country. With the rapid decrease in support for the Bulgarian Socialist Party, the successor of the Bulgarian Communist Party, that occurred in 1990, Bulgarian political life also became more fragmented. In Romania, by way of contrast, the continued dominance of old party leaders in the guise of the National Salvation Front effectively prevented much development on the part of other parties or movements.

Although the process is occurring at different rates in different countries, the trend is away from non-partisan groupings and towards more traditional party organizations. If, as certain analysts argue, women's concept of the political is a more diffuse one, and if women are more comfortable with non-partisan politics, this shift may be accompanied by a further decrease in women's participation in the future.

At the same time, traditional political parties continue to be weak throughout much of the region. Most of the very large number of political parties that have been formed or been recreated after the end of communist rule are weak and have few resources, in terms of finances or leadership, to attract a firm and sizeable group of voters or adherents. The advantages that might accrue to women by virtue of the proportional representation elements that are found to one degree or another in the electoral systems of all of these countries are thus vitiated by the limited power of most political parties to deliver the vote.

A further feature of the current political situation that deserves mention for its impact on women's participation is the importance of 'personalities', or individuals with high profiles, in political contests and political life in general. Given the absence of strong political parties with well-developed lower-level organizations to recruit and provide resources to support candidates, parliamentary as well as local-level elections have tended to turn on the extent to which candidates are already known by the public. Since, as noted earlier, few women emerged in leadership roles in the revolutions or negotiations that brought about the changes of regime, few have received the kind of press coverage or media attention that male leaders benefited from. Women were thus handicapped in the early post-communist elections by their lack of visibility at the national level. Lack of data prevents an assessment of the extent to which women were hurt by the tendency to rely on the equivalent of local-level 'notables' at lower levels at this time. But the fact that women were less likely than men to occupy positions of leadership and responsibility (even in areas, such as education and medicine, in which they predominated) during the communist period suggests that they would have been less likely to have been included in the group of alternative local leaders regarded as possible candidates to replace officials compromised by their co-operation with the communist regime.

Finally, women's political roles and a consideration of women's issues are also influenced by the magnitude and number of changes that the transition to post-communist rule and the market entails. The economic and political tasks that face those who are attempting to lead the countries of Central and Eastern Europe in the post-communist period are too well-known to need enumeration. In addition to the steps needed to create or recreate democratic governments, deal with the remnants of the old system in the behaviour and values of the population, reform bureaucracies, reinstitute market economies, reorient external economic relations, and deal with the negative residue of four decades of communist rule, the new leaders in the region have also faced a number of challenges originating in the external environment, including the impact of the Gulf Crisis and War, the disintegration of the CMEA trading system, and the breakup of the Soviet Union.

It is clear that many of the changes that have occurred since 1989 have been welcomed by the populations of Central and Eastern European countries. However, many of these changes have also increased the hardship of everyday life and reduced the resources available to governments to deal with pressing social and economic problems. Although the introduction of the market may improve economic performance in the long run, the end of subsidies, liberalization of prices, and the structural changes that economic reform has brought in many of these countries have led to a decrease in the living standard and an increase in the economic pressure felt by most families.

The end of communist rule has also seen the reappearance and in some cases intensification of old problems, such as ethnic conflicts, that could not be raised openly during the communist period. The civil war that broke out in Yugoslavia in 1991 is the most extreme of such tensions. However, ethnic and social conflicts have also increased in a number of other countries. Tensions between Czechs and Slovaks, for example, complicated the process of economic reform and constitutional revision in Czechoslovakia and led to the break up of the federation. New public issues, such as drug abuse and increased crime, have also come to the fore.

These changes are important to note, for, taken together, they result in a situation in which there is a great deal of uncertainty in almost every aspect of life. Thus, the process of being in transition, irrespective of the kind of institutions or policies that emerge, in itself is an important feature of public and private life at present. In addition to the daunting array of problems that leaders and citizens face in the political and economic spheres, which have caused many political leaders and women to see women's issues as secondary at present, the transition also carries psychological costs for individuals and families. Although there has been little systematic study of their effect, such costs may influence women's willingness and ability to be involved in politics both directly and indirectly. In the first case, the lack of certainty about the competence and procedures of particular governmental or other political bodies undoubtedly increases the costs of becoming politically involved. In the second, women's traditional roles in the home may well make them less likely to venture into additional outside activities at a time when running the household has become more complicated, if only because the accustomed ways of getting by that developed during the communist period have had to be changed to some extent, and in a situation in which family members are likely to be experiencing greater stress in other areas of their lives.

The magnitude of the problems these nations face as they attempt to deal with the legacy of forty years of communist rule has also had an impact on the way in which women's issues are perceived. As has been true in earlier historical periods in many of these countries, and as was true in the late communist period, many men and women view feminism, or an explicit focus on women's needs apart from those of society as a whole, as a luxury they cannot afford at present (see Bohachevsky-Chomiak 1985: 82–97; Freeze 1985: 51–63; and Garver 1985: 64–81). At times, these attitudes are expressed in an openly anti-feminist manner. Other leaders argue that securing democracy is the first precondition for achieving feminist objectives. Czechoslovakia's ambassador to the United States, Rita Klimová, noted in 1990, for example, that 'Feminism is a flower on democracy' (Ziková 1990).

Future developments in women's political involvement will depend in part on broader political developments in the region, and particularly on the extent to which political leaders succeed in institutionalizing democracy. Steps towards institutionalizing democratic procedures and norms clearly will contribute to successful transitions to democratic rule in the region.

Paradoxically, however, such steps may have negative implications for the development of more active political roles for women. For example, the experiences of women's movements in several Latin American transitions from authoritarian to democratic rule suggest that the solidifying of political alignments and the return to more routinized political patterns may decrease the space available for women or freeze them out of the political realm again. Thus, even in those cases in Latin America in which active women's movements had developed before the end of authoritarian rule, women and their concerns were once again marginalized as the new governments established their rule more firmly. (See Jaquette 1989, and Alvarez 1990, for discussions of these tendencies.)

It is clearly true, however, that a return to authoritarian rule in one guise or another will not lead to any positive change in women's political involvement or in the treatment of women's issues. An increase in the influence of forces that draw on the conservative, authoritarian traditions that prevailed in several of these countries in the interwar period would in all likelihood lead to a further decline in involvement by women. In the interwar period most of the states in the region allowed women to vote, but in reality women played a very small role in public life throughout the region (Garver 1985: 64–81; Wolchik 1985: 31–43). The restrictions that more authoritarian governments would enact on the political freedoms of all citizens would also affect women.

Thus, the change of regime in many of the countries in the region has created a space for women to articulate their concerns when they choose to do so, as well as better opportunities than before to raise new issues. The risk of being involved in politics is also less than it was previously, even though the end of communist rule has not removed many of the underlying barriers to equal utilization of such opportunities by men and women. While it is clear that the collapse of the communist systems has not been sufficient to ensure equal participation in political life by women or more attention to women's issues, the changes that have occurred do seem to be the necessary condition for the emergence of a form of politics and political systems in which women will have greater opportunities to articulate and defend their interests, whether through established interest groups, social movements, or some new form of corporatism.

FUTURE POSSIBILITIES

Current developments in these countries point in opposite directions in regard to the levels and kind of political involvement by women we are likely to see in the near future. Given the trends discussed above and the importance, in other transitions from authoritarian rule, of what goes on in the early part of the transition period, the situation is not encouraging. In many cases in Latin America and southern Europe, the fluidity of the early stage of the transition and the resulting greater space for new forms of politics and new groups in politics allowed women's groups greater influence than they had previously experienced. However, as is illustrated by the gradual decline in the importance of women's groups and actions as the situation normalized, even in these cases, the ability of groups to translate their temporarily greater influence into power in the emergent new political system depends on the resources, agenda, and organizational abilities of the group involved. It also depends on the kinds of political resources that are valued in the emerging political system, and on the extent to which women possess these or are interested in obtaining them (Jaquette 1989; Alvarez 1990). The myths, the perceptions of who has the right to enter politics, and the definition of what constitutes legitimate political issues that prevail in the early period also have an important influence on the nature and accessibility of political life once political structures and institutions solidify.

In the case of Central and Eastern Europe, the insistence on symbolic mobilization of women and the actions of the leaders of the official women's organization, as well as the decades-long experience of the population with the contradictions that the strategy of gender role change and other élite policies created for women, have reduced the interest most women have in politics in any form. The greater involvement of women at the outset of the transitions that occurred in several Latin American countries thus has little parallel. Central and Eastern European women, then, will start from a lower base as the political situation normalizes.

The continued influence of the past on women's political involvement has been compounded by the impact of current economic reforms and crisis. The need, as noted above, for women to find new ways of obtaining what their families need will continue as economic reforms continue. The overwhelming uncertainty that widespread social change brings also will persist for some time to come. Both of these features in turn may be expected to reinforce the attitudes discussed above concerning the inappropriateness or lack of utility of women's political activity. They may also deflect interest away from steps to pressure political leaders to deal with the issues of greatest concern to women.

On the other hand, there are several elements in the current situation that could engender higher levels of involvement on the part of women. The move towards capitalism and the market has already created, and will continue to create, new hardships for the populations of Central and Eastern Europe. Given their continued responsibility for the running of home and family on a day-to-day basis, and the lack of change in gender roles in regard to the division of labour within the home, these burdens fall most heavily on women. As developments in these countries to date illustrate, women will also bear a disproportionate share of the dislocations that economic transition is creating within the work-place (Wolchik 1992). As trends in Poland, Bulgaria, and the former East Germany, Czechoslovakia, and Yugoslavia reveal, levels of unemployment are higher among women workers than among their male counterparts. Women are also facing new obligations and pressures to perform better and to acquire new skills at the work-place as economic reform creates pressure on managers and entrepreneurs to operate profitably. The rejection of the old, communist-sponsored version of gender equality and the re-legitimization of traditional attitudes towards women and the family may result in more open discrimination against women workers and higher levels of sexual harassment at the work-place. Young, highly educated women are also likely to face greater difficulty than their male classmates in finding employment suited to their qualifications and interests in the current economic and political climate than they did previously. The motives these developments may create for women to organize to articulate and defend their interests will be supplemented by the many cuts in social services and social welfare provisions, and the increased cost of such services that austerity programmes and efforts to cut government budgets have already begun to bring in many Central and Eastern European countries.

Other, more political, factors may also help to mobilize women. Certain women's activists from Central and Eastern Europe have emphasized the deep commitment of women in the region to peace and disarmament. It is possible, then, that developments that threatened the peace in Europe or endangered the movement underway to create new security arrangements in the region could mobilize certain women.

However, it is more likely that domestic political issues will serve as a catalyst for greater involvement by women. In the early post-communist period, there have been mass protests by women centred on several kinds of issues. The first, and one of the most likely, sources of political mobilization of women are challenges to women's reproductive rights. Disparate regulations concerning abortion threatened to slow the process of German unification in 1990, and attempts to restrict access to abortion provoked mass protests not only in Czechoslovakia (Wolchik 1992) but also in Poland, where most citizens oppose restrictions, despite the role of the Catholic Church.

Developments in the region since the end of communist rule indicate that it is also possible to mobilize women around environmental issues. Certain women supported environmental groups and took part in protests concerning environmental issues during the communist period. Women's groups in Hungary, for example, organized independent protests concerning the environmentally unsound Gabčikovo–Nagymaros dam. Many women, particularly intellectuals, appear to be active in environmental groups in Bulgaria. In Czechoslovakia, a group of young Czech mothers in Prague organized a protest in which they pushed their babies in prams down some of Prague's main streets to protest against the contamination of the food supply by cancer-causing and toxic chemicals.

Ethnic tensions may be another, less positive, source of mobilization. In the course of the crisis that led to civil war in Yugoslavia, for example, Serbian women demonstrated in Belgrade against paramilitary formations. However, although the goal was ostensibly peace, the protest really served Serbian interests.

All of these cases give credence to the conclusions of the authors of the Czech study discussed above (Čermaková and Navarová 1990) that women can best be mobilized by perceived threats to their ability to care for their families or by direct challenges to their own rights. As Jaquette has argued in the case of Latin American women, Central and Eastern European women may be most likely to enter the political realm when they perceive the connection between political issues and their roles at home.

The activities of many of the women's groups that have formed in the region since the end of communist rule illustrate this tendency. New feminist groups have formed in most of these countries. However, the majority are small, set in urban areas, and have little support. Most of the new women's groups, in fact, are explicitly devoted to fostering women's domestic roles. However, at the same time that they deny that they are feminist—or, in many cases, political at all—many of these groups have sponsored actions that are in fact designed to improve women's qualifications, increase their knowledge of the current political and economic situation, or put pressure on public officials to resolve issues of special concern to women. By providing a space where women can meet to articulate and share their concerns, the new women's groups may foster recognition of common interests and the development of feminist consciousness. They may also lead women to take more formal, organized action on their own behalf. Such developments are most likely in urban centres in which educated, intellectual women are most concentrated, for it is these women who are most interested in political affairs and who are most likely to develop an interest in feminism.

Such women are also most likely to have contact with individuals and groups from other Western countries. As the result of the official sanctions against any form of independent organization that prevailed during much of the communist period and the backlash against the official goal of gender equality, there were few feminist groups in Central and Eastern Europe during the communist period and nothing that could really be described as a feminist movement. The small groups that did exist in Poland, Hungary, and Yugoslavia were formed by intellectual, urban women with extensive contacts with Western scholars and feminist ideas and materials.

It is clear that the strategies or organizational forms of feminist groups cannot be transferred intact from one country to another. It is also clear that the movement for change in women's situation must come from within each of these societies if it is to persist. Yet, historically, contact with other European intellectuals and societies has served as a conduit to introduce new ideas and tendencies to the countries in the region. The experiences of Latin American women also demonstrate the role that outside actors—in that case, agencies of the US government—can play in focusing greater attention on the needs and interests of women and in fostering the development of organizations devoted to promoting those interests (see Jaquette 1989). The importance of outside aid from the EC, other European governments, and the United States to the transitions now underway in Central and Eastern Europe raises the possibility that outside actors can aid those within Central and Eastern European countries who are concerned about women's issues, including both those who do and those who do not define themselves as feminist, in their efforts to keep such issues on the public agenda. At the very least, continued expressions of interest and support by outside groups can help to give greater legitimacy to the voicing of women's concerns within the region.

REFERENCES

ALVAREZ, SONIA E. (1990), 'Gender Politics in Brazil's Transition from Authoritarian Rule: Implications for Comparative Analysis', paper presented for a panel on 'Women's Participation in Democratic Transitions: Eastern Europe and Latin America', at the annual convention of the American Political Science Association, San Francisco, 30 August–2 September.

BARANY, ZOLTAN D. (1990), 'First Session of New Parliament', *Radio Free Europe Report on Eastern Europe*, 25 May, 30.

BOGUSZAK, MAREK, GABAL, IVAN, and RAK, VLADIMIR (1990a), *Česko-slovensko-leden 1990*. Prague: Skupina pro nezavislou sociální analyzu, January.

—— (1990b), *Československo-listopad 1990*. Prague: Skupina pro nezavislou sociální analyzu, November.

BOHACHEVSKY-CHOMIAK, MARTHA (1985), 'Ukrainian Feminism in Interwar Poland', in Sharon L. Wolchik and Alfred G. Meyer (eds.), *Women, State, and Party in Eastern Europe*. Durham, NC: Duke University Press, 82–97.

ČERMAKOVÁ, MARIE, and NAVAROVÁ, HANA (1990), 'Women and Elections '90', unpublished paper.

ČERMAKOVÁ, MARIE, and REŽKOVÁ, MILUŠE, (1990), 'Sociologický vyzkum a školství', *Sociologický časopis*, 26: 449–55.

COMISSO, ELLEN (1991), 'Property Rights, Liberalism, and the Transition from "Actually Existing" Socialism', *East European Politics and Societies*, 5(1): 162–88.

DEACON, BOB, and SZALAI, JULIA (1990), *Social Policy in the New Eastern Europe*. Aldershot: Avebury.

DE WEYDENTHAL, JAN B. (1991), 'Catholic Bishops Call for Cooperation between Church and State', *Radio Free Europe Report on Eastern Europe*, 17 May, 16.

DI PALMA, GIUSEPPE (1990), *To Craft Democracies*. Berkeley: University of California Press.

Elections (1990), 'Elections: National States of Leading Parties', Foreign Broadcast Information Service, FBIS-EEU-90-056 (22 March): 50–4.

FREEZE, KAREN JOHNSON (1985), 'Medical Education for Women in Austria: A Study in the Politics of the Czech Women's Movement in the 1890's', in Sharon L. Wolchik and Alfred G. Meyer (eds.), *Women, State, and Party in Eastern Europe*. Durham, NC: Duke University Press, 51–63.

GARVER, BRUCE M. (1985), 'Women in the First Czechoslovak Republic', in Sharon L. Wolchik and Alfred G. Meyer (eds.), *Women, State, and Party in Eastern Europe*. Durham, NC: Duke University Press, 64–81.

HEITLINGER, ALENA (1979), *Women and State Socialism: Sex Inequality in the Soviet Union and Czechoslovakia*. Montreal: McGill-Queen's University Press.

JANCAR, BARBARA WOLFE (1978), *Women Under Communism*. Baltimore: Johns Hopkins University Press.

—— (1985), 'Women in the Opposition in Poland and Czechoslovakia in the 1970s', in Sharon L. Wolchik and Alfred G. Meyer (eds.), *Women, State, and Party in Eastern Europe*. Durham, NC: Duke University Press, 168–85.

JAQUETTE, JANE S. (1989), *The Women's Movement in Latin America: Feminism and the Transition to Democracy*. Boston: Unwin Hyman.

'Kandidatní listina OF' (1990), *Příloha Tydeniku Forum*, 18/90: 2.

KOVACS, JANOS MATYAS (1991), 'Introduction: Ex occidente lux', *East European Politics and Societies*, 5(1): 1–4.

KULCSÁR, ROZSA (1985), 'The Socioeconomic Conditions of Women in Hungary', in Sharon L. Wolchik and Alfred G. Meyer (eds.), *Women, State, and Party in Eastern Europe*. Durham, NC: Duke University Press, 195–213.

MEŽNARIĆ, SILVA (1985), 'Theory and Reality: The Status of Employed Women in Yugoslavia', in Sharon L. Wolchik and Alfred G. Meyer (eds.), *Women, State, and Party in Eastern Europe*. Durham, NC: Duke University Press, 214–20.

NAVAROVÁ, HANA (1990), 'Impact of the Economic and Political Changes in Czechoslovakia for Women', Unpublished paper.

PUTNAM, ROBERT D. (1976), *The Comparative Study of Political Elites*. Englewood Cliffs, NJ: Prentice-Hall.

SCHOPFLIN, GEORGE (1991a), 'Post-Communism: Constructing New Democracies in Central Europe', *International Affairs*, 67: 235–50.

—— (1991b), 'Obstacles to Liberalism in Post-Communist Politics', *East European Politics and Societies*, 5(1): 189–94.

SCOTT, HILDA (1974), *Does Socialism Liberate Women?* Boston, Mass.: Beacon Press.

SIEMIENSKA, RENATA (1986), 'Women and Social Movements in Poland', *Women and Politics*, 6(4): 5–36.

ŠIKLOVÁ, JIŘINA (1990), 'Are Women in Middle and Eastern Europe Conservative?' Unpublished paper.

TAMAS, G. M. (1991), 'Farewell to the Left', *East European Politics and Societies*, 5(1): 92–112.

TÖKÉS, RUDOLPH L. (1990), 'Hungary's New Political Elites: Adaptation and Change, 1989–90', *Problems of Communism*, November–December: 44–65.

WOLCHIK, SHARON L. (1979), 'The Status of Women in a Socialist Order: Czechoslovakia, 1948–1978', *Slavic Review*, 38: 583–603.

—— (1981a), 'Ideology and Equality: The Status of Women in Eastern and Western Europe', *Comparative Political Studies*, 13: 445–76.

—— (1981b), 'Eastern Europe', in Joni Lovenduski and Jill Hills (eds.), *The Politics of the Second Electorate: Women and Public Participation*. London: Routledge & Kegan Paul, 252–77.

—— (1981c), 'Elite Strategy toward Women in Czechoslovakia: Liberation or Mobilization?' *Studies in Comparative Communism*, 14(2/3): 123–42.

—— (1981d), 'Demography, Political Reform, and Women's Issues in Czechoslovakia', in Margherita Rendel (ed.), *Women, Power and Political Systems*. New York: St Martin's Press, 135–50.

—— (1985), 'The Precommunist Legacy, Economic Development, Social Transformation, and Women's Roles in Eastern Europe', in Sharon L. Wolchik and Alfred G. Meyer (eds.), *Women, State, and Party in Eastern Europe*. Durham, NC: Duke University Press, 31–43.

—— (1989), 'Women and the State in Eastern Europe and the Soviet Union', in Sue Ellen Charlton, Jana Everett, and Kathleen Staudt (eds.), *Women, the State and Development*. Albany, NY: State University of New York Press, 45–65.

—— (1990*a*), 'Women's Roles in the Downfall of Communism in Central and Eastern Europe', paper presented at the 4th World Conference of Slavic Studies, Harrogate, July.

—— (1990*b*), 'Women in the Transition to Democracy in Central and Eastern Europe', paper presented at the annual meeting of the American Political Science Association, San Francisco, September.

—— (1991*a*), *Czechoslovakia in Transition: Politics, Economics and Society*. London and New York: Pinter.

—— (1991*b*), 'Central and Eastern Europe in Transition', in Young C. Kim and Gaston Sigur (eds.), *Asia and the Decline of Communism*. New Brunswick, NJ: Transaction.

—— (1992), 'Women and Work in Communist and Post-Communist Central and Eastern Europe', in Hilda Kahne and Janet Z. Giele (eds.), *Women's Work and Women's Lives: The Continuing Struggle Worldwide*. Boulder, Colo.: Westview Press.

—— (1992*b*), 'Women's Issues in Czechoslovakia', in Barbara Nelson and Najma Chowdhury (eds.), *Women and Politics Worldwide*. New Haven, Conn.: Yale University Press, forthcoming.

WOODWARD, SUSAN L. (1985), 'The Rights of Women: Ideology, Policy and Scoial Change in Yugoslavia', in Sharon L. Wolchik and Alfred G. Meyer (eds.), *Women, State, and Party in Eastern Europe*. Durham, NC: Duke University Press, 234–56.

ZUBEK, VOYTEK (1991), 'Walesa's Leadership', *Problems of Communism*, 40: 60–8.

2

Democratization and Women's Movements in Central and Eastern Europe: Concepts of Women's Rights

Barbara Einhorn

INTRODUCTION

The unique conjuncture of events that spelled the death of state socialism in autumn 1989 has been variously described as 'the end of history' (Fukuyama 1990) or 'the rebirth of history' (Glenny 1990). Its aftermath appears to be characterized by a selective historical view, excising the previous forty years of the state socialist experience and looking to earlier periods in the search for new self-definitions and values. While none would wish to recall the repressive lack of some basic freedoms, the stifling of creativity and individual potential which were the hallmarks of bureaucratized centrally planned societies, the total rejection of such societies—indeed, the wish to erase state socialist reality from the collective memory—implies both a loss of identity and a degree of disorientation with regard to the future.

In relation to women's status and women's rights, this entails the wholesale devaluing of state socialist legislation and social provision without regard for the fact that some elements of it may have been able to provide building blocks or stepping stones in an attempt to identify women's needs in the current economic, political, and social transformation process. The problem with total denial of the state socialist legacy is that any attempts to define women's needs and rights in the newly democratic societies of Central and Eastern Europe are beginning from scratch, as if, indeed, 1989 marked a hiatus after which history began afresh, without the encumbrance of memory, or of coming to terms with what went before.

With all of their limitations and contradictions, state socialist policies for the emancipation of women did mean that women's life experience on the two sides of the Cold War divide in Europe were very different. Women's labour-force participation, however much it may have been perceived as an obligation imposed from above rather than a right exercised as the result of autonomous choice, did give women in Central and Eastern Europe a different vantage point, a lived reality and a confidence from which it might have been, or perhaps still could be, possible to move forward in new

The author would like to thank the John D. and Catherine T. MacArthur Foundation in Chicago for supporting the research upon which this chapter is based.

directions in terms of defining the conditions for women's empowerment in the new united Europe.

The purpose of this chapter is to participate in the process of piecing together some sense of the actuality and the potential of women's past identity as the first stage in defining future strategies for women's rights, not only for women in Central and Eastern Europe, but as part of a collective process engaged in by and for women right across the uncharted regions of the new united Europe. Unfamiliar and shifting as the present political map of Central and Eastern Europe is, one thing seems clear. It would be a mistake to imagine that an unregulated market economy and an obsession with property rights could maximize women's welfare without an enormously enhanced set of institutionalized women's rights. The attainment of such rights, however, requires new forms of state intervention, the very notion of which is anathema at the present time, tainted as it is by association with what was perceived as a totally and oppressively interventionist state in the past. Hence there are difficulties in putting such discussions on the agenda. This chapter is written in the spirit of trying to evaluate what went before, and to compare it with the implications of the current transition period in Central and Eastern Europe for women's rights and women's movements.

WOMEN'S RIGHTS AND GENDER DIVISIONS UNDER STATE SOCIALISM

This section evaluates the state socialist legacy, highlighting its positive features in terms of legislation and social provision in favour of women, as well as its limitations in terms of defining women's 'emancipation', and the contradictions between legally enshrined equality and the inequalities encountered by women themselves in the course of their everyday lives.

It would be all too easy to follow the current Central and Eastern European practice of totally rejecting all that went before the *Stunde Null*, the year zero, of autumn 1989, rather than turning over each stone in order to see whether there may be elements in the pattern of state socialist policy upon which future campaigns for women's rights could fruitfully build. This is all the more so in view of the fact that previous studies of women's status in Central and Eastern Europe very often pointed to a level of legislative rights and social provision for women which in some respects seemed enviable from the perspective of Western feminists.

The positive record notwithstanding, there were two fundamental problems with state socialism's treatment of women's rights. The first was at the level of official discourse, in the limitations of the Marxist theoretical framework as it was adopted by those states. The second was at the level of implementation, namely that, even within the terms of that theoretical framework, there was a gulf between juridical rights for women and official rhetoric on the one hand, and the actual daily life experience of women in Central and Eastern Europe, on the other.

The state socialist interpretation of Marxian theories of women's 'emancipation', as the communists termed it, focused on economic rights to the exclusion of the gender rights highlighted by Western feminist movements in the area of self-determination, sexuality, and autonomy. Taking a somewhat narrow view of the line of argument developed particularly by Friedrich Engels and August Bebel, and excluding for example the 'heretical' questioning of the bourgeois family by Alexandra Kollontai, state socialism postulated that the necessary *and* sufficient condition for woman's emancipation was her participation in social production and her consequent economic independence from men. The state socialist formulation of women's rights therefore concentrated almost exclusively on rights such as the right to work and the right to equal pay for equal work, and stressed the equal educational opportunities and the creation of social amenities—especially child care, but also work-place canteens and public laundries—which would transform these paper rights into reality. Official discourse also encouraged women to exercise their political rights by participating in political and public life.

What this focus excluded from the parameters of official discourse (albeit not entirely from that of the legislation) was the private sphere and the personal. This followed from the notion that individual endeavour should be subordinated to the collective good, namely the advancement of socialism, which in everyday practice meant the fulfilment of the current economic plan. Hence issues of sexuality, autonomy, violence against women, and the gendered nature of the domestic division of labour were not subject to public scrutiny. This resulted in the much discussed 'double burden' under which women laboured—most of them working full-time outside the home, yet remaining responsible for the overwhelming majority of child care and domestic labour. Hence the public–private dichotomy that emerged with the development of Western capitalist societies was perpetuated within state socialism, with profound implications for the current transition period.

LEGISLATION AND IMPLEMENTATION

Many studies of women in various state socialist countries have noted the fact that legislation on behalf of women was progressive, an expression of a more general commitment to the achievement of an egalitarian social order (see Einhorn 1989; Heinen 1990; Molyneux 1982). In the former German Democratic Republic (GDR), the right to equal pay for equal work was contained in one of the early decrees of the Soviet Military Administration in 1946, while the 1950 Act for the Protection of Mother and Child and for the Rights of Women predated comparable UN decrees and contained the elements of almost all subsequent legislation on behalf of women. In the case of state regulation of the private sphere, all the state socialist countries introduced abortion rights at some period in their history. Most of them legalized abortion in the 1950s (Soviet Union, 1955; Hungary and Poland, 1956; Czechoslovakia, 1957), although several subsequently introduced regulations restricting access to legal abortions (Czechoslovakia, 1962; Hungary, 1973; Romania's 1967 de-legalization and attempt to enforce a policy of five children per woman is well-known). More recently, several again liberalized the conditions governing legal abortions (Czechoslovakia, 1987; Romania, 1989; Hungary, 1989). (For details of the legislation and practice in each country, see Heitlinger 1979; Szalai 1988; Fuszara 1991; Jankowska 1991; Castle-Kaněrová 1992; Corrin 1992.) GDR legislation came relatively late (in 1972) but contained a preamble which gave a nod in the direction of self-determination for women by conceding that they alone had the right to decide upon the number and timing of children they bore and on a termination of pregnancy as integral to that right (Einhorn 1989).

Nor was the family exempt from legal regulation. It was defined as the smallest cell of society, and the one responsible for reproducing the labour force. Parents had a duty to rear their children as future communist citizens. The GDR's Family Law of 1965 even stipulated that the marital partners should share equally the burdens of child care and domestic labour, and that each partner should stand back during some period in order to facilitate the other partner's career development or enhancement. In the case of the GDR, therefore, it could be maintained that the socialist state did attempt to modify and recast traditional attitudes and family structures. The fact that the gendered domestic division of labour remained largely unchanged may therefore be explained in terms of the desire to maintain the family as a non-politicized sphere, in a form of passive resistance to what was perceived as a ubiquitous state presence.

In general, however, emancipation for women in state socialist countries was defined primarily in terms of economic rights. In this area there was an impressive array of legislation which guaranteed their equality at the work-place, in education, in reproductive rights, especially in terms of maternity leave and child-care facilities. The implementation of these rights differed greatly between the countries of Central and Eastern Europe. In the former GDR in 1985, there were crèche places available for 72.7 per cent of all children under 3 and kindergarten places for 94 per cent of children aged 3–6. By contrast, there were crèche places in Poland in the same year for about 5 per cent and in Hungary for 14.4 per cent of children under 3, and kindergarten places for 85 per cent of the relevant age group in Hungary but for never more than 50 per cent in Poland (Einhorn and Mitter 1991: table 1).

In relation to maternity leave, all state socialist countries provided for a woman's job or an equivalent post to be held open for her to return to at the end of the leave. The length of optional child-care leave after the statutory maternity leave was increased to one year in the GDR and to three years in Poland and Hungary during the late 1970s and 1980s in an attempt to reverse the falling birth rate. In the second half of the 1980s the GDR and Hungary even extended the right to parental leave to fathers and/or grandmothers. The real differences between these countries lay in the level of material support to which a woman on extended child-care leave was entitled. In the case of Hungary, this was not high enough for many women to opt for the full three-year period, while in Poland there was no financial support at all after the initial statutory maternity leave had elapsed. This meant that only in the GDR, with its fully paid baby year, did reproductive rights and the level of child-care provision give women a real choice over whether and when to have children, and when to re-enter the work-force after childbirth.

State socialist policies on education have resulted in an unrivalled level of education among women in Central and Eastern Europe. Women comprised around half of students enrolled in tertiary educational institutions. Indeed, as a result of the policy of equal educational opportunity, women's educational attainment was such that in the GDR a policy of positive discrimination for boys was introduced at the secondary-school level in order to maintain an approximately 50–50 gender split among students entering tertiary education. The educational achievements of women in Poland are detailed by Białecki and Heyns in Chapter 5.

In Hungary, Poland, and Czechoslovakia, this achievement was qualified by problems for women arising from the lack of a unified secondary education system. Although the great majority of girls completed secondary education, girls tended to opt for general secondary schools specializing in the humanities whereas boys tended to choose technical secondary schools. This meant that girls often entered the labour force unqualified, hence making up the majority of unskilled workers on production lines, while boys had a vocational training by the time they left school. This skill differential laid the basis for the occupational segregation typical of those countries. In countries such as the GDR, where a large number of women attended technical tertiary institutions and were highly qualified in traditionally male-dominated professions such as engineering, the process of economic restructuring, with its concomitant enterprise closures and job redefinitions, will result in deskilling for a large number of women unless adequate quantities and types of retraining courses are introduced.

The second kind of problem with women's rights as practised under state socialism lay in the way they were implemented, even in the terms of the limited parameters within which they were conceived. I have detailed elsewhere (Einhorn 1989, 1991, 1992) the contradictions between the declaration of economic rights for women and the actual inequalities suffered by women in employment. These included a form of occupational segregation, career hierarchies, and the feminization and consequent devaluation in terms both of status and financial remuneration of certain professions such as medicine and law. Women were concentrated in certain industrial branches such as light industry and textiles, in retail and services, as opposed to the heavy industrial branches which were prioritized in terms of wages and investment. They also tended to be confined to a limited number of occupations. Young women continued to choose traditionally female occupations. Hence in 1987 more than 60 per cent of female school-leavers in the GDR began training for 16 out of a possible 259 occupations (Nickel 1990). In 1989, still using the GDR example, 99.8 per cent of those entering training as secretaries and 90.6 per cent of trainee shoemakers were women, whereas only 5.8 and 5.2 per cent of trainee machine builders and toolmakers respectively were women (Winkler 1990).

Few women made it to the level of managers. In 1980 in Hungary, only 12 per cent of managers of enterprises or directors of institutions were women, and 5.6 per cent of co-operatives were headed by a woman (Kulcsár 1985). Still in Hungary, a 1976 survey showed that 33 per cent of university instructors and assistant professors were women, but only 4 per cent of full professors (Koncz 1987). And although 77 per cent of teachers in the GDR were women in 1985, only 32 per cent of head teachers, and 7 per cent of university and college lecturers, were women (Einhorn 1989). One of the hangovers for women on waking from the initial euphoria of the 1989 'revolutions' resulted from the realization that such career inequalities had been greater than they themselves were aware. An example is the level of pay differentials. With women earning 66–75 per cent of men's wages, these turn out to have been remarkably similar to the pay differentials characteristic of West European countries (Einhorn and Mitter 1991).

In summary, it must be nevertheless conceded that women's rights enjoyed a place high on the agenda of state socialism. With all of the contradictions inherent in the state's handling of these rights, they did create a basis for women's empowerment. What is interesting in the current transition period is how the new democratic political parties and governments have dealt with this legacy. For the moment, it appears that issues of gender equity have disappeared altogether from the political agenda of the new democratic parties and governments in Central and Eastern Europe.

It is also the case that the double set of contradictions described in this section—that is, on the one hand the contradictions inherent in the theoretical definition of women's emancipation, and on the other the gap between positive legislation in favour of women's rights and their implementation in everyday reality—have led scholars and most recently Central and Eastern European women themselves to question the rationale of state socialist policies on women. East German feminists have spoken with

derision of the 'Mummy Policies', in other words the pro-natalist policies of the period since the mid-1970s. In Poland pro-natalist and pro-
employment policies alternated throughout the period following the Second
World War. As a result of newly available or more widely disseminated
statistics and analyses of the situation, there is a high level of disillusionment
among women in Central and Eastern Europe about the motivation of
state socialist governments in relation to women's rights. Were they simply
a means to an end? Were employment rights and the social provisions
that underpinned them introduced simply because of the economy's demand
for female labour, especially in the acute labour shortage of the immediate post-war reconstruction period, which later became institutionalized
in the shortage economy? Were maternity leave and child-care provisions simply a carrot to maintain levels of female employment while
also responding to negative demographic trends? There is a suspicion,
in other words, that policies on women's rights represented an instru-
mentalization of women in response to economic dictates and population
policies. The debate on this issue will undoubtedly continue during the
coming period of re-evaluation of and coming to terms with the state socialist
past.

DEMOCRATIZATION AND WOMEN'S POLITICAL
REPRESENTATION

What is striking about the first democratically elected parliaments and
governments in the former state socialist countries of Central and Eastern
Europe is the relative invisibility of women in them. From an average 33 per
cent representation in pre-1989 state socialist parliaments, women now hold
an average 10 per cent or less of parliamentary seats. Women comprised
13 per cent of deputies to the Sejm and 6 per cent of senators in Poland in
June 1989 (Kuratowska 1991), 8.6 per cent of MPs in the Czechoslovak
Federal Parliament in June 1990; held 7.2 per cent of seats in the Hungarian
parliament in March 1990 (Corrin 1992), 8.5 per cent in the Bulgarian
National Assembly in June 1990 (Veltcheva 1991), and only 5.5 per cent of
seats in Romania in May 1990 (Janova and Sineau 1992). In 1991 there was
only one woman minister, the General Auditor, in the Czechoslovak Federal
Government, and no Minister for Women's Affairs. In Poland there was one
woman minister, the Minister of Culture, until the government reshuffle of
December 1990. And the Polish Plenipotentiary for Women's Affairs, a post
at deputy ministerial level, was in 1991 simultaneously transmuted into
Government Plenipotentiary for Women and Youth, and moved sideways
from the Ministry for Labour and Welfare to the Prime Minister's Office. In
February 1992 the first and only holder of this post, Anna Popowicz, was

dismissed and the post abolished. In the former GDR, the post of Government Equal Opportunities Officer was abruptly abolished and Dr Marina Beyer, its incumbent, was summarily made redundant in late September 1990, on the eve of German unification.

There are various ways of interpreting this absolute numerical drop in women's representation. In past studies (including my own!) and present political commentary it has been common practice to assert that the ostensibly or at least numerically impressive level of female representation in the pre-1989 parliaments of Central and Eastern Europe was mere tokenism, achieved by the allocation of fixed quotas to the official women's organizations and quotas for women within political parties and mass organizations. Further, it was pointed out that the parliaments were not the real decision-making bodies and that women were conspicuous by their absence from the Politburos and held very few seats in the central committees of the various communist parties. Another view is that, indeed, there has been an absolute fall in women's representation, and that this is all the more striking in light of women's key role in the dissident groups whose activities helped to prepare the way for the 'revolutions' of 1989. Jiřina Šiklová points out that 18 per cent of Charter 77 signatories and 31 per cent of its spokespersons were women and comments bitterly: 'When we were dissidents, the men needed us and treated us well'; whereas what she calls, using a term coined by the sociologist Sonja Licht, the 'male democracies' of the current situation may well ignore women's needs (Šiklová 1990a, 1990b). Other analysts have pointed to this break in relation to the Hungarian situation, where women activists provided a large part of the core in the Dialogue peace group and in the environmental group which organized publicity and demonstrations against the proposed Danube Dam, both of which were instrumental in the democratization process (Béres 1991b).

The more I have pursued this question, and the more people I have interviewed about it in Central and Eastern Europe, the more clearly it emerges that there is an open question here. To what extent does this drop in female representation in the newly elected democratic structures represent a break with the past, and to what extent an element of continuity? Whatever the answer to this question, it is certainly evident that the current relative lack of female representation in the parliaments and governments of Central and Eastern Europe presents an objective handicap in terms of maintaining or introducing women's rights on to the political agenda.

Were women more politically active under state socialism than within the newly democratic structures, and if so, why? Why did they fail to take advantage of the new openings embodied by the creation of new political parties and the first democratic elections? Is their rejection of political involvement part of the general negation of what is seen as the too politicized past of the state socialist regimes, or have they been pushed aside by the men, as Šiklová suggests? Have they been paralysed by the overwhelming economic pressures of the current transition process, or is their political passivity akin to their stance within the stifling constraints of state socialism?

I would suggest the following five explanations. First, the question of tokenism aside, women undoubtedly were more politically active under state socialism, especially at the regional government, local council, and school board levels, where their representation was high. This may be a source of inspiration for future women activists, since Western political analysts too have suggested that women tend to find local community and local government level involvement both practically and ideologically better suited to them than the physically and conceptually further removed processes of central government. Second, this past political involvement may itself be seen as a partial explanation of the current lack of enthusiasm for political activism on the part of women. The present apathy or active disinclination represents in part a rejection of the pressure imposed on them by the state socialist regimes to take on positions of social or political responsibility in addition to their labour-force participation and responsibility for the major part of domestic labour. This has led to what I describe as women's triple as opposed to double burden under state socialism, a burden women are, not surprisingly, happy to shed as a first reaction in the current transition period.

Third, there is an element of truth in the interpretation that women have been pushed aside. In Czechoslovakia in 1990, all but one of the leaders of Civic Forum (1989–92) were men, and Civic Forum had no specific policy dealing with women's rights or women's needs in the current transition process. Nor are women politicians necessarily interested in defending women's rights. Indeed, Dr Jaroslava Moserová, a woman politician in the Czech National Assembly, expressed an 'allergy' to Western feminism and denied the idea that women in the 'moonscape' of her constituency in Bohemia's coal-mining area, with its dire environmental and economic problems, might have particular needs not synonymous with those of their menfolk (Moserová, personal interview, Prague, 1990).

In 1990 none of the Hungarian political parties had a policy on women, with the brief exception of the Free Democrats (SZDSZ), who had a short-lived women's group and a last-minute pre-1990 general election statement on women. There is a view expressed by male politicians in all of these countries that, given the pressing and grave problems of economic transformation, unemployment, and inflation, the issue of women's rights is at best of secondary importance, at worst a luxury or a non-necessity. The fact that there will be consequences of the economic transformation process that are specific to, say, women's employment, for which it might be important to formulate policies before rather than after the event, is an argument that scarcely impinges on their consciousness. A positive step in the Polish case has been taken by a cross-party group of women politicians in forming the Parliamentary Club of Women Deputies under the chair of Barbara Labuda. They see their function as monitoring women's interests and pressing for their inclusion in new legislation being passed by the Polish Sejm (Labuda, personal interview, Warsaw, 1991).

The fourth element in explaining women's apparent non-involvement in formal politics is the obvious one of lack of time. Studies have shown that women have a great deal less leisure time at their disposal than men as a result of the double burden of full-time labour-force participation and responsibility for 80 per cent of domestic labour, combined with the time spent in queuing for goods and gaining access to scarce services. In the present transition period it is becoming evident that the difficulties of providing for the family in a time of economic hardship represented by unemployment, steeply rising prices, and slashed subsidies are once again falling on women. There is also the element of shock at these totally new factors, and an uncertainty and fear of the future expressed by many women.

Finally, there is the question as to whether current passivity in political behaviour among women can be regarded as a simple continuity of the political cynicism engendered by state socialism's constraints. Irene Dölling has developed most fully the notion that the socialist state operated in a manner reminiscent of a pre-bourgeois paterfamilias. State socialism was a form of patriarchy, she argues, in which the all-powerful father figure brooked no disobedience from his children; hence there was no political space for the articulation of alternative political views and approaches. At the same time, the 'father state' was all-providing, which meant that women's rights were handed out from above rather than attained through struggle from below (Dölling 1991).

Developing this notion further, this dual aspect of the patriarchal socialist state engendered both a certain complacency, a taking-for-granted of women's rights, the legacy of which carries over into the present lack of engagement in defence of these rights, and on the other hand a passivity with regard to concerns previously treated as matters of state. It is scarcely surprising if, after over forty years of being treated as children in political terms, with acceptable political norms and behaviour as well as interpretations of both internal and international events prescribed for them by the state, women in Central and Eastern Europe have failed to become autonomous and active political subjects overnight. Nor is it surprising if, after years of enduring the hard life imposed by the double burden within a shortage economy, where many viewed their right to work as either an economic necessity in terms of the income needed to support the family or a state-imposed obligation, women breathe a sigh of relief at the possibility of being relegated to the domestic sphere, preferring to leave politics to the men. In addition, since their only experience is of full employment and of jobs awaiting them after extended child-care leave, women initially had no way of knowing that exercising choice in a decision to 'stay at home with the children for a few years' might result in their becoming long-term unemployed.

Thus, one must conclude that the dramatic drop in female representation in the newly democratic formal political structures results from a complex combination of causes, and can be seen as both a break with and a continuation of the past. On the one hand, the sphere of formal politics is itself regarded with mistrust by many, as having been 'tainted' by the non-democratic political process and the politicization of all spheres of life under state socialism. On the other, there is a growing sense among women that formal democratic rights are not necessarily synonymous with the real representation of their interests. The ideology of the present moment includes the oft-voiced opinion that politics is men's prerogative in a return to a 'natural order' in which women have primacy in the home, and men in the public sphere. Finally, most women themselves do not appear to feel that there are rights in jeopardy that might be worth fighting to retain; in other words, they do not appear to be conscious of the need to speak up or struggle on their own behalf. Indeed, they are often unaware of possessing needs distinct from those of men. It is as if the very fact that they have always been legally emancipated has led to a lack of self-definition in other terms. As Jiřina Šiklová puts it 'Many women in Czechoslovakia believe they are already emancipated, but they are not' (Šiklová 1990*b*).

IDEOLOGY AND THE ROLE OF THE FAMILY: SHIFTS IN THE PUBLIC–PRIVATE BOUNDARY?

The ideology of state socialism subordinated individual rights and aspirations to the collective good. However, this co-ordinated effort in favour of building socialism, which in practice meant fulfilment of the current economic plan, was always seen as being reproduced within the family unit. The family was defined as the smallest cell of society and simply renamed as the 'socialist family'. Some legislation, notably the 1965 GDR Family Code, aimed to alter the balance of power in gender relations within the family in favour of the egalitarian distribution of responsibility for child care and domestic labour. Nevertheless, on the whole, public policy refrained from attempts to regulate what went on in this private sphere. A form of tacit acknowledgement of the continuing gendered division of domestic labour, itself helping to entrench it, was the GDR's 'household day', a paid day off each month for doing housework which was available to women only (Einhorn 1989). Another example of state timidity in this sphere is the fact that early encouragement in *Für Dich*, the GDR's mass circulation women's magazine, of autonomy and forthright behaviour on the part of women within marriage was abruptly withdrawn in the late 1970s in favour of advocating tolerance and 'working through problems', in the face of an extremely high divorce rate.

The high divorce rate throughout the state socialist countries could be interpreted as a result of women's relative autonomy and economic independence. In 1989, for example, it was women who petitioned for 69 per cent of divorces in the GDR, which affected 38 per cent of all marriages (Winkler 1990). It also reflects the stresses arising from both partners working full-time, with little free time for themselves, each other, or their children. The high divorce rate was a clear indicator that not all was well within the family unit. Nevertheless, the family as an institution was never questioned, and as recently as 1988, 70 per cent of young people in the GDR responded to a survey of their aspirations by putting marriage and the establishment of a family high on their list of priorities (Winkler 1990).

There was also a certain idealization of the family resulting from its perception as a haven from the long arm of state socialist intervention. Indeed, this protection of the private sphere was explicitly granted to Hungarians by the former leader Janos Kadar in return for compliance in the public sphere. This helps to explain why the family was seen as the locus for private initiative (which played a central role in the second economy in Hungary) and for the development of individual autonomy and creativity. Its importance both as haven and as cradle of individualism tended to obscure the nature of gender relations within it.

This specific role of the private sphere in Central and Eastern Europe and its demarcation from the public sphere indicates a profound basis of difference with Western feminist analysis in which precisely the public–private split has been identified as a key source of gender inequalities. Hence there have been campaigns to break down the public–private dichotomy. The women's movement slogan that 'the personal is political' has had concrete results in forcing the state, via its agencies such as the judiciary and the police, to recognize and intervene to regulate cases of violence against women which occur behind closed doors in the hitherto sacrosanct sphere of 'domestic disputes'. The recent acknowledgement in a British court that rape within marriage is also a publicly recognizable crime represents further progress in breaking down this public–private divide. In Central and Eastern Europe, however, far from questioning the public–private dichotomy, the state socialist system had the effect of entrenching this divide, with the private sphere being idealized along classical nineteenth-century liberal lines as the source of individual autonomy.

In establishing her thesis that 'the root of inequality between the sexes lies in the dichotomy between private and public and the clash of values involved', Katherine O'Donovan cites John Stuart Mill's postulation of a sphere of action in which the state has only an indirect interest as the 'appropriate region of human liberty'. She further quotes Steven Lukes on privacy as a core idea of individualism: 'The idea of privacy refers to a sphere that is not of proper concern to others. It implies a negative relation between the individual and the state—a relation of non-interference with, or non-intrusion into, some range of his thoughts and/or action' (Mill 1910 and Lukes 1973; cited in O'Donovan 1985). It is in this latter sense particularly that the family played such an important role in Central and Eastern Europe in relation to what was perceived as the oppressive socialist state, and it is in this sense also that gender divisions within it could go unchallenged. The assignation of positive value to the private sphere also provides some explanation as to why women in Central and Eastern Europe are not protesting a return to the family as implicit in economic restructuring with its concomitant need to shed labour and also as explicitly propounded by the new state- and church-led ideologies.

Another reason for women's tacit acceptance of or apparent collusion in the notion that their primary or perhaps only sphere of responsibility is the private sphere lies in the belief expounded by many media commentators and shared by many Central and Eastern European women that their return home is an expression of an option or a right not previously open to them under state socialism. This view holds that women now have the freedom to 'choose' full-time motherhood (or, in effect, at this juncture in time, unemployment—the choice of terminology being also optional and ideology-influenced). It should be noted that, in all former state socialist countries except Hungary, the majority of the unemployed are women. Women's reaction to being made redundant is dulled by their relief at being able to shed, for a time at least, the burden of their double shift. This relief contributes to the current popularity, expressed in a recent Soviet opinion survey, espoused by the Hungarian Free Democrats (SZDSZ), or expressed in Czechoslovakia, of the notion of the 'family wage' (Molyneux 1990; Rosen 1990; Corrin 1992). It is difficult for women in the former state socialist countries to accept the idea that Western women's 'choice' to stay home is in fact mitigated by the necessity, all too familiar to women in state socialist countries, for a second income to support the family. In a similar vein, they tend to idealize the choice to work part-time or at home, a view that overlooks the frequently exploitative and/or unprotected conditions of casualization and part-time work in Western Europe.

There are also factors in the cultural and historical heritage of several of the state socialist countries which contribute towards women not seeing a return home as a defeat, or even as a retreat. On the contrary, women in Czechoslovakia, Poland, and Hungary see their position in the family as one of strength, from which they question the need for liberation. Eva Hauser cites the 'cult of motherhood' in Czechoslovakia, which women themselves are reluctant to give up, as the root of unequal gender relations (Hauser 1991). The Polish case is based on the role of women during the years of partition, when women worked to provide for and hold together the family while men went off on campaigns to liberate Poland from the yoke of its oppressors, often spending years away fighting or in prison camps. It is from this time that the image arises of the Polish woman as a strong, even heroic, defender of the family in the name of the Polish nation. This position of strength is, however, two-edged, based as it is on total subordination of the woman to the collective interest, that is to the well-being of the family and the destiny of the nation. It comes as no surprise, therefore, to learn that there are many examples in Polish literature of such self-sacrificing mothers and all-providing keepers of the hearth as carping and complaining victims (Uminska 1991). In Hungary, studies have pointed to the role of Hungarian women as the creators and mediators of informal networks essential for the acquisition of scarce commodities under state socialism, as well as tending the private plot and setting up the contacts essential to the operation of the second economy (Haney 1989; Szalai 1991).

But there is an alternative perspective which suggests that, despite women's relative power within it, the traditional family structure that has resurfaced, seemingly untouched by over forty years of the socialist experiment with egalitarianism, is semi-feudal and patriarchal. It is as though patriarchy in the public sphere, in the form of the patriarchal state, has simply been replaced by patriarchy in the private sphere, creating a continuity that hinders women's self-expression and autonomous development. Nor should it be overlooked that women's return to the family is occurring in a context of a general retreat of the state from social (welfare) provision. Concretely, this means for women that, once they become unemployed and therefore lose their right to a child-care place, finding a new job becomes more difficult. Indeed, there is a vicious circle whereby it is difficult to find a job without being readily available to start work, which a woman cannot do without a child-care place, to which she either is not entitled or cannot afford unless she has a job.

Devolution of state responsibility for child-care provision on to individual enterprises struggling to survive in the market-place means that, in the attempt to cut costs, the firms tend to shed work-place nurseries and crèches as 'optional extras'. In the former GDR and in Hungary, enterprises have passed these facilities over to the local authorities, themselves virtually bankrupt and unable to take them on. As a result, many child-care facilities have already been closed down and there are fears that more will follow. With the simultaneous removal of the massive subsidies which meant that child care was free with the exception of a nominal fee for the hot meals served at midday, there is thus a dual process at work which results in child care being both less available and priced out of reach. As early as 1990, there were reports in Poland of women 'voluntarily' giving up their jobs since they could no longer afford the child-care fees, especially for more than one child.

The withdrawal of the state from social and welfare provision means that the family, or more precisely the woman, becomes the provider as well as the consumer of welfare services, reminiscent of trends in Thatcherite Britain. This scenario will work in Central and Eastern Europe only so long as there is no shortage of female skilled labour, if unemployment benefits remain so nominal that they are not more expensive than employing women, or if married women do not claim unemployment benefit, as has been the case in Britain. It is unlikely that all three provisos will operate in the medium term, particularly in view of the already existing necessity in countries like Hungary for two or more incomes to maintain the family.

In the vacuum created by the demise of socialist ideology and its definition of emancipated women, we are witnessing the emergence of a form of national self-definition not in terms of the socialist state or its discredited egalitarian values, but in terms of individual enterprise and striving for profit (which in practice often means the sheer struggle for survival) within the community, defined in terms of the family within the wider ethnic or national identity grouping. Just as it is possible to interpret current Central and Eastern European idealization of the family and of women's role within it as akin to classical liberal views of the private sphere as the basis for individualism and freedom, so it is curious that the emerging ideological definition of the collective good appears to suggest a rejection of modern society (*Gesellschaft*) in the name of the ethnic or national community (*Gemeinschaft*). This opposition is not strictly accurate in the terms posed by Ferdinand Tönnies in the late nineteenth century, as he distinguished between the *Gemeinschaft* based on the household as a centre of production and consumption and the modern commercial society of the *Gesellschaft*, characterized by individualism and striving for profit by isolated individuals in an atomized market-place. But Tönnies's view of women's role certainly appears to have reverberations in relation to the present context. O'Donovan (1985) quotes him as stating: 'The realm of life and work in the Gemeinschaft is particularly befitting to women; indeed, it is even necessary to them. For women, the home and not the market, their own or a friend's dwelling and not the street, is the natural seat of their activity.' Current ideology, especially that promulgated by the Catholic or Orthodox Church, counterposes the need for individual responsibility and traditional moral and ethical values (which it sees as residing in the family) to the supposedly amoral collective ethic of state socialism.

Women are viewed by conservative parties and the Church alike in several Central and Eastern European countries as the guardians of traditional morality, entrusted with the sacred duty of bearing children 'for the nation' and rearing them in the spirit of national linguistic and cultural identity and ethical virtues. This ideological linkage between traditional patriarchal values, newly resurgent nationalism, and the Church is perhaps most clearly visible and most difficult to unravel in the Polish case. In Polish literature and culture the woman is equated with suffering Polonia, who in turn, in the figure of the Holy Virgin of Czestechowa, is named Queen of Poland. In both Poland and Czechoslovakia national identity is fiercely upheld precisely because of its historical fragility, as their respective territories have been for much of their history simply the staging posts in other people's campaigns (Němcová 1967; Szczypiorski 1990). This sense of an ethnic and cultural heritage to be retrieved after the period of state socialism has deeply affected current views of women's role in this renewal, in many cases appearing to instrumentalize them in the name of nationalism. The need to boost numbers in the ethnic group also provides one explanation for the almost universal attack on abortion rights.

REPRODUCTIVE RIGHTS

Control over one's own body and the autonomous power of decision-making about fertility has always been regarded as one of the central planks in Western campaigns for women's rights. It has been asserted that male dissident support for this right for women during the 1970s, particularly in Hungary, was motivated less by a concern for gender equity than by a concern 'to challenge the state's right to intrude upon private life' (Rosen 1990). This would provide a further instance of the way in which the status of the private sphere was elevated as a site of resistance to the oppressive public sphere of state socialism.

The availability of contraception in state socialist countries varied greatly. In the former GDR, although there was little choice, contraceptives (mainly the pill) were free and readily available to all women over the age of 16, regardless of marital status. Poland and the Soviet Union had a very high level of abortions in relation to live births because of the relative unavailability and/or poor quality of locally produced contraceptives; thus, abortion was used as a method of contraception (Fuszara 1991; du Plessix Gray 1991). Both Western and Eastern studies show that women resort to abortion not by preference, but as a last resort (Fuszara 1991; Der Spiegel, 20/1991). The right to terminate a pregnancy by means of a legal abortion was also variable in these countries. The 1956 Hungarian law sought to protect women's health from the threat embodied in illegal abortions; a 1973 regulation enforced compulsory counselling. Both the Polish Abortion Act of 1956 and the GDR's 1972 Abortion Act stressed the principle of self-determination in the form of the woman's right to decide (Fuszara 1991; Einhorn 1989). But, although Bulgaria, Czechoslovakia, Romania, and Hungary did legalize abortion in 1956–7, several of the state socialist countries—either from the outset, or at a later stage as part of natalist policies designed to counter the falling birth rate—limited the admissibility of abortion. Romanian strictures against contraception and abortion, and the pressure on women to produce at least five children, have been well publicized.

One of the striking features of the current transition period is that, in virtually every country in Central and Eastern Europe, women's previously legitimized right to decide on a termination of pregnancy is under threat in quite virulent terms. Posters in Croatia and inflammatory statements by church dignitaries such as Joseph Höffner, Cardinal of Cologne, Cardinal Glemp of Poland, and even Pope John Paul II himself on his April 1991 visit to Poland have equated abortion with the holocaust (Rosen 1990; *Der Spiegel*, 20/1991; Corrin 1992; Heinen 1992). This equation goes much further than simply denying women's right to decide or to have their health protected. It not only implies that women are morally irresponsible, but by extension suggests that they are united in a sinister international campaign of genocide against the unborn. That this is no fanciful notion on my part is underlined by a circular from the Polish Episcopate stating that 'we are dealing with systematic genocide—in peace time—via the massive murder of weak beings by strong beings' (cited in Heinen 1992). December 1992 saw a new 'Law on the Protection of the Foetus' in Hungary, where Christian Democratic Party (the smallest partner in the ruling coalition government, which controls the Ministry of Health) moves to modify the abortion law had led to the collection of petitions by the Hungarian Feminist Network in August 1990 (Corrin 1992). Abortion has been described as, 'at present, the number one women's social issue' in Czechoslovakia (Rosen 1990).

In Germany, there was a short period during 1990 when completion of German unification itself appeared to hang on the abortion issue. The temporary resolution of the problem consisted in a decision to defer the formulation and promulgation of a new all-German abortion law until the end of 1992. Laws in the former East Germany and West Germany were diametrically opposed. The 1975 Federal law, the so-called paragraph 218, made abortion fundamentally illegal, with certain exceptions; while the 1972 East German law provided for legal abortions on the woman's decision alone within the first twelve weeks of pregnancy. A 1991 opinion poll showed that 55 per cent of West Germans and 75 per cent of East Germans favoured either total legalization of abortion or the extension of the twelve-week regulation to all of Germany. Throughout 1991 and the first half of 1992 debate raged, and an inner-party dispute on the issue threatened to tear apart the ruling coalition of Christian Democrats (CDU), their fiercely conservative Catholic sister party in Bavaria, the Christian Socialists (CSU), and the smaller liberal party of Free Democrats (FDP) (*Der Spiegel*, 20/1991). Christian Democrat assurances that a ban on abortion would be accompanied by generous state provision to ease the burden of bearing and rearing children foundered on the strained state coffers of post-unification Germany. Federal Finance Minister Waigel, who also heads the arch-conservative Bavarian CSU, stated his refusal to fund the social package agreed by the CDU/CSU and the FDP as part of the Unification Treaty. This social package provided for the pill to be free on prescription, for an increase in child allowance, and for the right to a kindergarten place. All of these measures, but particularly the latter, would involve billions of Deutschmarks in investment, since the 100 per cent kindergarten place availability in the former GDR has already been diminished by kindergarten closures; moreover, provision in the former Federal Republic was always inadequate; Women's Minister Angela Merkel has estimated a shortfall in kindergarten places of 600,000 (*Der Spiegel*, 32/1991).

In summer 1991, six separate draft laws were submitted to the Bundestag (German Parliament). At one end of the spectrum, these portrayed abortion as a crime with almost no exceptions. The draft from the CDU/CSU was entitled 'On the Protection of Unborn Life', and the one submitted by forty-six independent parliamentarians—including only two women—inserted a new heading for paragraph 218: 'Killing of an Unborn Child'. At the other extreme lay the two drafts from Bündnis 90/Greens (a coalition including former GDR dissident groups and the UFV, the Independent Women's Association of the former GDR) and another from the PDS (Party of Democratic Socialism, the successor to the ruling Socialist Unity Party of the former GDR)/Left List coalition: both eliminated the infamous paragraph 218 from the Penal Code altogether and gave women the legal right to decide on an abortion.

Between these extremes lay the drafts from the opposition Social Democrats (SDP) and the FDP, both providing for abortion to be dealt with in the Penal Code, but to be exempt from criminal proceedings within the first twelve weeks of pregnancy. Their difference lay in the question of counselling; the SPD provided for a right to seek counselling while the FDP stipulated compulsory counselling with a three-day 'reflection period' between it and the abortion being carried out.

As it became ever clearer during the early months of 1992 that none of these six drafts could hope to get through the Bundestag with the necessary two-thirds majority, a cross-party group of female Bundestag members from SPD, FDP, Bündnis 90/Greens, and, most importantly from the point of view of gaining a majority, including CDU members, presented a seventh draft, based on a compromise between the SPD and FDP drafts. This compromise angered the CDU/CSU on the one hand, with its provision of a right to abortion within the first twelve weeks (albeit located within the Penal Code), and the UFV and many West German women on the other, with what they saw as its paternalistic insistence on compulsory counselling (*Der Spiegel*, 21/1992).

On 26 June 1992 the Bundestag passed a new law, legalizing abortion within the first twelve weeks of pregnancy with the proviso that the woman undergo compulsory counselling three days before a termination. This law was prevented from coming into force, however, by a group of conservative politicians who lodged an appeal against it with the Federal Constitutional Court. In May 1993, the Court pronounced the new law unconstitutional and abortion illegal, but declared that it would not be punished within the first twelve weeks of pregnancy. This paradoxical confirmation of the new law was limited by two conditions: that the woman undergo compulsory counselling whose prescribed purpose would be to deter her from a termination; and that health insurance schemes would not bear the cost of abortions on non-medical grounds, making legal abortions both more difficult to obtain, and the prerogative of those who can afford to pay. The Court's dictum has yet to be confirmed by the Bundestag, ensuring that the abortion debate is not yet over in Germany.

It is in Poland, however, that the fiercest battles have raged over the abortion issue. A church-sponsored new draft law in October 1988 would have banned abortion with no exceptions whatsoever and provided for a three-year prison term for the woman and five years for the doctor involved in performing the abortion. This sparked off mass demonstrations in the summer of 1989 and the creation of several grass-roots groups devoted to opposing the anti-abortion draft in the name of women's rights or democratic civil liberties. The level of public reaction has given rise to the ironic question as to whether the attack on abortion should be welcomed as a trigger for women's political activism (Fuszara 1991). The terms of the proposed draft were eventually rejected as too draconian by the Polish Senate and the bill was sent back for redrafting. A second draft of the proposed anti-abortion law providing for exceptions in cases of rape and danger to the woman's life was under consideration by the Polish Sejm in the early spring of 1991. By the summer of 1991 and two draft proposals later, the issue was deferred (Heinen 1990). Opinion surveys made it clear that the population was almost evenly divided over the issue, but that a majority opposed the criminalization of abortion (Jankowska 1991). There were many reports of church pressure, especially at the village level, including threats to withhold a Christian burial from parishioners who favoured maintaining the existing law. Such pressure is held responsible for the skewing of figures, especially on the number of women who expressed the view that abortion is a crime.

An aid programme initiated by French organizations, in collaboration with the Polish Ministry for Health and a wide spectrum of women's groups, has sought to introduce sex education into Polish schools, to reopen family planning clinics, and to import and make available on a large scale both contraceptives and contraceptive information (Heinen 1992). The recently formed Parliamentary Club of Women in the Polish Sejm planned to have abortion included in the Penal Code, in a formulation similar to that in the former West German law. This would make abortion fundamentally illegal, but with a set of precisely defined circumstances in which it could be legally performed. Barbara Labuda, President of the Women's Parliamentary Club, saw this approach as a realistic compromise and the only possible variant to a total ban likely to be accepted in the Sejm (Labuda, personal interview, Warsaw, 1991). The Catholic Church opposed a plebiscite being held on the issue, knowing that it would be lost, but claiming that moral and ethical issues cannot be subject to political decisions. Meanwhile, the re-introduction of the medical conscience clause in 1990 meant that many hospitals were refusing to perform abortions. On top of this, the Doctors' Association imposition (in the face of 90 per cent opposition from its members) of an ethical code banning doctors from performing abortions as of May 1992 effectively denied women access to legal abortions despite the continued validity of the 1956 law.

On 16 March 1993 a new abortion law came into force in Poland, providing for abortion only in the most limited circumstances: the pregnancy must be legally pronounced the outcome of rape, the foetus must be severely damaged, or three doctors must attest to the 'severe threat' to the mother's life. Doctors performing abortions in any other circumstances are liable to two years imprisonment.

Reproductive rights epitomize the borderline between the public and private spheres. On the one hand, reproduction is the result of a consensus reached in private by partners wishing to found a family. On the other, contraception and especially abortion have historically been subject to church and state intervention. The Catholic Church bases its objection not only to abortion but also to 'artificial' means of contraception on the belief that sexual relations should be confined to marital spouses and should have the sole purpose of reproduction. During the 1989 abortion commission proceedings in the Polish Sejm, the Church maintained that giving birth to children is 'the supreme mission of the woman' (Buxakowski; cited by Fuszara 1991). Catholic and other opposition to abortion is based on the notion of the right to life of the foetus from the moment of conception. Following this view to its logical conclusion renders abortion the disputed outcome of two apparently equal claims: the right to life of the mother if endangered by the pregnancy, and the right to life of the foetus. It is in the course of this seemingly insoluble dilemma that the state has historically intervened, in an attempt to regulate the outcome or at least to remove the burden of decision from individual women or doctors. It is a continuing subject of dispute as to whether and when the state has a legitimate interest in so intervening to protect life.

In the Polish case, opponents of the 1956 Abortion Act, which provided for legal abortion, claimed it was imposed by an oppressive socialist state intervening unjustifiably in the area of individual morality. In a bizarre twist to this argument, those who opposed the new draft criminalizing abortion were called 'communists', so that, ironically, those who deny women's right to decide are 'true democrats'.

Eastern and Western research on abortion has shown that criminalizing it does not lower the number of abortions performed: rather, it simply raises the level of female mortality. Further, this research demonstrates that women decide upon a termination as a last resort, and that their preferred first choice would be free access to contraceptives. Hence there is a real sense in which the way this issue is handled in the countries of Central and Eastern Europe, the kind of compromise reached, and the related policies on sex education and contraceptive availability will provide a measure of the status of women's rights in those countries, as well as of their level of humanity and democracy.

WOMEN'S MOVEMENTS

In evaluating the status of women in Central and Eastern Europe and the level of rights they enjoy, it is important to analyse the role played by the official women's organizations under state socialism. As in the case of political representation then and now, there is a striking difference between those organizations and the women's groups that are emerging in the newly open space created by the democratization process.

The women's leagues, councils and unions of the past were allegedly mass movements, but in practice they were bureaucratized semi-governmental organizations. Nevertheless, it would be a mistake to suppose that they had no popular support whatever. The activities of their network of local groups were well supported, particularly in country areas where they formed a focus for women's social and educational activities. Formed in the early post-war period with its acute labour shortages, their initial purpose was to encourage women's labour-force participation. In addition, they provided educational courses aimed at broadening women's political horizons, and others of a more practical nature, for example on home-making. In addition, they were in many cases responsible for formulating much of the early legislation on behalf of women. In later years their fixed quota of seats in the state socialist parliaments enabled them to monitor the implementation of women's rights in practice, both at the administrative and the work-place level.

It would be wrong, therefore, to see their role purely in negative terms, as evidenced by the mood of negation of the past which prevails in many quarters in Central and Eastern Europe today. However, it is true to say that retrospective evaluation of their role has shown them in a relatively negative light, and that they have been sufficiently discredited as regards both their structures and their activities as to render their attempts at a continued, albeit ostensibly 'reformed', existence as doomed as those of the former communist parties. Most of the reasons for the rejection of these organizations, and for the refusal to work with them by newly formed women's groups, stem from their past activities, the general feeling being that their activities were misdirected and irrelevant to the defence or promotion of women's rights.

In the former GDR, the German Democratic Women's Association (DFD) was set up in 1946. Since 1989 it has been denigrated as a 'knitting and crochet circle'. Beyond this, its possible role in the past in helping to crush any initiatives in the direction of autonomous women's activities has yet to be clarified. Furthermore, its lectures on domestic management, and the continuing focus of its activities on the tiny minority of GDR women who remained full-time housewives, were hardly the stuff of women's rights activists. In the latter years of the GDR the DFD played no role in identifying or challenging the contradictions between legislatively enshrined rights and societal reality, whether at the work-place or in the domestic sphere (Einhorn 1989). The Polish Women's League was established in 1945 with similar aims to the DFD in the GDR. Like the organizations in the other countries, it was established bureaucratically rather than in response to pressure from below, and its activities were seen as suspect, as 'window-dressing' (Fuszara 1991). Currently it is anxious to provide retraining courses for women and to co-operate with other women's groups and various French organizations in a campaign to make contraceptives available and to introduce sex education (Nowacka, personal interview, Warsaw, 1991). The Hungarian Women's Council was viewed as another arm of state control, a 'paper organization' which 'spoke on women's behalf but did not actively engage with issues affecting women' (Corrin 1992). Since 1989 Czech women have been horrified to discover that a large part of the enormous profits gained from their affiliated publishing house was spent by the Women's Union not on alleviating the material problems of women, but on restoring to its former glory one wing of the magnificent Renaissance palace in Prague where it has its offices. There is considerable resentment and the feeling that the Union did nothing for Czech women.

The acting president of the Czech Union in late 1990, like the president of the Polish League in 1991, asserted in an interview that her organization wished to work democratically in co-operation with new grass-roots women's organizations in the new pluralistic political landscape, and in defence of women's rights. Their intentions are mistrusted, however, especially in view of the fact that the leagues and unions still have access to considerable financial resources, in stark contrast to the tiny grass-roots groups, and can manipulate power through control of their still existing countrywide network of local groups.

The newly formed grass-roots democratic women's groups have problems of their own. On the one hand, the new democratic rights and the space to organize mean that there is every opportunity for self-definition and spontaneous organization. Nor is there a shortage of issues around which to mobilize. Yet the reality is that, far from becoming a mass movement, the new groups have remained tiny minority groups. This is true even in the case of Poland, where the draft anti-abortion law brought large numbers on to the streets and where the debate still rages. Yet the activists of Pro Femina, one of the main groups formed to defend women's right to choose, are few in number, weary, and discouraged (Jankowska 1991). A similar 'burn-out' after being thrust into activism on the abortion issue very shortly after it was founded is evident in the Hungarian Feminist Network (Corrin 1992).

On 3 December 1989 more than 1,200 women from over sixty women's groups in the GDR came together in a Berlin theatre, in a spirt of euphoric optimism, and formed the Independent Women's Association (UFV) as an umbrella group to press the government on women's issues (Einhorn 1991). By March 1991, the tremendous pressure of events surrounding unification, the total loss of identity this implied for the whole country and the individuals in it, together with the shock of unemployment and uncertainty about the future had left the UFV at its annual conference a relatively small group, riven with internal dissent, accused of being too intellectual and arrogant, too removed from the anxieties about the future of women factory workers, for example, or of older women made redundant long before retirement but with no hope of finding new employment.

The immediate aftermath of the 1989 'revolutions' saw a plethora of new, small, often single-issue groups. In the Polish case many of them were formed in response to the draft anti-abortion law, as described in the previous section. A few groups, like the Polish Feminist Association or some of the feminist groupings in the former GDR, had existed since the beginning of the 1980s, either within the framework of university-based seminar or discussion groups or, in the GDR case, under the umbrella of the Protestant Church which provided the physical and political space within which they could operate. The majority of the new groups, however, do not characterize themselves as feminist; indeed, many explicitly reject such an identification. This is true of Prague Mothers, a group formed with the specific aim of protesting environmental pollution in Prague in the name of their children's health. In Hungary, the Feminist Network debated long on the question of what to call itself when it was constituted in June 1990, deciding on the ultimate choice of 'Hungarian Feminist Network' for the rather negative reason that 'feminist' was one of the few words not used by, and hence not tainted by, association with the previous regime.

One of the reasons for this widespread 'allergy to feminism' (Moserová, personal interview, Prague, 1990) is a false identification of feminism with state socialist policies for women, now rejected as comprising what was perceived as the obligation to work and the resulting double burden, both felt to have been imposed from above without consultation with women themselves. In addition, the simplistic view that Western feminism is a form of warfare against men is contrasted with the view, widely held among dissidents in the 1970s and 1980s, that the 'us' pitted in defence of civil rights against the 'them' of the state were oppressed women and men in a community of shared interests. And, with the exception of limited access to Western feminist texts in the former GDR and the former Yugoslavia, rejection of Western feminism was based, as the Czech sociologist Hana Navarová points out, on total ignorance of that movement's multiplicity and debates (Navarová 1990).

One cannot escape the conclusion that the current position of the new women's movement in Central and Eastern Europe is not strong. On the one hand, it is operating in an environment that appears either oblivious to the need for defending women's rights or openly inimical to aspirations for women's autonomy and self-determination. On the other, the material pressures of economic transformation militate against mass activist involvement. A third element in their current status as tiny minority groups lies in their having been prematurely thrown into activism in defence of women's right to choose on the question of abortion. This instant activism had the effect of bypassing a more gradual process of self-definition as groups, and of defining their aims and strategies. For this reason, it would be wrong to interpret the present relative retreat from activism, for example into activities such as the translation and dissemination of Western feminist texts, as a sign of defeat. Rather, it should be seen as a period of reflection, creating space for the redefinition of women's needs and of the conditions for women's empowerment in the new democracies, as well as the reorientation of strategies for women's groups within that context.

CONCLUSIONS

The democratization process in Central and Eastern Europe means an increase in formal democratic rights in an atmosphere almost obsessively concerned with the promulgation of new legislation to establish the rule of law within a pluralistic democracy. Newly gained rights to freedom of expression and association create the space for women's self-organization in grass-roots groups, and for new formulations of women's rights by such groups. However, it is difficult in the present circumstances not to see the implications of economic and social transformation as involving a considerable loss of rights for women.

This chapter has shown, however, that the complex nature of change and of women's reactions to social and economic transformation, coupled with

72   B. EINHORN

the paradoxes in women's status at this juncture, mean that a one-sided pessimistic interpretation of women's situation would be misguided. Indeed, there may be strength and renewal to be gained from what at first appears as a defeat, or a retreat into traditional family values. What is important when analysing the position of Central and Eastern European women from a Western feminist perspective is the avoidance of the colonialist gaze so evident among Western businessmen and triumphalist politicians (Bassnett 1992). Feminist activists and scholars are not immune to a patronizing attitude in their evalua-tion of women's situations ('been there; done that; don't repeat the mistakes we have already made in the West'), nor to the false equation of the life experience of women under state socialism with that of women in Western capitalist societies. A hopeful view of the future would include careful research and East–West dialogue in a mutual learning process towards definition of the preconditions for a new Europe characterized by gender equity.

REFERENCES

BASSNETT, S. (1992), 'Crossing Cultural Boundaries; or How I Became an Expert on East European Women Overnight', *Women's Studies International Forum*, 15 (1): 11–15.

BÉRES, Z. (1991a), 'A Thousand Words on Hungarian Women', mimeo.

—— (1991b), 'Hungary in Transition: The Ecological Issue', mimeo.

CASTLE-KAŇEROVÁ, M. (1992), 'The Culture of Strong Women in the Making? Women in the Czech and Slovak Federative Republic', in C. Corrin (ed.), *Superwomen and the Double Burden: Women's Experience of Change in Central and Eastern Europe and the Former Soviet Union*. London: Scarlet Press, pp. 97–125.

CORRIN, C. (1992), 'Hungarian Women's Experience of Change', in C. Corrin (ed.), *Superwomen and the Double Burden: Women's Experience of Change in Central and Eastern Europe and the Former Soviet Union*. London: Scarlet Press, pp. 27–75.

DÖLLING, I. (1991), 'Between Hope and Helplessness: Women in the GDR after the "Turning Point"', *Feminist Review*, Special Issue no. 39 (Winter): 3–15.

DU PLESSIX GRAY, F. (1991), *Soviet Women Walking the Tightrope*. London: Virago.

EINHORN, B. (1989), 'Socialist Emancipation: The Women's Movement in the GDR', in S. Kruks, R. Rapp, and M. Young (eds.), *Promissory Notes: Women in the Transition to Socialism*. New York: Monthly Review Press, pp. 282–306.

—— (1991), 'Where Have All the Women Gone? Women and the Women's Movement in East Central Europe', *Feminist Review*, Special Issue no. 39 (Winter): 16–37.

—— (1993), *Cinderella Goes to Market: Citizenship, Gender and Women's Movements in East Central Europe*. London: Verso.

—— (1992), 'Emancipated Women or Hardworking Mums? Women in the former German Democratic Republic', in C. Corrin (ed.), *Superwomen and the Double Burden: Women's Experience of Change in Central and Eastern Europe and the Former Soviet Union*. London: Scarlet Press, pp. 125–55.

—— and MITTER, S. (1992), 'A Comparative Analysis of Women's Industrial Participation during the Transition from Centrally Planned to Market Economies in East Central Europe', consultancy paper prepared for UN Regional Seminar on 'The Impact of Economic and Political Reform on the Status of Women in Eastern Europe and the USSR', Proceedings, ST-CSDHA-19-UN.

FUKUYAMA, F. (1990), 'Are We at the End of History?' *Fortune*, 1 January.

FUSZARA, M. (1991), 'Will the Abortion Issue Give Birth to Feminism in Poland?' in M. Maclean and D. Groves (eds.), *Women's Issues in Social Policy*. London: Routledge, pp. 205–28.

GLENNY, M. (1990), *The Rebirth of History: Eastern Europe in the Age of Democracy*. London: Penguin.

HANEY, L. (1989), 'Privatization and Female Autonomy: The Hungarian Woman's Experience' (MA Thesis, University of California).

HAUSER, E. (1991), 'The Cult of Motherhood', *Everywoman*, July–August: 20–2.

HEINEN, J. (1990), 'The Impact of Social Policy on the Behaviour of Women Workers in Poland and East Germany', *Critical Social Policy*, 10 (2): 79–91.

—— (1992), 'Polish Democracy is a Masculine Democracy', *Women's Studies International Forum*, 15 (1): 129–38.

HEITLINGER, A. (1979), *Women and State Socialism: Sex Inequality in the Soviet Union and Czechoslovakia*. London: Macmillan.

JANKOWSKA, H. (1991), 'Abortion, Church and Politics in Poland', *Feminist Review*, Special Issue no. 39 (Winter): 174–82.

JANOVA, M. and SINEAU, M. (1992), 'Women's Participation in Political Power in Europe: An Essay in East–West Comparison', *Women's Studies International Forum*, 15 (1): 115–28.

KONCZ, K. (1987), 'Results and Tensions in Female Employment in Hungary', Mimeo.

KULCSÁR, R. (1985), 'The Socioeconomic Conditions of Women in Hungary', in S. L. Wolchik and A. G. Meyer (eds.), *Women, State and Party in Eastern Europe*. Durham, NC: Duke University Press, 195–213.

KURATOWSKA, S. (1992), 'Present Situation of Women in Poland', paper prepared for UN Regional Seminar on 'The Impact of Economic and Political Reform on the Status of Women in Eastern Europe and the USSR', Proceedings, ST-CSDHA-UN.

MOLYNEUX, M. (1982), 'Socialist Societies Old and New: Progress Toward Women's Emancipation?' *Monthly Review*, July–August: 65–100.

—— (1990), 'Perestroika and the Woman Question', *New Left Review*, no. 183 (September–October): 23–50.

NAVAROVÁ, H. (1990), 'What Did Socialism Give to Women?' mimeo.

NĚMCOVÁ , J. (1967), *Introduction to Czech and Slovak Short Stories*. London: Oxford University Press.

NICKEL, H-M. (1990), 'Frauen in der DDR' ('Women in the GDR'), in *Aus Politik und Zeitgeschichte*, Beilage zur Wochenzeitung *Das Parlament*, B16–17.

O'DONOVAN, K. (1985), *Sexual Divisions in Law*. London: Weidenfeld & Nicholson.

ROSEN, R. (1990), 'Women and Democracy in Czechoslovakia: An Interview with Jiřina Šiklová, *Peace and Democracy News* (Fall). 3–4, 35–8.

Šiklová, J. (1990a), 'Feminism, Post-Feminism, Sexism, and Women's Studies in Czechoslovakia', *Maxima* (Prague), no. 4: 6–7.

—— (1990b), 'Male Democracies, Female Dissidents', an interview with Ruth Rosen, *Tikkun*, 5 (6, 11–12): 100–1.

Szalai, J. (1988), 'Abortion in Hungary', *Feminist Review*, no. 29 (Spring): 98–101.

—— (1991), Presentation to the EC/IRFEC Workshop on 'The Impact of Political, Economic and Social Changes on the Position of Women in Eastern and Central Europe', Brussels, 24–25 January.

Szczypiorski, A. (1990), *The Beautiful Mrs Seidenmann*. London: Weidenfeld & Nicholson.

Uminska, B. (1991), 'The Portrayal of Women in Polish Literature', mimeo.

Veltcheva, V. (1991), 'Participation of Women in Political Life in the Republic of Bulgaria in the Process of the Democratization of Society', paper presented for UN Regional Seminar on 'The Impact of Economic and Political Reform on the Status of Women in Eastern Europe and the USSR', Vienna, 8–12 April.

Winkler, G. (ed.), (1990), *Frauenreport 90*. Berlin: Verlag Die Wirtschaft.

3

Women in East Germany:
From State Socialism to Capitalist Welfare State

Marilyn Rueschemeyer

INTRODUCTION: STATING THE PROBLEM

Since unification, the new states of the Federal Republic of Germany (FRG) that were formerly the German Democratic Republic (GDR) have faced a plethora of problems. The industrial production of East Germany has been reduced to half; wages are 50–60 per cent lower than in the western region. The new states do not have the financial resources to pay for many of the social benefits, cultural and educational subsidies, and other services that were provided before. Unemployment is high, and is increasing; by the summer of 1991, half of all those eligible to work no longer had stable employment.[1] Approximately 500 people were moving each day to West Germany with the intention of staying; most of those were young and skilled workers. Workers were crossing over to the western area, taking jobs for comparatively low wages, and then returning at the end of the day to what was once the GDR. Investment by West German firms in the East has been slow and hesitant.[2] In the spring of 1991 there were large protest demonstrations in several cities as well as strikes.[3] Even with impressive outlays of the federal government, many people in the East continue to feel as if they are poor relatives that are at best tolerated. They are inexperienced participants in a market economy.[4] Thus, many now reflect whether it was a good idea

---

[1] *The Week in Germany* (15 Feb. 1991: 5) reported that the German Institute for Economic Research calculated the unemployment rate in the former GDR to be around 10%. With 1.8 m people on reduced working hours in January, the Institute came up with a rate of 21%. Norbert Blüm spoke of a future rate of up to 50% according to the *Spiegel* (4 March 1991). If those on reduced working time, those who are under review and uncertain if they will have jobs at all, and those who were pressured to take early retirement are combined with the formally unemployed, half of the labour force was without a job in mid-1991.

[2] One factor that seemed responsible for this is the settlement of the property rights of former owners. This has been partially resolved by providing, in certain cases critical for the reconstruction effort, for compensation rather than restoration of title to former owners, thus not tying the property up in litigation.

[3] The Metal Workers Union, for example, succeeded in obtaining a gradual raise in this industry's wages so that by 1994 they will be equal to wages paid in West Germany. The success of the metal workers' action was important for the strength of the union in West Germany as well. On the other hand, unless increases in wages are generally subsidized by the federal government, there is danger of further job losses.

[4] For example, so many people have been besieged by unscrupulous salesmen selling corrupt insurance schemes that the government has had to extend the period for dissolving all such agreements.

to introduce a market economy so quickly—even in such journals committed to free-market policies as *The Economist*.

It has become increasingly evident that women more than any other group are affected by these developments. They face reduced employment opportunities and currently receive—or are threatened with receiving in the near future—fewer subsidies and other supports that in the past allowed them to combine work with family life. Women are now confronting a situation that involves a dramatic turnabout of expectations. Their social identity and self-conception are put into question as well as that familiarity with 'the turf' which is so important for the control over one's own life.

This chapter will assess the impact of political unification and economic restructuring on the position of women in eastern Germany, the former German Democratic Republic. It begins with a brief description of the status of women in the Federal Republic and in the German Democratic Republic before 1989. In both Germanies, important social policy developments affected women during the last forty years, and the pressures behind these changes are important for understanding present developments and tensions. The chapter comments briefly on women's political participation in the events of 1989 before turning to the gender-specific effects of unification and economic transformation.

WOMEN IN THE TWO GERMANIES: A COMPARISON OF DEVELOPMENTS AND POLICIES

After the Second World War, the two German states started out with very different orientations towards women. The male–female division of labour and traditional gender roles were quickly restored in post-war West Germany. This more traditional orientation was prevalent despite the equal-rights provision of the Grundgesetz of 1949, the constitution of the Federal Republic of Germany. There was an inherent tension between the principle of gender equality and the principle of freedom of contract which was guaranteed by the Grundgesetz to employers and workers, and there was tension between the equal-rights provision and the notion that the state should intervene as little as possible in the citizens' private sphere and in their social and economic lives (Rueschemeyer and Schissler 1990: 73). In 1957 West German family law was amended by the Act on Equal Rights for Men and Women. But two articles of the civil law remained in force which stated that the contribution of women to their families consisted mainly in doing housework, and that they were allowed to go out to work if this decision did not interfere with their duties as wives and mothers. It was only in 1977 that a new family law recognized marriage as a partnership.

During the 1950s and 1960s, there were campaigns against 'double-wage-earners' and many women were dismissed both from factories and from the civil service as soon as they married. Schissler notes that, although many women had to live their lives without a male breadwinner, these women were marginalized and two-parent families were presented as the norm (Rueschemeyer and Schissler 1990: 74–5). By 1985, 45 per cent of West German women were in the labour force, not a particularly high percentage in the western European community. That the labour market remained segregated according to gender can be vividly observed in the percentage of women in different occupations in the early 1980s. They were concentrated in service jobs and were dramatically under-represented in technical occupations: 71 per cent of all female employees in West Germany were in service occupations, 18.5 per cent were in manufacturing, 6.9 per cent in horticulture, fishery, and animal breeding, and only 1.6 in technical occupations (Schoepp-Schilling 1985: 125).

By 1980, under the pressure of the European community, the Equal Treatment Act was passed. Overall, there have been slow but impressive changes. This was partly due to the growing influence of the women's movement and the greater role of women in political parties (who could point to legislation in East Germany addressing some of the needs of working families as well as to the Scandinavian countries). Today, just over half of West German women are in the labour force. Women represent over 40 per cent of university students, typically in language and literature, though increasingly also in medicine and the law. By 1987 over half of the students in high school/*Gymnasium* and technical school were women. However, as in the former German Democratic Republic, their percentages in the highest executive positions remain low—less than 4 per cent—and they comprise only 7 per cent of the professors in the university. Their participation in the middle levels of management is higher but still limited, as it was in the former GDR; about a third of these positions are filled by women.

While state supports and family policies are far more developed in the Federal Republic than in the United States, measures advancing equal opportunities for women and child care were not as developed as in the Scandinavian countries. They were also less developed than in the GDR, where women's participation in the work-force was institutionalized. By the mid-1980s, working women in West Germany had a total of fourteen weeks' maternity leave, six before and eight after the birth, with a stipend and employer's supplement equivalent to the net wages or salary. From the fifteenth to the thirty-second week, there was a small stipend without the employer's supplement (FRG 1985: 70). The changes that were introduced in 1990 will be discussed later.

Abortion regulations are stipulated in para. 218 of the Criminal Code. A physician—not the woman's own—and review panel must agree that, because of the woman's health or because of a 'social indication', an abortion may take place. The interpretations of these regulations vary from state to state. While women in Hamburg, for example, have little difficulty obtaining abortions, women in Bavaria find it nearly impossible to have an abortion in their own state, and physicians have been criminally prosecuted there for performing abortions.

Although a number of West German women are able to afford private child care or have the help of relatives, only 3 per cent of children under the age of 3 are in public day care. The financing of public day care and support for it varies locally. Berlin, even with its established day-care system, fills fewer than a quarter of the requests by parents. About 80 per cent of all West German children between the ages of 3 and 6, however, are in *Kindergarten*. If a child becomes ill, women in West Germany can take only five paid days a year, and then only if the child is 8 or younger. This regulation, too, has now changed.[5]

In the GDR, as in West Germany, there was a severe shortage of men at the end of the Second World War. Almost immediately, the Soviet military administration established regulations stipulating equal pay for equal work; in 1949, the new constitution established gender equality in all areas of social life. At the same time, the labour force was further diminished by emigration, and the economic system of central planning generated a chronic labour shortage. That condition resulted in policies strongly favouring a high labour-force participation of women, although these policies were also flavoured at least by ideologies of the Weimar period. Nearly 90 per cent of all women eligible to work were studying or in the labour force before unification.[6] Public policy also supported an expanded system of occupational training. Seventy per cent of all women had completed an apprenticeship or more advanced vocational training, and women of 40 years and younger had achieved the same educational standards as men. Women comprised about half the college and university students; they concentrated mainly in economics, education, literature, and languages.

Although women entered the work-force in large numbers, it was only in the 1960s that the system of *Krippen* (for children under 3) and *Kindergarten* (for children 3–6) became fully developed in the GDR. There was increasing attention to women's participation in higher education, in political work, and in male-dominated occupations. Highly subsidized day care by the state included day-care centres supported by the state and enterprises, *Kindergarten*, school-lunch programmes and care after school. Over 80 per

[5] Interview with Hanna Beate Schoepp-Schilling, Berlin, summer 1991.
[6] A third of the women in the former GDR worked part-time, typically 6 rather than 8 hours a day. This percentage is similar to the percentage of women working part-time in West Germany, except that part-time work there may involve less than 15 hours a week with fewer benefits and poor pay.

cent of children aged 1–3 were in *Krippen* and nearly 90 per cent of those between 3 and 6 were in *Kindergarten*.

There were other supports encouraging women's participation in the work-force. In contrast to West Germany, East German parents were guaranteed forty days per year paid time off from work to care for ill children 14 years or younger. Furthermore, mothers of children under 16 and single women over 30 were allowed one paid day off per month for housework. Even with the interest of the GDR state in maintaining and increasing the birth rate, abortion during the first three months became legal in 1972. Contraceptives were free of charge. The state tried to encourage family life and childbirth through support from the state in the form of an interest-free loan which was reduced with the birth of each child; in addition, there was a small monthly stipend for each child. Women received a paid six-week leave before the birth of a child and a twenty-week post-natal leave, which was followed by paid parental leave until the child reached the age of 1 year, when they were entitled to collect 75–90 per cent of net pay. Women could then return to their jobs at the same level at which they had been employed before. For two or more children, the leave was extended to eighteen months. In the later years of the GDR these leaves could be taken also by the spouse or grandmother. Such policies helped to transform the lives of many women by increasing work opportunities and allowing them more choice in arranging their personal lives.

In the last few years, however, even before the opening of the borders, there was increasing and open discontent about issues of women that were still unresolved in the GDR. The official Democratic Women's Federation had started out in the Soviet zone of Germany as an effort to encourage women to join the work-force, transmit official ideology, and teach women needlework and all the other necessary skills they needed to run a good household. In later years it came to be regarded as an organization that did not address the real needs and frustrations of working women, even if it did important work with the elderly and made some improvements in the residential areas.

Complaints in the GDR revolved around a familiar theme: the difficulties of integrating work and family life, even with the expansion of day-care centres in the 1960s and housing availability in the 1970s and 1980s. The extensive use of shift work despite the complaints of workers about its effects on family life; the long work-day and, for many, a strenuous commute to and from work; the often uncoordinated schedules of men and women; the inadequacy of consumer goods and other services—these and other difficulties resulted in exhaustion and strain for both men and women.[7] Such difficulties were compounded by the unequal division of labour in the family,

---

[7] For more details, see Rueschemeyer (1981).

TABLE 3.1 Percentages of women in occupational leadership in the GDR

Sector	% in leadership positions	(% of all female employees in sector)
All sectors of society	about 33.3	
All sectors of the economy	1950: 8–10	
	1970: 20	
	1982: 30	(1983: 49.4)
Industry (all sectors)	1979: 20	
	1983: 16.6	(1983: 42.4)
Top positions in Kombinaten	1979: 2.3	
Deputy directors	1979: 12	
Leading positions at the third level	1979: 19.7	
Light industry	1983: about 50	
Agriculture	1976: 16.2	
	1979 & 1983: 16.6	(1983: 39.9)
Services (all sectors)	1983: 50	
Trade	1984: 58	(1983: 72.8)
Post and telecommunications	1983: about 50	(1983: 69.3)
Cultural and social sectors		
Education, science, culture	1983: 56.6	
Education		
Teachers	1970: 58.1	
	1982: 70.1	(1983: 76.7)
Principals	1970: 23.3	
	1982: 32.0	
Higher education including technical higher education	1983: about 33.3	
Of these, professors and instructors	1981: 7.5	
Health care (total)	1983: 56.6	(1983: 83.3)
Doctors	1982: 52	
Dentists	1982: 57	
Pharmacists	1982: 68	
Doctors in local public health services	1978: 20	
	1983: about 50	

Source: Meyer (1986: 306).

which was changing slowly; the changes that did take place were with the younger and more educated couples and concerned marketing and the care of children more than other household chores. For single women with children (a third of all children in the former GDR were born to single mothers), there were special problems. Aside from loneliness and the financial constraints of managing on a single income, those who lived in the new residential areas that surround urban centres complained about the lack of activities in the community for single parents, the difficulty of leaving the children and returning to the area again after the work-day, and the boredom of their lives.

East German sociologists working on the issues of women typically pointed to the small number of women in the highest leadership positions in industry, in universities and in politics, even if a third of all middle-level positions were

TABLE 3.2 Principal apprenticeship trades in the two Germanies: a comparison of East and West, and male and female, 1980s[a]

Trade	Male		Trade	Female	
	No.	%		No.	%
West Germany					
Motor mechanic	86,724	8.4	Saleswoman	66,166	10.2
Electrician	57,515	5.6	Hair stylist	62,041	9.6
Machinist	45,602	4.4	Saleswoman in		
Joiner	41,708	4.1	food trade	41,389	6.4
Builder	38,219	3.7	Office clerk	40,463	6.2
Painter/decorator	34,938	3.4	Doctor's assistant	37,936	5.9
Plumber	33,134	3.2	Industrial clerk	35,397	5.5
Clerk (wholesale,			Retail trade assistant		
import/export)	28,005	2.7	(2nd level)	27,323	4.2
Baker	24,125	2.3	Dentist's assistant	27,092	4.2
Toolmaker	22,060	2.1	Bank clerk	26,299	4.1
			Clerk (wholesale,		
			import/export)	20,453	3.2
TOTAL	1,029,113			647,764	
East Germany					
Maintenance mechanic	8,385	7.0	Saleswoman	9,592	10.2
Motor mechanic	7,623	6.4	Industrial clerk	6,901	7.3
Construction worker	6,334	5.3	Typist/stenographer	6,605	7.0
Electrician	6,277	5.2	Zoo technician/		
Fitter	5,805	4.8	mechanic	4,528	4.8
Machinist	5,045	4.2	Textile technician	4,235	4.5
Agricultural technician	3,990	3.3	Cook	3,208	3.4
Plumber	3,051	2.6	Dressmaker	2,671	2.8
Production technician	2,997	2.5	Railway technician	1,933	2.1
Cook	1,897	1.5	Machinist	1,875	2.0
			Chemical production		
			technician	1,772	1.8
TOTAL	118,679			93,739	

[a] Selected traits only.

Source: *Facts and Figures 1985* (Press and Information Office of the Federal Republic of Germany (Bonn)): 78.

held by women (see Table 3.1). There may have been discrimination in hiring. Despite the changes that had taken place in the GDR, many working women were still found in the more traditional occupations and free-time activities (see Tables 3.2 and 3.3).

THE TRANSITION

Women were active and involved in the dramatic changes that occurred in East Germany even before the borders opened. They became more involved in professional associations in the last few years, an indication, it seems, of their belief in actually being able to bring about some real social change. One interesting example involved elections in the Union of Artists. There was a great increase in the number of women elected to the district leadership. A third of the new people elected (half of all those in leadership positions were new) were women (Bildende kunst 1985: 434). The district elections did indeed have consequences for the National Congress elections, even if the changes were less far-reaching than anticipated (Rueschemeyer 1991).

Women took an active part in the demonstrations that erupted in cities throughout the GDR. Yet they felt it was imperative to organize an independent association to articulate the social policies and programmes they envisioned. This was due in part to what the women interpreted as insufficient support by the general opposition groups. In 1989 an independent women's movement was formed, a coalition of groups from all over the GDR which included communist women's initiatives as well as Christian women's groups (Weichert and Hoepfner 1990). Women actively participated in the Round Tables, where democratic political negotiation and administration took place during a temporary period of GDR government before the elections of March 1990. The Round Tables existed all over the country, either as coalitions or as replacements of the old leadership.

There were many meetings with West German women, under a variety of auspices—political parties, women's movements, feminist intellectuals, etc. It is not surprising that these revealed tensions between West and East Germany, as well as a growing number of divergent interpretations and understandings of the causes of remaining gender inequalities in the GDR. In the beginning, a number of GDR women involved in these meetings often felt that their point of view and their concerns were not respected, but that a feminist theology was presented to them, for them to take on as their own holy cause.

At one such meeting of Greens from East and West Germany, two western Green representatives criticized concepts of motherhood while their East German sisters—many of whom were single mothers—had attended the

TABLE 3.3 Share of employed females in the economic sectors (%)

Economic sector	Proportion of employed women in total number of employed				Proportion of economic sector occupied by women			
	1970	1980	1984	1985	1970	1980	1984	1985
Industry	42.5	43.3	41.9	41.7	32.3	33.0	32.1	32.1
Crafts	40.1	38.0	37.4	37.2	4.3	2.4	2.3	2.3
Construction	13.3	16.2	16.3	16.5	1.9	2.3	2.3	2.3
Agriculture and forestry	45.8	41.5	39.4	39.1	12.2	8.9	8.6	8.6
Transportation	25.5	27.4	27.0	26.9	3.0	3.2	3.2	3.2
Post and telephone	68.8	70.0	69.3	69.1	2.5	2.3	2.2	2.2
Retail trade	69.2	72.8	72.8	72.6	15.8	15.0	15.0	15.0
Other productive branches	53.7	55.1	55.0	56.1	2.6	3.5	3.4	3.3
Non-productive branches	70.2	72.9	73.2	73.1	25.4	29.3	30.9	31.1
Total	48.3	49.9	49.4	49.3	100.0	100.0	100.0	100.0

Source: (Nickel 1989: 53).

meeting with their children, who were being cared for in the very next room
by two young women. The East German women finally took over the meeting
to discuss their own issues.[8] What explains the differences between the two
groups? An interesting study of women members of the West German
Bundestag provides a clue. It indicates that the younger cohort of Greens—
compared with the somewhat older Social Democratic Party (SPD) women
who wanted to combine family and career and the even older Christian
Democratic Union (CDU) women who were generally more conservative in
orientation—have been more strongly influenced by feminist notions that
family commitments and women's equality are mutually exclusive and that
women should remain single to fulfil their potential (Kolinsky 1991).

Following the collapse of communism, issues concerning women's roles
became contentious. There was concern about maintaining abortion rights,
day-care centres, and the right to work, everything that had been gained by
women in the GDR. A *Spiegel* poll published on 1 January 1991 showed that
two-thirds of the East Germans interviewed considered the GDR ahead of
the FRG in matters of gender equality; nearly a third of West Germans
agreed. More than half of the East Germans, women as well as men, thought
that women had equal chances at work, while a third saw men getting
preferential treatment. Asked whether one should resign oneself to the fact
that day-care centres would no longer be guaranteed, two-thirds disagreed.[9]
With unification, voices that were less publicly heard in the old regime were
now being openly sounded, voices that were more in tune with the Christian
Democratic Party 'choirs' all over the land, accompanied by the appropriate
Blockflöten.[10] Now the appropriate goal of women should be to stay at home
and establish a family life that fits more with traditional values. This found
resonance with many women. Some talked about how hard it had been, how
their children and family life had suffered because of their working, because
their children were in day-care centres, and so on. For some, it is easier to
blame the difficulties of their children—the deep alienation of so many
young people—on these factors. The less skilled the women, the less
enthusiastic they were about their work. For those women who found it
difficult to combine work and family commitments, because of the incon-
venient location of day-care centres, work-place conditions, poor access to
markets, unhelpful attitudes of husbands, etc., the 'other life' became more
appealing.

There are also a variety of intellectual or professional reflections critically

[8] These remarks are based on observation of a meeting in Rostock in spring 1990. One long-
discussed problem was the lack of child-care facilities in West Germany.

[9] *Spiegel Spezial: Das Profil der Deutschen*, 1 (1991): 46,66.

[10] Here the word for a musical instrument also refers to the political parties in the former
GDR, which were not really independent of the dominant Communist Party. The suggestion
is that some former GDR citizens are conforming now to the CDU party line.

evaluating the women's policies of the GDR past. The state from its very beginnings was patriarchal in personnel and outlook. There was no real analysis of the problems and the restructuring that would have to take place on all levels of GDR life in order to create real gender equality.

At the same time, many recognize that individual women's lives were affected by their participation in work; that the work-place, especially for those in more skilled occupations, did empower them and did affect their sense of competence and independence, as well as providing financial resources and community outside the house. So, with all the attractions of that greener grass on the other side, there are many women who would not think of staying at home and not working, who search for a compatibility between work and the family—fewer hours at work, more time to be with the children, 'going out to lunch, playing tennis', as one East German SPD woman functionary fantasized.[11] In a poll by the Institute for Applied Social Research in Bad Godesberg taken in the autumn of 1990, only 3 per cent of 1,432 women between 16 and 60 in the new states described 'housewife' as a 'dream job'; 58 per cent thought that mothers with careers were 'just as good' as mothers who stayed at home. And of course, in a situation of financial and occupational uncertainties and instabilities, a retreat to the family nest could create more rather than fewer difficulties for households.

UNIFICATION AND RESTRUCTURING: THE IMPACT ON WOMEN

We still do not know how the employment of women and their social and economic situation more generally will develop, but we can sketch the reality of women's lives since unification. By 1991 a higher percentage of women than men had been laid off (52 v. 48 per cent), and women continue to be affected by high unemployment. By 1992, since the completion of this chapter, 63 per cent of all women eligible to work were unemployed. Women are strongly represented in light industry, textiles and clothing, electronics, chemistry and plastics—industries that have been adversely affected by unification. They are less represented than men in construction, transportation, and other industries which will necessarily receive support. Better educated women often filled administrative positions, many of which were related to the central economy and are likely to be decimated; they have been involved in cultural institutions, publishing houses, and so on, whose numbers continue to be reduced. This has affected the atmosphere at the work-place so that, even in 1990, women talked about the growing tension and decreasing rapport among their colleagues. In the view of many women,[12]

---

[11] During an interview in autumn 1990.

[12] Approximately two dozen women were interviewed in 1990–1 in Bern, Berlin and Rostock.

although they are formally represented by a union, they do not *feel* represented by anyone and have voiced complaints about exploitation, and not only in terms of salary. Some women said that they are afraid to open their mouths. Indeed, the Federation of German Trade Unions reports that infringements of the labour laws are common in eastern Germany. Ursula Engelen-Kefer, the deputy director of the West German Federation, stated that companies try to take advantage of the unfamiliarity of employees and workers' councils with the laws and that these problems would become even more serious when negotiated protection against dismissal runs out at the end of June 1991.[13]

The eastern German sociologist Hildegard Nickel predicts that training quotas for young women will no longer apply; interests and personal preferences will again acquire greater weight; the spread of technology will make the administrative spheres connected with these attractive to male labour, introducing competition in finance, marketing, and personnel management.[14] Because of the extreme situation, government measures are being initiated to deal with unemployment and job creation; these are mandated to benefit women in proportion to their share of the unemployed.

Eastern German women are likely to face discrimination when they apply for high-level jobs, and they have limited recourse for challenging such decisions. The EC stipulations are relatively weak. The present government coalition is discussing strengthening the laws against discrimination. Women's rights were also among the components introduced in West German labour negotiations during the last few years.

Anticipation of difficulties with day care and concern about the primary wage-earner provide good excuses for recruitment and hiring practices that favour men over women. And temporary and part-time work are less secure than full-time permanent employment.[15] The preference for hiring men is combined with the expectation that women will take care of 'family' matters.

The time women devote to confronting the new challenges of the market economy is a further factor inhibiting them from taking the time they need to search for work. Dealing with schools, medical care, and a different style of consumerism calls for a great deal of attention and energy. Even if both men and women see these tasks as vitally important, they are absorbing and enormously time-consuming. They also reinforce traditional notions of the gender division of labour.

[13] Interestingly, Engelen-Kefer noted that, although the East German courts were not yet fully functioning, 'some 40 union legal offices in Eastern Germany in some cases had to initiate more than 2,000 legal proceedings a month' (*The Week in Germany*, 26 April 1991: 5).
[14] Paper presented at the IREX sub-commission on women and work in the former GDR and the United States, Humboldt University, Berlin, 1991.
[15] As it stands, protection from being fired under federal law lasts from the beginning of pregnancy until some weeks after the birth (*Informationen*, no. 1, 1991: 28 and information from Dr Hanna Beate Schoepp-Schilling, Ministry for Women and Youth).

Single women with children among the unemployed face special problems. The special supports for these women—access to child-care facilities and *Kindergarten*—are endangered. Several proposals are being discussed now to ensure day care with support from the federal government. These proposals are being debated and face stiff opposition. In the meantime, the five new states are responsible for their own policies and financial support of day care while they face extreme budget difficulties generally. Even with continuity assured for a limited period of time, many parents are concerned about the loss of day care or expenses for day care they can ill afford. University students or students in vocational training will also face new problems. Students with children will no longer be able to count on child-care supports and other facilities.

These issues, combined with concerns about future abortion regulations, could theoretically play themselves out in the formation of a strong women's movement or in a heavy involvement of women in political parties. In fact, the independent women's groups are not very active and have not been able to mobilize women to any substantial degree. The formerly state-run Women's Federation, even after conducting secret elections and initiating new activities, has a very low membership.

What accounts for this weakness in the collective organization of women? Aside from the fact that many women are concerned with issues they consider more important now, the hesitancy to get involved is first of all related to the role of the state in the former GDR. It was the state that addressed the issues of women on its own terms, developed the policies that affected their lives, and presented the public interpretations of these policies and goals as well. There was no mechanism enabling women to be their own advocates. Thus, it is no surprise that women have limited practice in forming pressure groups and becoming their own advocates, even if these groups might be really important for what they want to accomplish.

Furthermore, they are unlikely to become active if they feel they have no impact. In the former GDR, there were strong tendencies to withdraw from public life and concentrate on the more private sphere. That inclination is likely to continue. It will be all the stronger among all those people—often highly qualified—who did get involved with the state and party in the past and are now seen as compromised.

Finally, inequality is rapidly increasing in the eastern part of Germany. Those who are relatively well off now experience gains in income as well as through social supports of the state, while the many others who lose in this process are the weakest and have the least power to organize. This applies to women generally and to those threatened with unemployment and single mothers in particular.

Such weakness of women's collective organization does not bode well for the chances of legislation and administrative action supportive of women's interests. The women's bureaux that were instituted in each community in the spring of 1990—with at least one full paid position in every community of more than 10,000 people—are no substitutes for political organization and influence.

Certain developments in the West German political parties would appear promising. The Social Democratic Party (SPD) now has as its goal a quota of 40 per cent women for all party offices, a goal they hope to reach by the year 2000. In public administration, the SPD has a 50 per cent quota as its goal which is presently being challenged in the constitutional court in North-Rhine Westfalia. In 1992, 26 per cent of Social Democratic deputies in the Bundestag were women. That compared with 13 per cent in the CDU/CSU, which has its own plan for a women's quota based on membership in the party, 19 per cent in the Free Democratic Party (FDP), half of the transformed communist party (PDS), and three women and five men in the Bundestag delegation of the Bündnis 90/Green coalition. Altogether, 20 per cent of the Bundestag members were women.[16] The large percentage of highly educated women, especially among the deputies of the SPD and the Greens, would seem to provide another potential support for policies fostering gender equality.[17]

Women active in the Federal Republic are turning to the state for measures, laws, and policies that address the issues of women. That in itself is not unusual, because West Germany is a *Sozialstaat*, with a long welfare state tradition. Any complete understanding of women's issues in Germany must take this into account, even though these welfare state policies may be quite conservative in their overall conception of gender issues. West German women are advocates on their own behalf, and they are skilled in this, though this does not mean that the forces that promote gender equality are winning all or even most battles. Some of the proposals have multiple consequences.

[16] In 1989, nearly 20% of the council seats in municipalities and cities with a population over 20,000 in the Federal Republic were held by women, compared with only 12.5% in 1984 (*The Week in Germany*, 15 June 1990: 6).

Kohl appointed four women to the new cabinet: Irmgard Adam Schwätzer (Free Democratic Party), Hannelore Rönsch (CDU), Angela Merkel (CDU), and Gerda Hasselfeld (CSU).

In the five new states, the Social Democrats (who in the West were, together with the Greens before their recent defeat, most progressive on women's issues) were successful only in the state of Brandenburg, the area surrounding Berlin. Regine Hildebrandt (SPD), the Brandenburg Minister for Social Policy, Labour, Families and Women, has become a heroine because she distributes birth control pills without cost, continuing the GDR policy.

[17] On the other hand Eva Kolinsky has suggested that with quota commitments the political parties in Western Germany were increasingly geared towards educated middle-class women, with the possible consequence that the lower stratum would be increasingly less integrated (Kolinsky 1991: 70). CDU Minister of Women and Youth Angela Merkel of eastern Germany is critical from another perspective. In 1991 she spoke out against the 'rigid quota system', suggesting that it was 'constitutionally questionable and ill-equipped to master the varied tasks of public administration and a flexible personnel policy' (*The Week in Germany*, 26 Apr. 1991: 2). Her political opponents have accused her of mouthing policies set forth by Chancellor Kohl and of not furthering the position of women.

Extending the eighteen-month parental leave to three years, moderately funded by the federal government, would increase the possibility of remaining at home and returning at a later period to work; but it may also mean a neglect of day-care centres, making it more difficult for both parents to seek employment. It may also lead to discrimination in hiring, against which, as mentioned above in connection with EC directives, there exists only weak protection. And it may result in channelling women into the household for several years. There is no consensus in West German society on these issues, and at this point most women in eastern Germany do not feel enough a part of the system to work in it on their own behalf.

Ironically, it seems that unification has created opportunities for West German women to push for gender equality that did not exist before. Many of the new policies mentioned above came about as a result of the tensions that developed after unification. Another example is the abortion issue, the much debated para. 218 in the Penal Code. In spite of intensive manoeuvring of Chancellor Kohl and the Christian Democratic Union (CDU),[18] there remained a good chance that the Penal Code would be liberalized. The agreement underlying the government coalition provided for a Bundestag vote according to each member's conscience on this issue and not along party lines. The FDP introduced a proposal that abortion be legalized for the first three months of pregnancy with only one condition—that the women have counselling. The SPD put forward the same proposal, only without conditions. Rita Suessmuth, Speaker of the Bundestag and one of the most popular CDU politicians, proposed a third way, which was considered somewhat more conservative but still more flexible than the current regulations, while the state of Bavaria pursued constitutional claims against the conservative regulation as too permissive. The majority of the governing Christian Democrats favoured a law similar to the one existing in West Germany but with fewer administrative reasons. The proposal reduced the reasons from four to two: medical reasons or 'psycho-social' emergency—to be determined by a doctor. In the autumn of 1991, the Bundestag established a special commission to consider the abortion issue (*The Week in Germany*, 27 September 1991: 1). In 1992 Parliament voted to allow abortion during the first three months of pregnancy after a consultation. These more liberal regulations were not, however, immediately upheld by the Constitutional Court.

During the early period of unification and restructuring, other policies that

---

[18] Kohl broke up the ministry on women, the elderly, and youth into three units. All heads are women and are said to be relatively weak. The abortion issue was taken out of Angela Merkel's (East German CDU) ministry for women and put in the ministry dealing with families. But Merkel, who declared her opposition to the liberal GDR regulation, runs a party commission on the issue. Other East German women with the same position also play key roles in the CDU strategy.

were being initiated included increasing the number of days allowed for sick-leave from five to ten (for single mothers, twenty) as well as raising the age of the sick child to include those 12 and under; previously in the Federal Republic, as mentioned above, parents were allowed to stay at home only if a child was 8 or younger. These measures, as well as an eighteen-month parental leave and the plans for its extension (with DM600 for half a year and then staggered according to income) were in response to tense reactions in East Germany to the loss of similar benefits. As important as these are, they may aggravate discrimination in hiring if stronger legal measures against such discrimination are not forthcoming.

As it is, the percentage of women in the highest positions in politics, economic institutions, and the university remains low in all parts of the country. These hurdles were not overcome in either West or East Germany.

Even with the possibility that women advocating gender equality will lose on issues they consider vital, there is a feeling of excitement about many of the policies that are now being discussed in the political arena. But these are discussions of *policies*. The *reality* for women in eastern Germany is characterized by a great deal of tension, insecurity, and even despair, both because of general economic and social conditions and because of their particular situation as women in the new states.

It is, however, through the political system that the supports for both men and women to play new and equal roles in both public and private life are most likely to be advanced. The hesitation of East German women actively to participate in shaping politics will endanger their interests in the long run. Furthermore, to be effective, it is necessary for East and West German women to find a way of joining forces. Without such co-operation, the participation of East German women will be weak. Unfortunately, the state of the Eastern German economy, the present preference for hiring men, and the absorption of many women into the 'private' sphere is leading to a vicious cycle of retreat from both the economy and the polity, and to even greater difficulties of reintegrating into the public sphere in the future.

REFERENCES

BILDENDE KUNST, (1985), 'Zu den Sektionswahlversammlungen der Bezirk-organisation des Verbandes Bildender Kuenstler der DDR', *Bildende kunst*, 10:434.
FRG (1985), *Facts and Figures*, Press and Information Office. Bonn: FRG.
KOLINSKY, EVA (1991), 'Political Participation and Parliamentary Careers: Women's Quotas in West Germany', *West European Politics*, 14(1): 56–72.
MEYER, GERD (1986), 'Frauen in den Machthierarchien der DDR', *Deutschland Archiv*, 19(3): 294–311.
NICKEL, HILDEGARD (1989), 'Sex-Role Socialization in Relationships as a Function of the Division of Labor: A Sociological Explanation for the Reproduction of

Gender Differences', in Marilyn Rueschemeyer and Christiane Lemke (eds.), *The Quality of Life in the German Democratic Republic: Changes and Developments in a State Socialist Society*. New York and London: M. E. Sharpe, 48–58.

RUESCHEMEYER, MARILYN (1981), *Professional Work and Marriage: An East–West Comparison*. London: Macmillan/New York: St Martin's Press.

—— (1991), 'State Patronage in the German Democratic Republic: Artistic and Political Change in a State Socialist Society', *Journal of Arts/Management/Law*, 20(4): 31–55.

—— and SCHISSLER, HANNA (1990), 'Women in the Two Germanies', *German Studies Review*, Special DAAD Issue, Winter: 71–85.

SCHOEPP-SCHILLING, HANNA BEATE (1985), 'Federal Republic of Germany', in Jennie Farley (ed.), *Women Workers in Fifteen Countries*. Ithaca, NY: Cornell University, ILR Press, 124–37.

WEICHERT, BRIGITTE and HOEPFNER, HELMUT (1990), 'Frauen in Politik und Gesellschaft', in Gunnar Winkler (ed.), *Frauen-Report '90*. Berlin: Verlag Die Wirtschaft, 199–227.

4

The Transition to Democracy in Bulgaria: Challenges and Risks for Women

Dobrinka Kostova

INTRODUCTION

During the forty-five years of Bulgarian state socialist development, women had major roles in three spheres: labour, family, and politics. In the sphere of labour, women entered many new jobs and professions. Women's role in the family was simplified owing to the availability of child care and to innovations in household appliances. In the sphere of formal politics, women's participation was facilitated by the application of quotas. During these years, much prejudice with regard to women was overcome through education and primarily through women's economic involvement. Women proved their abilities to pursue careers, and the employment of women enlarged their cultural interests. Although posing some problems in family life, women's labour activity became a source of new knowledge, skills, and experience. On that basis, the educational progress of their children and the development of their own personalities was enriched. Employment gave women a new status and new attitudes towards people and social realities. Their life options and their expectations increased.

The change in the traditional role of women would not have been possible without a parallel change in the role of men in labour and the family. During the period under consideration, the patriarchal family was gradually replaced by a complementary partnership. The nuclear-type family had emerged in Bulgaria after the Second World War. Before the state socialist revolution, Bulgarian women were strongly attached to their families. Later, some of the household chores and especially child care were transferred to kindergartens and schools because of women's full-time employment. Women's formal employment resulted in a diminution of their exclusive responsibility for family decision making, with a concomitant increase in the role of men in household duties and in the process of bringing up children. The more time women and men devote to employment, the more likely it is that the job will take precedence over non-economic roles, and over family satisfaction.

In this context, the period of transition starting in Bulgaria in November

I would like to thank Dr Valentine Moghadam for her comments on and assistance in editing earlier drafts of this chapter.

1989 with the downfall of Todor Zhivkov's regime is proving to be a time of constant changes in paradigms, attitudes, values, and behaviour. An overriding question is the transformation of women's roles and the degree of women's activity. Not enough time has elapsed for us to make definitive statements about changes in structures, in attitudes, and in women's roles. However, the economic, political, and even cultural changes that are taking place allow us to make observations, form hypotheses, and suggest trends. On the whole, women are in favour of the democratic reforms in Bulgaria. They are against violence and struggle. This approach has a strong influence on women's quantitative participation in the newly created parties and organizations.

Bulgarian women have always been active in economic, political, and social life, but the type and extent of involvement has varied during the different political periods. The curve of their job activity moves from predominant home work before state socialism to full labour employment in the period of state socialist development. The democratic revolution now offers opportunities for risk-taking, entrepreneurial, and qualified women to start private businesses. At the same time, the risk of becoming unemployed prompts women to seek security in the state sector. Both the fear of economic crisis and the sense that the transition to private entrepreneurship may improve the family's economic and social status seem to create strong family solidarity.

This chapter will review the negative and positive aspects of the situation of Bulgarian women during the period of state socialist development, and will show how these past contradictions provide the basis for both opportunities and risks during the transition period.

THE EXPERIENCE OF EQUALITY

The relationship between women's labour and family life and the emphasis on the one or the other depends to a great extent on the economic, social, and political growth of society. The latter is also the framework within which personal perceptions develop. Work and family roles differ according to social status, age, and personal preferences. While a woman's education and employment influences fertility decisions, the number and age of children also exert an influence on women's employment activity.

After the Second World War, Bulgaria underwent rapid industrialization. Farming, domestic services, clothing, and food production were greatly reduced as industry expanded. The result was a high demand for labour, which influenced the economic policy of the state proclaiming the necessity of female labour as a matter of principle in bringing about equality of the sexes. Through its social and economic policy, the state encouraged a model of full employment for men and women. Wages, which are a strong economic incentive, were a very important factor for full female employment. Many social benefits, notably child-care leave, were addressed to working women only (and later to grandparents, if they were still employed). Thus, social legislation became the second important element for women's employment.

The model of full female employment typical for the period of state socialist development did not solve the problems of women's emancipation. Although there existed a legal framework for labour rights (male and female), the conflicts between the two sexes were constantly reproduced. The most important factor was the model of egalitarianism administratively imposed on society by the ruling Communist Party. This model reflected party ideology and lacked an adequate economic and social basis. The country was poor, and a mechanism was necessary to motivate educated and capable people to take risks to move the economy forward. Instead, the principle of levelling was proclaimed as a state policy, and this benefited people on the lower rungs of the social ladder.

Women's emancipation was an integral element of the social programme of equality. It extended to work, political participation, and family benefits. Maternity allowances and child-care facilities were equal in amount and access for all Bulgarian families. A working woman was entitled to paid maternity leave of 120 days during pregnancy and the birth of her first child; for her second child the leave increased to 150 days, for a third child to 180 days, and for every subsequent child it was 120 days. If she so desired, a working mother could take paid child-care leave until her child was 2 years of age. Her job was kept up to the third year (*Labour Law* 1986: art. 163). Paid and unpaid parental leave could be used by the father or by one of the working grandparents (*Labour Law* 1986: arts. 164 and 165). If the child's parents did not use the maternity leave, the working mother was paid her whole wage plus 50 per cent of the minimum wage in the country. The three years of maternity leave was recognized as labour service.

In the state socialist system, the parents received child allowances monthly, the amount of which depended on the number of children in the family. Social policy was designed to encourage the birth of a second and third child. The allowances were received by the parents until the child reached the age of 16 (or 18 if the child was still studying). For handicapped children the allowances were doubled.

This legal framework of the social policy was established to solve some of the emerging problems connected with women's full-time employment, and sought especially to provide child care. Even then, it was very difficult for women to achieve psychological balance. The reason for this was women's traditional responsibility for child care, and the absence of adequate parental care of children as a result of full employment. Psychologists and sociologists both stress the importance of the development of the parent-child relationship in the formative years. Two major problems have been singled out: distancing between parents and children, and children's worsening health and social behaviour. These phenomena do not depend on parents' attitudes, behaviour, and activity alone, but on the way the socio-economic system is organized and the educational system functions.

The transition period already has had a great impact on changes in the family. In the first place, the economic function of the family is being restored through property rights and inheritance. This makes it very likely that the family could turn from a predominantly consuming unit into a more comprehensive economic unit, especially given the development or re-emergence of small firms and farms. This could lead to changes in family roles and thus in the role of women. With the rise of unemployment, the likelihood of women without a profession becoming involved in private family businesses will increase. This economic involvement of the family will change children's role and their requirements. The state socialist and pre-socialist Bulgarian system of values placed a premium on the higher education of children. Education is free and allegedly depends on children's abilities. In the transition period, the desire to overcome the economic crisis with as little loss as possible may alter family philosophy concerning children's education. The diversification of economic life leading to the development of small businesses, to the acquisition of different skills, and to a supply of cheap labour may influence parents' preferences towards adequate rather than higher education. The changing realities in the country could result in a shift from pure knowledge to the knowledge of how to adapt and benefit from the new political, economic, and social conditions, or how to acquire skills in practical work. Thus, an emphasis on economic relations within the family could result from liberalization of the relations in society. The changing model of society could be transferred to the family.

The principle of egalitarianism is the core of Decree 5 of 1987 of the Committee (now Ministry) of Labour and Social Affairs and of the Trade Unions. It defines the jobs suitable for women and the jobs from which they are banned. The jobs defined as forbidden to women are those that could be hazardous for their health and maternal functions. According to the first article of that Decree, women have to be given priority for jobs that are suitable for them if all other conditions are equal. The formal equality of opportunity in training and employment has an impact on, but does not radically alter, the real dynamics of women's occupational roles. The law has a general meaning, but the reality is different. Job equality of men and women cannot be achieved only through laws. It is necessary that the conditions for job realization be appropriate to the abilities and biological disposition of men and women. This could be implemented through a balanced male and female labour market participation in accordance with the economic growth of the country.

The pension law under state socialism was also based on formal equality. It required women to retire five years earlier than men for all labour categories. For the majority of Bulgarian women the retirement age was 55; mothers with five or more children were allowed to retire at the age of 40. In Bulgaria the average life expectancy for men is 68.1 years, while for women it is 74.8 years (*National Statistics* 1990*d*: 6). Bulgarian women spend approximately twenty years in retirement, which is very close to their number of years at work. That situation was beneficial because women did not receive very high wages; the longer retirement period was also a kind of compensation for the fact that women must combine jobs with household work.

In the process of transition to a market economy, the situation is changing. Now wages will become the main resource for meeting health, education, and pension needs. Thus, the earlier retirement of women will have a negative effect on their quality of life. This being the case, more flexible retirement arrangements have to be created. This problem is closely related to the negative demographic situation in the country, characterized by a definite increase of older people in the population and a constant trend of decreasing population growth rates. Twenty-five years ago the average age was 34 years, while in 1990 it was 37.3. The proportion of younger people (0–15 years) in 1990 was 20.2 per cent, whereas in 1980 it was 22.1 per cent (*National Statistics* 1990*d*: 5). The population growth rate in 1990 was negative (–0.4) for the first time in Bulgarian history (Minkov *et al.* 1991: 3). The generational structure of the Bulgarian population is worsening. This is due mainly to decreasing population growth, since life expectancy has been unchanged for the last twenty years.

These negative population trends have deepened since 1989 as a result of the difficult economic and political situation in the country. The data from Table 4.1 show that the fertility coefficient (the number of children born to the number of women of childbearing age) decreased significantly in 1990. A very important factor in this process in 1989 and 1990 is emigration. At the end of 1990 the number of people that had left the country was 458,000, of whom 240,000 had left Bulgaria in 1990 and the rest in 1989. The greater proportion of those leaving (55.3 per cent) were young people (aged 15–39), while at the age of 60 or more the percentage is just 7.9 (*National Statistics* 1990*d*: 5). This generational structure of the emigrants has a very negative effect on the reproduction of the Bulgarian population.

. The dynamics of both births and abortions show a stable proportion of abortions in the country (Table 4.1). At the same time, the number of abortions is higher than that of births. This is the consequence of a shortage of contraceptives. Although family planning exists and women have some control over their own fertility, the low level of sex education and above all the lack of availability and variety of contraceptives is a very important

TABLE 4.1 Births and abortions per 1,000 women of fertile age, Bulgaria, 1970–1990

	Births	Abortions
1970	63.5	64.5
1975	67.0	65.9
1980	60.4	72.9
1985	56.6	62.5
1988	55.6	62.6
1989	52.8	61.7
1990	48.6	61.6

Source: *National Statistics* (1991a: 12).

problem connected with women's health and the number of children they wish to have.

TRENDS IN THE FEMALE LABOUR FORCE, 1945–1990

The dynamics of women's employment in Bulgaria during the forty-five years of state socialist development show a constant increase of female labour participation (see Table 4.2). This time period may be divided in accordance to female recruitment into two sub-periods: (1) the late 1940s–late 1960s, and (2) 1970–89.

TABLE 4.2 Women in the Bulgarian labour force, 1934–1989 (%)

1934	1948	1962	1970	1980	1985	1988	1989
24.0	29.0	40.0	43.6	48.5	49.5	49.9	50.0

Source: *National Statistics* (1991b: 31); *Statistics 1939* (Sofia): 48.

The main characteristic of the first period is the rapid quantitative increase in working women, especially from the groups of peasants and housewives. This occurred in the context of industrialization and collectivization which required massive amounts of labour. Formulated in the ideological framework of sex equality, state policy prevented the continuation of the single-breadwinner family model. Economic realities and higher expectations further prompted full female employment.

The second sub-period is marked by the constant increase of working women. Certain branches of industry and agriculture saw increased female labour-force involvement, itself a result of the technological development of the Bulgarian economy: 81 per cent of all working women came to be employed in light industry, trade, education, finance, and health services.

TABLE 4.3 Education of workers in Bulgaria, 1990 (%)

	University	College	Professional secondary	General secondary	Primary
Total	9.6	5.1	15.8	24.9	44.6
Women	10.0	7.1	15.6	25.5	41.7

Source: National Statistics (1990a: 23, 25).

Half the women workers were secretaries, telephone operators, xerox operators, typists, and so on. There was a significant female–male differentiation in terms of professional structure. Women held 30 per cent of managerial positions but 82.8 per cent of all auxiliary positions. Professional women were concentrated in three areas: economics, health, and education. Over 90 per cent of accountants, teachers, nurses, and librarians were women (*National Statistics* 1990b: 16). Explanations for this pattern of gender differences in employment are rooted in the organization of labour itself and in the sexual division of labour in the family. According to some authors, occupational sex-typing is due mainly to educational and qualification differences (Kjuranov 1977: 207).

The data in Table 4.3 show a slight educational advance of women. However, the formal skill level of women is lower than that of men (*National Statistics* 1990c: 49–52). In the state socialist system, industrial occupations were better paid than many white-collar jobs, but more men were employed in the higher-paying industrial jobs, and at higher skill levels. This is one of the main reasons for income differences. An important characteristic of men–women labour participation is the wage differential. Tables 4.5 and 4.6 show the greater participation of women in lower wage groups and significant distinctions in male–female wages in the highest wage groups.

Since wages provide the bulk of most families' income, the recent fall in real wages has placed severe income pressures on most families, particularly the young ones. Together with wage problems, resulting from high interest rates and rising house prices at the beginning of 1991, the percentage of households owning their own homes dropped (*National Statistics* 1991b: 101).

The results of statistical studies and analyses show that at branch level the average earnings of women are lower than those of men. Given the equality of wages received by men and women for the same job, the reason for the differentiation must be sought in the gender differences of employment by categories. Furthermore, the proportion of women among workers is 46.7 per cent and among the specialists 68.0 per cent. The part of the female work-force in medical personnel is 84.5 per cent and among economists 83.1 per cent. This is not a new tendency in female employment. It shows that the economic changes in the country have not yet influenced the sectoral distribution of female labour. The differentiation is still based mainly on

TABLE 4.4 Wages in Bulgaria, 1990

Amount (*levas*)	Total (%)	Women (%)
0–165	3.5	4.6
166–180	3.0	4.2
181–200	5.2	7.3
201–220	5.8	8.1
221–240	6.6	8.7
241–260	7.0	8.9
261–280	7.6	9.4
281–300	8.6	10.0
301–350	16.6	17.4
351–400	12.3	10.1
401–450	8.3	5.4
451–500	5.4	2.7
501–600	5.5	2.1
601–700	2.4	0.7
701–	2.2	0.4

Source: National Statistics (1990*b*: 10–13; 1990*c*: 164).

TABLE 4.5 Average wages in Bulgaria according to branch, 1990

Branch	Average wage (*levas*)	Average wage for women (*levas*)
Industry	346	295
Construction	379	306
Agriculture	338	276
Forest production	265	232
Transport	391	306
Telecommunications	332	315
Trade	283	268
Others in production industry	325	304
Housing	294	258
Science	349	314
Education	296	285
Culture	279	259
Health and insurance	336	325
Finance	325	311
Management	368	333
Others in non-production industry	352	310

Source: National Statistics (1990*b*: 10–13).

qualification criteria, giving relatively better chances to men. It is also a consequence of the women's family responsibilities which tends to lead to a delay in their careers mainly as a result of maternity leaves.

The main conclusion from the wage analysis concerns the whole economic and financial policy of the state during the examined period. The aim was not to construct big differences between the male and female work-forces; a principal objective of state policy was to fix low wages for men in order to encourage women into employment. Its interest was to secure cheap labour in huge quantities.

This model of work-force employment in the transition period is about to collapse. The necessary efficient production can be realized by smaller numbers of workers. This will define future wage differentiation. At the same time, it will be the main condition for establishing a female labour market. In that sense, research programmes can be of great help to prove the real value of female labour, in the face of pressure for women to leave employment to take care of the household.

On the whole, forty-five years of state socialist development were characterized by full employment of the labour force. But in reality, full employment is difficult to regulate. Without the administrative approach, this kind of order would not have been possible. It determined educational quotas for a definite number of professions, particularly in the non-productive spheres (such as medicine, which stipulated equal shares of male and female students); the development of a system of three years' compulsory service for young people finishing vocational schools, colleges, and universities; overestimation of the administrative personnel; etc. This kind of a system did not favour the best professionals and workers. It also led to an absence of workers' motivation and to work alienation. Production efficiency and competitiveness were very low.

CHANGES IN BULGARIA 1989–1991: ADAPTATION AND RISK FOR
WOMEN

The transition to an economic system based on the rules of the market leads to significant turns in employment ratios and in social protection of labour. The economic crisis in the country calls for important structural changes in order to achieve competitive production and a new financial system. A few inefficient firms were shut down, and a number of other production units were closed because of pollution problems. For these and other reasons, such as the collapse of COMECON and the failure of centralized administrative regulation of the relations between the firms within the country, there has been a sharp rise in the rate of unemployment.

The formation of the labour market reflects the changes resulting from the economic reform. It is now unbalanced because of a large labour supply and a lack of corresponding demand for labour. The National Labour Bureau data show that on 31 May 1991 the number of unemployed people in the country reached 205,950. For the period July 1990–May 1991 unemployment increased 6.6 times, and from January 1991 to May 1991, 2.8 times. The number of unemployed women was 112,907. Among these, 60.6 per cent have lost their jobs through lay-offs; they will receive financial support for nine months, while the other 39.4 per cent do not receive any compensation. This is a negative effect of the law according to which compensations are received only in case of a worker being dismissed by an employer. Accustomed to full employment in the country, and at the same time ignorant of the labour laws, many women anticipating a dismissal left their jobs on their own initiative only to find out later that they were not eligible for financial compensation. In this largely spontaneous process of workers' release, the risks of women losing their jobs are considerable.

The data on unemployed women for the period July 1990–May 1991 (Table 4.6) show that the process was slowing down slightly, yet the overall figure was still higher than for male employees. In the period under review, the number of unemployed women increased 5.8 times. The regional distribution of unemployed women shows that their greatest number is in the region of Plovdiv (19,250), in the region of Sofia (15,345), and in Sofia itself (15,000). It should be noted that 60 per cent of all unemployed professionals are women. Young women's unemployment is a very important problem, as they form 54.8 per cent of all the unemployed in the age group up to 30.

The trend towards high female unemployment in Bulgaria is a result of two main factors. The first is related to the structural changes taking place.

TABLE 4.6 Number of women unemployed in Bulgaria, July 1990–May 1991

	No.	Portion of all unemployed
July 1990	19,499	62.8
August 1990	22,124	67.6
September 1990	26,270	67.4
October 1990	32,695	67.6
November 1990	39,231	66.3
December 1990	42,421	65.2
January 1991	47,046	63.5
February 1991	63,130	61.2
March 1991	79,136	58.7
April 1991	98,001	55.4
May 1991	112,907	54.8

Source: National Labour Bureau, (1991: 164).

The emphasis in the past on heavy industry—mining, metallurgy, mechanical engineering—is shifting to light industry in the transition period. The labour force released from these branches is being directed to light industry, which up to now has been highly feminized. The point of issue is the competitiveness of women. They are in an unfavourable situation for several reasons. If efficiency is the main aim of production, women will be away more often than men because of their child-care leaves. Despite their higher education (Table 4.3), their formal job qualifications are lower than men (*National Statistics* 1990c: 49–52). The job qualification coefficient for women is 0.386, while for men it is 0.441. The process of cutting down on staff is realized predominantly in non-productive sectors—administration, services, culture, etc.—where women predominate.

The second reason concerns technology. The demand for competitive production requires high technology. In that context, the younger generation will adapt more easily to the new labour requirements. The older employees, including women, will more often be released, and for them to find another job will be very difficult. The existing legal system allows employees who have three years or less to go before reaching the retirement age to retire earlier at a 10 per cent reduction in their pension (*State Gazette* 1990). This solution is partial. These women will have a steady income, but in the current situation of high inflation and price liberalization they are doomed to join the lowest social strata.

Unemployment has a very significant effect on women's position in society, on family relations, and on women's satisfaction in life. To women who for decades have perceived work as one of their most important roles in society, the loss of paid employment leads to severe distress. Job loss is regarded by some women as a collapse of their social perspective and value system in which labour has held a prominent position. As social policy up to now had simply fostered inactivity and adherence to its rules, in the new situation the lack of experience leads to loss of flexibility and security. This insecurity is strengthened if the family blames the woman's unemployment on her.

The models of behaviour of unemployed women are different. Some 20 per cent accept their family role as the main one (Bobeva *et al.* 1991: 74). Some unemployed women start their own private businesses; others turn to private firms in an attempt to find the same or similar work as they were doing before. Some women enrol in courses to gain more skills and widen their scope in order to become more competitive in the labour market. Financial reasons force others to accept jobs below their qualifications. Unemployment gives rise to negative psychological effects in some women, whose reaction is either passivity accompanied by deep depression, or activity sometimes combined with aggressiveness. The latter can manifest itself in migration but also in robberies, prostitution, and so on (*National Statistics* 1990d).

During the last four decades, women were influenced by the state's social and economic policy, which guaranteed full employment and job security based on a low but equal quality of life for the majority of population. This is why many women cannot now readily adapt themselves to unemployment in the first years of transition to a market economy. It represents a new challenge to the education system, to trade unions, and to personnel management in promoting self-confidence and important professional abilities.

The majority of Bulgarian women do not reject their involvement in child care and household chores. They consider these activities necessary for the benefit of their children and family life. While they could accept a delay in their labour market involvement and professional career, they could never accept being economically inactive. The data from a sociological survey with a representative sample of 1,600 women, conducted by the Institute for Trade Union and Social Science Research in 1991, give evidence about these attitudes of Bulgarian women (Table 4.7).

These data focus on the most important problems appearing in the relationship between the family and the economic activity of women. (In this question a condition is set: the answers should not concern the woman herself, her education, experience, or professional activities, but only her family duties.) The responsibility that the Bulgarian woman feels towards her family is a very important component in her value system. At the same time, only a small proportion of women reject work. And the reasons are not only financial. This is proved by the attitude of women in the case where a husband could earn enough to provide for the family: no more than 20 per cent of women would prefer to stay at home (Bobeva *et al.* 1991: 74). This indicates the disposition of Bulgarian women to work, a disposition that is economically, socially, and psychologically conditioned. The roots of this phenomenon could be found in the preference for economic independence,

TABLE 4.7 Should Bulgarian women work?

	Answers (%)
Yes, if they want to	25.0
Yes, after their children grow up	31.5
Yes, part-time	23.3
Yes, if they are not married	8.6
Yes, from time to time	3.0
No	6.2
No reply	2.4
Total	100

Source: Sociological survey, 'The Working Women in the Transition to Market Economy', ITUSSR, Sofia, 1991.

as well as in the high educational level, in the chances for social interactions at the work-place, and in the habit of working outside the family. To a certain extent, it is connected with the social memory of women's situation in peasant and working-class families before the state socialist revolution. In a predominantly peasant country, the majority of women were hard-working peasants, whose working day was not regulated and who generally worked without pay.

The recent emergence of a new model of the labour market, in which full employment is not really necessary, has not yet had any effect on women's attitude to work. Whether this value originated from or was influenced by the paradigm existing for forty-five years will be evident in women's future economic activity. From women's point of view, the desired model at the moment is guaranteed employment. Such a model depends on women's competitive abilities in the labour market. At the same time, the emerging new attitudes and expectations resulting from the changes in the labour market will influence female employment rates and the extent of female employment.

Despite the disposition to work, in the conditions of mounting un-employment the risks for women are greater than those for men. This is true in particular for young women expecting to have children or to have them very young. On the basis of a proposal made by the Tripartite Commission, consisting of representatives of the government, the trade unions, and the employers, Parliament approved a Decree that guarantees work to a husband or wife whose spouse is unemployed (*State Gazette*, vol. 32, 1991).

This decision is a very good example of the policy mechanism in Bulgaria in the transition period. The rationale behind it is to create a balance between the old and new social and economic realities, although the difficult economic situation of the country calls for urgent measures. The main characteristic of the transition is that it is no longer state socialist development. The new type of development cannot be realized without a transformation period needed to create new economic, social, and psychological values, skills, experience, knowledge, and flexibility. Even the best decisions from an economic or social point of view remain ineffective if they are not accepted and supported by the population.

The above-mentioned Decree presents a societal dilemma: from the perspective of enterprise development, the rule of guaranteeing work to at least one spouse, regardless of skill and qualification, is not viable. At the same time, if both spouses face unemployment, the quality of life for the whole family will decline rapidly. The approach of the Tripartite Commission is a compromise between policy necessities and the difficulties that citizens face in adapting to new realities.

CHALLENGES TO WOMEN MANAGERS

The initial stages of the market economy have shown that women are reluctant to break with the model of full employment. The structure of unemployment in Bulgaria up to May 1991 presupposed dissatisfaction at work in the female labour force. To some extent, the risks for women can be ruled out in the enlarging private sector. But as women do not have the necessary finance and are not inclined to take great risks because of their family commitments, only 5.8 per cent of the women interviewed are willing to start a private business (Bobeva *et al.* 1991: 30).

We can expect women in the private sector to be self-employed, or to assume managerial and executive positions. In these conditions, the new private sector may present women with risks connected with undeveloped health and pension insurance legislation. Very often, working hours are longer than recommended by the Labour Law. (Article 136 establishes 42.5 hours for a five-day working week and 46 hours for a six-day working week.) The longer working day is compensated by higher wages. This balance of interests between the private employer and the female work-force is very fragile and unfavourable to women in the long term in terms of health and the tension of the double burden.

Private business activity has so far attracted few Bulgarian women. Of 87,750 private firms established in 1989, only 145 (1.7 per cent) are owned by women. In 1990 the number of these firms increased to 5.5 per cent (*National Statistics* 1990b: 121). The motivation behind private entrepreneurship is interesting. The primary reason for starting up on one's own is independence, followed by professional interest in the chosen field, and financial necessities. The types of women-run firms repeat the typical branch differentiation of the private firms in the country in the first years of transition. The majority of businesses are found in the service sector (52 per cent); 20 per cent are in production, predominantly in light industry; and the rest are found in education and consultancy. A very encouraging survey finding is that 65 per cent of all businesswomen rely on their professional abilities, knowledge, and skills; 25 per cent on their personal attractiveness, and 29 per cent on the help of the relatives.

It is clear that women have fewer opportunities in managerial positions and career development. However, compared with female managers in the state-owned firms, women in the private sector feel more confident and more secure. This was shown by the results of a sociological survey representing economic managers and bank presidents in the state sector in 1990 (Kostova 1990).

Women managers represented 17.7 per cent of those interviewed. An important feature is that the majority of the male managers interviewed fell in the 50–60 age group, while among women the average age was 41–50 years.

This is probably due to women's earlier retirement age. At the same time, two-thirds of the female managers were activists of the former Communist Party (among male managers this was one-third); until 1990 this was a very important feature in leading positions. This suggests that women managers in state firms rely strongly on political factors for their success. Despite the fact that only 20.8 per cent of them rejected private entrepreneurs, only 14.9 per cent are ready to start their own businesses. The reasons for this reluctance were: the lack of proper abilities (26.7 per cent), lack of capital (13.3 per cent), and lack of strength (6.7 per cent). The most important factors in the quality of life for these women were: peace (70.4 per cent), meaningful life (5.6 per cent), and freedom (5.6 per cent). It is very important to note that none of the women consider family prosperity as an important life value, which was also mentioned in the survey. According to the women managers in state firms and banks, the most important life values were: tolerance (31.5 per cent), logical thinking (20.4 per cent), quick thinking (14.8 per cent), and independence (0.3 per cent). These qualities are very important in the responsible positions that such women occupy, but, probably because of their connections with the Communist Party in the past, they feel insecure and uncertain in the new situation where the party and its ideology have been rejected. The transition period is going to be a very difficult one for these women. It will be important that a *rational* purge be carried out to protect those women managers who possess excellent professional qualities and experience.

WOMEN IN POLITICS

The organized women's movement has existed in Bulgaria since 1857. The aim of the first organizations was the enlightenment and educational improvement of women. From then on, the leading women activists have always been intellectuals. The aims of these organizations were expanded with the increasing labour problems at the beginning of this century. After the Second World War women's groups were united into a National Women's Union, which later changed its name to the Bulgarian Women's Movement. The most crucial problem to be solved was women's illiteracy. Later this movement enlarged its activities to labour relations, labour–family conflicts, child development, and state social policy with regard to women.

The statistical data show that women were proportionally very actively involved in different political organizations. The proportion of women in the Fatherland Front was 50.5 per cent with 41.1 per cent as leaders. Women's involvement was quite similar in the Young Communist League—50.0 per cent of the membership and 38.4 per cent of the leadership. In trade unions women formed 46.4 per cent of all members, and 32.4 per cent were leaders.

TABLE 4.8 Candidates for Parliament: political party membership in Bulgaria, 1990
(%)

Sex	BSP[a]	Peasant Party	Freedom Movement	UDF[b]	Others
Men	89.3	91.4	90.3	92.2	85.8
Women	10.7	8.6	9.7	7.8	14.2
Total	100.0	100.0	100.0	100.0	100.0

[a] Bulgarian Socialist Party (regrouped former Communist Party).
[b] Union of Democratic Forces (anti-BSP, consisting of 16 parties).

Source: Sociological survey, 'Political Campaign 1990', ITUSSR, Sofia, 1990.

The proportion of women in Bulgarian Communist Party was 27.6 per cent (Gancheva et al. 1983: 129–31). According to one sociological survey, Bulgarian men and women devoted equal time to reading political news and watching television (National Statistics 1988: 280–5).

The participation of men and women as leaders in the transitional period, however, is different. The results of a survey investigating participation in the pre-election campaign for Parliament in June 1990 show that only 11.59 per cent of the candidates were women. The percentage of the elected women was 8.7, which is more than two times lower than in the previous Parliament, when the figure was 20.7 per cent. Women's party membership within different organizations is relatively similar (see Table 4.8). Only the Radical Democratic Party is led by a woman.

The explanation of the phenomenon, that while women are equal to men in their involvement with politics there are very few women leaders, is most probably to be found in the very practical approach of Bulgarian women to the democratic reforms. They put an emphasis on actions rather than status. This is very different from the model in the past. Now the emphasis is not on quantitative, but rather on qualitative, criteria. But there are also other reasons affecting women's political participation. One of them is the strong consolidation of the family in the difficult years of economic and social crises and the subsequent concentration of women's efforts on family rather than on social problems. This model of women's behaviour is also due to the fear that the transition to democracy could bring about violence and struggles.

CONCLUSION

During the forty-five years of state socialist development, women's labour-force participation was greatly enhanced. Full female employment overrode the family role. Maternity leave and child benefits were given to working women at their work-places. The high labour-force participation of women during their active reproductive state led to different role conflicts. These contradictions were solved mostly in favour of the occupational activity of women. But female emancipation through labour-force participation actually led to inequality between men and women because of women's much greater participation in family responsibilities.

The transition period has shown that the experiment called state socialism has failed in its promise to bring long-term prosperity and stability. But what follows is as yet unclear and probably will remain so for a long time. It is not possible at present to provide a complete picture of women's role in the process of the transition from a command economy to a market system. Some of the points made here are presented as hypotheses and informed speculations, and they can change.

The period of transition is a unique situation which offers risks and challenges for Bulgarian women, as for women in other societies in transition. Women will scrutinize their abilities, their different life-cycles, family requirements, and their own expectations. Setting one model of women's employment and self-realization against another is a wrong approach. It is necessary to create a legal, economic, and social framework to guarantee the equality of both men and women, allowing for their needs in different life cycles and giving them the right to choose their way of behaviour and activity. One hopes that the transition will bring about a political and economic model which allows a wider range of choices for women at all levels —micro, meso, and macro.

REFERENCES

BOBEVA, D., BARSASCHKI, S., DIMITROVA, A., and KIROV, D. (1991), *The Working Woman in the Transition Period, Sociological Survey*. Sofia: ITUSSR.
DEX, S. (1989), 'Gender and Labour Market', in D. Gallie, (ed.), *Employment in Britain*. Oxford: Blackwell.
GANCHEVA, R., IDOVA, M. V., and ABADJIEVA, N. (1983), *Hundred Questions and Answers for Bulgarian Women*. Sofia Press.
KJURANOV, C. (1977), *Social Classes and Social Stratification*. Sofia: Nauka i Izkustvo Press.
KOSTOVA, D. (1990), *The Economic Leaders in Bulgaria: Sociological Survey*. Sofia: ITUSSR.
Labour Law (1986), Sofia: Nauka i Izkustvo Press.
MICHEL, L., and FRANKEL, D. (1991), *The State of Working America*. M. E. Sharpe.
MINKOV, M., ILIEVA, N., NAIDENOVA, P., and TERZIEVA, V. (1991), 'General Directions of Demographical Policy', paper on conference 'The Women in the Transition to Market Economy'. (June) Sofia.
NAIDENOV, N., STOJANOVA, P., and KOSTOVA, D. (1990), *Political Campaign 1990, Sociological Survey*. Sofia: ITUSSR.

National Labour Bureau (1991), *Unemployment Figures*. Sofia: Ministry of Labour and Social Affairs.

National Statistics (1988), *Town and Village: Data*, ii. Sofia: Statistics Press.

—— (1990*a*), *Education and Qualification of the Work-Force and Working Conditions*. Sofia: Statistics Press.

—— (1990*b*), *Labour* (in English). Sofia: Statistics Press.

—— (1990*c*), *Labour Abilities and Realization of the Workforce: Representative Survey*. Sofia: Statistics Press.

—— (1990*d*), *Population*. Sofia: Statistics Press.

—— (1991*a*), *Quality of Life*. Sofia: Statistics Press.

—— (1991*b*), *The Economy of Bulgaria*. Sofia: Statistics Press.

State Gazette (1987), no. 45. Sofia.

—— (1990), *Pension Law* (corrections). Sofia.

—— (1991), no. 32. Sofia.

Statistics (1991), *Wages*. Sofia: Statistics Press.

5

Educational Attainment, the Status of Women, and the Private School Movement in Poland

Ireneusz Białecki and Barbara Heyns

The purpose of this chapter is to provide a sociological and institutional framework for understanding the links between gender and schooling in the countries of the Eastern bloc. The inital section will provide a brief overview of various aspects of the development of state socialist educational policy; the purpose is to describe how the institutions developed by the communist state dispensed schooling and the legacies that these institutions bring to post-communist societies. Then we will pursue the proposed reforms and institutional innovations that, thus far, can be said to characterize post-communist educational systems. The central question involves how the educational system differentiated gender roles and status, both before and after the 'revolutions' of 1989. The examples and the data are from Poland, but the model could be argued to apply equally well to the other Eastern European countries. Most analyses of the political and economic changes underway in the region deal with neither gender nor education, although both are crucial components of what might be termed civil society. Education can serve as a lens for viewing the impact of institutions and social policy on gender relations in both the past and the present. Educational policies in the past, we shall argue, contributed inadvertently to greater equality in the occupational structure; now, the economic transformation and the reform of education may contribute to a reversal of these trends.

Educational policy under state socialism was organized to further the interests of the state; the needs of the economy, as they were defined by central planning, were more important than individual aspirations. Much like the trends in the West, access to education expanded over time; the types of schools that were organized and promoted, however, were those believed to enhance the productivity and skills of the labour force. The favoured programmes emphasized applied vocational training, consisting of narrow technical skills and courses of study oriented towards the practical problems of production. Priority was given to the development of heavy industry, both to create a powerful and self-sufficient economic base and to develop a numerically dominant working class as the leading social force supporting the state socialist system. Vocational and technical skills were viewed as essential to the development of the economy. Technical schools, vocational schools, and training programmes closely linked to state socialist enterprises expanded dramatically in Poland throughout the 1960s and 1970s. At the university level, polytechnical schools and institutes grew more rapidly than institutions oriented towards the liberal arts. The university, in contrast, remained profoundly intellectual, abjuring the practical or the applied for the theoretical and the humanistic. In so far as one can link institutional patterns of education to the creation of class cultures, the universities created or perpetuated the 'intelligentsia' while vocational programmes were designed to enhance the status of the working class.

A major accomplishment of the communist regimes was the expansion of women's roles in both the economy and society. To be sure, the jobs and roles that women filled were generally not those with the highest prestige or power; the conditions of women's daily lives were, in general, much more difficult than in the West.[1] But the tacit assumption was that all members of a society, both male and female, should be involved in productive labour. Since education was the preparation necessary for socially desirable work, access was not restricted by gender. One of the paradoxes of educational development under communism is that the educational attainment of women expanded more quickly than that of men. In most developed countries, women have become an integral part of university communities and professional work, particularly since the 1960s. However, equal access to a university education was attained by young women in the Soviet Union and in Eastern Europe at an earlier historical period than was the case in either the rest of Europe or the United States. Moreover, this occurred without organized efforts by or on behalf of women and with little direct intervention by the state. Women successfully invaded élite educational programmes and institutions, seemingly with neither feminist ambitions nor economic incentives for prolonged study. Relative to Western women and the men in communist countries, the higher education of women increased dramatically under state socialism. If one takes the date at which university enrolments are equally divided between men and women as a crude measure of gender equity in higher education, the Eastern and Central European countries reached this benchmark point earlier than any country in the West, despite waning economic development. In the Soviet Union, over half of the post-secondary students were women well before 1950, while Bulgaria, Poland, and East Germany each reached this point by the mid-1970s. As Table 5.1 indicates, university training in Eastern Europe was close to 50 per cent female by the early 1970s, while it took the more economically 'developed' West at least a decade longer.

---

[1] The literature on women's roles in communist countries generally supports this point; for recent surveys, see Drakulić (1990), Moghadam (1990), Heitlinger (1985), and Wolchik (1989). For recent discussions of the status of women in Poland, see Bishop (1990), Bystydzienski (1989), Czarnecka (1989), and Siemieńska (1990). For the Soviet Union and more general theoretical perspectives, see Lapidus (1977), Scott (1974), and Stites (1981).

TABLE 5.1 Proportion of girls enrolled in post-secondary education in Western Europe and the state socialist countries, 1950–85 (%)

	1950	1955	1960	1965	1970	1975	1980	1985
Eastern Europe								
Albania	20	15	17	22	33	—	50	45
Bulgaria	—	—	40	43	51	57	56	55
Czechoslovakia	—	25	34	38	38	40	42	43
East Germany	23	29	25	29	43	52	58	54
Hungary	26	26	38	39	43	48	50	54
Poland	36	36	35	46	47	54	56	56
Romania	33	35	33	39	43	44	43	45
USSR	53	52	43	44	49	50	—	—
Yugoslavia	33	31	29	34	39	40	45	45
Western Europe								
Austria	21	20	23	24	29	38	42	45
Belgium	16	—	26	33	36	41	44	46
Denmark	24	28	35	35	37	44	49	49
Finland	37	42	46	49	48	50	48	49
France	34	—	40	38	—	48	—	50
West Germany	20	19	23	24	27	39	41	42
Greece	—	24	26	32	31	37	41	47
Iceland	18	23	21	27	25	37	50	53
Ireland	29	29	30	30	34	34	41	43
Italy	26	28	27	34	38	39	43	45
Luxembourg	—	20	31	33	42	42	35	34
Netherlands	21	25	26	25	28	33	40	41
Norway	16	18	21	34	30	38	48	50
Portugal	—	—	30	37	44	45	48	53
Spain	14	—	23	23	27	36	44	48
Sweden	23	29	33	41	42	40	—	47
Switzerland	13	15	17	20	23	27	30	32
UK	33	35	28	29	33	36	37	45
Other developed countries								
Australia	8	28	27	29	33	41	45	50
New Zealand	30	33	33	21	30	36	41	44
Israel	—	—	41	44	44	46	51	46
Japan	9	16	20	25	28	32	33	34
USA	32	34	37	39	41	45	51	52

Source: UNESCO, selected dates. School enrolment figures are based on the data files assembled by John Meyer and the school expansion project at Stanford University.

HOW STATE SOCIALIST EDUCATIONAL POLICIES FEMINIZED EDUCATION

In Central and Eastern Europe, as in Western countries, the postwar period witnessed an enormous expansion of education. In Poland the initial increase was in secondary, or post-primary, enrolments. At the end of the Second World War, among pupils who completed primary school before 1951, 31 per cent of girls and 46 per cent of boys started some form of secondary education.[2] Throughout the 1950s, secondary education expanded enormously. By the early 1960s, 60 per cent of girls were entering some type of secondary schooling and 68 per cent of boys. Young males still had a relative advantage in admission to secondary education; however, a larger percentage of the girls completed their studies: 39 per cent of the girls finished full secondary education, while barely 37 per cent of the boys received a secondary school diploma. The reason for this has to do with the organization of secondary education.

Roughly speaking, secondary education can be divided into three types of schools. First, there are the lower vocational schools, which are meant to prepare qualified workers for skilled and semi-skilled jobs, largely in industry. Second, there are two distinctive forms of full secondary education, both of which give students a diploma or certificate of graduation and the right to sit for the entrance examinations for higher education: the lyceum and the technikum. These two secondary programmes have quite different curriculum and educational goals. The lyceum consists of four years of traditional academic course work preparing the student for the university; the technikum, in contrast, requires five years to complete, and the major emphasis is on scientific and technical subjects. Both courses of study give the graduate the right to apply to higher education. Completing a degree in the technikum, however, in addition gives the graduate the diploma of technician in one of the sectors of the economy, whereas the lyceum grants only the secondary school diploma without any specialization or focused vocational training.

The expansion of secondary education in the 1950s had quite different impacts on male and female students. For the young women, the expansion meant a large increase in the enrolments in the lyceum. From less than one-tenth (8.4 per cent) of all female primary school-leavers before 1951, by the end of the decade the lyceum was admitting over one-fifth (21.4 per cent).

[2] These data, as well as others cited in this paper unless otherwise stated, are from the 1987–8 survey conducted by research team at the Institute of Philosophy and Sociology, Polish Academy of Sciences studying Social Stratification and Mobility Research in Poland. The team includes: Ireneusz Białecki, Henryk Domanski (head of the team), Krystyna Janicka, Bogdan Mach, Zbigniew Sawinski, Joanna Sikorska, Kazimierz M. Słomczynski (principal investigator), and Wojciech Zaborowski. The sample consists of 5,894 men (aged 20–65) and women (aged 20–60) in the civilian labour force.

No other form of secondary schooling experienced as large an increase in female enrolments. The technikum, for example, grew from 10.7 to 18.0 per cent, while lower vocational programmes increased by only 5 per cent, from 7.8 to 12.8 per cent of each cohort.

As for the males, the expansion of secondary schools meant, first of all, a substantial increase in vocational training. In the 1950s the technikum appeared to gain the most; the increases in enrolments here were the highest —over 11 per cent—and five times as great as the tiny increase in enrolment in the lyceum (2.2 per cent). Later, by the 1960s, lower vocational schooling expanded even more sharply, becoming the modal educational career for young males. Since then, the proportion of boys choosing this type of schooling has increased steadily. For most of the 1980s, over 50 per cent of boys leaving primary school entered and completed lower vocational education.

Since decisions regarding the choice of post-secondary education are determined to a very large extent by the social background of the pupils, it is worth while trying to learn what social origins coincide with what kinds of school choices. Both young men and women of intelligentsia origin (defined loosely by whether or not the student's father has a higher education diploma) tend to attend one of the schools offering a full secondary education, such as the lyceum or the technikum; about 75 per cent of the sons and 85 per cent of the daughters from these families do so. The girls, however, choose the lyceum more often than the boys. Girls of working-class origin are also more likely to choose full secondary school (lyceum or technikum) rather than lower vocational. The proportion of girls enrolled in lower vocational has increased since the late 1960s and in the 1970s, but the vast majority of students are still male. The same applies to girls of farm origin; they choose some kind of full secondary education over lower vocational schools, although in the 1980s the proportion choosing lower vocational did increase.

Males of working-class or farm origins, unlike their sisters, prefer lower vocational education over full secondary. What is more, the proportion of those choosing lower vocational secondary education grew steadily throughout the 1960s and 1970s, while the proportion opting for the lyceum was more or less constant over time, at around 5 per cent. As a result of these trends, in the late 1960s and 1970s some 26–28 per cent of girls of all backgrounds were attending the lyceum as their first choice of secondary school, while only 8–9 per cent of boys were doing so. These trends, operating individually and in concert, have brought about the feminization of the lyceum in Poland. Without compromising standards or mission, and without losing relative status, the lyceums became more than 70 per cent female. The lyceum has remained the single form of secondary education that offers the most favourable odds for successfully passing the rigorous entrance exams to higher education; 80 per cent of all university entrants are graduates of the lyceum in Poland, and this proportion has not changed very much over time.

The riddle of why female attendance at university was so high in state socialist societies is directly linked to the tracking of young women into the lyceum. The creation of vocationally relevant alternatives for males, alternatives that did not require or at times even disallowed higher education, left the domain of humanistic and non-technical schooling open to female penetration. Among the graduates of the lyceum, a higher proportion of males are admitted to university; however, the increasing numerical dominance of women in these secondary schools meant an increasing share of female applicants. In Poland, as in the West, female students tend to avoid technical fields, subjects that require preparation in maths or science, and specialized studies that appear narrow and vocational. Whereas in the West achievement in these fields predicts university attendance, in Poland it serves as a handicap. The majority of the graduates of the technikum choose to pursue jobs rather than go on to higher education. The state introduced numerous post-secondary programmes for women, such as teaching or nursing, that required less than the full five years of university needed to earn the *magister* degree; however, most of these feminized vocational programmes remained affiliated with the university.

The political objectives of the leaders of the centrally planned economy were the growth of heavy industry and an expansion of the working class. The policies to bring about these goals focused on the expansion of lower vocational education. Industrial workers were quite well paid in relative terms; the training provided in lower vocational schools signified good prospects for working-class boys. Girls from similar backgrounds were deprived of vocational training that was equally good. Moreover, it seems likely that the geographical network of vocational schools in traditionally female fields was not as good as that for boys. In contrast, the network of provincial lyceums was readily available. Furthermore, the appeal of operating complex industrial tools or large pieces of machinery may well have been less for girls. For some or all of these reasons, girls from disadvantaged social backgrounds chose the lyceum much more often than boys did. And consequently, the lyceum provided substantial educational mobility for young women.

In Poland, the crucial decision regarding which type of secondary school to be pursued after primary education is made quite early in the life course. For boys, these decisions tended to reproduce the vocational choices and the occupational histories of their fathers. The girls' decision to attend the lyceum offered less in the way of vocation, but it also closed off significantly fewer options. The curious fact is that women may have drifted into university simply because the array of post-primary vocational alternatives was unsatisfactory. The well-paved path from the lyceum to the university resulted in a growing number of young women seeking post-secondary training for occupations such as teachers and nurses and, subsequently, to larger cohorts completing higher education as well. This expansion of female enrolments in the university seemed to occur without any hint of affirmative action and with no indication that feminist aspirations or sympathies were in the air.[3]

As we have argued elsewhere, equality in access to higher education between men and women was an unintended consequence of state socialist educational policies (Heyns and Białecki 1993). The timing of school expansion, and the type and composition of the schools that were allowed to grow, fashioned distinctive educational careers for men and women. The dominant thrust of state socialist policy was clearly oriented towards training working-class men for jobs in heavy industry. Ironically, the feminization of higher education was a direct consequence of educational policies that were designed to further the interests of the proletariat. Instead of expanding possibilities for male workers, however, the vocational and technical tracks tended to limit their options—educationally if not financially.

We would like to extend this line of reasoning and consider a second hypothesis that links educational change to the state socialist labour market. The growing proportion of women who were employed in the service sector, in administrative positions, and in white-collar jobs generally was a consequence of the feminization of the lyceum. The lyceum supplied universities with a very large share of entrants; indeed, college preparation was its sole function. The graduates of the lyceum, whether male or female, were encouraged or almost obliged to continue their education. The expansion of women into professional and white-collar work that took place in the mid-1960s and the 1970s was the direct result of the feminization of higher education and the increasingly influential role played by women in secondary and post-secondary education.

Some of these occupations might well have been feminized in any event, irrespective of educational policy. The expansion of office jobs and administrative work in the East, like that in the West, offered numerous positions for women. It is common practice to upgrade the occupational qualifications for particular jobs when applicants are especially well trained. The fact is, however, that women moved into a wide variety of professional and service occupations in Poland. Feminization occurred in medical and specialized legal fields with well-established requirements for special credentials and training. In the case of health services, the growing numbers of medical students in the second half of the 1970s and increased professionalization

---

[3] As a result of these changes, the educational opportunities available to young women expanded much more than those available to young men. This had the effect of decreasing the variance of outcomes, or the distance between the poor and the privileged, more for females than for males.

led to a consistent advantage for women in the fields of pharmacology, stomatology, and even medicine itself.[4] Virtually all of the health and social service occupations were feminized before the 1980s. In certain semi-professions, such as nursing, a portion of the new recruits is being trained in schools of medicine. Teacher-training colleges produced large numbers of women teachers for both primary and secondary schools. Stomatologists and pharmacologists might never have reached as large a proportion of women if the lyceum had not recruited such a high percentage (over 70 per cent) of young women. The most dramatic expansion of women in medical schools occurred in the 1970s, largely as a consequence of increasing enrolment places in medical schools. Women were, it seems, the chief beneficiaries of the governmental decision to increase the number of doctors and other medical staff.[5]

The same process could be said to operate in the humanities and the social sciences. These fields manned, or perhaps womanned, the administrative apparatus of the communist state. To be sure, the positions of power were reserved for men, drawn from the ranks of *nomenklatura*; but in a host of professional and semi-professional fields, women dominated the official bureaucracies numerically. The university diploma in economics, or business vocational training at secondary level, were means to train accountants. Under state socialism, business and economics became female occupations because of the low status of the accountant at the state enterprise; the more prestigious posts in international trade, for example, remained male sinecures. The feminization of diverse occupations, such as sociologists, psychologists, editors, journalists, and so forth was, at least in part, an unintended side-effect of educational policies put in place in the 1960s and 1970s. As Table 5.2 indicates, female domination of the liberal arts and professional programmes in the universities dates from the 1960s.

One of the features of all centrally planned state socialist economies was full employment, combined with a permanent shortage of labour. That is why the percentage of women in the labour force in all state socialist countries was typically higher than in Western economies. Feminized secondary general education, i.e. the lyceum, enrolled more than one-fourth of all female primary school-leavers since the mid-1960s. We would argue that the feminization of many of the highly educated but *not* very well-paid positions within the professions was, at least in part, the result of the

---

[4] The over-representation of women in Polish medical schools was prevented by the decision of the rectors regarding *numerus clausus*: that is, the proportion of women admitted should not exceed 50 per cent in any department. See Sokolowska (1981) and Kennedy (1991).

[5] Medical schools in Poland consist of a six-year programme taught in special university departments. Although scientific, the lyceum generally gave a better education in biology and languages than the technikum.

TABLE 5.2 Proportion of girls enrolled in selected professional schools (day courses), Poland, 1960–1987 (%)

	Arts	Economics	Pedagogy	Law	Medicine	Humanities
1960	45.0	40.7	60.1	36.3	62.2	69.9
1970	48.0	62.3	70.6	48.5	66.0	75.5
1980	47.0	64.1	75.4	48.6	63.1	78.6
1985	48.7	57.1	72.5	46.3	61.9	74.3
1986	50.5	55.6	72.6	46.0	61.2	74.5
1987	50.8	55.0	71.6	46.5	62.5	74.0

Source: Głowny Urząd Statystyczny, *Rocznik Statystyczny Szkolnictwa*, selected years.

expansion of lower vocational education for males. The lyceum and the feminized specialties within post-secondary education created a reservoir of cheap but well-educated labour. Although some of the professional and service roles that were feminized consist of narrow, highly specialized jobs and occupational niches, such as accountants and economists, they are in fields that in the West remained well-paid, male-dominated enclaves.

The evidence regarding the impact of educational attainment on the status of women is rather mixed. Women surely did not reap the same monetary rewards for their educational degrees and credentials as men did in either the East or the West; moreover, the gender gap in income tended to increase with schooling rather than decline. In terms of occupational status, however, there is ample evidence that women played an increasingly important role in most professions and in the service sector. Between 1972 and 1982, the average levels of occupational attainment of women increased much more quickly than did those of men (Pohoski and Mach 1988). The patterns are similar when one compares 1982 and 1987 (Table 5.3), although the Polish occupational structure changed very little during the latter period.

TABLE 5.3 Changes in the occupational structure in Poland, employed persons 30–39 years old, by sex, 1972–1987

Occupational category	Men			Women		
	1972	1982	1987	1972	1982	1987
Professionals	19.9	23.1	19.5	19.6	28.7	26.5
Other white-collar	2.7	3.1	2.4	11.8	17.2	17.9
Skilled manual	50.8	54.7	58.1	17.3	20.0	27.8
Unskilled manual	10.9	4.6	5.7	19.9	15.2	15.5
Farmers	15.8	14.5	14.4	31.4	18.9	12.3
(No.)	(8,998)	(541)	(811)	(4,000)	(466)	(872)

Source: 1972 and 1982 from Pohoski and Mach (1988); 1987 tabulations are based on data collected by Słomczynski *et al.* (1986), IFiS, PAN.

In sum, the feminization of the service sector and of many of the educated occupations of the communist state was, we would argue, at least in part the result of the heavy reliance on lower vocational education and technical schools designed to enhance the skills of males. Although communist regimes espoused egalitarian ideals, class rather than gender was the highest priority; expanding educational opportunity was viewed as a means to advance educational opportunities for the proletariat or the peasantry. The educational attainment of women was an incidental byproduct of these policies. The aims of education were essentially utilitarian—to increase skills and human capital of males in order to advance the economic and industrial goals of centralized state planning. This emphasis on narrow, technically oriented education prevailed for most of the forty years of communist rule. Ironically, these policies helped women as a group far more than they helped the proletariat.

EDUCATIONAL TRANSITIONS

Given the roots of gender equality in education, one is forced to ask what patterns will prevail in the future. How will the transition from a command economy to a market economy affect schooling, women's status, and the patterns of employment by gender? It is, of course, too early to observe large changes in the institutional structures of education and employment. In July 1991 the Sejm passed an omnibus package of legislation about education, which will undoubtedly shape the functioning of the school system in the future. The new legislation permits substantially more decentralization in the control of both secondary and higher education, combined with possibilities for new programmes of study and new forms of schooling, both private and public, that did not exist under state socialism. It is too soon to assess whether and to what extent schools will take advantage of the new legislation to reform educational programmes. We can, however, observe the emergence of new educational programmes and explore some of the social and economic pressures experienced by state socialist educational institutions. We may even essay predictions about changes in educational opportunity based on the new economic, social, and legal context that is in the making. We can inspect the host of new programmes that aim to train or retrain managers and administrators in the use and interpretation of economic data. Finally, we can examine the educational hopes and aspirations of parents who are creating new schools to socialize their children for the new era. In each of these areas, it is possible to identify tensions between gender roles and post-communist institutions.

The data to be reported are based largely on interviews and on articles written by experts who are based in Warsaw. Warsaw is, of course, a place where the winds of political and economic transformation are fiercely blowing, but it is not altogether clear that it is the most reliable weather vane for social change in the country or the region as a whole. With this caveat, however, we will hazard some speculations regarding how changes in educational institutions will alter the status of women in post-communist Poland. These data suggest, although they cannot prove, that post-communist patterns will be less favourable to the educational and occupational choices of women. The three areas in which educational changes are suggestive of new trends are vocational education, independent secondary schools, and business education for adults.

In education, as in other fields, the process of transition has meant a fundamental questioning of all aspects of state policy. Both the intentions and the outcomes of the ideologies and the strategies for implementation that were adopted by the communist regime have come under attack. Much of the discourse is cast in the terminology that was embraced by the opposition movements in the 1980s, most particularly by the various branches of the Solidarity trade union. Education, for example, must be 'de-colonized', or established independently of state control. The themes are largely political; for example, virtually all proposed changes are argued to increase participation, democratic processes, and parent's control. In addition, new movements and ideas that resonate with the economic changes are also common. The logic of privatization has attracted a substantial following in educational as well as economic circles.[6] From the perspective of the new government, decentralization, combined with fiscal austerity, is the order of the day. The economic crisis has led to a Balcerowicz-type plan for education that implies few 'frills' and funds that are barely adequate to pay teachers' salaries.[7] Local school systems cannot hire new teachers; many have been forced to lay off part-time instructors.[8]

The administrative changes and the new policies for financing schools are the most salient aspects, but it is still too early to see to what extent these changes will influence the system directly. Key actors in the Ministry have been replaced by opposition leaders, and it seems clear that the role of the state in education will be diminished. The rationale for decentralization, for local control under the auspices of 'school councils', is in part economic and in part ideological. But to date, few if any of the local educational authorities have the means at their disposal to finance the revising of curricula, the

[6] The private schools in Poland prefer the term 'independent' or 'civic' schools. In Polish, privatization, or *prywatyzacja*, is generally applied only to strictly economic, profit-making organizations. However, these schools require parents to pay some tuition and to contribute a good deal to the organization and the planning of education.

[7] Balcerowicz was the Minister of Finance whose name is associated with the radical economic 'shock treatment' implemented in Poland in the first years of the non-communist government.

[8] Many of the part-time instructors were retired teachers with special skills and inadequate pensions.

purchase of books, the employment of new teachers, or a marked improvement of the quality of education.

At the same time, parental—and popular—expectations favour a complete restructuring of schools, at least in theory. How this could be brought off in the midst of an economic crisis is difficult to imagine. For the majority of parents, the transition to post-communist, maybe capitalist, society seems to have produced a chaotic and mercurial context for considering the education and future of their children. For a sizeable contingent of urban, relatively advantaged parents, school reform is essential. The school reform movement, however, seeks democratization through privatization.

The next three sections provide, by way of background, an examination of three significant developments in education in post-communist Poland. Understanding the evolution and the fate of vocational education, of private schooling, and of the numerous postgraduate courses in administration, management, and business education can provide a context for discussions of how women's roles are likely to be transformed.

VOCATIONAL EDUCATION[9]

As mentioned above, vocational education was one of the most conspicuous innovations developed by the communist educational system. In Poland and elsewhere, the communist state devoted substantial resources to expanding post-primary schooling, particularly the terminal, three-year programme of studies known as lower vocational education. Between the early 1960s, when these schools were introduced, and the mid-1980s, these programmes expanded threefold. Upon completion, the student earned a skill or craft designation (or, in slang, a *fach*) that entitled him or her to work in one of the appropriate industries or factories. These programmes were extremely specialized, and over time became quite narrow and inflexible; in Poland lower vocational education offered some training for over 240 different blue-collar trades.

Lower vocational programmes in Poland are quite diverse. Perhaps half of all vocational students were enrolled in programmes that were sponsored or affiliated, equipped and co-financed by large state enterprises. These programmes most resembled institutionalized apprenticeships, and included very little general education. The affiliation was, however, a good deal for both the students and the companies. The former were getting equipment, on-the-job training, and sometimes board as well as modest pay; the companies got cheap, underpaid labour for the duration of the training

---

[9] The data on vocational education programmes is indebted to discussions and information provided by Jan Szczucki, a member of the team studying the construction of expertise in post-communist Poland.

programme and then an opportunity to hire young workers who had been trained on the spot. At best, the skills that students learned translated directly into a job, or a promotion with a raise, when they finished their studies. In one large motor car factory outside Warsaw (FSO), 90 per cent of the newly hired workers each year were students from the vocational school connected to the plant.

Recession combined with unemployment is a new feature of the Polish economy. In the present situation, companies are not looking for a new labour force but are forced to lay off some of their existing workers. Moreover, many companies will not survive in the new economic climate. The Warsaw Steel Mill and the Ursus factory are on the brink of collapse; both closed their vocational schools in 1991. Even the firms that manage to weather the transition are unlikely to continue subsidizing vocational education; the school connected to FSO, for example, closed in early 1990. In a recession, state enterprises do not have money to support affiliated vocational schools. One of the first autonomous actions taken by many state enterprises when forced to cut costs was to cancel their vocational programmes. Before 1989, there were two places in Polish industry for each graduate of the vocational schools. Now exactly the opposite ratio holds: two graduates are available for every place. Vocational schools in the television industry (WZT), in food and dairy processing, in textiles, and especially in heavy industry have closed. Społem, one of the largest state-run firms that distributes and retails grocery and agricultural products, has terminated its vocational education programme as well. Some of these vocational programmes have been taken over by the Ministry and absorbed into the system of schools sponsored by the curatoreum; others, however, will simply be discontinued. Although systematic studies are sparse, there is evidence that the vocational programmes in other Eastern European countries are experiencing similar dislocation.[10]

As we have seen, vocational programmes in general were largely male; but even those that trained a substantial number of women—in the textile industry, for example—have been adversely affected. A large plant manufacturing semi-conductors just outside Warsaw (TEWA) has dropped its vocational education programme. As a result of the collapse of the Soviet market, many of the textile factories in Łódz are near bankruptcy or have suspended operations. The labour force in both these industries is heavily female.

A good many of the lower vocational schools in Poland probably *should* be closed, for both educational and economic reasons.[11] However, for most of

[10] In Hungary, the research of Eva Balazs (1991) suggests that the collapse of apprentice schools has increased the competition for places in the best secondary schools.

[11] For a particularly insightful evaluation of vocational education programmes in Poland, see Peter Grootings (1991).

the past decade, these schools absorbed over half of all primary school-leavers, and around two-thirds of the young males. Haunted by the spectre of growing unemployment, parents are anxious and confused about what sort of education will provide a secure future for their children. The closing of the traditional avenues of vocational training puts tremendous pressure on the schools that survive. In particular, the secondary schools that served as the primary alternative to lower vocational schooling, i.e. the lyceum and the technikum, are likely to be swamped with applicants. In Warsaw 20 per cent of the primary school-leavers traditionally enrolled in a lyceum; in the autumn of 1991, these schools accepted about 33 per cent of the school-leavers. In a period in which the state budget has little flexibility, it is difficult to know where the funds to support such an expansion will come from.

THE PRIVATE SCHOOL MOVEMENT[12]

One of the most fascinating developments in post-communist education has been the formation of a very active school reform movement. The themes and the rhetoric of proposed reforms echo those heard in the debates about economic and political transition generally. Institutions must be democratized and decentralized; the monopoly of the state over the provision of goods and services must be broken. The schools must become more responsive to the needs of individual parents and children. The curriculum needs a complete overhaul; all traces of ideological indoctrination must be expunged. The organization and financing of schools should be lodged in democratically organized community groups; schools should be controlled by the families, who can best monitor the education their children receive. And, finally, the most workable strategy for eradicating state control is to establish new, independent private schools, under the control of parents' groups.

Społeczne Towarzystwo Oświatowe (STO), which literally means the Social Education Association, is the paramount example of the school reform movement in Poland. It has had phenomenal success in challenging the monopoly of state schools and in creating alternatives. In the first year, 1989, 35 non-state or semi-state schools were in operation; in September 1991, 190 or more 'social' schools opened their doors. These schools are organized by some 36 different local educational associations and 160 educational foundations. STO currently claims over 10,000 members, as well as many sympathizers. The primary schools organized by STO are quite small and represent a tiny portion of the student population; the new secondary schools, however, are of primary interest here. Without exception, these new

---

[12] The information regarding the independent schools movement is from interviews with members of the Ministry, from a number of Warsaw activists, and from selected issues of the STO journal, *Edukacja i Dialog*.

schools are élite lyceums, offering university preparation and a modified version of the standard lyceum curriculum. In Poland there are only 900 lyceums; numerically, then, the 100 new private lyceums constitute a significant proportion of the total number of schools, although they do not yet enroll 10 per cent of the students. At least part of their popularity and their dramatic growth is due to an increasing demand for this type of education.

The term 'social' as applied to private education in Poland is curious. The term is used in contrast to 'state', and it includes virtually all independent or non-state education, whether religious or non-denominational. 'Social' is sometimes translated as 'civic' or even 'public' education. Only a handful of the new private schools are wholly supported by private funds, but all proclaim the right to establish autonomous educational institutions, subject to democratically elected self-government. Politically, these schools must meet standards of educational quality that apply to state schools. Economically, the financing arrangements require the state to pay approximately half the costs of the civic schools, while parents pay the rest. The new schools can, by law, be run by 'non-state self-governments, legal or lay persons', but virtually all the new schools are still fiscally dependent on the state.[13] In practice, social schools are run by foundations, private companies, the church or one of the various convents, and individuals.

The style and the rhetoric of STO clearly owes much to the political opposition in Poland. The success of the movement is surely attributable in part to the collapse of the communist state, although the organization itself antedated the Round Table talks and the change of government. STO as an organization was the result of the decision made in 1987 to try to register an association of parents explicitly claiming the right to control the education of their children and to establish private schools. In theory, these rights were guaranteed by Polish law, under a statute passed in 1961; but official permission was needed in order to exercise such rights, and such permission had never before been granted. In December 1987, neither the Ministry of National Education nor the twenty-three signers of the petition asking for official sanction believed that an organization like STO would be allowed to exist.

When the Ministry turned down the petition for registration, the fledgling organization appealed the decision through the courts. After a brief legal battle, STO and two affiliated groups in Wrocław and the Małopolska region

---

[13] In January 1990, the Minister of National Education agreed that the state should subsidize social schools, to the amount of half the current costs per child in the state schools in the region; schools sponsored by foundations or business concerns do not qualify for state subsidy, although denominational schools do. The tuition paid by parents is quite modest by Western standards, amounting to between $10 and $12 per month; however, even fees of this order represent 10% of the average monthly salary.

won their suit; in December 1988 they were formally registered with the intent of establishing private schools. The stage was set for private alternative schools under the auspices of democratic, non-state control and authority. STO was registered as an official organization, but opening such schools still had to be formally approved.

The first petition requesting official permission to open a private school was submitted to the Ministry of National Education in June 1988. The minister responded quickly and, as predicted, rejected the petition, arguing that it would be against the Polish Constitution to collect fees for education. The Krakow parent, Anna Jeziorna, who had submitted the petition then appealed this decision to the High Administrative Court. This case understandably attracted considerable attention; it was the first time in which a group of concerned parents had challenged the right of the Ministry to determine where and how their children would be educated. The timing was, of course, fortuitous. Plans for the Round Table talks were under way, and Solidarity was about to be reinstated as a key actor in the negotiations between state and civil society. The political changes were not lost on the legal system. On 23 February 1989, at almost the same moment that the Round Table talks were beginning, the High Court handed down its decision; the state administration was wrong to deny parents the right to organize schools. Parents did have the legal right to open private schools in the People's Republic of Poland. The right to found private schools, as it turned out, would outlive the 'People's Republic'.

The 'social' or civic schools take democratization as their most fundamental purpose and the lack of it their principal grievance with state education. The chief impetus behind STO, and a central motif in the schools that have been formed, is democratic education. Although STO does not endorse any particular educational philosophy except democratic pluralism, the STO schools share basic assumptions. The ideology of the 'social' schools is quite similar to that of progressive education in the West: teachers should attend to individual differences and to the needs of particular children. Parents should be actively involved in the education of their children at every stage. Schools should be open institutions, fostering community participation and parental involvement. The only sure way to rid schools of communist dogma, and to change the passive and conformist attitudes and behaviour associated with the past, is to establish new and different institutions. As in state schools, religious training will be offered to all students, although it is likely to be less popular in STO schools. The curriculum should be modernized, although for STO members this does not mean that standards should be lowered or the curriculum intellectually diluted. These secondary schools maintain the traditional prerequisites for admission to university. The parents who have so ardently supported the new schools do not want their children to be at a competitive disadvantage with the graduates of state schools.

Ironically, thus far it seems easier to privatize state education than state industry; and it has been easier to found new schools than to alter the organization and structure of those already in existence. Educational policy under communism was both highly centralized and quite hierarchic. It is not yet clear what organizational framework will define the governance of education in the future. It is possible that the new private schools will become models for education generally; it is possible that they will not survive the present economic crisis. The current government clearly favours local control and local funding. New public educational boards, school councils, are in place. These boards are democratically elected, and members are equally divided between parents, teachers, and students. The councils also often include a few eminent leaders from the community, either religious or lay. These boards are mandated to provide local oversight; they can propose educational policies, and they now control that part of the school budget that is locally collected. At present, however, only the new 'social' schools receive a significant portion of their funds from non-state sources. In the state schools, the local boards are not particularly responsive to parent or community groups yet; at the same time, parent and community groups often have no idea how to use them to improve the quality of education or to influence programmes.

The civic schools incorporate forms of education that were unavailable under state socialism, even in the best lyceum. The schools have been organized by and for parents with élite aspirations, if not backgrounds. As a result, both the formal and the informal curricula are conscious of the status of education. In the area of sports, for example, several new schools offer tennis and swimming.[14] In contrast, the best state socialist schools gave students soccer and gymnastics. Soccer, like most team sports, requires minimal individual coaching and much less expensive equipment for each student. Gymnastics can be taught in a vacant room furnished with a few mats; when the weather is inclement, these courses provided good indoor exercise, but at relatively low cost. The supplemental athletic activities in civic schools provide access to training that, under state socialism, were reserved for private classes paid for by parents.

There are no blueprints available for shaping post-communist society or post-communist educational policy; more to the point, 'social' schools have elicited an uncommon amount of energy and activity from parents. The STO 'Koła' or 'circles' organizations pursue democratic decision-making in their schools and communities. The thrust of their efforts, however, seems to be oriented towards discrediting the state in all aspects of educational planning

[14] The first civic high school in Warsaw supplements the state curriculum with the teaching of 'swimming, skiing, skating, horseback riding, and the rudiments of self-defence' (*Edukacja i Dialog*, 26/27, March/April 1991: 31).

and control. Privatization in education does represent a democratic alternative to traditional state schools; the question remains, however, whether such schools will support equality and the public interest.

POST-COMMUNIST EDUCATIONAL PROGRAMMES: ADULT EDUCATION[15]

The most visible changes that have occurred in the field of education, and those most directly linked to the growth of private enterprise, are the proliferation of new training programmes in management and business administration, and in foreign languages. Virtually all of these programmes are privately funded, and most charge a hefty tuition fee. There are now forty-seven new programmes in operation, with diverse sponsorship and the title 'International Business School'. These programmes offer not so much continuing education as a retooling for the market economy. In part, such programmes are designed to retrain managers and administrators from the state sector; in part, they aim to provide skills in marketing, accounting, business English, and capital accumulation for budding entrepreneurs. The most respectable programmes are affiliated with either a university, a foundation, or a large foreign enterprise that hopes to develop business contacts in Poland. Sometimes the fees for such programmes are paid by a foreign consulting firm, hoping to recruit a local labour force; sometimes the purposes are strictly altruistic. Advertisements in newspapers and on television promise to provide the training and contacts for starting a successful private business. A typical programme offers a short but intensive training period, followed by a trip or exchange with a foreign university or firm. While one should be wary of the claims and the credibility of many of these new schools and programmes, Western universities and foundations have undoubtedly contributed to the proliferation of them.

EDUCATION IN TRANSITION: GENDER AND EQUALITY OF OPPORTUNITY

What will be the consequence of these new post-communist institutions and policies on educational attainment? Will the new institutional forms outlined

[15] These results are based on several dozen open-ended interviews with the directors and managers of new business programmes in Warsaw, conducted in the summer of 1991 by Dina Smeltz and Pauline Gianoplus. This work is part of the ongoing project on 'The Construction of New Expertise: Education, Professions and Elites in Post-Communist Poland', by Michael D. Kennedy, Ireneusz Białecki, and Barbara Heyns, and is funded by the National Council for Soviet and Eastern European Research, 1991–2.

above endure? What impact do the new educational trends augur for women's status in post-communist Poland? What will become of the large number of women with considerable human capital who have never reaped the full economic benefits of their education?

Although definitive answers to such questions cannot yet be given, some speculation seems in order. With respect to secondary schooling, it is clear that more students will abandon, or be abandoned by, the lower vocational programmes in industry that offered an easy vocational transition to adult roles. A shift in enrolments from lower vocational education to lyceum and technikum schools can already be observed, at least in Warsaw. The growth of the lyceum will most probably mean an especially large increase in male enrolments. Although the majority of students in these schools are still female, the new non-state schools, and those offering the most élite education, are becoming masculinized, or at least de-feminized, more quickly than traditional state programmes. The secondary schools are likely to diversify their educational missions and clientele as well. Partly as a result of decentralization and local control, communities will increasingly have to define what type of educational programmes meet the needs of the community and what can be supported. The new private schools are one response to these trends. One can imagine an educational system in which these institutions become models for high-quality educational programmes in the state sector; or a system in which innovation and reform remain 'privatized'. At present, these schools are most concerned with retaining political independence and some measure of fiscal control. Will males reclaim the lyceum, displacing female students in the educational tracks that lead most directly to the university? Although it is too early to conclude that this is inevitable, such an outcome cannot be ruled out. If one judges by the preferences and educational ideologies expressed by STO members, many post-communist parents believe that the returns to higher education are likely to increase substantially in future.

With respect to the overall status of women, the issues raised by educational and economic transitions are interesting but very complex. It seems likely that the demand for lyceum and for post-secondary education of all sorts will increase. Moreover, it seems likely that young men and women will increasingly be competing for scarce positions in both the lyceum and the university. The reasons for this are several. First, the declining utility of lower vocational programmes will increase the demand for alternative programmes of schooling. A significant portion of these new recruits will be males, drawn from the ranks of those who would have become technicians or qualified workers under state socialism. A larger pool of lyceum graduates will put pressure on the universities to either expand or admit a larger proportion of male students. The same could be said of the professions and the service sector generally. The élite professions are likely to become better paid and therefore more desirable positions for men. The incumbents of the occupations and jobs in administration and the service sector will also face increasing competition from new entrants, some with university degrees and some without.

The evidence for these claims rests on the patterns of attendance in the new élite private schools and the attitudes expressed by the rectors and directors of the new programmes in the university. Although the private schools do not explicitly endorse any change in the gender composition of schools, the new private secondary schools offer, uniformly, *lyceum-type university preparation*. They aim to satisfy parents' demands for an élite education combined with special attention to children with difficulties or problems in adjusting to school. Despite grass-roots organizations and 'bottom-up' support, STO is basically a movement of 'middle-budget intelligentsia' families, who value education and place a high priority on it for their children.[16]

National enrolment data are not yet published for the period since 1989, although special tabulations provided by the curator of schools in Warsaw is instructive. Table 5.4 provides data on the gender composition of all state secondary general schools in Warsaw and of the new private schools, both for all students and for those in their first year. The differences are consistent and significant. The traditional lyceum enrolment has increased. Although the majority of students are still young women, an increasing share are male. The private non-state schools, which are without exception oriented towards university preparation, are significantly more likely to be male than are the state schools, although even in these élite schools the majority of students are female. Moreover, the first-year class has a larger proportion of male enrolment than later classes.

The role of the numerous new adult education programmes in post-communist society is still ambiguous. At present, these programmes appear to attract a higher proportion of males than their counterparts in the university, but they are also admitting students from a fairly broad age range. Reliable enrolment figures by gender which could be compared with these applications are difficult to come by. Moreover, many, perhaps the majority, of the new business schools will probably not survive. As the number of schools and programmes have proliferated, applications to individual schools have fallen off, perhaps as a result of competition between the programmes. Although virtually all of the new schools are promising to provide special skills for the post-communist era, it is not clear how many will make good on these promises. Few of the private business schools have either the time

---

[16] This conclusion is reached by virtually all of the Polish observers of the civic schools; the quotation, however, is from Andrzej Witwicki, the former secretary-general of the Civic Educational Association (Witwicki 1990).

TABLE 5.4 Students in state and non-state general secondary schools (lyceums), by sex and year of study, Warsaw, 1990–1991 (%)

	Independent schools	State schools	Total	(No.)
First year				
Male	45.1	36.4	37.2	(7,706)
Female	54.9	63.6	62.8	(4,558)
Total	100.0	100.0	100.0	
(No.)	(1,039)	(11,225)		(12,264)
All other years				
Male	38.5	36.5	36.6	(9,652)
Female	61.5	63.5	63.4	(16,732)
Total	100.0	100.0	100.0	
(No.)	(980)	(25,404)		(26,384)
Total lyceum students				
Male	41.9	36.5	36.8	(24,438)
Female	58.1	63.5	63.2	(14,210)
Total	100.0	100.0	100.0	
(No.)	(2,019)	(36,629)		(38,648)

or the inclination to track their graduates or evaluate the outcomes of their programmes, much less to assess their impact on gender inequality.

With respect to the management and language training programmes, the results are similar. Both applicants and enrolments appear increasingly likely to be male. To be sure, women still constitute the majority of students in the language training and business programmes, as one would expect, given their superior educational qualifications. Although the image of these programmes has post-communist appeal—based on their entrepreneurial, international focus—it is not yet clear whether they will be significant factors in the economic mobility, or even economic stability, of their graduates. But they certainly aspire to recruit and assist soon-to-be-successful new business leaders and managers. The directors of these programmes reported, with some satisfaction, that they are receiving a larger number of applications from males than previously. Indeed, we were told that this was a very important phenomenon because it proves that business and economics are once again 'serious' fields of work and study. The Warsaw programmes that we studied range in composition from over 60 per cent female to 70 per cent male. The programmes with the largest proportions of males are those that restrict admission to those currently managing state enterprises; but even foreign languages, a traditionally female area, has a higher proportion of males than in the past.

SUMMARY AND CONCLUSIONS

In summary, we have argued that the educational policies in state socialist countries favoured the substantial growth of vocational and technical education. The vocational and technical schools attracted and enrolled a disproportionate share of males and a growing share of all male primary school-leavers. As a consequence, the non-technical and non-vocational programmes became feminized. In particular, the lyceum enrolled and absorbed a steadily increasing number of young women pursuing post-primary schooling. The lyceum was not, however, a vocational track; the primary option for graduates was continuing on to higher education. In the West, élite preparatory academies lost their monopoly on access to colleges and universities; in Poland, the educational transformations, combined with an emphasis on vocational schools, allowed the lyceum to retain status while becoming dominated numerically by females. Higher education, in turn, enrolled a larger percentage of females than in most Western institutions. Although the evidence is not yet fully assembled, it seems likely that the higher proportions of women with advanced educational degrees in Eastern Europe and the Soviet Union is the unintended result of vocational policies, rather than the product of policies aimed to create gender equality.

Second, we argued that the feminization of the lyceum led to more female enrolments in the post-secondary training colleges and universities at an earlier period than occurred in the West. Although the economic returns to education under state socialism are quite low and generally do not favour women workers, there have clearly been noticeable improvements in the occupational status of women. In particular, higher education appears to have contributed significantly to the high proportions of women in the professions and to the feminization of the service sector. Again, these patterns are typical for Eastern countries, and they suggest the importance of investigating educational policies as well those specifically directed at the labour force in order to understand the relationships between gender and employment under state socialism.

These trends provide a fascinating contrast to the patterns of education and attainment in Western countries. Moreover, the process of economic and social transition provides a ready-made laboratory for studying whether the underpaid and feminized occupations will gain income and status or, alternatively, lose a portion of their heavily female labour force. Education is a lens for studying these processes and a strategy for examining gender and status relations generally. In so far as one can form an early impression of these processes, it seems clear that the lyceum will become a more gender-balanced institution, in both the state and the private sectors. It also seems likely that there will be greater competition between males and females for university places.

The prestigious secondary schools that are growing the most quickly and that seem to have the greatest appeal to post-communist parents are lyceums; moreover, the new private lyceums are attracting an increasing number and an ever-larger proportion of male students.[17] One may expect that, as the returns to education and to occupational position change, and presumably increase, there will be increasing tension as to how such rewards are distributed. Given the linkages between education and employment, it seems likely that the transformation occurring in education and vocational training will be matched by changes in the labour market. Considering the gendered nature of the occupational structure, this tension is likely to involve competition and perhaps conflict between Polish males and females over both occupational positions and occupational rewards.

REFERENCES

ADAMSKI, WLADYSŁAW, and BIAŁECKI, IRENEUSZ (1981), 'Selection at School and Access to Higher Education in Poland', *European Journal of Education*, 16: 1.

—— and GROOTINGS, PETER (eds.) (1989), *Youth, Education and Work in Europe*. London: Routledge.

BALAZS, EVA (1991), 'Social Chances within the Transforming Secondary School System', paper presented at Hungarian Sociological Association meeting, Budapest.

BIAŁECKI, IRENEUSZ (1982), *Wybor Szkoly a Reprodukcja Struktury Spolecznej* (Educational Choice and the Reproduction of Social Structure). Warsaw: Ossolineum.

—— (1986), 'Wykształcenie i Ruchliwość zawodowa' (Education and Social Mobility), chapter 1 in *Przemiany Ruchliwości Społecznej w Polsce*. Warsaw: Polish Academy of Science, Institute of Philosophy and Sociology, 51–110.

BISHOP, BRENDA (1990), 'From Women's Rights to Feminist Politics: The Developing Struggle for Women's Liberation in Poland', *Monthly Review* (November): 15–34.

BYSTYDZIENSKI, JILL M. (1989), 'Women and Socialism: A Comparative Study of Women in Poland and the USSR', *Signs*, 14(3): 668–84.

CZARNECKA, CHRISTINE (1989), 'Women in Poland's Workforce: Why Less than Equal is Good Enough', *Comparative Labor Law Journal*, 11: 91.

DOMAŃSKI, HENRYK (1990), 'Labor Force Segmentation in Poland', *Social Forces*, 69(2): 1–21.

DRAKULIĆ, SLAVENKA (1990), 'In their Own Words: Women of Eastern Europe', *Ms.* (July/August): 36–47.

GŁOWNY URZĄD STATYSTYCZNY STATYSTYKA POLSKI (1988), *Rocznik*

---

[17] We should point out that many of the STO organizers that we have interviewed are convinced that the new schools have the same gender composition as the state schools, although they have not actually collected any data. The best state lyceums are most evenly balanced between males and females; perhaps the impression of the parents in the private school movement are based on a contrast between STO schools and the most exclusive state schools; or perhaps the data for all of Poland will be less compelling.

Statystyczny Wojewodztw, 1988. Warsaw: Głowny Urząd Statystyczny, Statystyka Polski Seria: Stystyka Regionalna.

GROOTINGS, PETER (1991), 'Modernisation of Vocational Education and Training in Poland', Working Paper for the Task Force on Training and Human Resources, Warsaw, January.

HAUSER, EWA, HEYNS, BARBARA, and MANSBRIDGE, JENNIE (1993), 'Feminism in the Interstices of Politics and Culture: Poland in Transition', in Nanette Funk and Magda Mueller (eds.), *Gender Politics and Post-Communism: Reflections from Eastern Europe and the Soviet Union.* London: Routledge.

HEITLINGER, ALENA (1985), 'Women in Eastern Europe: Survey of Literature', *Women's Studies International Forum*, 8(2): 147–52.

HEYNS, BARBARA (1991), 'Church and/or State: Educational Policy in Post-Communist Poland', paper presented at Hungarian Sociological Association meeting, Budapest, June.

—— and BIAŁECKI, IRENEUSZ (1993), 'Educational Inequalities in Postwar Poland', in Yossi Shavit and Hans-Peter Blossfeld (eds.), *Persistent Barriers: A Comparative Study of Educational Inequality in Fourteen Countries.* Boulder, Colo.: Westview Press.

KACPROWICZ, GRAZYNA (1987), 'Inequality in Access to Education: An Analysis of Social Origin of Students', *Sisyphus: Sociological Studies*, iv. Warsaw: Polish Scientific Publishers.

KENNEDY, MICHAEL D. (1991), *Professionals, Power and Solidarity in Poland: A Critical Sociology of Soviet-Type Society.* New York: Cambridge University Press.

KORALEWICZ, JADWIGA, BIAŁECKI, IRENEUSZ, and WATSON, MARGARET (eds.) (1987), *Crisis and Transition: Polish Society in the 1980s.* New York: St Martin's Press.

LAPIDUS, GAIL (1977), *Women in the Soviet Union.* Berkeley, Calif.: University of California Press.

MOGHADAM, VALENTINE M. (1990), 'Gender and Restructuring: Perestroika, the 1989 Revolutions, and Women', World Institute for Development Economics Research, Working Paper no. 87, November.

PESCHAR, JULES L. (1991), 'Educational Opportunities in East–West Perspective: A Comparative Analysis of the Netherlands, Hungary, Poland and Czechoslovakia,' *International Journal of Education Research*, 15: 107–21.

POHOSKI, MICHAŁ, and MACH, BOGDAN W. (1988), 'Trends in Social Mobility in Poland, 1972–1982', *Polish Sociological Bulletin*, 3: 19–37.

SAWINSKI, ZBIGNIEW (1986), 'The Prestige of Education', in K. M. Słomczynski and T. K. Krauze (eds.), *Social Stratification in Poland: Eight Empirical Studies.* Armonk, NY: M. E. Sharpe; reprinted from *International Journal of Sociology* 16 (1–2).

SCOTT, HILDA (1974), *Does Socialism Liberate Women?* Boston: Beacon Press.

SIEMIEŃSKA, RENATA (1990), *Płeć Zawód Polityka: Kobiety w życiu publicznym w Polsce* (The Political Organization of Gender: Women in Polish Public Life). Warsaw: Instytut Socjologii, Uniwersytet Warszawski.

SKÓRZYŃSKA, KATARZYNA (1990), 'Report on the Situation of the Non-State Schools in Poland', unpublished paper, Independent Department of Innovation and Non-State Schools, Ministry of National Education, June.

SŁOMCZYNSKI, KAZIMIERZ M. (1983), *Pozycja zawodowa i jej zwiazki z wyksztal-ceniem* (Occupational Status and its Relation to Education). Warsaw: Institute of Philosophy and Sociology of the Polish Academy of Sciences.

—— and KRAUZE, TADEUSZ (eds.) (1986), *Social Stratification in Poland: Eight Empirical Studies.* Armonk, NY: M. E. Sharpe.

SOKOLOWSKA, MAGDALENA (1981), 'Women in Decision-Making Elites: The Case of Poland', chapter 6 in Cynthia Fuchs Epstein and Rose Laub Coser (eds.), *Access to Power: Cross-National Studies of Women and Elites.* London: George Allen & Unwin, 90–114.

STITES, RICHARD (1981), 'Women and Communist Revolutions: Some Compara-tive Observations', *Studies in Comparative Communism*, 14(2/3): 106–22.

SWIDLICKI, ANDRZEJ (1988), *Political Trials in Poland 1981–1986.* New York: Croom Helm.

SZCZEPAŃSKI, JAN (1964), 'Sociological Aspects of Higher Education in Poland', in S. Ehrlich, J. Szczepanski, J. Tepicht, and S. Zawadzk (eds.), *Social and Political Transformations in Poland.* Warsaw: Polish Scientific Publishers, 255–80.

WESOŁOWSKI, WŁODEK, and KRAUZE, TADEUSZ (1980), 'Socialist Society and the Meritocratic Principle of Remuneration', in G. Berreman (ed.), *Social Inequality: Comparative and Developmental Approaches.* New York: Academic Press, 337–48.

WITWICKI, ANDRZEJ (1990), 'The Avalanche Has Started', *Education and Dialogue* (December): 14.

WNUK-LIPIŃSKA, ELZBIETA (1989), 'The Educational Performance of Univer-sities in Poland', *Innovation*, 2(1–2): 143–52.

WOLCHIK, SHARON (1989), 'Women and the State in Eastern Europe and the Soviet Union', in Ellen M. Charleton, Tana Everett, and Kathleen Staudt (eds.), *Women: The State and Development.* Albany, NY: State University of New York.

ZAHORSKA, MARTA, and SAWIŃSKI, ZBIGNIEW (1990), *Szkoły Społeczne na tle szkółpaństwowych: Raport z badania ankietowego* (Social Schools for Everyone: Report and Survey Results), conducted by Demoskop under contract to the Ministry of National Education, Independent Department of Innovations and Non-State Schools, Warsaw, December.

PART II

PERESTROIKA AND WOMEN
IN THE SOVIET UNION

6

Gender and Restructuring: The Impact of Perestroika and its Aftermath on Soviet Women

Gail Warshofsky Lapidus

INTRODUCTION

The past few years have brought far-reaching changes in the position of women on the territory of the former Soviet Union. The accession of Mikhail Gorbachev to the Soviet leadership in March 1985, and the inauguration of increasingly radical political and economic reforms, had dramatic, though largely unintended, consequences for women's roles. On the one hand, the cognitive and political changes associated with glasnost democratization progressively undermined many of the taboos that had long constrained the discussion of gender issues and, by creating unprecedented opportunities for social and political activism, permitted the emergence of genuinely autonomous feminist organizations.

At the same time, the mounting economic crisis precipitated by the Gorbachev leadership's erratic economic policies drove sheer economic survival to the top of women's agendas. Rampant inflation and the disintegration of the consumer sector produced growing hardship and increasing social strain, while economic breakdown and rising unemployment made women its major victims. Moreover, the erosion of the central government's authority and resources, and the emergence of increasingly autonomous republics and even localities as major foci of decision-making, led to a *de facto* decentralization of policy-making and resource allocation which also had important consequences for women. The crumbling of all-Union authority, and with it the very pretence of uniform nationwide policies with respect to the whole range of issues—from job security to social welfare benefits to the availability of day care—resulted in increasing differentiation of women's positions from republic to republic and in the growing influence of local conditions, traditions, and needs.

The collapse of the Soviet Union in 1991 and the emergence of fifteen new states on its former territory opened a new chapter—indeed, fifteen separate chapters—in the evolution of women's roles. In the Baltic States and in Russia, where efforts to construct democratic political systems and launch the transition towards a market economy have proceeded furthest, restructuring has brought new challenges as well as opportunities for women. In other successor states, however, women's roles have been affected to a

138   G. W. LAPIDUS

greater extent by political and ethnic strife, economic collapse, or the attempts to relegitimize former power structures in neo-traditional terms.

In order to place these recent developments in the proper context, this chapter will briefly review the major patterns of women's employment and family roles established over several decades of Soviet rule, and the policy debates that they precipitated in the late Brezhnev era, before turning to a more detailed examination of the impact of perestroika and its aftermath on women.[1]

THE HISTORICAL LEGACY

The role of women in the Soviet labour force was shaped by a distinctive set of ideological assumptions and historical developments that influenced Soviet policy to the very end. Central to the Soviet approach—as it was to Marxist and Leninist theory—was the conviction that women's entry into social production held the key to the creation of a genuinely state socialist society. The family, by contrast, was initially seen as the very antithesis of the factory, the embodiment of tradition and backwardness—as Bukharin put it, the 'most conservative stronghold of the old regime' (Geiger 1968: 52).

In the view of the revolutionary Bolsheviks, it was necessary to deprive the family of its economic base and to redirect its energies and loyalties from private to public domains, replacing its most important educational and social functions with publicly provided services. The nationalization of industry and the collectivization of agriculture would divest the family of its economic power; the expansion of public education and institutional child care would diminish its influence over the socialization of children; and the creation of public laundries and dining rooms would complete the shift of family functions to the wider society and would free women for participation in the labour force. The economic independence of women was the guarantee that women would enter both work and family roles on an equal basis with men.

Maternity itself was to be transformed into a social function. Early Soviet policies therefore recognized the potential contribution of women to both production and reproduction, and attempted to provide conditions for the simultaneous performance of both. The initial Soviet approach sought women's equality through a shift of functions from the private domain to the public rather than, as in contemporary feminist strategy, through a redefinition of male and female roles.

Stalinist priorities, however, precluded any major shift of family functions to the larger society. On the contrary, the family's importance for social stability, economic performance, and population growth received increasing

[1] For a more extensive treatment, see Lapidus (1978; 1988).

official recognition. Simultaneously, Stalin's industrialization strategy, with its extreme emphasis on heavy industry at the expense of consumer industries and services, compelled the household to provide itself with a wide range of goods and services that are normally shifted outside it in the course of economic development. Rising female employment outside the household supplemented rather than replaced female labour within it.

Soviet norms and institutions thus ultimately rested upon the premiss that women, but not men, had dual roles. On the one hand, female employment was encouraged by measures that accorded women equal rights with men, expanded their educational opportunities and professional training, and shifted some of the additional costs of female labour from the individual enterprise to the larger society. At the same time, the growth of female industrial employment was exceptionally dependent on special arrangements to accommodate the continuing heavy burden of family responsibilities. The effort to make female occupational roles permeable to family needs created especially sharp differences in the conditions of male and female labour. The result was a distinctive pattern of linkages between the family and the occupational system that had fundamentally different consequences for women and men.

FEMALE LABOUR AND THE SOVIET ECONOMY

The ideological goal of full female participation in social production was transformed into a pressing economic need by the inauguration of rapid industrialization under the First Five-Year Plan in 1928. Rapid economic expansion created a rising demand for industrial labour, while falling real income and a growing shortfall of males increased the supply of female labour. The demand for female labour was given added impetus by the Second World War, when a new influx of women workers replaced the millions of mobilized men. The cumulative casualties of war and civil war, of collectivization, purges, deportations, and, ultimately, of the Second World War, had created a severe deficit of males. In 1946 there were only 59 men for every 100 women in the 35–59 age group. This demographic imbalance affected the supply of, and demand for, female labour by obliging large numbers of women to support themselves. Political deportations and wartime losses made wives and widows heads of households; in addition, the scarcity of men deprived a large proportion of Soviet women of any opportunity to marry. Female-headed households made up almost 30 per cent of the total in 1959.

The gradual return to demographic normality in the post-war period, combined with the steady improvement of living standards, might have been expected to diminish the pressures for high female employment. Yet the

140   G. W. LAPIDUS

TABLE 6.1 Average annual numbers and percentages of female workers and
employees, 1922–1989

	Total no. of workers and employees ('000)	No. of female workers and employees ('000)	Women as % of total
1922	6,200	1,560	25
1926	9,900	2,265	23
1928	11,400	2,765	24
1940	33,900	13,190	39
1945	28,600	15,920	56
1950	40,400	19,180	47
1960	62,000	29,250	47
1970	90,200	45,800	51
1980	112,480	57,700	51.2
1989		58,700	50.6

Note: Women constituted 55% of the total population in 1959 and 63.4% of the age cohort
35 and over; by 1985, the figure had dropped to 53%.
Source: TsSU SSSR (1972b: 345, 348; 1975b, 28–9; 1977: 470; 1979: 178–9; 1980: 387–8,
391; 1981: 160; 1985a: 409) Zhenshchiny v SSSR (1980: 70), Zhenshchiny v SSSR (1990: 48).

continuing reliance on an extensive strategy of economic development
required a steady influx of new labour resources. Between 1960 and the early
1970s, an additional 25 million women were added to the Soviet labour force,
raising their numbers to above 51 per cent of the total. By the 1970s over
87 per cent of working-age women were either employed or studying full-
time; their average length of employment rose from 28.7 to 33.5 years
between 1960 and 1970; and the average number of non-working years
dropped from 12.3 to 3.6 (Kotliar and Turchaninova 1975: 106–7). The only
major untapped reserves of female labour in the USSR were found in the
Central Asian and Transcaucasian republics, where female participation rates
outside agriculture—especially among the local nationalities—remained
extremely low (Ubaidullaeva 1987).

High female participation rates were partly the result of official policies
aimed at drawing housewives into the work-place to offset the growing labour
shortage. But they also reflected severe economic pressures: Soviet wages and
pensions were too low to support a family of dependants on the income of a
single breadwinner. The average monthly wage in the 1970s, for example,
was less than two-thirds of what was required to support a family of four at
even the officially recognized level of 'material well-being', and opinion
surveys of women factory workers clearly demonstrated that economic need
was the major determinant of female employment.[2] Moreover, 'economic

[2] For studies showing that family income and female labour force participation were inversely
related, see Kharchev and Golod (1971: 38–69); Osipov and Shchepan'skii (1969: 444, 456).

need' is itself relative; despite economic improvements in the 1960s and 1970s, rising aspirations outran rising incomes. In addition, rising wages increased the opportunity cost of not being employed, encouraging women to prefer employment to either larger families or more leisure. Similarly, as educational attainments and professionalism rose, labour force attachment was strengthened.

Soviet ideology reinforced these economic pressures by emphasizing the intrinsic value of work, as well as its contribution to economic independence, social status, and personal satisfaction. The role of 'mere housewife' was sharply devalued by Soviet ideology; Soviet surveys indicated that relatively few women would withdraw from the labour force even if it became economically feasible, although expanded opportunities for part-time work would have been welcomed by some (Iankova 1975: 43; Mikhailiuk 1970: 24; A. L. Pimenova 1966: 36–9).

PATTERNS OF FEMALE EMPLOYMENT

The massive scale of female participation in Soviet economic life did not, however, eradicate the differences between male and female workers in the distribution of income, skill, status, power, or even time. Women predominated in economic sectors and occupations with low status and pay, and were under-represented in the more prestigious professions and in managerial positions. In industry, as in the economy as a whole, women were heavily concentrated in a relatively small number of areas, and significantly under-represented in others. Women constituted over 80 per cent of food and textile workers and over 90 per cent of garment workers, but less than 30 per cent of the workers in coal, lumber, electric power, and mineral extraction.

Moreover, in industrial employment, as in the professions, women were concentrated at lower levels of the occupational pyramid. Although Soviet data are scanty, they clearly indicate that, even as women began to enter the middle and upper ranks of industry, they continued to predominate in low-level, unmechanized, and unskilled jobs. Thus, in a typical industrial city studied in one Soviet survey, approximately 4 per cent of the women workers were highly skilled; 30 per cent were of average skill; and 66 per cent were low-skilled, compared with 31, 50, and 19 per cent, respectively, for men (Sonin 1973: 362–3). Similarly, in a group of machine-building enterprises studied by another Soviet research team, almost 95 per cent of the women workers, but only 5 per cent of the men, occupied the three lowest skill classifications; no women at all were found in the highest classification (Kotliar and Turchaninova 1975: 67–8). Nor did technological progress automatically bring greater equality. Rather, increasing mechanization not

142   G. W. LAPIDUS

TABLE 6.2 Distribution of Soviet full-time workers and employees in various age groups, by wage levels, March 1989
(% in each earnings interval)

Roubles earned per month	Age group				
	16–24	25–29	30–39	40–49	50+
Men					
Under 80	4.1	1.4	0.8	0.8	2.4
80–90	4.5	2.1	1.3	1.2	2.9
91–100	4.9	2.2	1.3	1.2	2.3
101–120	10.0	5.7	3.7	3.3	5.6
121–140	9.5	6.8	4.5	4.1	6.1
141–160	12.5	10.1	7.1	6.4	8.5
161–180	11.3	10.7	8.9	8.2	10.9
181–200	10.2	10.5	10.0	10.0	10.1
201–220	6.4	8.0	8.2	8.1	7.6
221–250	8.3	11.2	12.7	13.3	11.5
251–300	8.5	12.4	15.7	16.6	13.4
301–350	4.2	6.9	9.2	10.0	7.8
351–400	2.4	4.4	5.9	6.1	4.3
Over 400	3.2	7.6	10.7	10.7	6.6
Women					
Under 80	6.7	3.5	2.6	2.9	6.3
80–90	13.9	8.5	5.8	5.4	9.1
91–100	9.5	6.9	4.8	4.2	5.7
101–120	18.9	15.3	11.5	10.2	12.2
121–140	14.1	14.5	12.1	10.0	10.5
141–160	12.3	14.1	13.2	11.9	11.2
161–180	7.7	10.6	11.5	11.4	10.8
181–200	5.6	7.6	9.5	9.6	8.1
201–220	3.4	5.0	6.6	7.1	5.9
221–250	3.4	5.5	7.8	9.0	7.1
251–300	2.7	4.7	7.4	9.2	6.9
301–350	1.0	1.9	3.4	4.2	3.1
351–400	0.4	0.9	1.7	2.2	1.5
Over 400	0.4	1.0	2.1	2.7	1.6

Source: TsSU SSSR (1990: 71–2).

infrequently widened the gap between men and women workers as newly mechanized and automated work went primarily to males.

Women were better represented among technical specialists than among skilled workers in industry. They occupied a particularly prominent place in teaching and medicine, although even here the proportion of women declined at higher levels. But women were still largely absent from positions of managerial authority. To be sure, the proportion of women among enterprise directors did rise, from a mere 1 per cent in 1956 to 9 per cent in 1975, and to 11 per cent in 1985; but women did not move into management to the extent that their training, experience, and proportion of the relevant age cohort would warrant.

Women were also virtually absent from the Soviet political élite. Until the final collapse of the Communist Party, women were far less likely than men to become party members, and after 1918 their proportion in the party's central committee never exceeded 5 per cent. Only two women have ever been members of the Politburo, and only one was named to Gorbachev's newly created Presidential Council.

THE EARNINGS GAP

The uneven distribution of women across economic sectors and occupations, combined with their under-representation in positions of high skill and responsibility, resulted in a considerable gap between male and female earnings. The publication in 1989 of the first Soviet figures on distribution of wages by age and sex largely confirms earlier Western estimates that average full-time female earnings were only 65–75 per cent those of males (TsSU SSSR 1990: 71–2; for Western estimates, see Lapidus 1982: pp. xxi–xxvii; Ofer and Vinokur 1981).

The wage disparity was all the more surprising in view of official assertions that women were guaranteed equal pay for equal work, and in light of the fact that the educational attainment of much of the female industrial labour force actually exceeded that of males, that female labour force participation was more continuous in the USSR than in the West, and that virtually all employed women worked full-time.

TABLE 6.3 Estimates of mean monthly wages and Gini coefficients for Soviet men and women of various age groups, 1989

Age band	Men		Women		Female wage as % of male
	Gini	Mean (Rb/mo.)	Gini	Mean (Rb/mo.)	
16–24	0.212	229	0.214	163	71.2
25–29	0.187	270	0.200	184	68.1
30–39	0.172	304	0.202	212	69.7
40–49	0.167	308	0.205	224	72.7
50+	0.195	270	0.233	205	75.9

Note: A lognormal curve was fitted to the data in the table by a minimum Kolmogorov–Smirnov estimator.

Source: Alexeev and Gaddy (1991: 28–9).

Several factors account for this wage disparity. First, economic sectors and industrial branches with high wage levels and greater wage differentials— such as heavy industry and construction—were precisely those in which women were under-represented; those that had a high concentration of female employees—light industry and the services—were also those in which lower wage levels and narrower differentials prevailed. For example, in construction, where women constituted 28 per cent of the labour force in 1985, monthly earnings averaged Rb236.6; in public health and physical culture, where females made up 84 per cent of the work force, they averaged Rb132.8.

Second, blue-collar occupations were more highly rewarded than most white-collar ones, even when white-collar employees had higher levels of educational attainment. For example, in 1985 the average wage of industrial workers was Rb211.7 a month, and of white-collar personnel in industry, Rb164.6 (TsSU SSSR 1986: 397). Thus, the large-scale movement of women into white-collar and professional occupations in the USSR, brought with it a sharp decline in their status and pay relative to skilled blue-collar workers.

Soviet sources often attributed the earnings gap to differences in the qualifications and productivity of male and female workers, but this explanation is not sufficient. Although Soviet law required that equal work receive equal pay, there was no mechanism to ensure that women were placed in positions commensurate with their training and skills. Women were thus frequently overqualified for the jobs they held. A study of industrial enterprises in the city of Taganrog came to the startling conclusion that 40 per cent of all female workers with higher or secondary specialized education occupied low-skill industrial positions, compared with 6 per cent of comparable males; only 10 per cent of these highly educated women, compared with 46 per cent of their male counterparts, occupied high-skill positions. Most striking of all was the fact that the distribution of the male labour force as a whole, without respect to education, was more favourable than the distribution of this highly educated female contingent (Gruzdeva 1975: 94; Zdravomyslov et al. 1967). Finally, the possibility of direct wage discrimination cannot be completely ruled out. A Western analysis of unpublished Soviet wage data in the 1970s concluded that only one-fourth of an average male–female wage differential of Rb40 per month could be attributed to the combined effects of sex differences in distribution across education, age, economic sector, and levels of skill or responsibility (Swafford 1978: 661–5).

It is often argued—in the Soviet Union as in the West—that these patterns reflect not discrimination, but fundamental differences in the occupational preferences of men and women. Soviet studies made it abundantly clear that from early childhood boys and girls diverged in their educational and occupational choices. Fewer adult women expressed an interest in a career as opposed to a job, and in choosing a job women attached more weight to convenience than to content. Yet these individual choices were made within a socially structured context of opportunities and costs.

Three features of the Soviet system deserve to be singled out for their role in shaping women's preferences and choices. First, sexual stereotyping of occupations was sustained by official attitudes and policies. Measures that restricted women's employment in heavy or dangerous work considered unsuitable or 'harmful to the female organism', and encouraged their entry into suitably 'female' occupations, served to channel female labour. Although the rationale for particular classifications was sometimes questioned, the distinction in principle between 'men's work' and 'women's work'—based on biological and psychological stereotypes—went unchallenged. Soviet labour economists routinely wrote of the need to create working conditions that corresponded to the 'anatomical–physiological peculiarities of the female organism and likewise to the moral–ethical temperament of women'.

Second, female occupational choices were profoundly influenced by the continuing identification of both creativity and authority with men. As many Soviet sources testify, women who pursued demanding careers encountered subtle but widespread prejudices, which impeded their professional mobility and limited their accession to positions of responsibility. To cite just one example, two prominent male scholars argued,

The increase in the number of women with scholarly degrees accounts for the decrease in the number of those who really develop science . . . The 'rebellious' spirit, the predisposition to search for new, non-traditional methods in science, are more typical among men than women . . . Therefore, the broad feminization of science contributes to the slackening in the development of new branches of science, even if women make their contribution in the accumulation of facts. (Sokolov and Reimers 1983: 77)

(See also Posadskaya 1992.) According to other Soviet studies, women were widely, though erroneously, believed to have less initiative and creativity than men, and to be less suited for managerial positions (Pavlova 1971).

Throughout the 1970s, complaints that insufficient attention was paid to recruiting women for responsible positions occurred with monotonous regularity in official pronouncements. At one meeting of a provincial Communist Party committee, the under-recruitment was explicitly attributed to the presence of 'a certain psychological barrier': 'On the one hand, a number of leaders fear to entrust women with responsible positions, and on the other, women themselves demonstrate timidity, doubting their strength and refusing under various pretexts, a transfer to leadership positions' ('Povyshat' politicheskuiu proizvodstvennuiu . . .' 1975: 44). Dubious about the utility of further exhortation, and impatient with the slow pace of change, one labour specialist proposed a more radical solution: the adoption of sexual quotas, with the number of women in managerial positions to be proportional to the number of women working under their jurisdiction (Tolkunova 1967: 103).

A third social determinant of the pattern of female employment was the explicit treatment of household and family responsibilities, culturally and in legislation, as primarily and properly the domain of women. Thus, the fundamental assumption of Soviet economic and family policy—that women, and women only, have dual roles—effectively assigned women a distinctive position in both the occupational and the family systems.

FEMALE WORKERS AND THE FAMILY

Just as family roles affect the scope and pattern of female employment, so women's work affects many aspects of family life, including patterns of marriage and divorce, fertility, and the family division of labour. Soviet scholars tended to share the view of Western sociologists that education, occupational status, income, and social participation are resources that directly influence family authority; and they contended that, by reducing disparities in these areas between men and women, state socialism guaranteed the independence of women in marriage, enhanced their power within the family, and produced a more egalitarian pattern of family life.

Patterns of marriage and divorce in the USSR offered some support for this view. Early marriage, a high marriage rate, a large male–female age difference at the time of marriage, and a low divorce rate usually indicate women's limited status and opportunities outside the family relative to the value attached to their reproductive potential within it. Such a pattern still predominates in the largely rural and Muslim regions of Soviet Central Asia. By contrast, access to education, employment, and independent income, typical of the more developed, European regions of the USSR, tends to enhance a woman's freedom to enter or leave marriage by reducing the relative value of the resources gained through marriage. Thus, the proportion of married women is considerably lower in the Russian Republic than in Uzbekistan; the mean age of marriage is higher; the age disparity between spouses is considerably smaller, and the rate of divorce substantially higher.

Female employment also affects family structure through its influence on childbearing. Studies in the 1960s and 1970s showed that non-working women had 20–25 per cent more children than their working counterparts; and the latter had 2.5 times as many abortions (Strumilin 1964: 140; Musatov 1967: 321; Nemchenko 1973: 35–6; Shlindman and Zvidrin'sh 1973: 74). This difference helps to account for the inverse correlation of urbanization with birth rates. Urban women both desired and expected fewer children than rural women, and women in large cities expected to bear fewer children than their counterparts in small cities; the figures reached an alarming low of 1.69 in Moscow and 1.55 in Leningrad in the mid-1970s (Belova 1975: 109, 129; Borisov 1976: 72–7; Sysenko 1974: 36–40).

Birth rates also vary with educational attainment, occupational status, and professional skill. White-collar mothers have far fewer children than industrial workers, and industrial workers have fewer than collective farmers. Among workers, family size is inversely related to skill level. The highest proportion of third, fourth, and fifth children was found among unskilled workers and those with low qualifications; relatively few large families were found among workers with high qualifications or with engineering and technical skills (Sysenko 1974: 37, 40; Belova 1975: 146).

The tendency for increased female education, employment, and qualifications to be associated with lower rates of marriage, later marriage, higher rates of divorce, and declining family size, and for stable family patterns and high birth rates to be found among the least 'liberated' Soviet women, provoked growing concern in the Brezhnev era. In seeking to reverse these trends, Soviet scholars and planners noted with interest that most women had fewer children than they appeared to desire. Some concluded that specific obstacles—limited financial resources, poor housing, and crowded pre-school facilities—were responsible for low urban birth rates, and that measures to alleviate these problems would have a positive effect on fertility. But Soviet investigations of the relationship between income and fertility yielded contradictory results: subjective perceptions of family needs played a crucial mediating role. Not surprisingly, then, the efforts of the 1970s to strengthen the family and reverse the declining birth rate had disappointing results.

Numerous Soviet scholars also argued that women's entry into the workforce resulted in greater female authority within the family, greater male participation in housework, and a more egalitarian pattern of family decision-making. Yet this assertion is disputed by a voluminous body of Soviet time-budget investigations. They demonstrated that, although men and women devote roughly equal time to paid employment and sleep, working women spent on average 28 hours per week on housework compared with about 12 hours per week for men; men, by contrast, enjoyed 50 per cent more leisure time than women. Within the family, a sharply defined sexual division of labour also persisted. A first category of activities, such as gardening and repairs, was predominantly male; a second, including shopping and cleaning house, was predominantly female but was shared to some degree by males; a third group of activities, including cooking and laundry, was performed almost exclusively by women. In short, nearly 75 per cent of domestic duties fell to women; the remainder were shared with husbands and other family members (Iankova 1970a: 43; Slesarev and Iankova 1969: 430–1).

Several additional conclusions could be drawn from these studies (Lapidus 1978: 256–8). First, male–female differences in the allocation of time were apparent even among single students living in dormitories. Second, this basic male–female differential increased with marriage: the amount of housework performed by husbands did not offset the time spent on such work by wives. Third, there was a positive relationship between female employment outside the home and male help within. Fourth, the male–female differential was sharply increased with the birth of a first child. Finally, educational level seemed to have an important effect on the allocation of time to domestic chores, but not necessarily on the participation of males in them. A study of time use among workers with higher or specialized secondary education found that, although the total amount of time devoted to housework was lower, the male–female differential was actually larger than that found in worker families of lower educational qualifications (Gruzdeva 1975: 9). Even high female educational attainments failed to obliterate sharp sex-role differences; the five most prevalent daily activities of women with specialized education differed far more from those of comparable males than from the activities of women with only four grades of schooling.

The time devoted to housework by males varies with the demands of their work roles and with their job and educational levels. Blue-collar males actually devoted more time to housework than their white-collar counterparts. The latter—particularly those engaged in demanding careers—devoted more time to work, study, and social participation, and less time to household chores, than any other category.

Women's educational efforts virtually ceased with the birth of a child, but family responsibilities had little apparent effect on the ability of male workers to continue their studies. As two Soviet authors explicitly recognized, men combined employment with study by limiting the time they devoted to family chores—at the expense of other members of the household, who, in effect, subsidized these educational pursuits (Gordon and Klopov 1972: 200–1).

In light of these patterns, it was unrealistic to assume that further economic development would bring a dramatic decline in women's household responsibilities or a sharp increase in leisure time. As a distinguished Soviet sociologist argued, women do not simply shed their former duties as development occurs; they acquire new ones. Higher standards of housekeeping and childrearing create new responsibilities, and the breakup of extended families means that tasks once shared between two generations of women now fall exclusively on one (Iankova 1970a, 1970b).

Nor would reductions in female working time automatically yield the increase in leisure that many Soviet writers anticipated. The shift from a six-day to a five-day work-week in 1967 yielded a comparatively greater increase in male leisure than in female, as did an experiment with shortening the work-day of women factory workers (Gordon and Rimashevskaia 1972: 24, 62–79; Porokhniuk and Shepeleva 1975: 102–8; V.N. Pimenova 1974: 131). In both cases, men took advantage of the opportunity to reduce their share of household chores, while women devoted more of the additional time to child care and domestic responsibilities than to study, social participation, or leisure pursuits. By freeing males from the performance of routine household and child-care chores, women workers in effect advanced the occupational mobility of males at the cost of their own.

THE INTERDEPENDENCE OF WORK AND FAMILY ROLES

This profile of the Soviet female labour force has pointed to the ways in which the interaction of women's work and family roles contributed to a sharp differentiation between the activities of male and female workers. For men and women alike, work and family roles were inversely related and tended to compete with each other for time and energy, but for women family roles were primary, and that defined the nature and rhythms of female employment. The consequences were frankly acknowledged by a Soviet analyst:

Women do indeed choose easier jobs, with convenient hours, close to home and with pleasant co-workers and managers, but not because they lack initiative. They choose these jobs because their combination of social roles is difficult. (Pavlova 1971)

Soviet women's family responsibilities intruded into the work-place—and were accommodated by it—to a degree unusual in Western industrial societies. Provisions for pregnancy leaves, for leave to care for sick children, for nursing infants during work hours, and for exemptions of pregnant women and mothers from heavy work, overtime, or travel were predicated on the view that childrearing and other 'exclusively female' family responsibilities took a certain priority that work arrangements should accommodate. Women were explicitly encouraged to view work from the perspective of their roles as wives and mothers.

This limited insulation of female work roles from family roles resulted in characteristic patterns of female behaviour. As two Soviet specialists observed, 'The women value jobs requiring simple automatic responses that can be performed adequately despite . . . mental distractions [of house and children]' (Kharchev and Golod 1971: 63–4). Women workers were less demanding than their male counterparts, as is generally true of workers whose mobility is blocked and whose work satisfaction depends less on the content of their jobs than on working conditions. Under these circumstances, it is understandable that married women were seriously under-represented in enterprise activities requiring additional commitments of time and energy, as well as in volunteer movements and in public affairs generally.

The effects of this sexual division of labour both on the job and at home were not altogether benign. As the massive participation of women in full-time paid employment eroded the traditional rationale for a sexual division of labour within the family, it increased the level of conflict between men and women over the division of domestic tasks. These rising resentments, in the view of Soviet analysts, contributed to alcoholism and high divorce rates and were a potential source of disenchantment with the institution of the family itself.

A second source of strain was the extreme tension between female work and family roles, resulting in the deliberate limitation of family size. As one Soviet writer noted:

The current decline in the birth rate has certain negative consequences—e.g., it will contribute to the manpower shortage—but it also has some positive aspects. It can be viewed, in part, as a spontaneous response by women to their excessive work load and lack of equality with men—a response that consists of eliminating the single factor over which they have the greatest control. The falling birthrate is an important —in fact indispensable—lever that women can use in their effort to achieve full equality with men. (Riurikov 1977: 119)

For the Brezhnev leadership, these were alarming trends. By impinging on a wide range of economic, political, and military concerns, they compelled fundamental reconsideration of the whole spectrum of policies involving female work and family roles.

POLICY DILEMMAS AND OPTIONS UNDER BREZHNEV

By the 1970s, the Brezhnev leadership faced a policy dilemma brought on by mutually contradictory processes. By opening a new range of educational and professional options for women, Soviet policy encouraged them to acquire new skills, values, orientations, and aspirations that competed with their traditional domestic roles. At the same time, the high value attached to the family, the critical social roles assigned to it, and the large investments of time and energy needed to sustain it seriously constrained women's occupational commitments and achievements. The resulting 'contradictions', in the language of Soviet analysts, between the occupational and family roles of working women had an extremely high economic, demographic, and social cost. They adversely affected women's health, welfare, and opportunities for professional and personal development, and led to increased family tensions and a declining birth rate (Kharchev 1970: 19; Shishkan 1976: 38). Enlisting the aid of social scientists as well as several newly created legislative and administrative bodies, the Brezhnev leadership searched for a strategy that would use scarce labour resources more effectively, while also reversing the decline in birth rates in the developed regions of the USSR.

A first group of proposed measures aimed at redistributing female labour resources by removing women from employment in unsafe and unhealthy conditions, transferring them from low-skilled, non-mechanized, and heavy labour to more skilled and suitable jobs, and achieving a demographically more balanced regional labour market by providing a better mix of 'men's' and 'women's' work. A number of critics also urged that upgrading the skills of women workers be given higher priority and increased incentives, and that vocational programmes be adapted to the schedules and responsibilities of working mothers (Kostakov 1976: 101–60; Kotliar and Shlemin, 1974: 110–19; Sergeeva 1976: 37–46).

A second group of proposals focused on improving the working conditions of the female labour force. In particular, they called for stricter legislation and better enforcement of labour laws protecting women from hazardous work. Other analysts even advocated introducing differentiated work norms, urging that women be assigned reduced work norms, and even a shortened working day, without loss of pay, in compensation for their unpaid work at home (Iankova 1975: 44–6; Iuk 1975: 122; Sakharova 1973). A third group recommended improving the supply of consumer goods and everyday services to reduce the strain of women's dual role. Many studies argued that investments in refrigerators, public laundries, or rapid transit systems would generate savings of time that would more than compensate for initial investments. Calls for the more rapid expansion of pre-school facilities, and even for the introduction of private and co-operative arrangements, were coupled with reminders that the lack of such facilities contributed to underemployment of women, high rates of turnover, and lowered productivity.

Taken together, these three groups of recommendations amounted to an agenda for slow but incremental reform to reduce the conflict between 'men's' and 'women's' work. They rested on the assumption that a combination of technological progress and socio-economic reform would obviate the need for more far-reaching changes in the structure of family or work.

Some Soviet experts, however, argued that the problem would, in fact, require a more radical response. One option aimed at increasing the birth rate at any cost through an all-out effort to elevate the social status and material rewards associated with reproduction, even if this resulted in a decline in female labour-force participation (Urlanis 1974: 283). The central and most controversial aspect of this pro-natalist position was its desire to transform maternity into professional, paid, social labour. Financial subsidies, tailored not to the direct costs of children but to the opportunity cost of female labour, would be offered to induce new mothers to withdraw from the labour force for up to three years; a sliding scale of benefits tied to wage levels would ensure a more equal distribution of births among different social strata. The costs of such a programme, its advocates argued, would be offset by its long-term contribution to the labour supply and by the more immediate savings generated by a cutback in public nurseries. Critics, however, viewed this approach as an unacceptable step backward.

A radically different set of policy options derived from the premiss that the more effective use of female labour, and not stimulation of fertility, was the overriding priority. Arguing that work was of critical importance to women's social status and personal development as well as to the economy, its proponents urged increasing the equality of men's and women's economic roles.

'Women have no need of "light work", but of qualified work, commensurate with their professional preparation and training, their education, and their talents,' insisted one commentator (Berezovskaia 1975: 12). Recognizing that women's 'double burden' reduced their ability to raise their skill levels and to undertake more responsible duties, this approach called for a more equal sharing of family responsibilities (Iurkevich 1970: 192). But even the most outspoken advocates of women's interests during the Brezhnev years emphasized the biological and psychological differences between men and women, and attached high value to women's family and maternal roles.

Emphasizing that new attitudes were a precondition for new patterns of behaviour, and refusing to treat them as purely private and personal matters, a number of writers also called for a more systematic intervention by state, party, and public organizations to inculcate egalitarian values. Moreover, they insisted that the more immediate problems faced by working mothers with young children would be alleviated by an expansion of part-time work at a much lower cost than the extended maternity leaves proposed by the radical pro-natalists (Martirosian 1976: 54–61; Novitskii and Babkina 1973: 133–40; Shishkan 1971: 42–7). Clearly, the introduction of part-time work on a large scale would have raised a host of complex problems (Moses 1983). It would have been far more feasible in routine white-collar and service occupations than in highly skilled technical positions or supervisory jobs. In all likelihood, it would have increased the concentration of women in low-skilled and poorly remunerated jobs. And, if experiments with shortened work-days were any indication, it would have forestalled a more equal division of household responsibilities.

Although the Brezhnev leadership was relatively slow in coming to an awareness of these economic and demographic issues, they gradually came to occupy an important place on the political agenda. Overall, the measures introduced under Brezhnev sought to strike a balance between a labour-extensive strategy and a labour-intensive one. On the one hand, they encouraged high female participation rates by raising minimum wages, expanding the child-care network, modifying the pension system, and exploring the possibilities for expansion of part-time work. At the same time, concern over declining birth rates was evident in the family allowance programme introduced in 1974, which extended maternity leave benefits to female *kolkhoz* (collective farm) workers, liberalized sick leave for parents of young children, and expanded partially paid maternity leave to a full year. In this as in other areas, however, the Brezhnev leadership failed to act with the vigour and decisiveness necessary to address the problem adequately.

But whatever policy measures were adopted during these years, they reflected the concerns and priorities of the party leadership rather than of women themselves. Women remained the subjects, not the agents, of policy change.

WOMEN UNDER PERESTROIKA

To attempt even a broad sketch of the impact of perestroika on Soviet women is a daunting task. The contradictory nature of the political and the economic trends, the breathtaking speed of events, and the growing diversity of outcomes in different regions and republics preclude simple generalizations about the period 1985–91.

It remains unclear whether Gorbachev had any new approach in mind to women's issues when he launched his attempt at reform. Some of his early initiatives gave women's issues higher visibility — his advocacy of the promotion of more women in political life, and his appointment of Aleksandra Biryukova to the party's powerful Secretariat; his role in the creation of a national women's organization intended to link the Soviet Women's Committee to a broad nationwide network of local women's councils; and his emphasis on the need for new attention to social and family policy. The prominent role and unprecedented visibility of his wife Raisa, however controversial, also altered the ethos of family secrecy and male domination traditionally surrounding the General Secretary of the Communist Party.

Gorbachev's early economic policies had more ominous implications for women. The effort to promote more rapid economic growth and increased technological innovation by stimulating greater competition within the workplace carried with it the prospect of massive dismissals of redundant workers and growing wage differentiation. Coupled with Gorbachev's call for an expansion of the service sector, they suggested the prospect of a long-term shift in female labour force participation from industrial to service employment (Kostakov 1986; N.K. Zakharova, *et al.* 1989). But Gorbachev's economic reforms remained limited and contradictory; the most enduring legacy of the Gorbachev era proved to be the intellectual, political, and spiritual liberation that the reforms unleashed.

The impact of glasnost on the discussion of women's issues was particularly dramatic. Not only did this dialogue radically broaden in its scope, frankness, and forms of discourse, but a whole series of issues that were previously taboo — including prostitution, rape, contraception and homosexuality — became legitimate topics of analysis and debate. Among the many dramatic departures from past practice, a first Gay–Lesbian Film Festival was held in Moscow in August 1991. And, just as terms like 'command–administrative system' and 'totalitarianism' were incorporated into the political lexicon, concepts such as 'patriarchy' or '*muzhkratia*' (male-dominated bureaucracy) became a staple of feminist discourse.

The change in discourse was accompanied by increasing legitimation of socio-economic and public opinion research focusing on women's position; for the first time it was recognized to be important as an academic and policy enterprise. Two newly created research institutes, both directed by distinguished women scholars (Tatyana Zaslavskaya and Natalya Rimashevskaya), provided a home for such work, but the most radical new departure was the creation within Rimashevskaya's institute of the first Centre for Gender Studies, headed by the young feminist scholar Anastasia Posadskaya.

The process of democratization, which unleashed an unprecedented wave of socio-political activism across the Soviet landscape, not only drew many women into new social, environmental, political and national movements; it also gave impetus to the emergence of a variety of new forms of feminist organization and mobilization (Buckley 1990). Some took the form of small-scale and relatively informal women's groups devoted largely to consciousness-raising and to the study and dissemination of feminist literature, often Western in origin. Others, like the clubs of women journalists, women writers, women scholars, or women entrepreneurs, were based on professional ties, often within a single city, and devoted to improving the status and conditions of women in a given field. Yet a third type was represented by the creation of women's sections within larger organizations or political movements not specifically concerned with women's issues—the women's group of Sajudis, the Lithuanian Popular Front, or the loose organization of women deputies to the Supreme Soviet are examples of this genre. Finally, there were more explicit political action groups, some of which, like the Soviet Women's Committee, had long been part of the establishment but were now attempting to adapt to new conditions, whereas others, such as the organization of mothers pressing for changes in military practices, were the result of spontaneous efforts to deal with new issues.

The more open and competitive political milieu, however, not only created new opportunities for independent action; it also resulted in a decline in female representation in national and republican legislative bodies. The first quasi-competitive elections, held in 1989, which partly dismantled the old quota system guaranteeing a certain proportion of seats to women as well as to members of other social categories, resulted in a sharp fall in the proportion of female deputies—from 33 to 16 per cent at the all-Union level. Moreover, a majority of these were selected for 'reserved seats' by public organizations such as the Soviet Women's Committee. In the 1990 republican and local elections, where 'reserved seats' were largely eliminated, women candidates fared even more poorly, winning under 6 per cent of the seats in Russia's Congress of People's Deputies and under 10 per cent in most other republican legislatures. Some of the women who gained political prominence during these years have proved themselves effective and genuine political actors rather than token appointees.[3] But the combination of unfavourable electoral arrangements, the widespread resistance to the idea of female politicians, and the mounting burden of everyday life on women created by the dislocations of perestroika were serious obstacles to an expansion of women's political role in the new politics of the perestroika era.

WOMEN AND RESTRUCTURING IN POST-SOVIET RUSSIA

The end of the Soviet system, and the emergence of fifteen new states on its former territory, opens a fundamentally new chapter in the history of women's roles. While the legacy of the Soviet past—both its institutions and its attitudes—will weigh heavily on the future of this entire region, women's roles in the new states are likely to be shaped ever more powerfully by the divergent political orientations, economic priorities, and cultural identities these post-communist societies pursue. In facing the simultaneous challenge of state-building and nation-building, the moral and political vacuum created by the collapse of communist ideologies and parties is being filled—here as in Eastern Europe—by various forms of nationalism, which frequently converge with social and religious conservatism in redefining women's roles.

Our consideration of the impact of post-Soviet developments will therefore be confined to Russia, which, along with the Baltic states, has moved furthest towards the creation of democratic political institutions and a market economy. Moreover, because the major changes in Russia's political institutions—and the role of women in them—occurred before independence, and have changed relatively little since then, our primary focus will be on the impact of recent economic changes.

Although the new Russian government of Boris Yeltsin launched a serious programme of economic reform in early 1992, a variety of institutional and political obstacles have limited both the scope and the pace of these reforms in comparison with Poland, Hungary, and the Czech Republic. Even the limited degree of price liberalization and privatization, however, have aggravated the economic crisis inherited by the Yeltsin government and magnified by the breakup of what was once a unified economic space. By early 1993 Russia was suffering from severe inflation verging on hyperinflation, a sharp decline in GDP, and a massive budgetary deficit.

[3] Marju Lauristan, Galina Starovoiteva, Kazimirez Prunskiene, and Klara Hallik are examples of such figures.

The impact of inflation has been particularly injurious to pensioners, a great majority of whom are women. The budgetary crisis, and the unravelling of the central government more generally, has forced the curtailment or elimination of subsidies to a broad range of programmes, from educational and cultural institutions to day-care centres. As these trends continue, they are likely to compel the withdrawal of growing numbers of women, and especially mothers of young children, from the labour force.

Until now, state enterprises have largely resisted the pressures towards lay-offs and closures by resorting to part-time employment and unpaid leaves. Although the levels of unemployment remain very low by European standards—under 1 per cent in October 1992, according to somewhat sketchy official figures—women constitute a high percentage of the total: i.e. roughly 70 per cent, and up to 90 per cent in some regions (RFE/RL Research Report, 4 December 1992: 5). The vast majority are women with higher education, and the cutbacks are particularly sharp in the administrative apparatus and among engineers and technicians (Rimashevskaya 1992: 72; Interlegal 1992: 8). While a growing number of workers are shifting from the state to the often lucrative private sector, many of the new opportunities for women are in poorly paid secretarial and service employment rather than in supervisory or entrepreneurial roles.

The process of privatization has been disadvantageous for women in still other ways. The old, almost exclusively male, *nomenklatura* has largely managed to transform its political power into property rights in the emerging market system, accumulating capital for entrepreneurial activities. At the same time, opposition to the privatization of land by a conservative coalition has prevented ordinary workers or peasants from becoming independent farmers on any significant scale. Moreover, the voucher system, adopted as an instrument of privatization, is particularly advantageous to the management and employees of well-endowed industrial enterprises who are able to become owners of the newly created joint stock companies, while the largely female-dominated institutions of the cultural establishment or service sector offer no comparable opportunities to acquire potentially valuable property rights.

The process of transition from a centralized command system to a market economy is inevitably a painful process. But its negative impact on women can be mitigated—and its costs and benefits more equitably distributed— by strategic intervention on the part of an effective government enjoying a measure of public trust. The necessary conditions for such intervention are largely absent in Russia today. Bitter conflicts over political power, and indeed over the very identity and borders of the Russian state, prevent the stabilization and consolidation of democratic institutions, let alone the adoption of coherent legislation on major issues. Moreover, the unravelling of central authority and the growing autonomy of regional and local actors make the implementation of even the most enlightened legislation highly problematic. Under these conditions, there is little prospect of actions by the central government capable of alleviating the difficulties of transition; indeed, political disarray is compounding them. It may well be that local and regional governments could prove a more promising focus for such efforts.

REFERENCES

ALEXEEV, M. V. and GADDY, C. G. (1991), 'Trends in Wage and Income Distribution under Gorbachev: Analysis of New Soviet Data', *Berkeley–Duke Occasional Papers on the Second Economy in the USSR*. Durham, NC: Duke University (Department of Economics), 25: 28–9.

All-Union Conference of Women (1987), *Pravda*, 1 February.

ANDRIUSHKIAVICHENE, I. (1970), 'Zhenskii trud i problema svobodnogo vremeni', in N. Solov'ev, Iv. Lazauskas, and Z. A. Iankova (eds.), *Problemy byta, braka i sem'i*. Vil'nius: Mintis, 78–86.

ANTOSENKOV, E. G., and KUPRIIANOVA, Z. V. (1977), *Tendentsii v tekuchesti rabochikh kadrov*. Novosibirsk: Nauka.

ARTEMOV, V. A., BOLGOV, V. I., and VOL'SKAIA, O. V. *et al.* (1967), *Statistika biudzhetov vremeni trudiashchikhsia*. Moscow: Statistika.

BARANASKAIA, N. (1969), 'Nedelia kak nedelia', *Novyi mir*, 11: 22–55.

BELOVA, V. A. (1975), *Chislo detei v sem'e*. Moscow: Statistika.

BEREZOVSKAIA, S. (1975), 'Prestizh: zabota nasha obshchaia', *Literaturnaia gazeta*, 12 (June): 25.

BERLINER, J. S. (1987), *Soviet Female Labor Force Participation: A Regional Cross-section Analysis*, Monograph 177. Cambridge, Mass.: Harvard Russian Research Center.

BLIAKHMAN, L. S., ZDRAVOMYSLOV, A. G., and SHKARATAN, O. I. (1965), *Dvizhenie rabochei sily na promyshlennykh predpriiatiiakh*. Moscow: Ekonomika.

BORISOV, V. A. (1976), *Perspektivy rozhdaemosti*. Moscow: Statistika.

BREZHNEV, L. I. (1977), 'Rech' tovarishcha Brezhneva, L. I.', *Pravda*, 22 March: 1–3.

BUCKLEY, M. (ed.) (1986), *Soviet Social Scientists Talking: An Official Debate about Women*. London: Macmillan.

—— (1990), 'Gender and Reform', paper presented at workshop on '*Perestroika* in Historical Perspective', King's College, Cambridge, 16–19 July.

CHUIKO, L. V. (1975), *Braki i razvody*. Moscow: Statistika.

DIRZHINSKAITE, R. (1975), 'Sovetskaia zhenshchina: aktivnyi stroitel' kommunizma', *Partiinaia zhizn'*, 20: 23–8.

DOGLE, N. V. (1977), *Usloviia zhizni i zdorov'e tekstil'schchits*. Moscow: Meditsina.

GEIDANE, I. M., GOSHA, Z. Z., and ZVINDRIN'SH, I. V. *et al.* (1976), *Balans vremeni naseleniia Latviiskoi SSR*. Riga: Zinatne.

GEIGER, K. (1968), *The Family in Soviet Russia*. Cambridge, Mass.: Harvard University Press.

158   G. W. LAPIDUS

GORBACHEV, M. S. (1986), 'Politicheskii doklad Tsentral'nogo Komiteta KPSS XXVII s'ezdu Kommunisticheskoi partii Sovetskogo Soiuza', *Pravda*, 26 February.

GORDON, L. A., and KLOPOV, E. V. (1972), *Chelovek posle raboty*. Moscow: Nauka.

—— and RIMASHEVSKAIA, N. M. (1972), *Piatidnevnaia rabochaia nedelia i svobodnoe vremia trudiashchikhsia*. Moscow: Mysl'.

GRUZDEVA, E. B. (1975), 'Osobennosti obraza zhizni "intelligentnykh rabochikh"', *Rabochii klass i sovremennyi mir*, 2: 91–9.

—— and CHERTIKHINA, E. S. (1975), 'Zhenshchiny v obshchestvennom proizvodstve razvitogo sotsializma', *Rabochii klass i sovremennyi mir*, 6: 133–47.

—— —— (1983), *Trud i byt sovetskikh zhenshchin*. Moscow: Politzdat.

GUSEINOV, G., and KORCHAGIN, V. (1971), 'Voprosy trudovykh resursov', *Voprosy ekonomiki*, 2: 45–51.

IANKOVA, Z. A. (1970a), 'O bytovykh roliakh rabotaiushchei zhenshchiny', in N. Solov'ev, I. Lazauskas, and Z. A. Iankova (eds.), *Problemy byta, braka i sem'i*. Vil'nius: Mintis, 42–9.

—— (1970b), 'O semeino-bytovykh roliakh rabotaiushchei zhenshchiny', *Sotsial'nye issledovaniia*, 4: 76–87.

—— (1975), 'Razvitie lichnosti zhenshchiny v sovetskom obshchestve', *Sotsiologicheskie issledovaniia*, 4: 42–51.

Institute obshchestvennoe issledovanie (1984). *Sotsial'nye posledstviia razvoda*. Moscow: Sovietskaia sotsiologicheskaia assotsiatsiia.

Interlegal Research Center (1992), 'Women's Discussion Club', mimeo, February, p. 8.

IUK, Z. M. (1975), *Trud zhenshchiny i sem'ia*. Minsk: Belarus'.

IURKEVICH, N. G. (1970), *Sovetskaia sem'ia; funktsii i usloviia stabil'nosti*. Minsk: Belorusskii gosudarstvennii universitet.

KHARCHEV, A. G. (1964), *Brak i sem'ia v SSSR*. Moscow: Mysl'.

—— (1970), 'Byt i sem'ia', in N. Solov'ev, I. Lazauskas, and Z. A. Iankova (eds.), *Problemy byta, braka i sem'i*. Vil'nius: Mintis, 9–22.

—— (1972), *Zhurnalist*, 11.

—— (ed.) (1977), *Izmenenie polozheniia zhenshchiny i sem'ia*. Moscow: Nauka.

—— (1986), 'Issledovaniia sem'i: na poroge novogo etapa', *Sotsiologicheskie issledovanie*, 3: 22–33.

—— and GOLOD, S. I. (1969), 'Proizvodstvennaia rabota zhenshchin i sem'ia', in G. V. Osipov and I. Shchepan'skii (eds.), *Sotsial'nye problemy truda i proizvodstva*. Moscow: Mysl', 416–38.

—— —— (1971), *Professional'naia rabota zhenshchin i sem'ia*. Leningrad: Nauka.

KOSTAKOV, V. G. (1976), *Trudovye resursy patiletki*. Moscow: Politizdat.

—— (1986), 'Chelovek i progress', *Sovietskaia kultura*, 1 February: 3.

KOTLIAR, A. E. (1973), 'Voprosy izuchenia struktury zaniatosti po poly v territorial'nom razreze', in A. Z. Maikov (ed.), *Problemy ratsional'nogo ispol'zovaniia trudovykh resursov*. Moscow: Ekonomika, 400–53.

—— and SHLEMIN, A. (1974), 'Problemy ratsional'noi zaniatosti zhenshchin', *Sotsialisticheskii trud*, 7: 110–19.

—— and TURCHANINOVA, S. I. (1975), *Zaniatost' zhenshchin v proizvodstve*. Moscow: Statistika.

—— *et al.* (1982), *Dvizhenie rabochii sily v krupnom gorode.* Moscow: Finansy i statistika.

KPSS v tsifrakh (1986), *Partiinaia zhizn'*, 14: 19–32.

LAPIDUS, G. W. (1978), *Women in Soviet society.* Berkeley: University of California Press (revised edn. forthcoming).

—— (ed.) (1979), 'The Female Industrial Labor Force: Dilemmas, Reassessments, Options', in A. Kahan and B. Ruble, *Industrial Labor in the USSR.* New York: Pergamon.

—— (ed.) (1982), *Women, Work and Family in the USSR.* Armonk, NY: M. E. Sharpe.

—— (1988), 'Women and Family Roles in the USSR', in B. Gutek *et al.*, *Women and Work*, iii. Newberry Park, Calif.: Sage, 87–121.

MANEVICH, E. L. (ed.) (1971), *Osnovnye problemy ratsional'nogo ispol'zovaniia trudovykh resursov v SSSR.* Moscow: Nauka.

MARTIROSIAN, E. R. (1976), 'Pravovoe regulirovanie nepolnogo rabochego vremeni', *Sovetskoe gosudarstvo i pravo*, 10: 54–61.

MIKHAILIUK, V. B. (1970), *Ispol'zovanie zhenskogo truda v narodnom khoziaistve.* Moscow: Ekonomika.

MOSES, J. (1983), *The Politics of Women and Work in the Soviet Union and the United States.* Berkeley, Calif.: Institute of International Studies.

MUSATOV, I. M. (1967), *Sotsial'nye problemy trudovykh resursov v SSSR.* Moscow: Mysl'.

NECHEMIAS, CAROL (1992), 'Transition to Democracy: The Issue of Women's Participation', paper presented at American Association for the Advancement of Slavic Studies annual convention.

NEMCHENKO, V. (1973), 'Mezhotraslevoe dvizhenie trudovykh resursov', in D. E. Valentei *et al.* (eds.), *Narodonaselenie.* Moscow: Statistika.

NOVIKOVA, E. E. (1985), *Zhenshchina v razvitom sotsialisticheskom obshchesive.* Moscow: Mysl'.

—— MILOVA, O. L., and ZALIUBOVSKAYA, E. V. (1988), 'Sovremennaia zhenshchina na rabote i doma (opyt sotsial'no-psikhologicheskogo obsledovaniia', *EKO*, 8: 127–37.

NOVITSKII, A., and BABKINA, M. (1973), 'Nepolnoe rabochee vremia i zaniatost' naseleniia', *Voprosy ekonomiki*, 7: 133–40.

OFER, G., and VINOKUR, A. (1981), 'Earnings Differentials by Sex in the Soviet Union: A First Look', in S. Rosenfielde (ed.), *Economic Welfare and the Economics of Soviet Socialism.* Cambridge University Press, 127–62.

OSIPOV, G. V., and SHCHEPAN'SKII, I. (eds.) (1969), *Sotsial'nye problemy truda i proizvodstva.* Moscow: Mysl', 416–38.

PATRUSHEV, V. D. (1966), *Vremia kak ekonomicheskaia kategoriia.* Moscow: Mysl'.

PAVLOVA, M. (1971), 'Kar'era Ireny', *Liternaturnaia gazeta*, 13 (22 September).

PEREVEDENTSEV, V. I. (1982), *270 millionov.* Moscow: Finansy i Statistika.

PETROSIAN, G. S. (1965), *Vnerabochee vremia trudiashchikhsia v SSSR.* Moscow: Ekonomika.

PIMENOVA, A. L. (1966), 'Sem'ia i perspektivy razvitiia obshchestvennogo truda zhenshchin pri sotsializme', *Nauchnye doklady vysshei shkoly: Filosofskie nauki*, 3: 35–45.

PIMENOVA, V. N. (1974), *Svobodnoe vremia v sotsialisticheskom obshchestve*. Moscow: Nauka.

PISHCHULIN, N. P. (1976), *Proizvodstvennyi kollektiv, chelovek i svobodnoe vremia*. Moscow: Profizdat.

PLECK, J. H. (1977), 'The Work–Family Role System', *Social Problems*, 4: 417–27.

POROKHNIUK, E. V., and SHEPELEVA, M. S. (1975), 'O sovmeshchenii proizvodstvennykh i semeinykh funktsii zhenshchin-rabotnits', *Sotsiologicheskie issledovaniia*, 4: 102–8.

POSADSKAYA, ANASTASIA (1992), 'Self-Portrait of a Russian Feminist', *New Left Review*, 195: 3–19.

'Povyshat' politicheskuiu proizvodstvennuiu aktivnost' zhenshchin: s plenuma ivanskogo obkoma KPSS' (1975), *Partiinaia shizn'*, 16: 39–45.

Programme of the Communist Party of the Soviet Union (1986), Moscow: Novosti.

PRUDENSKII, G. A. (ed.) (1961), *Vnerabochee vremia trudiaschikhsia*. Novosibirsk: Sibirskoe otdelenie AN SSSR.

REZNIK, S. D. (1982), *Trudovye resursy v stroitel'stve*. Moscow: Stroiizdat.

RIMASHEVSKAYA, N. (1992), 'Changes in Social Policy and Labor Legislation', *Sociological Research*, September–October: 70–79.

RIURIKOV, I. B. (1977), 'Ieti i obshchestvo', *Voprosy filosofii*, 4: 111–21.

—— (1983), 'Mestorozhdenia schast'ia', *Pravda*, 9 July: 3.

RZHANITSYNA, L. (1979), 'Aktual'nye problemy zhenskogo truda v SSSR', *Sotsialisticheskii trud*, 3: 58–67.

SAKHAROVA, N. A. (1973), *Optimal'nye vozmozhnosti ispol'zovaniia zhenskogo truda v sfere obshchestvennogo proizvodstva*. Kiev: Vishcha shkola.

SERGEEVA, G. P. (1976), 'O professional'noi strukture rabotaiushchikh zhenshchin', *Planovoe khoziaistvo*, 11: 37–46.

SHISHKAN, N. M. (1971), 'Nepolnyi rabochii den' dlia zhenshchin v usloviiakh sotsializma', *Nauchnye doklady vysshei shkoly: Ekonomicheskie nauki*, 8: 42–7.

—— (1976), *Trud zhenshchin v usloviiakh razvitogo sotsializma*. Kishinev: Shtiinsta.

SHKARATAN, O. I. (1967), 'Sotsial'naia struktura sovetskogo rabochego klassa', *Voprosy filosofii*, 1: 28–39.

SHLAPENTOKH, V. (1984), *Love, Marriage and Friendship in the Soviet Union*. New York: Praeger.

SHLINDMAN, S., and ZVIDRIN'SH, P. (1973), *Izuchenie rozhdaremosti*. Moscow: Statistika.

SHUBKIN, V. N., and KOCHETOV, G. M. (1968), 'Rukovoditel', kollega, podchinennyi', *Sotsial'nye issledovaniia*, 2: 143–55.

SLESAREV, G. A., and IANKOVA, Z. A. (1969), 'Zhenshchina na promyshlennom predpriiatii i v sem'e', in G. V. Osipov and I. Shchepan'skii (eds.), *Sotsial'nye problemy truda i proizvodstva*. Moscow: Mysl', 439–56.

SOKOLOV, B., and REIMERS, I. (1983), 'Effektivnye formi upravleniia nauka', *EKO*, 9: 72–87.

SOLOV'EV, N., LAZAUSKAS, I., and IANKOVA, Z. A. (eds.) (1970), *Problemy byta, braka i sem'i*. Vil'nius: Mintis.

SONIN, M. I. (1973), 'Aktual'nye sotsial'no-ekonomicheskie problemy zaniatosti zhenshchin', in A. Z. Maikov (ed.), *Problemy ratsional'nogo ispol'zovaniia trudovykh resurov*. Moscow: Ekonomika, 352–79.

Sovetskaia sotsiologicheskaia assotsiatsiia (SSA) (1972), *Dinamika izmeneniia polozheniia zhenshchiny i sem'ia* (3 vols). Moscow: Institut konkretnykh sotsial'nykh issledovanii AN SSSR.

STRUMILIN, S. G. (1964), *Izbrannye proizvedeniia*, iii, *Problemy ekonomiki: truda*. Moscow: Nauka.

SWAFFORD, M. (1978), 'Sex Differences in Soviet Earnings', *American Sociological Review*, 5: 657–73.

SYSENKO, V. (1974), 'Differentsiatsiia rozhdaemosti v krupnom gorode', in D. I. Valentei *et al.* (eds.), *Demograficheskii analiz rozhdaemosti*. Moscow: Statistika.

TATARINOVA, N. I. (1971), 'Zhenskii trud', in E. L. Manevich (ed.), *Osnovnye problemy ratsional'nogo ispol'zovaniia trudovykh resursov v SSSR*. Moscow: Nauka, 161–94.

TOLKUNOVA, V. N. (1967), *Pravo zhenshchchin na trud i ego garantii*. Moscow: Iuridicheskaia Literatura.

'Trud i byt zhenshchin' (1978), *EKO*, iii.

TRUFANOV, I. P. (1973), *Problemy byta gorodskogo naseleniia SSSR*. Leningrad: Leningradskii gosudarstvennyi universitet.

Tsentral'noe statisticheskoe upravlenie pri Sovete Ministrov SSSR (TsSu SSSR) (1972a), *Itogi vsesoiuznoi perepisi naseleniia 1970 goda*, ii. Moscow: Statistika, ii.

—— (1972b), *Narodnoe khoziaistvo SSSR: 1922–1972*. Moscow: Statistika.

—— (1975a) *Naselenie SSSR 1973*. Moscow: Statistika.

—— (1975b), *Zhenshchiny v SSSR*. Moscow: Statistika.

—— (1976), *Narodnoe khoziaistvo SSSR v 1975 godu*. Moscow: Statistika.

—— (1977), *Narodnoe khoziaistvo SSSR 60 let*. Moscow: Statistika.

—— (1979), *SSSR v tsifrakh v 1978 godu: kratkii statisticheskii sbornik*. Moscow: Statistika.

—— (1980), *Narodnoe khoziaistvo SSSR v 1979 godu*. Moscow: Statistika.

—— (1981), *SSSR v tsifrakh v 1980 godu: kratkii statisticheskii sbornik*. Moscow: Finansy i statistika.

—— (1985a), *Narodnoe khoziaistvo SSSR v 1984 godu*. Moscow: Finansy i statistika.

—— (1985b), *Zhenshchiny i deti v SSSR*. Moscow: Finansy i statistika.

—— (1986), *Narodnoe khoziaistvo SSSR v 1985 godu*. Moscow: Finansy i statistika.

—— (1990), *Narodnoe khoziaistvo SSSR v 1989 godu*. Moscow: Finansy i statistika.

UBAIDULLAEVA, R. (1987), *Selskaia zhizn*, 24 March: 2.

URLANIS, B. (1974), *Problemy dinamiki naseleniia SSSR*. Moscow: Nauka.

VANEK, J. (1975), 'Time Spent in Housework', *Scientific American*, 5: 116–20.

VOLKOV, A. (1983), 'Rozhdaemost i "defitsit zhenikhov"', in E. Vasileva (ed.), *Rozhdaemost': izvestnoe i neizvestnoe*. Moscow: Finansy i statistika, 13–17.

WOODRUFF, D. (1991), 'The "Woman Question" and the State Question: Current Soviet Debates', seminar paper, Political Science 241A, University of California, Berkeley.

ZAKHAROVA, N. K., *et al.* (1989), 'Kak My Reshaem Zhenskii Vopros?' *Kommunist*, March: 55–65.

ZDRAVOMYSLOV, A. G., ROZHIN, V. P., and IADOV, V. A. (eds.) (1967), *Chelovek i ego rabota*. Moscow: Mysl'.

ZHENSHCHINY v SSSR (1980), *Vestnik statistiki*, 1: 69–79.

—— (1986), *Vestnik statistiki*, 1: 51–67.

ZVINDRIN'SH, P. P. (1983), 'Stabil'nost' brakov i rozhdaemost'', in E. Vasileva (ed.), *Rozhdaemost': izvestnoe i neizvestnoe*. Moscow: Finansy i statistika, 61–9.

7

Changes in Gender Discourses and Policies in the Former Soviet Union

Anastasia Posadskaya

INTRODUCTION

Changes in gender relations were less visible during the initial period of restructuring in the USSR, in 1985–9. During this period the most entrenched perceptions of Soviet reality received ideological reappraisal, after a pluralistic vision of past, present, and future had been declared. The official 'line' towards women changed at least twice: first, women were politically demobilized by Gorbachev's declared aim 'to let them have some rest from production work', and then they were mobilized by the revival of the women's councils structure. Neither of these political intentions brought any real changes.

The real turning-point occurred in 1989, during the first free parliamentary elections, and in 1990, when the course towards the market economy received legal status, especially when the law on small business development was adopted in August. Since that time the gender dimension of restructuring has become evident: women's participation in the new political and economic structures is insignificant, and their share in the polity and the economy has been decreasing dramatically.

The visibility of gender bias in the restructuring process produced the possibility and the necessity for changes in the discourse on women. Two opposite approaches have become evident. Each has a different social meaning of women's issues, and different ideas on how to resolve them. In the first approach, the so-called 'natural specificity' of women is the main dimension to be governed by social policy. The second approach considers the *social* construction of differences between sexes, that is their changing character. Consequently, the concept of gender has been adopted. Words such as 'equality', 'women's emancipation', and 'solidarity' have negative connotations for public consciousness, because of their association with the communist past. The word 'gender' itself has to be imported into the Russian language in order to overcome the negative stereotypes of the former orthodoxy.

In this context, it is appropriate to pose the following question: is the situation for women during restructuring absolutely hopeless, or are there grounds for future positive changes? This chapter will review the record, examine changes in gender discourses and legislation, and offer policy recommendations.

GENDER ISSUES IN THE CONTEXT OF RESTRUCTURING

The changes brought into being by the process of perestroika need elaboration. Since April 1985 it has become increasingly evident how complicated, multi-faceted, and controversial this process is. The crisis of the 'totalitarian' system had economic, cultural, and political dimensions. We felt that we did not know the truth of our past and present; the creative potential of the nation had collapsed; the economy was unbalanced; public control was formal rather than real; the military complex was a prioritized, huge, closed and powerful empire; people did not believe in any ideals. Depending on their place in the social hierarchy, perestroika had different meanings for different social groups: workers and employers, the elderly and the young, urban and rural populations, metropolitan and peripheral residents, women and men. But what we should admit is the fact that the gender dimension of the social reconstruction was and is less visible and less debated, especially during the first four years of perestroika, than other aspects of the reconstruction. Of course both before and during perestroika there existed a special policy on women. But it was the party policy, and as such it could only represent the party approach to women's issues. In public debate the question of women would arise, but only in connection with other problems —economic, demographic, or moral. In these public debates women were viewed instrumentally, as a means to solve perceived economic, demographic, or moral problems. So the question is: if it is no longer the Communist Party that designs social strategy, will women be able to formulate their political agenda themselves, or will they continue to be the objects rather than the agents of their social being?

The period of restructuring has shown that all the changes that have occurred in our society affect men and women differently, and are particularly unfavourable to women. Women dramatically lost their usual one-third representation in the Parliament and local *soviets*; they are not regarded as serious candidates for recruitment to the modernized and privatized sectors of the economy; the possibility of combining employment and family responsibilities is becoming more limited owing to the closing down of crêches; new legislation on the family by the central government and local administrations presupposes and encourages women's family attachment rather than career options. The recently introduced official registration of the unemployed revealed that women with higher and secondary technical education form the majority of those losing jobs; these women are correspondingly less in demand for new jobs. So the labour market, just being formed, is already two-sided, in so far as a secondary labour market and marginal position has emerged for women. The status of women at this time is confusing and in a state of flux. The sphere of public life, which was always so easily accessible, is changing extremely rapidly: it is now easy to leave, but not so easy to enter. We may well ask: does privatization mean women's exclusion from the public sphere and relegation to the private household sphere?

The gender aspect of perestroika should not be confined to discourses on employment and the family. Perestroika has led to changes in political structures and in cultural practices. The process of women's objectification is manifested by the usage of a woman's body as a commodity: widespread pornography and prostitution are now common. With regard to religion, the rise of religiosity also has its gender aspect: it means the resurgence of traditional attitudes towards gender relations. There has been a growth in clerical fundamentalism which has followed from nationalism and national separatism. Political decentralization, therefore, which has also followed from perestroika, might have less than desirable consequences for women. This would include the education of girls in a manner compatible with the national identity ('a real Russian woman', or an 'authentic' Muslim, Georgian, Armenian (etc.) woman), with a strong emphasis on traditional values.

But perestroika not only disappointed women; it also gave them hope. First, in revealing the truth of women's lives, and providing serious examination of women's position in society, perestroika helped to make an ideological appraisal of the achievements and failures concerning 'the Woman Question' in the USSR. Secondly, after years of state socialist symbolic equality, which discredited the language of gender emancipation, women have a possibility to bring back into public debate the issue of emancipation and gender equality. Thirdly, by formulating an alternative programme of women's integration into the process of social reconstruction, women may be able to control and transform the direction of current changes.

Supporting the transition to global thinking, perestroika provided the possibility for assimilation of the ideas of major social movements, such as the Green, peace, and feminist movements. Awareness of feminist ideas, both nationally and internationally, opens the way to the ideological reappraisal of women's experience under state socialism, and prepares the political agenda for the real woman's movement in the USSR and other former communist countries.

Perestroika was a challenge. With respect to women it was a threefold challenge: in terms of their past, present, and future. For decades the experience of the Soviet Union in resolving 'the Woman Question' was considered a model for other countries. After acknowledging the reality of women's lives under state socialism and during the perestroika period, we should answer the following questions:

- What did we lose—the illusions or the ideals?
- Why did Soviet women, despite having achieved nearly the highest levels of labour-force participation, educational attainment, and political representation in the world, continue to occupy secondary and sub-ordinate social positions?
- Under what conditions are the high levels of women's labour-force participation, education, and political representation also the criteria for women's emancipation?
- Did legal gender equality contribute to concealing *de facto* gender inequality?
- What was the evolution of the Soviet's state policy on women, and what was the transformation of the emancipation/equality ideal?
- What happened to the language of women's emancipation, and how did it affect the discourse on gender issues and the opportunities of women during the period of perestroika?
- Was the rise of patriarchal gender aspirations and discourses during the reconstruction period caused by the character of this reconstruction, or was it rooted in the pre-reconstruction era?

CHANGES IN THE LAWS ABOUT WOMEN AND FAMILY: INTEGRATION OR EXCLUSION?

It is well known that legal equality between men and women was the immediate concern of the Soviet government following the Bolshevik revolution of 1917, when all the old laws restricting women's rights were abolished and the principle of equal pay for equal work regardless of sex was introduced. A special decree on civil marriage abolished the inequality between spouses in the family. Marriage was proclaimed to be a voluntary union of free persons enjoying equal rights. Women and men obtained equal property and parental rights. All Constitutions of the Soviet State included special articles on gender equality. In the 1920s, the Communist Party actively promoted the policy on women by creating the special departments for work among women within the structure of the party all over the country. But in the 1930s, the fate of many other important social problems befell 'the Woman Question': it was proclaimed 'solved' by the Stalin Constitution of 1936, and hence closed for any critical interrogation. For the next two decades, women were also deprived of the right to abortion.

In spite of the proclaimed equality, Soviet law always regarded women as a 'specific labour force' because of their maternity function, and hence made special provisions 'to help women to combine paid employment with maternity' by ensuring paid maternity leave. After the mid-1950s, however, a new tendency became clear: women began to receive an increasing number of benefits related not to the physiological process of birth, but to maternity as a socially defined function of women. One might say that the construct Mother-Woman became the permanent focus of the party's concern and assistance.

Article 35 of the current Constitution states that women and men have equal rights in the USSR. But the article has the following extension:

Exercise of these rights is ensured by according women equal access with men to education and vocational and professional training, equal opportunities in employment, remuneration and promotion, in public, political and cultural activity, as well as by special labour and health protection measures for women; by providing conditions enabling mothers to work; by legal protection, and material and moral support for mothers and children, including paid leave and other benefits for mothers and expecting mothers, and gradual reduction of the working time in production for women with small children.

The formulation of this Article reflects the general contradiction of the legal provisions on women. On the one hand, it states that women are provided with equal opportunities in the spheres of employment, education, training, politics, culture, and so on. At the same time, owing to their reproductive function, women are assigned to a number of benefits; these in effect provide for women a different opportunity structure, which contradicts the statement on provision of equal opportunities. Over the last two decades the practical realization of this Article has been mostly related to its 'maternity benefits' part.

Perestroika was a time of active legislative activity, comprising all spheres of social life. Beginning in 1985, we witnessed several attempts to make radical economic transformations in order to draw the country out of economic stagnation. The laws on state enterprise, on co-operative and individual labour activity, and on the rights of working collectives gave more freedom to the production units, but failed to improve the economy. None the less, it was clear for gender researchers (Zakharova *et al.* 1989:59) that, even if economic reform succeeded, the gender consequences would be adverse for women. Consequently we advocated new approaches to the legal provisions on women which would neutralize the negative effect of the economic reform. We warned that women would make up the majority of the unemployed; that the enterprises would use their new economic independence to close down pre-school day-care facilities attached to them; that the emerging labour market would be two-sided and unfavourable to women; that there would be dramatic short- and long-term consequences for gender relations within the family, for the ideology of education, and for the perception of men's and women's social roles. We insisted that, with respect to the legal regulation of women's involvement in production, the orientation should be changed. It was suggested that changes should be twofold. On the one hand, special provisions promoting women's equal opportunities in production should be adopted at the state level. On the other hand, affirmative actions are needed to promote men's participation in family responsibilities in order to make the opportunity structure more gender-neutral. The importance of women's involvement in the decision-making process was also accentuated.

Unfortunately, the changes that occurred after the first free elections to the Soviet Parliament and then to the republican and local legislative bodies confirmed the above predictions. First of all, the share of women in the Parliament fell dramatically, from 33 to 15.6 per cent, as a result of partial abolition of the quota for women. Half of the women deputies were nominated by the public organizations, which was the Communist Party's move for bringing more loyal deputies to the Parliament. Most of these women were nominated by the Soviet Women's Committee, the organization attached to the Communist Party, which for over forty years spoke on behalf of all Soviet women. Understandably, these women were unable to formulate the new women's agenda directed at the integration rather than exclusion of women in the restructuring process. Accustomed to the traditional approach to women's issues, they set up the Committee on the position of women with regard to the protection of family, maternity, and childhood, and the corresponding executive body in the Soviet of Ministers.

The activity of these two bodies resulted in the adoption of two main decisions: (1) 'On Urgent Measures to Improve the Position of Women, Protection of Maternity and Childhood' of 10 April 1990, adopted by the Supreme Soviet of the USSR, and (2) the decision of the Soviet of Ministers of 2 August 1990, 'On the Additional Measures to Provide the Social Protection of Families with Children in View of the Transition to the Regulated Market Economy'. Unfortunately, the concrete provisions of the above stated decisions covered only traditional issues on women and family areas; women's labour conditions; provisions related to childbearing and rearing; benefits for women with family responsibilities; special measures to avoid poverty of families with children. It should also be noted that, after the attempted coup in August 1991, all central USSR bodies ceased to exist, including the committees on women in the USSR Parliament. Nevertheless, it is useful to examine the main provisions of the new legal codes which were being discussed in the latter stage of perestroika.

Labour conditions

The labour conditions of women are some of the oldest areas of legal regulation. It includes such issues as the prohibition of night shifts for women, the banning of women from jobs with hazardous working conditions, limits for lifting and carrying weights, and additional remuneration for work in harmful jobs (such as benefits in income, working hours, leave, and retirement age).

Despite the legal prohibition, there was always a strong economic motivation, on the part of both administration and women, to keep women on such jobs. Since the 1930s, the State Labour Committee has been issuing the 'Lists of Jobs Banned to Women'. Nevertheless, in 1991 more than 8,000 women were occupied in the jobs that were legally closed to them; over 4 million women worked in conditions that violated the requirements and rules of labour protection; in industry, 44 per cent of women were working in shops doing heavy work in unhealthy conditions.

It is clear that a new approach is needed to handle this problem of labour conditions. First of all, jobs with hazardous working conditions should be banned not only to women, but also to men. For example, in industry men make up 56 per cent of those working under hazardous working conditions, and in construction, 83 per cent. At the same time, the 'reproductive' justification for the existence of the 'List of Jobs Banned to Women' is also relevant to men: it is known that certain harmful working conditions, for example vibration, may lead to men's infertility. Moreover, men's life expectancy in the Soviet Union in 1989 was 64.8 years and women's was 74.0. That means that enterprises should eliminate hazardous working conditions rather than offer additional benefits to workers enduring them. At the same time, women should be motivated to upgrade their skills and thus increase their wages. The current enactments still require that a new 'List of Jobs Banned to Women' be enforced. Moreover, it is stated that a 'List of Jobs Recommended to Women of Childbearing Age' should be worked out. I very much doubt that the criteria for such jobs will be free of gender stereotypes. One can easily suspect that the programme of women's removal from hazardous working conditions during the marketization of the economy might turn into the programme of the removal of women from production.

The existence of the list of banned jobs has another negative consequence for women. Because women have to persuade management to hire them for such positions, they have to agree upon a lower rate of pay as a price for the risk the management takes in violating the law.

Benefits for women with family responsibilities

These benefits are the right to work part-time, to work flexible working hours, and to have paid days off work for family responsibilities. The legislation extant in 1991 contained more and more provisions for women with children. The number and ages of children are the criteria for assignment of benefits. In the past women with children under 12 years of age had the formal right to apply to the management to transfer to part-time work although the majority of women were at full-time jobs. Now management *must* provide a woman with a part-time job if she wants it.

The notion of part-time work in the ex-command economy might have an interesting gender interpretation. Full-time working was the absolute norm under state socialism. Alternatives to this pattern were considered deviations from the norm. Women, who had the right to 'deviant' work behaviour, were regarded as a specific, irregular part of the labour force. On the other hand, men were socially regarded as a normal, correct, and regular part of the labour force.

We should admit that these benefits have been mostly symbolic; in the past, neither women nor employers were interested in part-time work. Now, however, the introduction of this provision carries some rather contradictory implications. A move to the market economy means that: (a) enterprises will be less willing to admit administrative regulation and thus will avoid the obligation to provide a woman with a part-time job should she need it; but at the same time, (b) enterprises will be motivated by the profit concern to hire a certain proportion of their labour forces on a part-time basis, especially in the service sector. The meaning of part-time work is also changing: it may often be considered not as a benefit but as a form of under-employment. That is why under new conditions the law assigning part-time work only to women with small children makes no sense.

Maternity and parental leave provisions

As of January 1991, maternity leave could be taken by the father, grand-parent, or other person taking care of the child. It would be fair to say that this provision is one of the rare progressive changes in the current legislation on women and family. Unfortunately, by now its significance has only the value of an ideological break-through. In order to motivate a significant number of men to take the leave, special affirmative action measures should be introduced. Under conditions when women's wages are on average much lower than men's wages—and as they will probably fall still further—it is probably unrealistic to expect fathers to take the parental leave willingly. Another factor discouraging men from using this provision is the gender-stereotyped consciousness of Soviet people, which is ever increasing in the transition to a market economy.

At present, the total length of the parental leave is three years and three months, with eighteen weeks' partially paid leave and up to three years' unpaid leave. The parent's job has to be retained for her or him during this absence. We have numerous evidence that recently this provision has become problematic: as a result of redundancies and the closure of enterprises, women often do not have a job to return to.

Another innovation in respect of maternity leave is the size of the partial payment. Previously it was a fixed allowance making up about 50 per cent of the country's minimum wage. Now it is equalized to the level of the current official minimum wage and is index-linked to inflation. However, by now there is no regular official announcement of the minumum wage level. Mothers whose job records are of less than one year or who have not worked at all are entitled to the partially paid leave at the level of half of the regular minimum wage.

One of the negative consequences of this provision is the closure of child-care facilities for children under 3 years of age under the pretext that mothers should use their parental leave. So in practice, the long maternity leave limits women's opportunity structure and excludes them from the 'public' sphere.

Special measures to avoid poverty of families with children

Before perestroika, the main measure to alleviate the poverty of families with children was the 1974 provision to pay a family allowance of Rb12 per month to families with children, if the average monthly income per capita was less than the official minimum of Rb50. This measure had a serious drawback: the payment of allowances started a year after the onset of actual hardship.

The negligible amount payable and the complicated application procedure of this allowance made it an ineffective one. In December 1990 a woman became entitled to a maternity allowance three times the official minimum wage, which is paid right after the delivery. Families with average per capita income not more than double the amount of the official minimum wage are entitled to a monthly allowance equal to 50 per cent of the minimum wage for every child between $1\frac{1}{2}$ and 6 years old. Single mothers receive a monthly allowance of 50 per cent of the official minimum wage for every child up to 16 years of age. Children of soldiers who serve in the armed forces are covered by a monthly allowance equal to the minimum wage over the period of the father's service. A parent with a one-year job record or none at all prior to the child's birth is entitled to an allowance of half the official minimum wage up until the child is 18 months old. This provision, in effect since January 1991, is a measure compatible with the reality of forced unemployment or underemployment. If a mother (or father) is a student, she/he receives a grant as a lump sum after the child's birth.

As was mentioned above, indexation of the minimum wage is not yet the regular practice. What would be more helpful than financial aid is the direct provision of products, goods, and services, which are very scarce. For example, at present families with less than Rb60 average per capita income per month do not pay for pre-school facilities (in the state sector). For any family with four or more children, the fee is reduced to 50 per cent. Two-year-old children from families with more than three children or with less than Rb50 per capita income monthly are also cared for free of charge. Children of school age from such families receive free lunch and school uniforms. (*Note*: in April 1991, the scale of these provisions was changed owing to the extraordinary official price increases for all basic goods and products, with simultaneously fixed monthly compensation of Rb60 per adult and Rb40 per child.)

These measures are of course better than nothing, but are still not enough, especially in view of the current high inflation. The tendency to associate the size of the family allowance with the level of the official minimum wage, but not with the actual wage of a parent caring for the child, makes this provision both minimal and gender-biased. It is understandable that, when the woman's average wage is one-third less than the man's, women will automatically be the ones taking parental leave. That is why we may say that the introduction of parental (as distinct from maternity) leave is a rather symbolic measure.

We may conclude that most changes in the law on women and the family are not directed at the social integration of women in the restructuring process. There are no provisions to increase women's participation in the decision-making process, or to eliminate unjust and unfavourable levels of remuneration to women in the feminized labour-force sectors; there are no special programmes for women's retraining. The current legislation helps women to leave rather than enter and re-enter the labour market. Furthermore, the law reproduces constructions of femininity and masculinity and their differential distribution in production and between production and reproduction. The women's sphere is legally organized as a sphere of 'the other', abnormal, 'specific'; the men's sphere is the realm of norm, regularity, order. The protectionist character of the law regulating women's labour conditions bears mainly a symbolic meaning, reproducing the notion of women's labour-force attachment as a specific and perhaps unusual one. By imposing different benefits on women, the law ensures woman's dependency on the charity of the state, limits her opportunity for self-determination and autonomy, and turns her into a social invalid.

We have to conclude that the proclaimed legal equality between men and women is rather a façade buried in the numerous legislative norms oriented at reinforcing the division between women's and men's spheres, excluding women from the public sphere and pushing them to the private sphere. In order to turn the law into an instrument of women's social integration, fundamental changes are needed, changes that the legislative bodies cannot bring about.

TWO APPROACHES TO 'THE WOMAN QUESTION'

It is not easy to elaborate on 'the Woman Question' when there are no explicitly described perspectives regarding the relevant arguments, justifications, and explanations. Usually points of view arise indirectly in general discussions, in the appraisals or condemnations of personalities, social processes, and prospects for the future. It seems that only researchers with a strong feminist orientation can provide a consistent and explicit perspective on 'the Woman Question'. Despite personal differences, these perspectives share the perception of social determination of gender differences, and might together be summarized as an egalitarian (or feminist) approach. The other approach, based on the idea of natural specificity of gender inequality, which is spread among specialists working in different fields, might be called a patriarchal approach.

This manner of theorizing approaches to 'the Woman Question' was first suggested by Posadskaya (1989); later it was developed by Zakharova *et al.* (1989). I now suggest revised versions of these two approaches, with additions prompted by the latest developments.

The patriarchal approach

Briefly, the essence of this concept is as follows. The world is based on some natural foundations, and to destroy them is extremely dangerous, for this will sooner or later lead to the destruction of society itself. The division of functions between man and woman is precisely such a natural foundation. As the primary goal of life, woman by her very nature is intended to be a mother, the keeper of the hearth. Man, however, is decreed by his gender to be a real person, the breadwinner, the worker in society, to implement the link between the small community—the family—and the larger one— society as a whole. As it applies to our history, 'patriarchal' consciousness is inclined to connect all negative processes with the fact that an orientation towards women's work in production as the main sphere of life activity destroyed the maternal instinct and led to a severe decline of temperaments and a crumbling of the foundations of the family. Children, the elderly, and husbands were left without a woman's care and kindness, and as a result children grew up like orphans in the presence of living parents; the elderly were abandoned in the villages; and husbands became weak-willed, feminized, subordinated; and so on.

For the improvement of society, the supporters of this line of thought propose to shorten woman's work-day; to give domestic, maternal labour the status of socially necessary and productive work with appropriate payment and inclusion in the general earned length of service; to allot women a completely free paid day each week for domestic duties, to extend paid leave for the care of a child; and, for mothers of three or more children, to exempt them from the obligation of working in public production with suitable guarantees and so forth. It is believed necessary to cease propagandizing the ideal of the emancipated women via the mass media, since this is destructive to family and society, and, on the other hand, to give greater attention to a healthy image of life, to successful, happy families in which relationships are built on the natural functions of woman and man. Demands are put forward to employ more decisively such measures as the strengthening of parental rights, the criminalization of prostitution, and the creation of a special service for monitoring moral conduct. It is proposed to push through the appropriate legislative changes quickly.

Within the framework of the patriarchal approach, four subtypes can be distinguished: moral, economic, demographic, and political. The moral approach is represented by authors, journalists, and all those who write on so-called 'women's', 'village', and 'moral' subjects and which might be well characterized by the above description. The economic approach is represented mainly by specialists, for whom the process of the intensification of the economy and the human role in it appear to be the basic themes of research (thus I call this approach 'economic'). Women's problems are seen as reflections of economic problems; as a factor of production, women's work efficiency is not great because of their frequent absences, and they have much lower qualifications. This is why a reduction in the levels of their employment in public production is required. The most consistent representatives of this approach believe that only by removing inefficient workers (and this means female workers first of all) is it possible to attain high economic efficiency. In order to ease the 'exit' from public production for such a woman, it is proposed to give her additional job benefits: shorter working hours and extended maternity leave (with the latter included in earned length-of-service).

The first steps of marketization show that the advocates of this perspective are now ready for its practical implementation. At KAMAZ, the biggest truck factory in the country (located in Tataria), the percentage of female workers dropped from 52.5 to 45 in only two years, between 1989 and 1990 (Posadskaya and Zakharova 1990). At the same time, KAMAZ provides every woman employee with children of pre-school age with an allowance of Rb100 per month when she is not working. When the KAMAZ Deputy General Director was asked what his strategy was concerning women's promotion after such a long leave, he replied: 'Our strategy is to remove all women from production.' The President of the prosperous exchange ALICE believes that women do not have any managerial or entrepreneurial ability. The perception that business is not a woman's realm, and that women should be provided with specific women's jobs, is now widespread. It seems to be a reaction to the years of state protectionism towards women.

The third approach—demographic—is characterized above all by its emphasis on the reproductive aspect of women. Analysing the declining birth rate in the more economically developed regions of the country, the demographers maintain that ultimately this may lead to depopulation, unless special demographic policies are designed. Inasmuch as statistics give evidence that the level of the birth rate, as a rule, is inversely proportional to the level of women's employment in public production, the demographers believe it necessary to grant all women the same benefits: extended paid leave for child care, shorter working hours, and so on.

Finally, there is a new political approach, which became evident during the free elections to the Parliament of the USSR (1989) and republican parliaments (1990), when women suffered a dramatic drop in their representation. This perspective is a reaction to the quota system for keeping the number of women (as well as workers, peasants, and certain other social groups) in the *soviets* at a fixed level. This system was mostly favourable to specific types of women known as 'iron ladies' or 'obedient puppets'. Very often, these were women with low education, living in villages or small towns, and belonging to a limited range of occupations, such as 'noted' textile workers or milkmaids. This period produced a negative stereotype of women in politics, which was an additional obstacle for women seeking to be elected.

Thus, the political approach is based on the viewpoint that politics is not for women (a notion unfortunately shared by many politically active women), and that where women do manage to reach the high level of decision-making, their activity should be limited to certain fields: education, health, social (public) policy. Interestingly, these were the spheres of lower priority for the Soviet state, and are much less involved in the process of power and resource distribution. To repeat a well-known aphorism, 'Where there are women, there is no power; where there is power, there are no women.'

The egalitarian (feminist) approach

Those who represent it (and I count myself in their number) are not inclined to examine in particular the 'women's' aspect of moral, economic, political, or demographic problematics. On the contrary; all these appear appear as indicators of the position of woman in society, that is, her social status. We proceed on the assumption that the so-called natural division of labour between man and woman is socially constructed. (As Shulamit Firestone put it, 'Nature made woman different from a man; society made her different from a human being.') And the process of changing the old division of functions is the process of destroying old social conditions, and not of undermining societal structures in general. A new, egalitarian relationship between the sexes, replacing the patriarchal one, is founded not on the relationships of master and subordinate, assigned by tradition and elevated to the rank of 'natural law', but rather on relationships that are mutually complementary in society and in the family, which can only be realized in the objective and subjective 'space of free choice'. And this social—material and spiritual—environment, in which all a priori notions about a person (class, background, sex, age, politics) are removed, is the environment in which a person is measured against herself, against her own scale—not against some scale set in advance.

During perestroika researchers often cited the words of Lenin—that equality of the sexes does not mean equating woman with man in terms of the heaviness of labour or the extent of exertion—believing that we have gone too far in just such an 'incorrect' equality/equation. They concluded by talking about 'the need for a fuller inventory of the character of the female work-force' ('character' here meaning everything that is 'by nature itself intended for woman . . .').

When speaking of an egalitarian interpretation of the Marxist understanding of the principle of equality, we must note that it does not advocate the idea that society must strive towards the obliteration of all social differences between man and woman. (Such an approach is manifest only in the rhetoric of early socialist utopias.) Exactly the opposite: the necessity of systematic, active work to create equal social conditions of development is emphasized. It is not a question of reducing or transforming a person into a uniform, sexless creature, but of *removing social barriers, which prevent a person from showing his/her worth as an individual*. One such barrier is the stereotype of gender, which oversimplifies and reduces an individual to the level of realization of her/his 'natural traits' as a woman or a man. Thus, movement is assumed towards a more developed, complex, and social consciousness based on equality of opportunity for self-actualization, in keeping with today's accent on development through the growth of varied, humanistic orientations towards a clear identity.

Any society examines its world-view system as it applies to its own needs, and the extent to which that society may adequately adapt such a system largely depends on the level of development of society itself. The specific conditions for the realization of communist reforms in our country were connected with incomplete, and at times faltering, execution of Marxist and Leninist principles in resolving 'the Woman Question'. The main emphasis was put on involving women as fully as possible in public production, and it was precisely this quantitative indicator that came to be considered the basic criterion for the successful solution. In fact, the process left unresolved such classic conceptions as transforming housework into a field of public labour, encouraging new attitudes between the sexes, and a new type of division of labour in housework. The subsequent 'double burden' phenomenon was unavoidable, and, as in all countries undergoing industrialization, it 'works' to discredit the emancipation of women. All this did not lead us to overcome our patriarchal relationships; on the contrary, in a certain sense it strengthened them, leaving the woman with the old rota of 'her' duties in the family and reproducing it on the level of society in general. Naturally, if we really want to achieve social equality, it is necessary to resolve 'the Woman Question' in its full scope.

However, experience shows that, where significant successes have been achieved in the development of trade, public nutrition, and services (that is, in the collectivization of housework), these achievements have not been sufficient in themselves to overcome the attitude towards a woman as a 'second-class worker'. It seems that, both in theory and practice, the most important perspective remains unbroached: it is impossible to emancipate *only* women. Emancipation is, at a minimum, a two-sided process. Both men and women must be able to enter the spheres previously excluded from them: career development for women, and the home and family for men. Building a consistent policy to this end and trying to influence the public opinion are, in our view, necessary steps for a resolution of 'the Woman Question'. And it is important to take them at once.

It seems fundamentally important to stop criticizing men's insufficient participation in the housework and children's education, and to start creating real material conditions *for men* for such participation. The 'mono-functionalism' developed and consolidated in general consciousness leads to a great loss both for society and for the individual male. Indeed, the sphere of his vital activities in the family is tied to his role as breadwinner. Even if a man wants to realize himself in greater measure in the family sphere, if this is closer to his personal disposition, he generally may not do so, as society does not recognize such a right for him. He could not take advantage of additional parental leave or leave for child care if a need were to arise. But, indeed, nature assigned woman only one function: to give birth. Care and the education of children, however, are functions for both parents. The man's position is even more unequal at the dissolution of marriage. Even though the Constitution acknowledges the equality of man and woman in all spheres of activity, in 99 out of 100 cases the child stays with the mother after divorce, regardless of the particular circumstances of any given case. And after divorce only one thing is really demanded (and often wanted) from men: financial support. Often they are simply cut off from the education and mental and emotional development of the child, becoming ex-fathers.

Parenthood involves both spouses equally; it is important to proceed from this premiss, working out measures of demographic policy. It is important that all benefits that society is in a position to grant (provided they are not connected with distinctive physiological features of men or women) are given to the family *as a whole*—or even, perhaps, that a few benefits are provided specifically for fathers, for example paid leave during mother's hospital stay after birth. A number of countries do have a system of hospital stay after birth. A number of countries do have a system of paternal benefits: Denmark, Sweden, Greece, West Germany, Finland, and Brazil. In Bulgaria, for example, the benefits are granted to any member of the family, including the grandmother and grandfather. As a member of the Swedish parliament, Mai Britt Teorin, observed, worldwide recognition of Sweden's achievement in involving women in higher administrative and political activities is explained by, among other things, the social support for parenthood—not only for women, but for men as well.

Of course, we are not denying gender differences as such, when we speak of protecting women and men from the traditional perception of their roles, which are grounded in cultural and, in part, legal norms. Replacing the 'difference of necessity' (as we call it) is another concept: the 'difference of freedom', which assumes a whole range of possibilities for an individual to fulfil his or her full human potential, on the basis of free choice. Employment relations and the legal norms regulating them must promote the formation of this new character, so that it develops *thanks to* them, rather than *in defiance of* them.

In order to support such an approach legislatively, it is important, in our view, to expand Article 35 of the Constitution of Russia with a section that would guarantee not only to women but also to men the possibility of combining the functions of parent and worker. A special commission ought to review both the Employment Law and the Codex on Marriage and the Family. It is important to bring to light and eliminate any legal norms that lead to direct or indirect discrimination against women in the sphere of employment and against men in the sphere of the family. Specially developed government measures are needed, guaranteeing the rights of men and women in connection with actual economic, demographic, and social policy.

This conceptualization of the feminist perspective is a simplified one, since at present only a few researchers explicitly identify themselves with feminism: Tatiana Klimenkova, Olga Voronina, Valentina Konstantinova, Natalia Zakharova, myself, and, among journalists, Olga Lipovskaya.

Within the same socio-deterministic perspective, some feminists (including myself) are more egalitarian; that is, they put more stress on the importance of men's emancipation. Others are more sceptical about possibilities to change the nature of patriarchal society (Tatiana Klimenkova), or are especially concerned with the introduction of feminist values in society (Valentina Konstantinova). But all agree that, without development of an independent women's movement and of the feminist research/training institutions (women's studies), feminism in Russia will remain an élite and purely theoretical perspective.

CONCLUSIONS

The general conclusion is quite depressing. So far, perestroika and economic reform constitute a masculine project. Women are invisible in the sphere of decision-making; they play a role of objects rather than active agents of current changes. We are witnessing the process of accelerating separation between the public and private sphere, whereby women are being excluded from the public and included mainly in the private sphere. In this process the family is used as a form of positive exclusion, as a form of control and subordination of women. The current situation is not produced solely by the restructuring itself, but is deeply rooted in the system of patriarchy which existed before and during the period of state socialism. Perestroika revealed only a symbolic character of professed gender equality.

Does this mean that the situation is hopeless, or is there any justification for optimism? Restructuring is a painful process, especially for women. But this is the only time in our history when women do have an opportunity to formulate their own agenda, to turn policy *on* women into policy *by* women. If women do not seize this opportunity, restructuring will have failed. One of the lessons from the attempt to resolve 'the Woman Question' under state socialism is that we should distinguish between symbolic and actual equality. This would permit us to bring back the issue of gender emancipation to the academic and public debate, and to the agenda of women's movement. Another lesson is that 'the Woman Question' cannot be resolved automatically, as a consequence of socio-economic and political development. This should be a concern for the rising independent women's movement. Russians are being given a chance. The destiny of 'the Woman Question' in time of restructuring will very much depend on the possibility of political integration around such issues as un(under)employment, reproductive rights, and private and public violence against women. The experience of the international woman's movement and adaptation of feminist ideas are also of vital importance. Whether women of the former Soviet Union will be able to take up this chance before they lose all their rights is an open question.

REFERENCES

Constitution of the Union of Soviet Socialist Republics (Principal Law) (1977), Moscow: Novosti.
Decision of the Supreme Soviet of the USSR (1990), 'On Urgent Measures to Improve the Position of Women, Protection of Maternity and Childhood', *Pravda*, 12 April.
Decision of the USSR Soviet of Ministers (1990), 'On the Additional Measures to Provide the Social Protection of Families with Children in View of the Transition to the Regulated Market Economy', *Pravda*, 2 August.
KLIMENKOVA, T. (1988), 'Philosophical Issues of Neo-Feminimism of 1970s', *Voprosy Philosophii*, no. 5.
LIPOVSKAYA, O. (1991), 'A Woman as an Object of Consumption', *Iscusstvo Kino*, no. 6.
NOVIKOVA, E. (1985), *A Woman in the Developed Socialist Society*. Moscow: Mysl'.

POSADSKAYA, A. (1990), 'Socio-Economic Problems of the Labour Activity of Women', [M.Sc.] dissertation, Moscow.

—— and ZAKHAROVA, N. (1990), *To be a Manager: Changes for Women in the USSR*. Geneva: ILO.

Position Paper to the State Programme on the Position of Women, Protection of Family, Maternity and Childhood (1990), Moscow.

Protection of Health in the USSR (1990), Statistical Data. Moscow.

SERGEEVA, G. (1987), *Employment of Women: Problems and Prospects for the Future*. Moscow.

VORONINA, O. (1991), 'Woman's "Destiny": Myth, Ideology, Practice', *Iscusstvo Kino*, no. 6.

Woman and Society: Reality, Prospects for the Future, Perspectives. (1991), Moscow.

ZAKHAROVA, N., POSADSKAYA A., and RIMASHEVSKAYA, N. (1989), 'How We Decide the Woman Question', *Communist*, no. 4.

8

Glasnost and 'the Woman Question' in the Mirror of Public Opinion: Attitudes towards Women, Work, and the Family

Valentina Bodrova

This chapter represents a quantitative and a qualitative analysis of the results of three nationwide polls concerning women's status in the family, at work, and in management during the period of perestroika. In contrast to many investigations of this subject that were carried out in the USSR, the findings described here are based on the opinion of respondents who represented the population not of a separate town, region, or enterprise, but of the whole of the country. This chapter therefore sheds light on some of the problems of women's status in the former Soviet Union, problems that have their roots in previous development and that also arise from the restructuring of the political, economic, and social life of the country.

PERESTROIKA, GLASNOST, AND 'THE WOMAN QUESTION'

The current epoch is one of radical changes in women's social status towards an ever wider recognition of their equality with men. However, the actual achievement of gender equality is a complicated and controversial social process for all countries, including the former USSR. Thus, despite the Soviet Union's sufficiently lengthy experience in attempting to resolve 'the Woman Question', women are still unequal within the framework of the system of social relations: female labour is unequally distributed in social production; women are insufficiently represented in the bodies of power, particularly in the uppermost echelons; family roles and duties entail a 'double burden' for women.

Perestroika in the USSR permitted us to look at 'the Woman Question' in a new way and to attempt to evaluate, with an unbiased attitude, the solution of the problem and to reflect upon the future. Glasnost, which resolutely deserts settled dogmas, opened our eyes to the real and complicated status of women in our society.

I wish to thank O. Podkolodnaya and V. Sanzonov for co-operation in the elaboration of questionnaires and for joint processing of the materials derived from the polls, and Valentine Moghadam for editorial assistance.

With perestroika came recognition that the achievement of genuine equality between men and women was an urgent task of the state, and that we needed an appropriate social and economic strategy towards that end. The latter could not be drafted without a knowledge of economic, ideological, and moral–ethical aspects, as well as a determination of the population's attitudes to a wide range of issues involving the position of women in the family, at work, and in management, and possible ways of changing some of these attitudes.

In this context, the All-Union Public Opinion Research Centre conducted two nationwide polls in 1989, based on a representative sample of the country's population on the subjects 'Women in the Family' and 'Women at Work and in Management', and one in 1990 on the subject 'Labour Activity of Women'. The polls were carried out in towns as well as villages and involved male and female members of the population over the age of 16.

The poll 'Women in the Family' was conducted in September 1989 and involved the following republics: The RSFSR, the Ukraine, Moldavia, Kazakhstan, Latvia, Lithuania, Georgia, Kirghizia, and Tajikistan. In all, 1,611 of the inhabitants of twenty-two towns and eight rural areas in these republics were polled.

The poll 'Women at Work and in Management' was held in December 1989 and involved the following republics: the RSFSR, the Ukraine, Armenia, Estonia, Kazakhstan, Kirghizia. In all, 1,516 of the inhabitants of twenty-four towns and eleven rural populated areas in these republics were polled.

The third poll, on 'Labour Activity of Women', was held in August 1990 in the following republics: the RSFSR, the Ukraine, Estonia, Georgia, Uzbekistan and Tajikistan. In all, 2,604 of the inhabitants of thirty-one towns and thirteen rural populated areas were polled.

The information given by these three polls is comparable, as in each case the sample was representative of the population of the whole of the USSR.

The purposes of the above-mentioned polls may be extensively reduced to the following:

1. To clarify the population's attitude to the question of women's status in the family
2. To determine the most acute problems that women have in performing their family responsibilities
3. To determine which aspects of women's labour-force participation are, in the opinion of the population, the most problematical
4. To obtain the public's opinion on the main reasons for the differences between men's and women's status in the spheres of employment and management and on the possible measures to be taken for improving women's status

5. To determine the population's attitude towards the participation of women in management

6. To determine the public's opinion on whether women should orient themselves towards family or career

The results of these polls enabled us to establish that the population was highly interested in solving the issues involved in the status of women in the family and at work. This is testified to at least by the fact that most of those who were approached voiced quite definite ideas concerning a variety of aspects of women's lives, as well as the forms of state assistance that should be available to women and the family.

The framework of this chapter is insufficient for looking into all inter-relations that came to light in analysing the respondents' answers. Therefore we will dwell only on those of interest from the point of view of the subject we chose, that is, the achievement of women's social equality.

WHAT IS MORE IMPORTANT FOR WOMEN — FAMILY OR WORK? OR PERHAPS SOMETHING ELSE?

There are three points of view on the combination of occupational and family life roles.

The first one—primary orientation towards occupational activity—could mean, in the extreme, ignoring family and refusing to have children. The second is a primary orientation towards family, or, in the extreme, a withdrawal from work. The third approach is to combine occupational and family roles with a differing priority given to occupational and family values corresponding to varying stages of the life cycle. The choice of any of these three viewpoints is an inalienable human right. Nevertheless, depending on the economic strategy, society will sometimes call on women to 'mobilize' and to 'take active part in social production', and at other times to 'go back' to the home. The corresponding ideology is either one of equality between men and women, or one of 'natural destination'.

With the onset of perestroika and of economic reforms, many women became dissident workers; the 'overemployment' of women came to be seen as a central 'Woman Question'; and segments of society began a clarion call for women to 'return' to the family and 'free' themselves from excessive toil in the sphere of production. We thought it would be interesting to learn our respondents' opinions on the subject. Would they agree that women should work less than men, or perhaps not work at all?

In order to clarify which point of view on the employment of women in social production prevails among the population nowadays, in the 1989 survey 'Women at Work and in Management' the following question was posed: 'How do you value the fact that the majority of women in this country are engaged in the spheres of production and the national economy?' In the 1990 survey 'Labour Activity of Women' the question was as follows: 'What is more important nowadays for the majority of women—family or work? Or perhaps something else?' The time difference between these two surveys is less than a year—December 1989 and August 1990. Let us compare the replies to the questions. First we shall analyse the replies to the questions posed in the 1989 survey. Possible expected answers were as follows:

- All able-bodied women must work.
- Women who have families should not work away from home.
- Women must have a choice: to work or not to work.

The distribution of replies to this question indicated that only one-third of those polled adhered to either extremist view of women's professional work: 15 per cent of respondents considered that all able-bodied women should work, whereas 18 per cent believed that women with a family and children should not work at all outside the family. Thus, the polls showed that extremist positions are not supported by the majority of the population. More popular, though, is the view that women should be able to choose levels of their economic activity to their liking. This idea was shared by two-thirds of those polled.

The results obtained, it seems, reflect society's growing understanding of the difficulties involved in a woman's combining her work with her family duties, but they also reflected the changes in the traditional view of professional labour as an inalienable part of the life and activities of the majority of women in the Soviet Union. The opportunity of an alternative choice (to work or not to work) was rated the highest by people in the younger age brackets with one or two children; typically, they had a comparatively high educational status and rather favourable material and living conditions. Older people more often adhered to extreme ideas. The cited interrelations are defined as aspects characteristic of the life cycle of the respondent's family (age and the number of children) and are also due to the softening of the existing stereotypes concerning the employment of women along with the growth of the respondents' social status and material level. Persons with a relatively high cultural level, as a rule, have a more democratic attitude to issues pertaining to the status of women, including those involving their professional activities.

An interesting fact is that those who had three or more children more often than others called for women's obligatory participation in socially useful work. In our view this is due not only to the salience of economic need for this section of the population, but also to another factor detected by a number of researchers: a greater interest of mothers of large families in socially useful labour (work outside the family) and their interest in resuming professional activities and restoring social contacts broken long before because of childrearing.

In the next poll, 'Labour Activity of Women', conducted in 1990, the replies to the question 'What is more important nowadays for the majority of women—family or work? Or perhaps something else?' indicated a tendency to strengthen the ideology of 'woman's natural destination'. The following results were obtained:

- Family the most important—35.8 per cent
- Family more important than work—18.1 per cent
- Family and work equally important—36.9 per cent
- Work more important than family—2.3 per cent
- Work the most important—1.0 per cent
- Neither family nor work important, but something else—0.8 per cent
- Hard to say—5.4 per cent

These figures tell us that orientation towards professional work was supported by an insignificant number of respondents—3.3 per cent; that 36.9 per cent of respondents felt that family and work are of equal importance for women; and that the view that family is the most important collected the majority of votes—53.9 per cent—and here the opinions of men and women coincided. Those respondents whose ages were 25–29 were orientated towards the family role of woman more often than the others—70.7 per cent, both married and single, though the percentage of unmarried persons upholding this view was somewhat lower. As in the 1989 poll, 'Woman at Work and in Management', unanimity in preferring a family role over an occupational one for women can be explained by the fact that this age group incorporates the majority of women with young children. They are the ones who find it most difficult to combine professional work and family duties, and both they and their associates are aware of this situation. Besides, this age group belongs to the generation that has experienced the full-time employment of their mothers in the national economy and does not wish to repeat their experience of 'super-employment': a double working day in conditions of underdeveloped infrastructure.[1]

Apparently, those respondents who felt that family is most important for

[1] Brief information on employment of women in the USSR is provided in confirmation of the above given data. In the 1920s and 1930s, women from the domestic and small individual business sectors were considered a part of the national economy. This process was completed in the 1960s and 1970s. In 1959, according to the general census of USSR population data, women's employment level in social production was 68.4%; by 1970 the number of women workers and office employees increased by 18 million to 46 million, and the proportion of women in employment reached 82%. In this period (the 1960s and 1970s) the process of involvement of women was supported by middle-aged and retired persons, who had been previously busy in the domestic sphere and individual farms. In the 1970s and 1980s the level of women's employment in what was called 'social production' reached 90–93%; at the same time, some 7.5% of women were engaged in studies or training. During these years the number of men and women engaged in the national economy was approximately equal; and the proportion of women workers and office employees from 1970 was invariable, averaging 50–51% for the next 18 years. In 1989 it fell to 48%.

women (35.8 per cent) supported the idea of making women return home to the family, when the following question was posed in the 1990 poll: 'Which point of view on the issue of women working away from home do you agree with?' The response to the choice of answers reflects three approaches to the issue of women working away from home:

- It is time to make women return home to the family—36.7 per cent
- Women must work equally with men away from home—6.8 per cent
- Women should work away from home if they wish to—49.7 per cent
- Hard to say—7.0 per cent

From the point of view of respondents' family status, the replies of married, unmarried, and divorced persons were similar. But the opinions of men and women did not coincide: 30.8 per cent of women respondents supported the idea of making women return home, and 41.8 per cent of male respondents. The opinion that women should work away from home if they wish to was more often supported by women (54.7 per cent) than by men (45.2 per cent), and by highly educated people (58.8 per cent) than by those who graduated from vocational schools or did not finish school (ninth form or less) (44.2 per cent).

EQUALITY: FROM REALITY TO DREAM—A GREAT DISTANCE?

Even before the advent of perestroika and glasnost, we had encountered difficulties with the classical paradigm of 'the Woman Question', and its solution. That there was an absence of real equality between men and women in the USSR although they are formally equal came to be widely recognized. With the onset of glasnost, there were ample opportunities for an open discussion of 'the Woman Question'. It became an open secret that in the Soviet Union, as elsewhere, many working women were employed in hazardous environments, despite protective labour legislation; that their salaries and wages were on average lower than those of men; and that there was a gap in skill achievement between men and women in industrial occupations.

The polls we conducted proved that the population as a whole could see with sufficient clarity the lack of equality between men and women both in their occupations and in the family. Thus, according to a considerable part of those questioned in the 1989 poll, 'Women in the Family', women possess fewer opportunities than men not only for raising their educational and occupational levels and for leisure-time activities or rest and recreation outside the family, but generally for restoring their physical and emotional energy after their working day. Answering the question, 'Which spouse in the contemporary family enjoys more opportunities for restoring strength after work?', 58 per cent of the respondents said the husband, and only 4

per cent the wife. Meanwhile, in their evaluation of the married couples'
opportunities for self-education, approximately half of those approached (46
per cent) said men had more such opportunities, and only 5 per cent said
that their wives did. The correlations were roughly similar in the answers
about the spouses' opportunities for rest and recreation outside the family
(respectively, 44 and 3 per cent), promotion at work (42 and 5 per cent) and
rest at leisure (41 and 5 per cent).

The majority of participants in the 1989 poll 'Women in the Family'
considered that the status of women in the family was more infringed upon
than that of men; hence the greater number (59 per cent) of those who were
sure that men were satisfied with their status in the family compared with
the smaller percentage of satisfied women (47 per cent). And 33 per cent of
the women but only 20 per cent of men questioned voiced dissatisfaction.
One explanation of this could be the fact that the aim of only 46 per cent of
married respondents was real partnership in the first place, whereby neither
spouse had absolute power in the family. As to the distribution of those who
thought that families should be dominated by one spouse, the ratios for
families 'ruled' by either the husband or the wife were approximately equal
(about 20 per cent).

However, when we pass on from rule in the family to rule in society, the
picture radically changes in men's favour. There were many more men than
women on executive posts in the Soviet Union. For instance, practically
every second man with a higher or secondary education was an executive (48
per cent) while the level for women was as low as 7 per cent. In this
connection, the respondents to the 1989 poll 'Women at Work and in
Management' were asked about their attitude to women's participation in
administration: 51 per cent of the polled persons said that women should
take part in the administration on an equal level with men. The sum total
of the supporters of inequality was small—36 per cent—while 7 per cent
believed that there should be no woman executives at all, and another 4 per
cent, on the contrary, thought that a majority of executive posts should be
given to females. Twenty-five per cent of those approached said that women
should be in the minority among executives.

In response to the question put in the 1990 poll, 'Labour Activity of
Women' ('Who, in your opinion, stands a better chance in promotion at work
—men or women?'), 64.5 per cent of respondents considered that men stood
a better chance in comparison with 4.5 per cent of those who thought that
women did. Those who thought that chances were approximately equal for
both men and women constituted 22.3 per cent of respondents, and nearly
10 per cent found this question difficult to answer. The opinions of men and
women diverged but the difference was not substantial: 65 per cent of male
and 60.9 per cent of female respondents felt that men had the better chances,
irrespective of respondents' family status and age. Heads of enterprises,

TABLE 8.1 Replies to the question, 'Who, in your opinion, stand a better chance in promotion at work—men or women?'

(% of respondents)

Groups of workers	Men do	Women do	Chances are approximately equal	Hard to say
Heads (deputy heads) of enterprises, offices, organizations	55.6	9.7	33.3	1.4
Heads of subdivisions of enterprises (section, laboratory, shop)	77.1	1.0	20.8	2.1
Specialists in technology (higher or secondary education)	73.3	3.2	17.5	6.0
Specialists in the sphere of science, culture, education, health protection (higher or secondary specialized education)	74.7	0.9	19.7	4.7
Office employees representing technical and service staff (typist, laboratory assistant, accounting clerk)	61.6	2.6	28.4	7.4
Qualified worker	63.3	5.8	22.2	9.1
Unskilled, auxiliary worker	52.7	2.7	32.1	12.6
Others	66.7	0.0	26.3	7.0
Total	65.6	3.8	23.1	7.8

Source: the poll 'Labour Activity of Women', 1990.

technical specialists, intellectual workers, and unskilled workers equally were in favour of men's advantages (see Table 8.1).

Why was public opinion so unanimous? Could it be that women as workers deferred to men and were less inclined to take up new ideas at work? There was no unanimity on these problems among respondents.

In the 1990 poll the replies to the question, 'Do you agree with the fact that women as workers defer to men?' divided into two contrary opinions: 40.4 per cent of respondents agreed and 41.3 per cent disagreed with this assertion, while 18.3 per cent of respondents found it difficult to say. Women themselves thought that they were better workers than men: more than a half (52.9 per cent) of them considered that they did not yield to men in this respect; whereas only 29.2 per cent of men considered women as workers to be equal to them. The opinion of the population on women's inclination towards new ideas was as follows: only 16 per cent of respondents thought that women were inclined to new ideas to a greater degree, and respondents aged 25–29 were especially sceptical: only 6.7 per cent of them adhered to this opinion.

According to 60–65 per cent of respondents, the major cause for women's unequal participation in the managerial system and promotion at work was household duties, which take up so much of women's time, and the lack of aspiration for promotion at work. In the 1989 poll 'Woman at Work and in Management' the question, 'Why do women more rarely than men become executives?' was posed, and in the 1990 poll the question was put as follows: 'Why is it, in your opinion, that not all the women achieve the official position which they would like?' A comparison of replies to the questions (remember that the time gap between the polls was less than a year) suggests a strengthening of the 'woman coming back to family' ideology (see Table 8.2). Whereas in December 1989 59.7 per cent of respondents felt that women had fewer opportunities for an executive role because of the amount of time spent on domestic chores, in August 1990 64.9 per cent of respondents named circumstances connected with family duties as the main cause for women's unequal access to promotion at work. According to other VCIOM polls conducted during 1989–91, it was obvious that household duties, and especially food shopping, required more effort and time than in previous years. In this situation women may have become less interested in promotion at work. The number of respondents who noted this fact more than trebled in 1990 in comparison with 1989. (See the replies to the questions in Table 8.3, third line.)

At the same time, it should be noted that men, more often than women, said that women were in an unequal position in the managerial system by reason of lack of talents needed to make an executive (15 per cent of men against 6 per cent of women). It is also of interest that lack of such talents or of a desire to work as an executive were mentioned mainly by young people without children and with comparatively high social and educational levels, whereas chores as a barrier to promotion were complained about by middle-

TABLE 8.2 Replies to the question, 'Why is it, in your opinion, that not all women achieve the official position which they would like to?'
(% of respondents)

	%*
Not all women strive for promotion at work	39.6
Women lack sufficient skill to lead	16.4
Family and upbringing of children take a lot of time	64.9
Women don't have enough persistence and purposefulness	14.1
Relatives are in opposition	8.7
Men colleagues are prejudiced	10.9
Women colleagues envy them	11.8
Other reasons	1.7
Hard to say	14.8

* The sum total exceeds 100%, as respondents could give several answers.
Source: the poll 'Labour Activity of Women', 1990.

TABLE 8.3 Replies to the question, 'Why do women more rarely than men become executives?'

(% of respondents)

	%*
Women are less interested than men in promotion at work and in becoming executives	11.0
Women have fewer abilities for executive role	10.0
Women have fewer opportunities for executive role due to household chores	59.7
They unjustly do not nominate women for executive posts	17.2
Other reasons	1.1
Hard to say	7.9

* The sum total exceeds 100%, as respondents could give several answers.

Source: the poll 'Women at Work and in Management' (1989).

aged people with two children, by persons with general secondary and specialized education, and by executives. In the meantime, characteristically, middle-aged and older people with comparatively low educational levels working as executives more often than not were against the idea of women executives, or believed that women should be in a minority among such executives, whereas younger and more highly educated respondents stressed the need for women's equal participation in the managerial system. A more critical approach to the abilities of women executives, detected during the polling in young people with comparatively high professional status, must in many respects be connected not only with less life experience but also with the changes in their system of values, which now places a higher premium on the family, on spending more time with their children, and so on.

While noting the inequality of women in practically all spheres of social activities, the majority of those polled said that the reason was women's many responsibilities and the notorious 'double burden'.

THE 'DOUBLE BURDEN' — THE CENTRAL 'WOMAN QUESTION'?

In the decades before perestroika, there had been a trend towards democratization of the spouses' roles. But these changes were reflected mainly in men's and women's mental attitudes; whereas the real distribution of family roles, and particularly family duties, lagged far behind the recommendations for modifications in this sphere. It was discovered that, in the majority of the families approached, men either never did any chores or did a smaller part of the household work. That was reported by approximately half of the men and women in their answers to the question, 'What portion of the chores is done by the man?' Apart from that, comparatively more negative were the evaluations of participation in household chores by men in the 30–39 age bracket with children, with high educational and professional levels, and with comparatively favourable material and living conditions.

In many countries, most families combine their family duties with outside work, which apparently is always difficult for women, for the family, and for society as a whole. According to public opinion at the time of the polls, most negative were such consequences of women's 'double burden' as a chronic strain on women's emotional and physical well-being (56 per cent of the respondents), women pointing it out more often than men. It was felt that women's continuous physical and moral stress had unfavourable effects on all spheres of their activities. It was related to the family's lack of strength and the poor moral education of children (one-third of the respondents), to the low productivity of women's labour (13 per cent of those approached), and to other aspects. Meanwhile the first two problems (stress and the family's lack of strength and poor moral education of children) particularly bothered people in the 30–39 year age bracket with three children (38 per cent), as well as widows, people in the older age group, those without children, and those with a comparatively high social and professional status. (People in this last group seemed mostly to adhere to an overall approach of women combining their production and family duties and in particular to the influence of the working women's overwork upon relations within the family.) The insufficient productivity of female labour was more often pointed out by middle-aged persons with two or more children—that is, respondents whose period of highest professional activity coincided with a heavy family load, including childrearing.

It should be noted that a major reason for working cited by women with children was the 'impossibility to live on the husband's earnings alone', which was mentioned by 80 per cent of those questioned. This indicates that public opinion regarded a mother's freedom of choice of options in life as an ideal situation, but difficult to realize. The respondents also mentioned reasons other than economic need, for example women's striving for material independence (14 per cent) or desire for an interesting job (9 per cent). We could add that the two last reasons were cited more often by persons from the youngest and the oldest age groups having no children or large families, and by those with a high social–professional status. The interrelations mentioned above seemed to hinge not only on the growth of the educational and material levels entailing the importance of professional work, but also on the specifics of the stage in the life cycle of the concrete population categories, and in particular on the absence of small children in such families.

WHO SHOULD BE ASSISTED?

While answering this question in the 1989 poll 'Women in the Family', respondents obviously proceeded from common sense which says that one should assist first those who are in a worse position. The result was that nearly half the respondents (46 per cent) said that women were more in need of assistance, while only 2 per cent of those polled said that men should be assisted first.

Our 1990 survey, 'Labour Activity of Women', showed that public opinion could see no way of radically altering women's status to achieve gender equality by one single project. Most respondents called for a wide set of steps and a specific policy aimed at changing women's working and living conditions. Answering the question 'Which measures should be taken to most effectively help a woman to fill a post she would like to fill?', 60.8 per cent of respondents said that it was necessary to eliminate the necessity of women having to perform laborious work outside the home (e.g. mass production factory work); whereas the opinion of 56.6 per cent of respondents was that facilitation of housework could be the best measure (development of public utilities, improvement of domestic appliances and food supplies, etc.). Some answers reflected new democratic attitudes: 7.5 per cent of the respondents believed that legislation was necessary to reserve a certain quota of leading posts especially for women; and 11.5 per cent of the respondents had no objection to an independent women's movement to protect the rights and interests of women.

As to the priority of the steps to be taken for the improvement of women's positions, 66 per cent of those approached called for more benefits for women at their work-places (shorter working-days and weeks, longer leaves, etc.); while 21 per cent of the respondents supported the idea of creating conditions under which women would not *have* to work outside the family.

Such distribution of the answers was most telling, in our view. It testified to the fact that public opinion by no means supported the idea that women should stop working to devote themselves wholly to family problems. In respondents' view, another way out should be devised (that is, humanization of working and living conditions) since only in this way would women be able to combine career and family functions without harm to themselves, their families, and their jobs.

It is interesting to note that, although two-thirds of those polled called for giving women a real opportunity to make their own decisions concerning whether or not to work, while devising some ways of improving working women's positions, an insignificant portion of those polled felt the need for conditions that would make it unnecessary for women to work at all. The majority of the respondents enumerated as optimal the most traditional solutions for the problem: that is, a reduction of women's employment and family loads. We may explain this phenomenon not only in terms of a recognition of economic need as a reason for female employment (four-fifths of those approached considered that women work because it is impossible to live on their husband's salaries or wages alone), but also in terms of a general unwillingness of the large part of the population to support fundamental changes in women's social status, namely withdrawal to the sphere of domesticity.

It should be noted that the opportunity for women to stay at home was supported largely by people from the younger age brackets without children and with comparatively high educational and material levels (such as specialists in technology and the humanities), while additional benefits at work were called for by middle-aged and older people with two or three minors and a secondary general and specialized education. Most often, the need to make it easier for women to do the housework was noted by young and sufficiently educated respondents without children who may be more inclined towards a rationalization of work and a democratic distribution of family duties.

The 1989 poll 'Women in the Family' showed that such benefits related to the working regime and conditions, as labour carried out at home and on a flexible time schedule lacked popularity. (They were supported by 10 and 8 per cent of the respondents, respectively.) This was perhaps due, first of all, to the fact that, although a flexible schedule makes it easier for women to do the chores and care for children, it gives them no additional leisure time. So far as working from home is concerned, for a majority of women this form of employment often deprives them of the opportunity to work in their speciality; it further deprives them of valued social contacts.

Most of those polled (46 per cent) supported the idea of a paid leave to care for a child until the age of 3. Twenty-eight per cent of those approached felt it was of primary importance for the mother to stop working for one or more years. Another 27 per cent of the votes were cast for paid leaves to care for the child with the sum of payment amounting to half of the salaries or wages. And finally, 23 per cent of respondents supported the idea of admitting the mother's labour in caring for the child as socially important, in the form of remuneration and an old-age pension. The data obtained sufficiently and vividly testified to the fact that for the time being, in the population's opinion, the importance is growing of the possibility of reducing productive loads for women with minors. The priority given by a vast proportion of the respondents to paid or part-paid leave for child care was above all a consequence of understanding the importance of a mother's care in the first years of the child's life, as well as of the growing desire of women to take care of and morally educate their children themselves. This form of assistance was rated the highest by people in the 25–29 year age bracket (54 per cent) having two or three minors (respectively, 49 and 53 per cent), with a higher education (51 per cent), specialists in technology, natural sciences, and the humanities (respectively, 52 and 54 per cent).

The polls also shed light upon another important aspect. The country's population generally adheres to a sufficiently comprehensive approach to the solution of the problem of the status of women, seeing that assistance to women is impossible without assistance to the family. Thus, a significant number of the respondents noted that assistance is due to the family as a whole (41 per cent), not to individual members of the family. Meanwhile in the young age group (20–29 years) and in population groups with sufficiently high educational rates and social and professional status, the share of those who gave priority to assistance to the family was higher than that of those who gave priority to assistance to women alone. For instance, the portion of the former in the 20–24 year age bracket was 53 per cent, whereas among people with a higher education and specialists in technology and natural sciences the proportions were 51 and 56 per cent respectively.

From the point of view of a large part of the respondents (69 per cent), elimination of shortages of consumer goods was the most important way of assisting the family. Another 42 per cent of those polled called for increasing the output of all kinds of housing utensils at reasonable prices. This was in fact another criticism of the short supply of consumer goods. About one-third of the respondents said that assistance to the family would also be promoted by improvements in the living and communal conditions and in public transport; nearly one-fourth believed this could be accomplished by expanding the network of services and increasing the number of services provided; and one-fifth said that the most important way to assist the family was to widen the network of crèches and kindergartens and improve their quality.

The rank ordering of ways to assist the family differed insignificantly between groups of population. For instance, families with several minors attached more importance to improvements in the system of pre-school moral education, while married couples with relatively high educational and social status deemed it important to produce more electrical and other household utensils and to prove more services. All of the suggestions cited here are indicators of the dissatisfaction of the population with the state and quality of their living conditions. One is at a loss to choose priorities in this case, because living conditions, services, crèches and kindergartens are painful issues in the Soviet Union. A majority of votes were cast for solving the issue of 'consumer goods in short supply', but it is most doubtful that this solution would render all families stronger. Meanwhile, there is no doubt that consumer goods in short supply do not render the family stronger or improve the state of both women and men.

Then again, the family must be assisted in specific ways, said many people covered by the 1989 poll 'Women in the Family'. Thus, assistance to strengthen intra-family relations also presupposes 'educating men so that they would change their approach to the chores at home' (13 per cent of the respondents said it was a panacea). The importance of such a step was more often stressed by respondents from the youngest (up to 20 years old) age group (19 per cent), the respondents with two or three minors (respectively, 14 and 15 per cent), with a comparatively high educational level (about 15 per cent, on the average), and specialists in the humanities (17 per cent). The listed interrelations seemed to be brought about by the mentioned specifics of certain stages of the family life cycle, as well as by the demands of the young and of respondents with sufficiently high cultural and material levels, towards the distribution of family duties between the spouses.

Many respondents said the salaries or wages of one of the working spouses in the family (man or woman) must be drastically raised if the other one is to be enabled to leave work. This proposal, which had previously been voiced by economists and demographers, was rather widely supported (42 per cent) among various strata of the population. The research indicated that the idea was more widely supported by middle-aged and old people (more than 45 per cent), those with two or three children (respectively, 43 and 46 per cent), with a higher (44 per cent), and with a general secondary education (45 per cent).

While discussing the possible ways to apply such approaches in practice, 35 per cent of those polled said that men alone should work, while women should devote themselves to the family. Fifteen per cent of respondents adhered to directly opposing viewpoints: although the two groups considered that both spouses should work, one group (9 per cent) preferred a major part of the household chores to be done by men, whereas the other (6 per cent) said they were the duty of women. Interestingly, 1 per cent of the respondents announced that women alone should work, while the chores should be done by men. And finally, 43 per cent of the respondents supported the idea that 'both spouses should equally work and do the chores'. Despite a sufficiently convincing 'victory' by the egalitarian approach in this case, the existence should be noted of a representative 'opposition' in the form of supporters of 'returning women to the family'. In our opinion, the struggle between the 'egalitarians' and the 'traditionalists' will intensify, especially as women's status undergoes changes in the context of our country's transition to new economic conditions.

WOMEN AND PERESTROIKA

In our view, a most pressing issue is that of the forthcoming changes in the status of women that are to be brought about by a radical economic reform. Answering the question, 'How does working women's status change in new economic conditions?' (from the 1989 poll 'Women at Work and in Management') two-fifths of the respondents said that the new economic conditions caused neither specific hopes nor apprehensions, since the status of working women had not changed sufficiently. The share of 'pessimists' (those who felt that woman's status in connection with the reform is worsening), numbering 12 per cent, equalled the proportion of 'optmists' (those who believed that woman's status in connection with the reform is improving). It should be noted that the negative phenomena related to women's professional activities under new economic conditions were pointed out more often by people from the youngest and the oldest age groups, as well as by respondents from large families whose material level was rather low. Meanwhile the positive changes were mostly underlined by middle-aged people with comparatively high social and material levels.

Such interrelations seem to testify, above all, that the difficulties related to the restructuring of the economy were felt above all by the categories of workers with insignificant professional experience (young people, mothers of large families), those with low levels of educational and professional training, people about to retire, and people with insufficient material levels (young people, pensioners, and large families).

It is of interest that men on the whole were more critical of the changes in the status of working women under new economic conditions. Thus, 15 per cent of male respondents noted negative changes in that respect, whereas women 'pessimists' numbered 10 per cent.

It should also be noted that the share of those finding it difficult to answer in a definite way a question about the state of women in the new economic situation is significantly high (35 per cent); this must testify to the fact that the role of the reform in women's working and living conditions not only was controversial but that it had not yet manifested itself to the full.

MEN AND WOMEN

Were there significant gender differences in responses? It seemed to us a priori that, in answering at least some of the questions, men would 'attack' women and vice versa. However, the research failed to support the idea. Even in cases where it would be natural to assume opposite positions, male and female respondents shared views that were close to each other.

Thus, in answering the question about who should be assisted in the family, 49 per cent of men and 49 per cent of women said the wife should, and as few as 3 per cent of men and 1 per cent of women 'felt sorry' for the husband; 9 per cent of men and 17 per cent of women said that in assisting the family the government should 'educate men to change their approach to family duties and chores', and in both groups this method occupied seventh (i.e. the last) place among all those to choose from.

It is only natural that painful and controversial issues in relations between the sexes also came to the surface. For example, 24 per cent of women and

14 per cent of men believed that their families were dominated by women (wives), whereas the male (husband's) domination was marked by 25 per cent of men and 14 per cent of women. Apart from that, the polls showed that women were apt to somewhat overestimate (by 6–9 points) conditions for self-education, rest, and leisure outside the family, promotion and leisure-time activities of men (comparatively with their own estimates), whereas men to about the same degree (by 7–10 points) overestimated the extent of equal opportunities for men and women.

In spite of the listed differences, the results we obtained on the whole testify that, at least in 1991, gender did not determine respondents' approaches to 'the Woman Question' or to methods of tackling problems associated with women's roles and status.

'FROM PATRIARCHY TO EGALITARIANISM'?

We were interested to know how widespread 'patriarchal' and 'egalitarian' sentiments were in our society. Having analysed the respondents' answers, we concluded that, while the solution to problems related to women's professional and social activities is dominated by the egalitarian approach, patriarchal trends grow more obvious when issues relate to women's status in the family. And it is also important to note that in this case the patriarchal approach manifested itself not only in terms of the 'ideology' of marital relations, but also in terms of the methods of solving family issues. Thus, 39–63 per cent of our respondents in fact supported the idea of family 'struggle', whereas 22–46 per cent of those approached called for equality and mutual assistance of the husband and wife.

Also important in its own right was the fact that we effectively failed to construct social profiles of the typical 'traditionalist' (a person with a patriarchal conscience) and 'egalitarian'. The levels of education, profession, and high material level, in fact, failed to play the role of social indicators that would have enabled us to put our respondents into definite groups. Sometimes people from older age groups voiced much more radical ideas (for example, emphasizing choice) than did the younger and the highly educated specialists. Besides, sufficiently often in the process of our analysis we came up against situations when aims were set by respondents 'the egalitarian way', whereas the suggested means for their achievement were purely 'patriarchal'.

In our view, this suggests that a restructuring is underway in all social relations, including relations between men and women. Public opinion polls on problems of woman's social status confirmed the fact that a transition to real equality of men's and women's opportunities will be very lengthy and painful for both men and women and for the whole of society.

9

Comparative Study of Women's Work Satisfaction and Work Commitment: Research Findings from Estonia, Moscow, and Scandinavia

Kaisa Kauppinen-Toropainen

INTRODUCTION

The economic and political changes under way in the former Soviet Union raise interesting questions about the possible impact of 'Westernization' on the occupational structure and on aspects of women's employment. Will women's labour-force participation and attachment change dramatically? Will new definitions emerge of 'men's work' and 'women's work'? Will conditions of work improve or deteriorate? The answers to these questions lie in the future; as long as the situation remains fluid in the former Soviet Union, we can only speculate as to how women's employment will be affected. But important clues reveal themselves when we examine the existing patterns and conditions of women's employment. In particular, analysing the subjective dimensions at the micro level—women's work satisfaction and work commitment—may suggest something about female labour-force attachment at the macro level. This chapter presents the main findings of a research project on women's work satisfaction and work commitment in Estonia and Moscow. As this project is part of a larger comparative project which includes women workers in Michigan (USA) and Scandinavia, the findings are presented in a comparative perspective.

WOMEN'S LABOUR-FORCE PARTICIPATION

Women have always worked (Kessler-Harris), especially Soviet women (Lapidus 1978; Sacks 1988; du Plessix Gray 1990; Rimachevskaya 1991). In 1985 the Soviet Union claimed the highest female labour-force participation rate of any industrial society, with 87 per cent of working-aged women engaged in full-time work or study. At that time, they constituted 51 per cent of the total labour force (Lapidus 1988).

Similarly, in the Nordic countries women's labour-force participation is

I wish to thank Dr Ludmilla Yasnaya from the Russian Academy of Sciences for her contribution in making the study of the Russian physicians possible.

high: in 1987 85–90 per cent of Danish, Finnish, and Swedish women and 80 per cent of Norwegian women aged 25–54 years belonged to the labour force (Nordic Statistical Secretariat 1989, Haavio-Mannila 1992). In Estonia the proportion of employed women was 88 (Puur 1989). In the Nordic countries in 1989, the percentage of women among the employed varied between 45 and 48 per cent (Haavio-Mannila 1992). It was considerably higher, however, in Estonia (55 per cent) and the Russian Federation (52 per cent) (Rimachevskaya 1991). In Scandinavia, unlike the former Soviet Union, many employed women have part-time jobs. Even in Finland, where part-time work is less common than in other Scandinavian countries (Niemi 1991; Haavio-Mannila and Kauppinen 1992), women work fewer hours than did women in the former Soviet Union.

CROSS-CULTURAL DIFFERENCES IN THE SEX SEGREGATION OF WORK

In Scandinavia as well as in the Soviet Union and the United States, the labour market is strongly segregated according to sex: there are distinctive men's and women's occupations, jobs, and work tasks. In Finland in 1986, about half of all employed men and women worked in occupations where 90–100 per cent of the workers were of the same sex; 11 per cent of the men and 14 per cent of the women worked in occupations where the sex composition was more balanced; and only 6 per cent of the women and 4 per cent of the men worked in occupations where the proportion of workers representing their own sex was less than 20 per cent (Kauppinen et al. 1989). Examples of women's gender-non-traditional occupations are: engineer, manager of a private business, technician, police officer, auto mechanic. The term 'token' is used to refer to men and women who work in jobs and work in places that are dominated by the opposite gender (Kanter 1977).

The expansiveness of sex segregation of work is similar in the other Nordic countries. In 1985 sex segregation was most extensive in Norway, followed by Sweden, and then Finland and Denmark. Sex segregation was somewhat less pronounced in Denmark: 65 per cent of the Danish women were employed in female-dominated jobs (Nordic Council of Ministers 1988, Haavio-Mannila and Kauppinen 1992). Similarly, in the United States over two-thirds of the employed women were concentrated in occupations where 70 per cent or more of the workers were women (Frank Fox and Hesse-Biber 1984; Reskin and Hartman 1986).

In the former Soviet Union too, women were concentrated in a number of industrial branches, and were under-represented in others, even though half of all industrial workers were women. (In Scandinavia, women's share among the industrial workers is less than 20 per cent.) Women constituted over

80 per cent of the food and textile workers, and over 90 per cent of the garment workers. These industrial branches are female-concentrated in Western countries, too. In a typical industrial city studied in a Soviet survey, about 4 per cent of the female workers were highly skilled; 30 per cent were of average skill; and 66 per cent were low-skilled, compared with 31, 50, and 19 per cent, respectively, for men (Lapidus 1988).

Even though the overall picture regarding the expansiveness of sex segregation of work is quite similar from country to country and from one political system to another (Gutek *et al.* 1986; Reskin and Hartman 1986; Kauppinen *et al.* 1989), there are important cross-cultural differences. The most striking is that in the former Soviet Union—unlike in Western countries—women are well represented in the technical speciality fields (Lapidus 1988; Koval 1989). In Estonia, female engineers made up 74 per cent of all technical specialists, and in 1985, women with a university-level technical degree made up 45 per cent of the engineers (Kandolin *et al.* 1991). In the Soviet Union, the proportion of women engineers was 58 per cent in 1989 (Rimachevskaya 1991).

In Scandinavia, as in the United States, the technical fields have traditionally been male-dominated and exhibit a pervasive masculine culture (Hacker 1981; Cockburn 1985; Kauppinen *et al.* 1989; Williams 1989). Engineering is said to have the dubious distinction of being the most male-dominated of all professions in the United States; in 1984 only 3 per cent of the engineering professionals were women (McIlwee and Robinson 1990). In Scandinavia a small fraction of engineers are women. In 1986, in Finland 7 per cent, and in Sweden 8 per cent, of the engineers with a university-level degree were women. In 1981 in Denmark, 3 per cent of engineers and architects were women (Nordic Council 1988; Kauppinen *et al.* 1989; Haavio-Mannila 1992).

It is evident that in the former Soviet Union the mathematical and technical sciences were not as strongly male-labelled as has been the case in the Western world, where women's so-called 'maths anxiety' has been a psychological barrier preventing many women from entering the technical speciality fields. (Consequently, these fields lack the genuine female viewpoint.) It is to be hoped that 'Westernization' in the former Soviet Union and in other East European countries will not mean women's feminization in the sense that they start avoiding mathematical and technical sciences.

Another unique feature of the former Soviet Union was that the medical profession has been female-dominated, whereas in the Western world it has typically been a high-status male occupation. In the USSR women's participation in the medical and health care sector in 1985 was as high as 87 per cent (Lapidus 1988; Koval 1989). However, Lapidus (1988) claims that the proportion of women declines at the higher levels of the occupational pyramid.

In the United States, 10 per cent of the physicians were women in 1984

(Frank Fox and Hesse-Biber 1984), and in 1989 the proportion had risen to 15.6 per cent (Riska and Wegar 1989). In Finland in 1991, 42 per cent of the medical doctors were women, while in 1980 the percentage was 34 per cent and in 1970, 27 per cent. Today, more women than ever are entering the medical profession (Riska and Wegar 1989). In 1991, 63 per cent of young doctors under the age of 30 were women, while every fourth doctor was a woman in the age group of 50–59 years. In other Nordic countries, women's interest, in the medical field has been somewhat less pronounced than in Finland, even though the trend is the same (Riska and Wegar 1989).

THE AIM OF THE STUDY AND DATA COLLECTION

The aim of this study was to explore how women professionals in Moscow and Estonia on the one hand, and in the Western countries on the other, experience their work and life situations in general. The idea was to find both similarities and dissimilarities in women's work-related experiences, work satisfaction, and work commitment.

The focus was on the experiences of women engineers: in the Western countries they represent women in a 'token' situation—women in a minority position as regards gender at their workplace—while in the former Soviet Union their work situation as technical specialists was less unique. Accordingly, the study inquired about cross-gender interaction at work, work satisfaction, and work commitment.

Seventy-eight women engineers in Estonia were surveyed by questionnaire in 1989 and 1990. These results will be compared with the results of a survey of women engineers in Scandinavia and the United States who had been surveyed with the same quesionnnaire.

In addition to the study of women engineers in Estonia, a survey of female and male medical doctors in hospitals and health care centres in Moscow was conducted in the winter of 1991. The survey dealt with working conditions, work satisfaction, and general life satisfaction, as well as salary differences between men and women. Altogether, 185 female and 56 male doctors were surveyed by myself and my Russian colleague in Moscow. A similar study carried out in Finland in 1988 was used as a model (Juntunen et al. 1988)— thus, the Finnish, Estonian, and Russian results can be compared.

In 1986–7, thirty-three Finnish female engineers were personally interviewed in the metropolitan area of Finland. Female engineers in Denmark and Sweden were surveyed with the same questionnaire in 1988. A mailed questionnaire was sent to women engineers belonging to the engineers' professional association in each country. Sixty-two Danish engineers and 65 Swedish engineers were included in the study. The response rate among the Danish engineers was 53 per cent and among the Swedish engineers, 62 per cent.

In 1988–9, a new data-set was added by interviewing women engineers in the United States (Michigan). The women in this study represented the US automotive industry near Detroit. The interviews were mostly based on group interviews consisting of ten or fifteen women during each interview session. Eighty-three engineers were included in the American sample.

The sample representing the Estonian engineers was collected in 1989–90 among women technical specialists in Tallinn and Tartu. I myself visited one of the work sites in Tallinn with my Estonian research assistant who could also communicate in Russian. The questionnaires (which were first translated into Estonian and then Russian) were personally handed to the women at their work sites. The women normally filled out the questionnaires at home and returned them to the research assistant; however, some women preferred to be interviewed, in which case the questionnaires were filled out by the research assistant during the personal interviews. Altogether, 78 women engineers were surveyed for the Estonian sample. The sample consisted equally of Estonian- and Russian-speaking women.

BACKGROUND DATA

The Estonian women were older than the other women, their median age being 43, while the Finnish and the US women were significantly younger, their median age being 36 and 32, respectively (Table 9.1). In Finland the engineers were least often married or co-habiting with someone, while the Estonian women were least often mothers of young children: 71 per cent had older children living at home. The Finnish and the US engineers were most often childless, but if they had children they were young; thus they faced the challenge of combining work and the intensive demands of family life.

In each country, the women said that they performed more household tasks than their spouses. The least sharing took place in the Estonian families, while in Denmark and Finland the household duties were more equally shared. Also, the general Soviet statistics show that men in the former Soviet Union were old-fashioned regarding their family duties and were reluctant to participate in household work (Haavio-Mannila and Rannik 1987; Sacks 1988; du Plessix Gray; Niemi 1991).

This lack of sharing household chores may explain why marital happiness among the Estonian women was significantly lower than in any other country. Other studies have shown that the more sharing there is between the spouses, the happier the marriages are, especially according to the women's own judgements (Haavio-Mannila et al. 1984; Kauppinen-Toropainen and Kandolin 1991).

TABLE 9.1 Background factors of the female engineers ($N = 321$)

	Finland	Denmark	Sweden	Estonia	United States	F-test/ chi-square test
Mean age (years) mean	36	40	38	43	32	***
Married or co-habiting (%)	52	76	74	70	61	n.s.
Have children living at home (%)						
Under 7 years of age	21	31	46	9	20	***
Over 7 years	9	42	25	31	6	
No children	70	27	29	60	74	
Shares household tasks with the spouse (%)[a]						
I do more	47	50	-	81	62	**
We do equally	53	43	-	15	36	
My spouse does more	0	7	-	4	2	
Marital happiness (%)						
Fairly or very happy	65	75	87	42	96	***
Not happy/not unhappy	29	6	9	46	2	
Fairly or very unhappy	6	17	6	12	2	
N	33	62	65	78	83	

[a] Those who are married or co-habiting.

n.s. not significant.
** $p < 0.01$.
*** $p < 0.001$.

CROSS-GENDER INTERACTION AT WORK

Seventy-eight per cent of the US female engineers, 65 per cent of the Danish female engineers, and 69 per cent of the Swedish female engineers said that their immediate workplace colleagues, i.e. the persons who performed the same sort of work as themselves, were men (Table 9.2).

In Estonia, women's professional interactions were significantly more gender-balanced; 47 per cent said that their immediate work-place colleagues were either men or women, and 45 per cent mentioned a female colleague; only 6 per cent of the Estonians said that they had exclusively male colleagues. In contrast, none of the US engineers could mention a female colleague performing the same kind of work as she did. The situation was very much the same in the Scandinavian work-places. In Finland, however, 15 per cent of the women had female colleagues and co-workers.

The question of personal friends is a measure of work-place culture from a subjective point of view. Table 9.2 shows that women often had personal

TABLE 9.2 Cross-gender interaction of the female engineers ($N = 321$)

	Finland	Denmark	Sweden	Estonia	United States	Chi-square test
Professional contacts (%)						
Only/mostly women	15	2	2	45	0	***
Both men and women	12	42	23	47	19	
Only/mostly men	69	55	69	6	78	
No daily contacts	3	2	6	1	2	
Has personal friends among workmates (%)						
Only or mostly male friends	3	5	10	1	0	**
Only or mostly female friends	9	13	8	27	6	
Both male and female friends	76	57	55	51	78	
No friends	12	25	27	20	16	
Own supervisor is a man (%)	97	87	85	83	98	*
Sexual harassment						
Physical advances (%)	19	7	-	0	30	n.s.
Looks and gestures (%)	29	8	-	5	46	***
Verbal harassment (%)	37	15	-	0	49	**
Written material, posters, etc. (%)	6	3	-	5	22	*
N	33	62	65	32[a]	83	

[a] 46 engineers did not answer the question.

n.s. not significant.
* $p < 0.05$.
** $p < 0.01$.
*** $p < 0.001$.

friends among their workmates. Having friends bears an intrinsic value in itself, but friendship can also have an instrumental value, e.g. when it functions as a buffer between difficult life conditions and thus alleviates depression and feeling bad (Haavio-Mannila 1992). In a highly praised book, the writer Francine du Plessix Gray (1990) emphasizes the meaning of friendship networks for Russian women as a 'survival strategy'. Her own observation is that women's friendship survival networks consist mostly of other women in the family and at the work-place.

Thus, not unexpectedly, the Estonian women, more often than the other nationalities, mentioned women as their personal friends among their workmates. This may be due to the fact that Estonian work-places were more female-dominated; it may also be that the women actively sought each other's company for instrumental as well as emotional support. The Finnish and US engineers, more often than the Danish and Swedish engineers, had gender-mixed friends, which, in turn, may relate to the women's younger age.

With regard to the gender of a supervisor, the situation was quite similar in the various countries: 98 per cent of the US engineers interviewed, 85 per cent of Swedish, and 83 per cent of Estonians had a male supervisor. The fact that women do not advance as easily as their male co-workers is referred to as the 'glass ceiling' phenomenon: there are stereotyping and preconception barriers which prevent women's advancement at work (Epstein 1988). This problem is confronted by women regardless of culture, gender composition of the work-place, or political system. According to Soviet statistics, only 7 per cent of the women with university or technical college degrees occupied executive and managerial positions compared with 48 per cent of men with similar qualifications (Posadskaya and Zakharova 1990).

A recent questionnaire study at the KAMAZ manufacturing plant in the Russian Federation revealed that 72 per cent of the men and 68 per cent of the women preferred a man to a woman as their supervisor (Posadskaya and Zakharova 1990). One-fifth of the men and 28 per cent of the women said that the sex of the supervisor was irrelevant. A small proportion preferred a woman over a man as a supervisor.

In Finland in 1989 and 1990, the same question was asked of a representative sample of employed men and women. One-fifth of the women and one-quarter of the men preferred a man over a woman as a supervisor. For most of the respondents the sex of the supervisor had no relevance. However, even in Finland, very few expressed a preference for a woman over a man as a supervisor (Lonka et al. 1989).

We may speculate why women are preferred less often to men as a supervisor. One reason relates to the long history and tradition that accords men the more powerful positions in the society—which, in turn, maintains the sex/gender hierarchy and gives men more authority and dignity (Epstein 1988; Williams 1989; Haavio-Mannila et al. 1991). It may also reflect the fact that the image of a female boss has a negative stereotype—a woman is seen as bossy, fussy, and too controlling—and people do not want to work under such supervision. Kanter (1977) has mentioned that a female superior, in a given organization, has less formal and informal power than a male superior —the woman has a more marginal position—which also explains why people prefer not to have a woman as their superior.

Anastasia Posadskaya and Natalia Zakharova (1990) have noted that the qualities that are combined with supervisory and managerial roles— assertiveness, independence, competitiveness—are seen in Russia as masculine and over-emancipating. Thus, 'real women' do not want to see themselves as possessing such qualities. For women, the problem of being labelled as 'over-emancipated' or 'masculine' (Rimachevskaya 1991; Lauristin 1992) presents a serious psychological barrier, which exists in the

Western world too, and hinders many women from realizing their potential at work.

There are other factors explaining this complex social phenomenon. It is, however, vital to learn why these psychological and institutional obstacles—which are present in the Western societies, too—could not be overcome in the former Soviet Union, even though the ideology for many years claimed equality between the sexes and emphasized women's public and political activity (Sacks 1988; Haavio-Mannila 1992). Also, it is surprising that, although Soviet women had better access to male-dominated occupations than women in the Western world, and even though women professionals worked jointly with their male peers, this did not markedly change the image of a 'real woman' (Lauristin 1992).

Table 9.2 gives the results relating to sexual harassment. The measure of sexual harassment was composed of four items concerning whether the women felt that they had received the following forms of unwanted sexual attention at their job: physical advances (deliberate touching, leaning over, cornering, or pinching); sexually suggestive looks or gestures; verbal harassment (sexual teasing, jokes, remarks, or questions); and unwanted material, posters, and texts of a sexual nature. The questions were based on studies done in the United States (Tangri *et al*. 1982; Gruber and Björn 1982). In Sweden the question was open-ended; thus, the results are not comparable. Altogether, 6 per cent of all those questioned mentioned sexual harassment.

In American work-places sexual harassment was far more common than eleswhere. Least harassment was mentioned in Estonia: only 5 per cent of the Estonian women had had experiences of sexually suggestive looks and gestures, compared with 46 per cent of the US engineers mentioning this form of harassment. Gruber's (1990) analysis of eighteen surveys of sexual harassment in the United States showed that, on average, 44 per cent of working women had been sexually harassed at work, the range in different studies extending from 28 to 75 per cent.

The fact that sexual harassment was far less common in Estonian work-places than elsewhere may reflect differences in the work-place culture regarding cross-gender interaction; i.e., men and women are more accustomed to working together as professionals. It may also reflect that, particularly in the United States, the question has been a more active topic for public discussion; thus, the women can more easily answer questions referring to it (Högbacka *et al*. 1987); Hagman 1988). Perhaps women in American work-places are more sensitive to signs of sexual harassment, which, in turn, reflect higher rates (Kauppinen-Toropainen and Gruber 1991).

It appears that issues dealing with sexuality have been tabooed in Estonia (Kandolin *et al*. 1991) and in the former Soviet Union (du Plessix Grey 1990); thus, women may have found these questions too intimate to answer. In fact, the interviewer noted some reluctance among the Estonian women to discuss openly issues relating to sexuality. (One-third of the Estonians did not answer this set of questions at all.) Also, it was evident that the women tended to attribute harassment problems to natural differences between the sexes, such as 'Boys will be boys' (Kauppinen-Toropainen and Gruber 1991).

Another difference was that the Estonian women were significantly older than the Finnish and the US women, who had the most experiences of sexual harassment. Other studies have proved that young and single women tend to be more often targets of unwanted sexual attention than older and married ones (Högbacka et al. 1987; Hagman 1988; Gruber 1990). One further explanation is that, since the work-places in Estonia were less male-concentrated than in any other country, women had less daily contact with men. According to the contact hypothesis (Gutek et al. 1990), an individual's experience of social–sexual behaviour at work is a function of the amount of contact the person has with the opposite sex.

For the most part, the forms of sexual harassment were mild, the most common form being verbal harassment. Even though mild, however, sexual harassment lowered women's work satisfaction; also, our other studies have shown that, the more women report sexual harassment on their job, the more stress symptoms they tend to have (Högbacka et al. 1987; Haavio-Mannila et al. 1988; Kauppinen-Toropainen and Gruber 1991). On the basis of these results, it is important to encourage a sexually neutral work-place atmosphere. Sexual harassment decreases the well-being of women and hinders collegiality and friendship between men and women at work.

JOB SATISFACTION, LIFE SATISFACTION, AND THE QUALITY OF WORK

The Estonian engineers reported significantly less job satisfaction than those in any other country (Table 9.3): 55 per cent of the Danish engineers, 33 per cent of the Finnish, and 36 per cent of the US engineers, but only 16 per cent of the Estonians, agreed with the statement that they were very satisfied with their work. The same pattern was evident when asked whether the women enjoyed their work: while over 68 per cent of the Finnish and 65 per cent of the Danish engineers enjoyed their work a lot, only 11 per cent of the Estonian engineers felt the same way. The Estonians also found their work less challenging and rewarding than did the other women engineers.

When asked whether the women had positive or negative attitudes towards themselves—a question adopted from Rosenberg's Self-Esteem Scale (Rosenberg 1979)—the Estonian women had the least favourable and the US women the most favourable picture of themselves: 17 per cent of the Estonians, but 64 per cent of the US women engineers, completely agreed

TABLE 9.3 Work satisfaction and self esteem of the female engineers ($N = 321$)

	Finland	Denmark	Sweden	Estonia	United States	Chi-square test
'In general, I'm very satisfied with my work' (%)						
Agrees completely	33	55	-	16	36	***
Agrees to some extent	39	29	-	28	43	
Difficult to say	21	8	-	37	8	
Disagrees to some extent	6	8	-	12	7	
Disagrees completely	0	0	-	8	5	
'I enjoy my work' (%)						
Agrees completely	68	65	41	11	43	***
Agrees to some extent	23	20	39	41	40	
Difficult to say	3	8	12	27	7	
Disagrees to some extent	3	7	6	14	7	
Disagrees completely	3	0	2	8	2	
'My work is interesting and challenging' (%)						
Agrees completely	45	61	46	23	45	***
Agrees to some extent	42	29	40	24	40	
Disagrees to some extent	9	10	12	45	14	
Disagrees completely	3	0	2	8	1	
'I have a positive attitude toward myself' (%)						
Agrees completely	39	22	24	17	64	***
Agrees to some extent	58	69	52	42	27	
Disagrees to some extent	3	5	21	32	8	
Disagrees completely	0	3	3	8	1	
N	33	62	65	78	83	

*** $p < 0.001$.

with the statement that they have favourable attitudes towards themselves. The Danish, Finnish, and Swedish engineers fell in between these two groups: the Scandinavian women had a moderately positive picture of themselves. One-third of the Estonians disagreed with the statement that they had positive attitudes towards themselves. Ambivalence and even negativism in the Estonian women's attitudes towards themselves may be a sign of the women's general low life satisfaction. It may also be a symptom of difficult living conditions which threaten women's sense of coherence and self-acceptance.

In contrast to the dissatisfaction found among the Estonian engineers, a large proportion (63 per cent) of the medical doctors in Moscow were satisfied with their work (Table 9.4). They were also strongly committed to their work: 81 per cent would not consider changing their profession. Moreover, they found their work purposeful and meaningful.

Even though the medical doctors were more satisfied with their professional lives, their general life satisfaction was extremely low (there were no gender differences): 71 per cent said they were either dissatisfied or very dissatisfied

TABLE 9.4 Work satisfaction and general life satisfaction of the Moscow medical doctors ($N = 240$)

	Men	Women	Chi-square test
'I get a lot of satisfaction from my work' (%)			
Almost always	9	11	n.s.
Often	58	51	
Sometimes	31	35	
Never	2	3	
'How meaningful do you find your work?' (%)			
Very meaningful	38	29	n.s.
Somewhat meaningful	53	50	
Not very meaningful	7	16	
Not meaningful at all	2	5	
'I would be willing to change my profession' (%)			
Yes	9	3	*
Possibly	9	16	
No	82	81	
'How satisfied are you with your life?' (%)			
Very satisfied	0	2	n.s.
Satisfied	27	28	
Dissatisfied	41	43	
Very dissatisfied	33	28	
'How satisfied are you with your salary?' (%)			
Very satisfied	2	3	n.s.
Satisfied	9	7	
Dissatisfied	27	36	
Very dissatisfied	62	54	
'How often do you feel tired after a working day?' (%)			
Almost always	15	31	**
Often	54	49	
Sometimes	26	20	
Never	5	0	
'Have your stress-coping skills changed?' (%)			
Deteriorated greatly	13	30	***
Deteriorated to some extent	32	39	
No change	36	19	
Improved	20	11	
N	55	185	

n.s. not significant.
* $p < 0.05$.
** $p < 0.01$.
*** $p < 0.001$.

with their life in general. This result was the opposite of the Finnish women doctors' answers to the same question: their general life satisfaction was very high (Juntunen *et al.* 1988).

The low general life satisfaction reflects the many social changes taking place in Soviet society which challenge people's well-being and threaten their ability to control their lives. The women doctors complained significantly more often than their male colleagues about being tired after a working day, and felt more strongly that their ability to cope with stressful situations had significantly deteriorated. A difficult situation takes its toll on everyone's happiness, which is reflected especially by the high stress and fatigue of women professionals.

SALARY DIFFERENCES

The Moscow women medical doctors were very dissatisfied with their salaries (Table 9.4), the average salary being about Rb300 per month at the time of the survey in the winter of 1991. (There were no gender differences in salary dissatisfaction.) Fifty-four per cent were very dissatisfied and 33 per cent were dissatisfied with their salaries. The women's salaries were 25 per cent lower than the men's, even though the women were significantly older than the men and had practised medicine significantly longer. The men's average monthly salary was about Rb400. As was predicted from previous studies (Lapidus 1988), the women's speciality fields in medicine were different from those of the men. The women worked more often as pediatricians, general practitioners, and gynaecologists, while the men's speciality fields more often were anaesthesiology, surgery, psychiatry, and neurology. Women's speciality fields were less rewarding than the men's.

The pronounced salary differences between the sexes was true for the Estonian engineers also: 41 per cent of the male engineers, but only 3 per cent of the female engineers, earned over Rb320 per month (in Tallinn in 1988); 33 per cent of the women, but only 9 per cent of the men, earned Rb180–219 per month (Kandolin et al. 1991; Haavio-Mannila 1992). In 1988 in Estonia, the average monthly salary of all workers and employees was, according to the official statistics, Rb250 (Rahvamajandus 1989, cited by Haavio-Mannila 1992).

Furthermore, in the Soviet Union as a whole, women's salaries and wages were much lower than men's. In 1989 it was estimated that full-time women's earnings averaged 65–75 per cent of those of men (Haavio-Mannila 1992). According to Soviet statistics, women with university or technical college degrees earned 70 per cent of the average salary of men with the same qualifications (Posadskaya and Zakharova 1990). The highest salaries were earned in manual and manufacturing work. Intellectual and managerial work was evaluated in the middle of the scale. The lowest paid occupations were information and accounting, education, health, and physical and social care (Rahvamajandus 1989, cited by Haavio-Mannila 1922).

The salary difference between the sexes is not unique for the Soviet Union and Estonia: there is a wide gender gap in salaries all over the world. In the Scandinavian countries, the salary difference is about 75–85 per cent, but there is great variation across various occupations (Nordic Statistical Secretariat 1989). In gender-non-traditional occupations, women tend to earn better than women in status-comparable female occupations; however, 'token' women never reach the same salaries as their more successful male colleagues (Kauppinen-Toropainen et al. 1989).

Gender differences with regard to salary were also demonstrated between spouses. In Estonia, the wives' salaries were about 60 per cent of those of their husbands (Haavio-Mannila and Rannik 1990). At the KAMAZ manufacturing plant, the average monthly pay for female technical specialists was Rb185 (in 1990); their spouses' average salary per month was considerably higher—about Rb300 per month. This means that women's salaries were 61 per cent of men's salaries at KAMAZ (Kauppinen-Toropainen and Gruber 1991).

These results show that women are 'sandwiched' between two situations in which their earnings are lower than men's: one at the work-place, and the other in their own family as the less-earning spouse—a situation that exists in the Western world, too (Hochschild 1989; Kauppinen-Toropainen and Kandolin 1991). This status difference at home, coupled with women's lower status at the work-place (which seems to have been exacerbated over the years), shapes women's career patterns and may negatively affect their commitment to their profession, especially if they have families needing care.

Even though the status difference at home and at the work-place applies to women professionals in the Western countries, we may argue that Soviet women are especially burdened by it and vulnerable to its consequences. This is true for several reasons. Firstly, traditional sex roles are entrenched in Soviet society (du Plessix Gray 1990; Posadskaya and Zakharova 1990). Secondly, family life is strongly female-centred, and men are reluctant to participate in housework (Sacks 1988; Haavio-Mannila and Rannik 1987; Niemi 1991). Consequently, women have restricted opportunities to negotiate new strategies in cross-gender interaction at home. Thirdly, housework is time-consuming and burdensome owing to the lack of household appliances (Koval 1989). Fourthly, women fear that they are not regarded as genuinely 'feminine' if they compete with men at work and expect their husbands to participate more actively in family life (Posadskaya and Zakharova 1990; Lauristin 1992). Also, women lack supportive professional networks which enhance women's self-image in the work-place as well as in the family.

CONCLUSION

These results confirmed that, in general, working life in the former Soviet Union was sex-stereotyped even though women there have better access to male-dominated occupations than their counterparts in the Western countries, and even though educated Soviet women professionals work shoulder to shoulder with their male professional peers. Nevertheless, opportunities for women lag far behind those for men. This situation is reflected in women's lower positions in the hierarchical structure and in the great difference between men's and women's earnings. Also, women do not have positive female role models for advancement at work.

There were similarities and dissimilarities in women's work-related experiences. Engineering proved to be female-dominated in Estonia, while in the other countries it was typically male-dominated. In the Scandinavian countries, as in the United States, the technical fields have typically been male-dominated and exhibit a pervasive masculine culture. Thus, the Estonian women were not in token situations at their work-places, whereas most of the Scandinavian and US women engineers were, working as the only female professionals in male-dominated work settings. It is to be hoped that, along with 'Westernization', women in the former Soviet Union and Eastern European countries do not start avoiding technical and mathematical sciences; it is important to have women specializing in these areas in order to preserve the feminine viewpoint and expertise.

Our results showed that Soviet women have become increasingly critical about their working conditions, salaries, and advancement opportunities. They felt dissatisfaction and stress because their jobs were uncreative, repetitive, and lacked possibilities for career development. The preliminary comparisons also indicated that female medical doctors were more strongly committed to their work than female engineers. This may relate to the fact that the medical profession is people-oriented, while the engineering is material- and things-oriented; other studies have shown that women get much satisfaction from working with and helping other people (Gilligan, 1982; Gilligan and Pollak 1988). However, the women doctors' general life satisfaction was very low, and they felt that their stress-coping skills had greatly deteriorated.

The low work commitment and general frustration of the Estonian women may reflect women's disillusionment with the past ideology which for many years promised a lot but filled their everyday lives with hardships and difficulties. The empty promises hit the women especially hard. The declarations about equality did not change the everyday facts of working life which continued to favour men's advancement and give them privileged treatment.

It is not surprising, therefore, that there exists, among well educated Estonian women, much interest in housewifery. To some women housewifery offers an alternative or a refuge from the way of life that was for many years forced on them by the state. Now the women want to become what they call 'real women' and take care of their homes and families (Lauristin

1992). A recent study presented at the Estonian Sociological Association meeting claimed that 22 per cent of young Estonian women surveyed in 1990 would seriously consider becoming housewives and staying at home with their children instead of pursuing careers (Vöörmann 1992). The result indicates that many years of enforced public activity have not created a genuine work identity for women.

In order to increase women's work commitment and interest in their own work outside the home, it is important to create qualitatively challenging work opportunities for women. It is also important to provide women with more flexibility to manage their own lives. One solution is the Scandinavian model, which emphasizes women's public activity, but also gives women opportunities to care for their children when they are small and need attention. This system also encourages men's participation in child care (Haavio-Mannila and Kauppinen 1992). Our results show that women have become increasingly critical about their work and working conditions. Discouraging attitudes and sex-stereotyping treatment lower women's work satisfaction and work involvement. The key issue is high-quality work and supportive and encouraging work-place management.

REFERENCES

COCKBURN, C. (1985), *Machinery of Dominance: Women, Men and Technical Know-How*. London: Pluto Press.

DU PLESSIX GRAY, (1990), *Soviet Women: Walking the Tightrope*. New York: Anchor Books/Doubleday.

EPSTEIN, C. F. (1988), *Deceptive Distinctions: Sex, Gender, and the Social Order*. New York: Russell Sage Foundation.

FRANK FOX, M., and HESSE-BIBER, S. (1984), *Women at Work*. New York. Mayfield.

GILLIGAN, C. (1982). *In a Different Voice*. Cambridge, Mass.: Harvard University Press.

—— and POLLAK, S. (1988), 'The Vulnerable and Invulnerable Physician', in C. Gilligan, J. V. Ward, and J. M. Taylor (eds.), *Mapping the Moral Domain*. Cambridge, Mass.: Harvard University Press, 245–62.

GRUBER, (1990), 'Methodological Problems and Policy Implications in Sexual Harassment Research', *Population Research and Policy Review*, 9: 235–54.

—— and BJÖRN, L. (1982), 'Blue-Collar Blues: The Sexual Harassment of Women Autoworkers', *Work and Occupations*, 9(3): 271–98.

GUTEK, B., LARWOOD, L., and STROMBERG, A. (1986), 'Women at Work', in C. L. Cooper and I. Robertson (eds.), *International Review of Industrial and Organizational Psychology*. New York: John Wiley, 217–34.

—— COHEN, A. G. and KONRAD, A. M. (1990), 'Predicting Social–Sexual Behaviour at Work: A Contact Hypothesis', *Academy of Management Journal*, 33 (3): 560–77.

HAAVIO-MANNILA, E. (1992), *Work, Family, and Well-Being in Five North and East European Capitals*. Jyväskylä: Academia Scientiarum Fennica.

—— and KAUPPINEN, K. (1993), 'Women and the Welfare State in the Nordic Countries', in H. Kahne and J. Z. Giele (eds.), *Women's Work and Women's Lives: The Continuing Struggle Worldwide*. Boulder, Colo.: Westview Press.

—— and RANNIK, E. (1987), 'Family life in Estonia and Finland', *Acta Sociologica*, 30 (3/4): 355–69.

—— JALLINOJA, R., and STRANDELL, H. (1984), *Family, Work, and Emotions*. Helsinki: WSOY (in Finnish).

—— KAUPPINEN-TOROPAINEN, K., and KANDOLIN, I. (1988), 'The Effect of Sex Composition of the Workplace on Friendship, Romance, and Sex at Work', in B. A. Gutek, A. H. Stromberg, and L. Larwood (eds.), *Women and Work*, iii. Newbury Park, Calif.: Sage Publications, 123–37.

—— —— —— (1991), 'Gender System of the Working Life', *People and Work*, 5 (3): 185–96. (in Finnish with English and Swedish summaries).

HACKER, S. L. (1981). 'The Culture of Engineering: Woman, Workplace and Machine', *Women's Studies International Quarterly*, 4 (3): 341–53.

HAGMAN, N. (1988), *Sexual Harassment on the Job*. Helsingborg: Wahlström & Widstrand (in Swedish).

HOCHSCHILD, A. (1989), *The Second Shift: Working Parents and the Revolution at Home*. New York: Viking.

HÖGBACKA, R., KANDOLIN, I., HAAVIO-MANNILA, E., and KAUPPINEN-TOROPAINEN, K. (1987), *Sexual Harassment in the Workplace: Results of a Survey of Finns*, Equality Publications Series E 2, 9–42. Helsinki: Ministry of Social Affairs and Health.

JUNTUNEN, J. et al. (1988), *Stress and Burnout in the Medical Profession*, Finnish Medical Association Publications, no. 13 (in Finnish with English summary).

KANDOLIN, I., RANNIK, E., and HAAVIO-MANNILA, E. (1991), 'Work and Well-being among Blue-Collar and White-Collar workers in Estonia and Finland', *Sociology*, 28 (1): 15–24 (in Finnish with English abstract).

KANTER, R. (1977), *Men and Women of the Corporation*. New York: Basic Books.

KAUPPINEN, K., HAAVIO-MANNILA, E., and KANDOLIN, I. (1989), 'Who Benefits from Working in Non-traditional Workroles: Interaction Patterns and Quality of Work', *Acta Sociologica*, 32 (4): 389–403.

KAUPPINEN-TOROPAINEN, K., and GRUBER, J. E. (1991), 'Sexual Harassment: A Cross-National Study', paper presented at the American Psychological Association Meetings at San Francisco, August 1991.

—— and KANDOLIN, I. (1991), 'Integrating Work and Family Orientations', *People and Work*, 5 (3): 295–312 (in Finnish with English and Swedish summaries).

KESSLER-HARRIS, A. (1982), *Out to Work*. New York: Oxford University Press.

KOVAL, V. (1989), 'Working Women: Common Problems', *Soviet Life*, March: 24–5.

LAPIDUS, G. (1978), *Women in Soviet Society*. Berkeley: University of California Press.

—— (1988), 'The Interaction of Women's Work and Family Roles in the USSR', in B. A. Gutek, A. H. Stromberg, and L. Larwood (eds.), *Women and Work*, iii. Newbury Park, Calif.: Sage Publications, 87–121.

LAURISTIN, M. (1992), *In Eastern Europe: A New Female Role?* paper presented at the 'Women Can' conference in Stockholm, May 1992.

LONKA, S., MARKKULA, M-L., and TUOMI, A. (eds.) (1989), *The Finnish Woman at Work, at Home and for Herself*. Helsinki: A-lehdet Oy (in Finnish).

McILWEE, J., and ROBINSON, J. G. (1990), 'Women in Engineering: A Promise Unfilled', paper presented at the American Sociologian Association Meetings in 1990.

NIEMI, I. (1991), *Time Use in Finland, Latvia, Lithuania and Russia*, Studies 182. Helsinki: Central Statistical Office of Finland.

Nordic Council of Ministers (1988) *Women and Men in the Nordic countries*. Copenhagen: Norden 58.

Nordic Statistical Secretariat (1989), *Nordic Statistical Yearbook 1988*, no. 27. Stockholm: Nordic Council of Ministers and the Nordic Statistical Secretariat, Nord 114.

POSADSKAYA, A., and ZAKHAROVA, N. (1990), *To Be a Manager: Changes for Women in the USSR*, Discussion Paper no. 65. Geneva: Training Policies Branch of ILO.

PUUR, A. (1989), *Female Labour Force Participation in Estonia*, Estonian Inter-universitary Population Centre, RU 8, Estonia.

RESKIN, B. and HARTMAN, H. (1986), 'Explaining Sex Segretation in the Workplace' in B. Reskin and H. Hartman (eds.), *Women's Work, Men's Work*. Washington DC: National Academy Press, 37–82.

RIMACHEVSKAYA, N. (1991), 'Socio-Economic Changes and Position of Women in the Union of Soviet Socialist Republics', paper presented at Soviet–Finnish Seminar on the Impact of Social Changes on the Status of Women: Moscow, 'Uzkoje', 3–5 June 1991.

RISKA, E. and WEGAR, K. (1989), 'The Position of Women in the Medical Profession in Finland: Integration or Separation', in R. Silius (ed.), *Women in male-dominated occupations*, publications from the Women's Studies Center at the Åbo Akademi, no. 5, 14–52 (in Swedish).

ROSENBERG, M. (1962), 'The Association between Self-Esteem and Anxiety', *Journal of Psychiatric Research*, 1: 135–52.

—— (1979), *Conceiving the Self*. New York: Basic Books.

SACKS, M. P. (1988), 'Women, Work and Family in the Soviet Union', in M. P. Sacks and J. G. Pankhurst (eds.), *Understanding Soviet Society*. Boston: Allen & Unwin, 71–97.

TANGRI, S., BURT, M. and JOHNSON, L. (1982), 'Sexual Harassment at Work: Three Explanatory Models', *Journal of Social Issues*, 38 (4): 33–54.

VÖÖRMAN, R. (1992), 'Relationship between Education and Social Status', paper presented at the meeting of the Estonian Sociologists Association, Tallinn, 17–18 January.

WILLIAMS, C. L. (1989), *Gender Differences at Work: Women and Men in Nontraditional Occupations*. Berkeley: University of California Press.

PART III

10

Women's Economic Status in the Restructuring of Eastern Europe

Monica Fong and Gillian Paull

INTRODUCTION

A major objective of the reform programmes in the countries of Eastern Europe is the reallocation of human resources to more productive uses. The aim of this chapter is to consider the likely impact of economic reform on the future economic role and status of women in Eastern Europe. This question has received surprisingly little attention, as other issues have demanded higher priority by those involved in the reform process in Eastern Europe on the presumption that the effects of the transition are gender-neutral. The analysis explores available data to determine whether reform programmes are gender-neutral in their effects or whether female labour is likely to bear a disproportionate share of the costs of restructuring. Special measures and approaches to overcome the higher cost for women are proposed where they are likely to occur.

Policies to discourage discrimination and to facilitate female labour supply as well as general policies to enhance the quality and quantity of available labour resources may be required to ensure a more efficient functioning of the emerging labour markets in the East European economies. Measures to broaden women's economic roles both during the transition phase and in the longer term must, of course, also be considered from the point of view of equity or parity, but that is not our direct concern here.

Two caveats are in order. The chapter draws upon seven countries, grouped into Czechoslovakia, Hungary, and Poland in the east and Yugoslavia, Romania, Bulgaria, and Albania in the centre. All have similar economic and political structures and a shared objective of economic reform towards a market-oriented economy, but the reform process is progressing at very different rates across the region and considerable cultural and economic differences remain. Thus, generalizations are broad-brush and tentative.

The second caution relates to the availability of data. The labour market information systems for generating the data needed to monitor a market economy have not yet been put in place. This study is based on existing information: incomplete and fragmented data, not available across all countries and usually not gathered with female labour participation issues in mind. The scope of the analysis is further limited by the availability of data at a highly aggregate level that does not permit detailed analyses of the labour market. Moreover, East and West European data in this area are often not strictly comparable, making the assessment of similarities and differences approximate.

THE CHANGING ROLES OF WOMEN IN EMPLOYMENT

Overview of labour-force participation

In order to assess changes in female employment under the reform process, a brief overview of past trends is necessary. Since the end of the Second World War women's participation in the labour force has risen rapidly, and at least 80 per cent of all women between the ages of 16 and 54 in the region now work.[1] With the exception of Yugoslavia, women account for nearly half the labour force. (Yugoslavia's lower labour-force participation rate for women masks a difference across republics, ranging from a rate of 71.8 per cent in the republic of Slovenia to 18.5 per cent in the Kosovo Autonomous Province: World Bank 1991i). Inclusion of women on child-care leave in some cases increases the participation rate further. For example, in Hungary, adding the number of women on child-care leave results in an activity rate of around 80–82 per cent, almost the same as that of men. In most countries labour-force participation rates by age indicate almost no gap in the childbearing ages.

During the 1980s employment rates for women in Eastern Europe increased significantly, while those for men stagnated or fell in most cases, resulting in a growing share of women in employment. One factor explaining this increased participation of women was the reduction of real household income, which forced more women to become second earners in the family at that time.

A comparison with labour-force participation rates in OECD countries indicates that the Eastern European rates for men do not differ significantly, but female participation rates are considerably higher. For example, the participation rate for women in Hungary is twice that of Greece and the rate in Romania is twice that of Spain. Only Finland, Norway, and Sweden approach the East European rates of female labour-force participation (see Table 10.1).

---

[1] Data for Eastern Europe are usually given as employment rates rather than labour-force participation rates and the usual distinction between the two does not apply. For the purposes of this paper the terms have been used interchangeably. Note also that the labour-force participation rates for Czechoslovakia and Poland are comparable with other East European countries, although they appear lower, since they are given as a proportion of the entire population aged 15 and above rather than of the working-age population.

TABLE 10.1 Labour-force participation rates in Eastern Europe, by sex[a] (%)

Country	Year	Total	Male	Female
Czechoslovakia	1985		77.6	62.1
Hungary	1980	79.5	87.4	70.7
	1985	78.5	82.5	74.1
	1990	79.7	83.6	75.2
Poland	1978	67.3	76.6	58.7
	1988	65.3	74.3	57.0
Yugoslavia	1981	62.9	74.7	51.3
	1985	63.9	74.5	53.4
	1989	64.5	73.3	55.6
Romania	1980	83.3	88.9	77.1
	1985	82.7	86.2	78.7
	1989	84.2	87.3	80.6
Bulgaria[b]	1987	70.1	68.5	71.7
Albania[c]	1980	80.8	78.2	82.7
	1985	82.0	79.9	84.5
	1990	84.0	82.0	86.3
Comparative rates				
Austria	1988	66.9	80.3	53.7
Canada	1988	76.0	85.4	66.6
Finland	1988	76.9	80.8	73.0
France	1988	65.5	75.4	55.7
Germany[d]	1988	68.8	82.9	54.4
Greece	1988	59.3	75.6	43.4
Ireland	1988	61.0	83.9	37.6
Italy	1988	61.2	78.8	43.9
Norway	1988	80.1	87.2	72.8
Spain	1988	58.3	77.3	39.4
Sweden	1988	82.3	84.4	79.4
UK	1988	75.4	87.2	63.5
USA	1988	76.1	85.5	66.9
OECD Europe	1988	66.2	80.9	53.5

[a] The labour-force participation rate is the proportion of economically active labour force compared with the population of working age, except for Czechoslovakia and Poland which show the proportion aged 15 and over.
[b] Figures for Bulgaria use 1988 population figures and 1987 employment figures for the state socialist sector only.
[c] Figures for Albania are for the year-end.
[d] Germany is the former Federal Republic of Germany.

Sources: Venerova (1991) (Czech.); Lado (1991), Adamik (1989) (Hun.); World Bank (1991*d*) (Pol.), World Bank (1991*i*) (Yug.), World Bank (1991*g*) (Rom.), World Bank (1991*f*) (Bul.), *Albania Statistical Book* (1990) (Alb.), OECD (1990).

TABLE 10.2 Female employees as a percentage of all employees in Eastern Europe, by sector

	Czechoslovakia 1988	Hungary 1988	Poland 1989	Yugoslavia 1990	Romania 1988	Bulgaria 1988	Albania 1989
Total	46.0	45.8	45.7	41.6	40.0	49.9	46.7
Productive sphere	41.3						
Agriculture	39.7		27.8	27.6	24.1		52.4
Agriculture and forestry		39.9					
Forestry			18.5	11.6	22.3		
Industry	40.8	43.2		37.7	41.3		44.5
Industry and mining							
Mining and manufacturing		37.2					
Construction		19.0	20.0		12.8		8.9
Water management				12.2			
Civil engineering				11.4			
Nonproductive sphere	60.0	62.7					
Trade		65.4	69.7	51.9	61.7		53.1
Home trade	75.7						
International trade	65.4		76.5				
Education	71.6		61.0		70.0		
Culture and the arts	52.1				48.7		
Education and culture				54.9			52.7
Science and research	38.1				45.9		
Research and development			48.3				
Housing			42.8	18.9			
Health service	78.8						
Social care	89.0						
Health service and social care			81.4	76.2	76.0		78.8

Community services				
Transport and tele-communications		43.1	25.7	28.2
Telecommunications	16.0	53.3	17.1	
Communications				58.7
Transport		12.3		24.4
Sport and recreation				55.3
Catering and tourism			60.5	
Public administration and justice				64.4
Government and political organizations			54.1	
Finance and insurance		66.1		84.5
Financial and other services			53.9	
Administration		40.9		
Crafts			23.8	

Notes: Figures for Poland and Albania are for the socialized sector only. Figures for Romania exclude co-operative and private-sector employment.

Sources: Okruhlicova (Czech.); Lado (1991) (Hun.), World Bank (1991*d*) (Pol.), Pesic (1991) (Yug.); World Bank (1991*g*) (Rom.), World Bank (1991*f*) (Bul.), *Albania Statistical Book* (1990) (Alb.).

Employment by occupation and sector

Despite higher female labour-force participation rates than in most other countries, East European countries show similar patterns of differentiation by sector and by hierarchy to those pertaining for the rest of the world (Table 10.2). The distribution of women and men in state and private enterprises also shows some differences. In Hungary, Poland, and Yugoslavia the majority of women are employed in the state sector, but substantial proportions are employed in private agriculture in Poland and Yugoslavia and in the co-operative sector in Hungary.

Women dominate employment in the service sphere, particularly in the education, health, and social care sectors, and they also constitute the majority of workers in the trade, culture and arts, communications, and finance sectors. This occupational concentration has resulted from a combination of factors including an association between the 'feminization' of sectors and a decline in the status and also wages of these sectors. In Hungary, nearly a third of female employees are employed in the service sector and nearly a third in industry, while in Poland over 40 per cent of women in the nationalized sector are employed in the services. Over half of the female workers in the state sector are employed in industry in Romania, but over 20 per cent are employed in the service sector (see Table 10.3). In Czechoslovakia, Venerova (1991) reports that almost half of all female workers are employed in services, one-third in industry, and one-fifth in agriculture.

Women are also under-represented in management positions. Recent data comparing the relative position of men and women are sparse, despite

TABLE 10.3 Distribution of female employment in Eastern Europe, by sector (%)

	Hungary 1988	Poland 1989	Romania 1988
Industry	29.1		52.7
Mining and manufacturing		28.5	
Construction	3.0	3.1	2.4
Agriculture	16.4	3.6	5.2
Transport and telecommunications	5.1	5.4	3.8
Trade	15.3	15.4	12.0
Services	29.4	40.9	20.9
Other	0.8	2.3	3.2
Waterworks and supplies	0.9		
Total	100.0	99.2	100.2

Notes: Figures for Poland are for the state socialized sector only. Figures for Romania exclude co-operative and private-sector employment.

Sources: Lado (1991) (Hun.); World Bank (1991*d*) (Pol.); World Bank (1991*g*) (Rom.).

frequent reports that women's representation at higher levels of economic decision-making remains extremely low. Lampland (1989) reports that, in the case of Hungary, 37 per cent of men with advanced degrees work as upper- or middle-level managers, while only 12 per cent of women do so. Of those with middle-level degrees, 35 per cent of men hold middle-management positions, compared with 8 per cent of the women.

These data relate to the official or formal economy. Statistical information on the role of female employment in the 'informal', 'parallel', or 'second' economy is not available. Although essentially market-oriented, this activity operated under strong state restrictions and functioned mainly on a part-time basis, serving as a source of supplementary income for workers with official full-time employment. The size of this second economy varied considerably between the countries, being very limited for example in Czechoslovakia, and of great importance particularly in Poland, and we can only speculate on the differing roles of men and women in this sector. When these activities become part of the official private sector, as many are expected to, statistical information on them will become available; if they remain in the informal sector to avoid taxes, social security, and labour regulations, they will continue to elude official information systems. Thus, female participation in this small and dynamic sector of the economy may continue to elude us for some time to come.

Unemployment

Throughout Eastern Europe, unemployment has traditionally been very low, but now it is beginning to emerge in substantial numbers or to rise from previous low levels across the region. In proportion to their labour-force participation, women are over-represented among the unemployed, in most countries constituting more than half of the unemployed. In countries where the main cause of unemployment is job loss, the share of men and women in the unemployed is not substantially unequal, for example in Hungary and Poland. In countries where new labour-force entrants are an important element in unemployment, the share of women is relatively higher, despite declines over the last decade—for example Yugoslavia and Albania. Available evidence on re-employment possibilities in Hungary and Poland suggest that women are likely to remain unemployed for longer periods than men. If this pattern continues, the share of women among the unemployed can be expected to increase substantially in the future, as new unemployed are added to the pool of unemployed women and most remain there.

In *Czechoslovakia*, available data indicate that the unemployment rate remains at a low level: 1.5 per cent in January 1991. However, this figure conceals an increase in the *number* of unemployed of by two-thirds. Unemployment figures by sex, currently not available, are expected in the

very near future. Estimates for the Slovak Republic suggest similar levels for
women: 58 per cent. Unemployment by qualification and age alone, from
the same source, suggest that those with a middle level of education
constitute the largest share of the unemployed and that younger age groups
have a greater risk of unemployment than older cohorts. Government
forecasts indicate an increase in unemployment to an average rate of 5–8 per
cent for 1991 as a whole; other estimates range from 3 to 12 per cent in
1991–2 (Economist Intelligence Unit 1991*a*; Riveros 1991).

In *Hungary*, the unemployment rate has risen continuously since the
registration of unemployed persons began in January 1986. Unemployment
levels remained below 1 per cent in the 1980s, but have since risen to
3.4 per cent by April 1991. It is estimated that unemployment may peak
at between 7 and 14 per cent during 1991 (World Bank 1991*b*). The female
share of unemployment is just over 40 per cent, lower than women's 46 per
cent labour-force participation rates. The male unemployment rate for
January 1990 was 2.9 per cent compared with a female unemployment rate
of 1.7 per cent. Unemployment varies by skill: unskilled levels have the
highest rate of unemployment, although their numbers now equal those of
the skilled unemployed. At lower skill levels men are at greater risk of
unemployment than women; however, the data suggest that women may be
more vulnerable to unemployment relative to men at the highest skill level
(Nagy and Sziraczki 1991; Lado 1991).

In *Poland*, unemployment began to increase rapidly at the beginning of
1990 and by April 1991 had reached nearly 1.4 million and an unemployment
rate of 7.3 per cent. Contrary to predictions made before the January 1990
stabilization programme, employment has declined mainly as a consequence
of a generalized contraction in output rather than as a result of massive lay-
offs through sectoral restructuring (see e.g. Coricelli and Revenga 1991).
Current estimates indicate that unemployment may peak at between 1.8 and
2.5 million in 1991–2 (World Bank 1991*e*).

In Poland women suffer a larger share of unemployment: they constitute
58 per cent of the unemployed, while their share in the labour force is
46 per cent. These figures reflect an increase in the number of unemployed
school-leavers, of which women constituted 58 per cent; for general secondary
school-leavers, women constituted 82 per cent of the unemployed (see
Table 10.4). Figures for both sexes combined indicate that the 18–34 age
group and those with a secondary level of education constitute the majority
of the unemployed (see Table 10.5). Kuratowska (1991) reports that the
majority of unemployed women in December 1990 fell into the 31–40 age
group and that there were many more unemployed women than men in this
age cohort.

Not all of the unemployed are entitled to unemployment benefits.
Housewives, whom Gora *et al.* (1991) estimated to make up 18.7 per cent

TABLE 10.4 Unemployed school-leavers in Poland, by sex, 31 December 1990

	No. of school-leavers ('000)	% female
Tertiary	8.9	51.0
General secondary	21.4	82.3
Vocational secondary	49.5	66.2
Basic vocational	84.4	47.5
Total	164.2	58.0

Source: World Bank (1991*d*); Gora *et al.* (1991).

TABLE 10.5 The unemployed in Poland, by age, educational level, and work experience

Age structure	%	Educational level	%	Working experience	%
15–17	1.4	Tertiary	8.5	Less than 1 year	24.8
18–34	60.0	Secondary	41.9	1–10 years	58.6
35–54	35.0	Vocational	33.5	More than 10 years	16.6
55+	2.4	Unskilled	16.4		

Source: Gora *et al.* (1991).

of the registered unemployed in February 1991, were acknowledged as unemployed but were not entitled to benefits. The increased registration of individuals not entitled to benefits may also reflect an increase in the participation rate of secondary workers or the movement into the formal economy of those who have lost work in the 'second' economy, as a result of the recession.

Women can be at a considerable disadvantage in finding new jobs. In Poland vacancies have traditionally been classified by sex, and recent data in some areas show a steady increase in the number of jobless per vacancy, with the number of vacancies for males outnumbering those for females 3 : 1. The prospects for re-employment for unemployed women thus appear to be much worse than for men.

Unemployment in *Yugoslavia* has increased from traditionally low levels, (1.1 per cent in 1953, 2.3 per cent in 1961, 3.3 per cent in 1971) (World Bank 1991*i*) to 8.6 per cent in 1981 and to 12.8 per cent or nearly 1.4 million unemployed in 1990. Unemployment is forecast to reach 1.8 million in 1991 (Economist Intelligence Unit 1991*e*). The rate of unemployment, like the labour-force participation rate, varies considerably across the republics, from 2.8 per cent in Slovenia to 28.5 per cent in Kosovo (World Bank 1991*i*).

The rate of unemployment for women has been considerably higher than that for men: in 1989 the male rate was 9.3 per cent while the female rate was 14.6 per cent. As the share of women in the labour force has increased to 41.6 per cent, the share of unemployment has also decreased slightly during the 1980s, from 56.7 per cent in 1981 to 53 per cent in 1990. During the previous decade, the share of the unskilled among the unemployed has fallen, while those with high-school qualifications and above have constituted an increasing proportion. The majority of the unemployed are those with no previous work experience and those who have been looking for work for over a year.

Unemployment has traditionally not been a large problem in *Romania*, but there are indications that higher levels of unemployment are beginning to emerge. Here women are the majority of the unemployed, estimated at 85–90 per cent of those looking for work. In September 1990 the unemployment rate was less than 0.5 per cent, with 50,400 registered unemployed. In the last quarter of 1990 unemployment reached approximately 100,000, including 70,000 school-leavers. Estimates of future levels range from the official forecast of 462,000 in 1991 to 4 million unemployed by 1995 (Economist Intelligence Unit 1991*d*).

In *Bulgaria* in July 1990 there were 22,400 registered unemployed, of whom approximately 63 per cent were women and half were between the ages of 30 and 50. By February 1991 the unemployed had reached 136,000, and by April the unemployment rate was 4.6 per cent, with the proportion of women remaining over 60 per cent. Given that women constitute marginally less than half of the labour force, the unemployment rate for women is clearly higher than that for men. In 1991 the World Bank estimated that the unemployment rate would rise to 6.7 per cent at the end of 1991 and 10.9 per cent by 1993 (World Bank 1991*a*).

Unemployment registered at employment offices in *Albania* has followed a steady upward trend during the 1980s to reach a rate of 2.3 per cent by the end of 1990, according to official statistics. The share of women in the unemployed has fallen from 75 per cent in 1980 to just under 60 per cent in 1990.

In Eastern Europe in 1991 unemployment was still lower than in many West European countries, but women had higher rates of unemployment than men. In part this is a visible echo of higher female employment and unemployment in the structure of centrally planned economies; in part, it reflects a scarcity of female job vacancies in the emerging employment exchanges and a difficulty in finding new employment, which could result in an ever-expanding pool of female unemployment. This is therefore a major area for future monitoring and action (see Table 10.6).

Earnings

Traditionally in Eastern Europe, wage differentials have been very narrow and differences in earnings by skill and occupation have been small.

TABLE 10.6 Unemployment in Western Europe, by sex, 1990

Country	Number unemployed			Rate of unemployment (%)		
	Total	Males	Females	Total	Males	Females
			(% of total unemployed)			
Finland	88,000	54,000	34,000	3.4	4.0	2.8
		(61.4)	(38.6)			
France	2,504,700	1,148,700	1,355,900			
		(45.9)	(54.1)			
Germany (FRG)	1,872,000	962,600	909,400	7.2	6.3	8.4
		(51.4)	(48.6)			
Norway	112,000	66,000	46,000	5.2	5.6	4.8
		(58.9)	(41.1)			
Spain	2,441,200	1,166,100	1,275,100	16.3	12.0	24.2
		(47.8)	(52.2)			
UK	1,664,500	1,232,300	432,200	5.9	7.6	3.5
		(74.0)	(26.0)			

Sources: ILO (1991); World Bank (1991*h*).

A widening of wage differentials may be expected as a result of the economic reforms, and any inequalities now present are likely to increase.

Despite this tradition and legislation enacted on equal pay, however, the gap between men's and women's wages in Eastern Europe is considerable, and shares many characteristics with Western wage differentials. The average compensations of women are 68.9 per cent that of men in Czechoslovakia, 73.4 per cent in Hungary, 76.7 per cent in Poland, and 86.9 per cent in Yugoslavia (see Table 10.7). Data available on wage differentials by sex for manufacturing in Western Europe range from 67.8 per cent in the UK and 69 per cent in Ireland to 79.2 per cent in France and 85.5 per cent in Norway (ILO 1991). Examining wage differentials by economic sector indicates that the average salary for women is lower than that for men across all branches of economic activity. The earnings gap is lowest in Poland and highest in Hungary. The greatest disparity between men's and women's wages is found in industry (see Table 10.8).

Wage differentials by educational level show smaller disparities for secondary school and university graduates in Czechoslovakia, Poland, and Yugoslavia (see Table 10.9). Analysis by age shows smaller differences at younger ages and an increased differential with age and labour-market experience. More generally, the lower average pay for women is due largely to women not working in the well paid areas, such as the mining or steel industries, and because they hold fewer supervisory posts.

TABLE 10.7 Female average earnings in Eastern Europe as a percentage of male average earnings, by hierarchical position

	%
Czechoslovakia	
Total	68.9
Manual workers	65.4
Operational and service workers	74.1
Technical workers	67.6
Leading and administrative staff	65.1
Other workers	70.1
Hungary	
Total	73.4
Skilled	75.8
Semi-skilled	78.8
Unskilled	84.3
Yugoslavia	
Total	86.9
Chain manual work	78.8
Machine work	74.5
Professional and technical work	88.5
Managerial and administrative work	76.6

Notes: Figures are for average earnings for Czechoslovakia, monthly average wage (1987) for Hungary, and salary level (1986) for Yugoslavia.

Sources: Venerova (1991) (Czech.); Central Statistical Office (1989) (Hun.); Drakulic (1991) (Yug.).

TABLE 10.8 Female average earnings as a percentage of male average earnings in Eastern Europe, by sector

	Czechoslovakia	Hungary Blue-collar	Hungary White-collar	Poland
Industry	65.4	64.5	52.1	
Construction	71.0	65.2	55.6	82.0
Mining				56.2
Agriculture	83.2	67.7	54.8	87.3
Water management				
Science/research	72.6			80.2
Trade	76.0	76.2	66.8	83.4
Transport		69.5	56.7	83.6
Services		75.8	64.2	
Education	72.1			81.4
Health services	66.1			79.8
Culture/arts				89.7
Finance/insurance				91.8

Notes: Figures are for average earnings for Czechoslovakia, monthly wage in the non-private sector (1989) for Hungary, and monthly compensation (1990) for Poland.
Sources: Venerova (1991) (Czech.); Szalai (Hun.), Gora *et al.* (1991) (Pol.).

TABLE 10.9 Female average earnings as a percentage of male average earnings in Eastern Europe, by education

	%
Czechoslovakia	
Elementary education	69.2
Skilled	69.5
Secondary school	74.7
University-trained	86.6
Poland	
Elementary	74.0
Lower technical	71.7
Secondary	79.2
Technical	77.5
Secondary (+)	80.8
University	81.4
Yugoslavia	
Total	86.9
No school or 1–3 grades of primary school	87.3
Completed secondary school	86.4
Junior or senior college	85.5

Notes: Figures are for monthly compensation (1990) for Poland and salary level (1986) for Yugoslavia.

Sources: Venerova (1991) (Czech.); Gora *et al.* (1991) (Pol.); Drakulic (1991) (Yug.).

Summary

The participation of women in the labour market has been almost equal to that of men in Eastern Europe, but the form has been very different. Segregation across occupations by sex has left women in the poorer paid and less prestigious sectors, and they are also under-represented in the managerial and higher-level positions. This partly explains the lower earnings of women relative to men. The share of women in unemployment where it has existed has traditionally been higher than that for men. The evidence suggests that this may become more pronounced during the transition phase, owing to a lower probability of re-employment. Overall, the current position of women in employment in Eastern Europe may be described as a secondary work-force, occupying less desirable positions of administrative support and more prone to unemployment during downturns in the demand for labour.

Sufficient data are not yet available to determine the effect that reform has had on the position of women with respect to unemployment. Nevertheless, it is clear that the differences in employment and unemployment, occupational patterns, earnings differentials, and the education, skills, and qualifications described above will affect the impact of economic restructuring on men and women. Secondly, the current labour-market characteristics of the female population reflects the gender biases present but assumed absent under the state socialist economies. These biases will continue to affect the response of both employers and employees under the reform, unless specific action is taken to remove them.

The factors affecting labour demand and supply during the transition period will be reviewed below in order to determine the probable impact of the reform process on women in the labour market.

LABOUR DEMAND FOR WOMEN

The statistical evidence of the effect of the reform process by sex is not yet in. Potential developments in labour demand are ambiguous as to their effect on the position of women. In some respects, the restructuring process could favour women's employment. Although women will lose jobs in the administrative and clerical positions of many enterprises, the declining sectors in the economy are male-dominated and the expanding areas are those traditionally dominated by women, both by experience and education. This is especially true for younger women. In addition, women have administrative and entrepreneurial skills which can prove advantageous in the private sector. One of the objectives of the reform measures is to minimize employers' costs, including the wage bill. As shown above, women have on average earned less than men in Eastern Europe and therefore may be more willing to continue to accept lower wages. Assuming that other factors are equal and that women can be hired at a lower cost than men, labour demand will be greater for women than men.

However, women have had a higher risk of job loss and are facing greater difficulties in attaining re-employment. Traditional classification of employment along sex lines, cultural traditions, and the strong value placed on women's domestic responsibilities may create a preference for men on the part of many employers. Younger women are particularly likely to be affected by these factors because of the (mis)perception that they have extensive child-care responsibilities. This could be mitigated by other factors, including the ability to retrain, to take advantage of other employment services, or to switch occupations. It will also depend, to some degree, on women's willingness to become self-employed.

The distribution of job losses

Loss of employment will be caused both by a dismissal of excess employees and by the closing of uncompetitive firms. This lay-off of workers will be distributed unevenly across different sectors in the economy and across different types of occupations and employees within sectors. Women's loss of employment will depend upon the concentration of women both across and within sectors and occupations.

The initial data indicate that the pattern of women's employment across sectors before the transition period does not predispose them disproportionately to loss of employment—quite the contrary. In Czechoslovakia the main reductions in employment in 1990 occurred in the industrial and construction sectors (Bouse 1991). In Hungary the most serious declines in production in 1990 occurred in mining, iron and steel, engineering and light industry, particularly textiles (Economist Intelligence Unit 1991b). Throughout the last decade, the share of services in the Hungarian economy has been increasing at the expense of agriculture and industry and this shift became more pronounced in 1990 (Nagy and Sziraczki 1991). In Poland, light industry and textiles are being hard hit by economic changes, but, again, the output decline in the service sector is smaller than in other areas. In 1990 employment in the socialized sector in agriculture and forestry fell by 21 per cent, in mining, manufacturing, and construction by 10.7 per cent, and in services by only 5.9 per cent (Kwiatkowski 1991). In Yugoslavia employment is expected to decline particularly in heavy industry, production of metal products, transport equipment, and electrical appliances (World Bank 1991i). In Romania the first wave of unemployment occurred mostly in construction and heavy machinery (Celac 1991). Overall, the concentration of men in employment in heavy industry and agriculture and their low representation in the services suggest that men will be more vulnerable to employment loss. However, light industry and textiles in particular are high-risk areas for female unemployment.

There are also indications that managers will concentrate staff reductions initially in administrative support occupations, which are dominated by women. As a result, even in sectors dominated by men, employment loss may affect the minority of women within the sector; for example, cuts in production in heavy industry may result in reductions in employment in the firms' overstaffed and overdeveloped administrative departments.

Information concerning the actual criteria for the selection of employees to be made redundant during the process of labour-force reductions within an enterprise is poor. In the case of Hungary, Nagy and Sziraczki (1991) report that companies are tending to use four methods to reduce the size of the work force: (1) by introducing a recruitment ban; (2) by systematically targeting elderly employees; (3) by raising disciplinary standards; (4) through lay-offs based on selection criteria of discipline, reliability, and efficiency.

Employees with low qualifications, employees with regular absenteeism (including women with small children and workers with health problems), and less performance-orientated employees are therefore at greater risk. In addition, those workers whose long-term commitment to their job is judged to be doubtful are at high risk, such as young men before compulsory military service or young women before marriage. In the case of Poland, Sopniewska (n.d.) reports that women, together with commuters, workers who own small farms, elderly people, leavers of company trade schools, and the disabled, are among the first to be laid off.

Government regulations on dismissals

Government regulations on dismissals in most countries currently specify the length of notice required and the size of severance payments. In some cases, as in Hungary, workers and their representatives have legal rights to take part in decision-making issues relating to redundancy, including the selection principle. In several countries there are bans on the dismissal of pregnant women, mothers on maternity leave or with young children, and single mothers. In Czechoslovakia this ban also applies to men who are single parents. In addition, a proposal current in Eastern Europe involves the prohibition of the dismissal of a worker if another member of the household is already unemployed, although the practical implementation of this may be problematic. If women constitute a disproportionately large share of the unemployed for other reasons, such a regulation could preserve the employment of working husbands at the expense of other women; as more and more women become unemployed, more and more husbands would retain employment under this rule. At present, government regulation of redundancy policy does not appear to be biased against women, but careful consideration of the gender effects needs to be given to future proposals, including the example above.

Hiring and new employment

By sector. As is the case with employment loss, the relative re-employment of men and women will depend, to some degree, upon which areas of the economy are growing and are likely to expand in the future. Throughout Eastern Europe, employment is likely to expand in consumer goods and service industries, particularly in financial services, commerce and trade, and information technology. These are precisely the employment areas that women have traditionally dominated, and this may advantage women in several ways. First, on the basis of past work experience, on average, women will be better qualified for employment in these areas. Second, these careers have a female 'stereotyping': employers are familiar with hiring women for positions in these sectors and there are female role models in the occupations, encouraging other women to seek employment in such jobs. Third, women have oriented their education and training towards these sectors. Finally, a preference on the part of women for service occupations in general may reflect women's involvement in caring and services more generally from adolescence onwards. However, it should be emphasized that the restructuring process and the reallocation of resources will take time, and any benefits that may accrue to women in employment will appear only with a considerable time lag.

We must also bear in mind, however, that the past is no longer a valid model: throughout the years of central planning, most countries in Eastern Europe experienced a labour shortage. In the radically different situation of excess labour supply, gender preferences in hiring may come to the forefront for the first time and women could find it more difficult than men to obtain new employment.

In many countries, job vacancies may specify the desired gender and 'men only' advertisements are becoming more widespread. For example, in the Slovak Republic in Czechoslovakia in February 1991 there were 7,563 vacancies, but only 29 per cent were for women (Okruhlicova 1991). In Hungary in 1988 and 1989 the vast majority of vacancies for manual jobs were 'men only', although the situation was less discriminatory for non-manual vacancies.[2] Lado (1991) reports further that the better the job offered, the more likely it will specify 'men only'. Foreign joint ventures openly prefer men to women in their advertisements and many companies prefer men for their higher managerial positions. In Poland, data for some areas in April 1991 show 17 unemployed men for each vacancy for men, but 59 unemployed women for each vacancy for women (Kwiatkowski 1991; Central Statistical Office 1991). In this situation, the probability of obtaining new employment for a man is more than three times greater than for a woman.[3]

By education.   Limited female access to education has been virtually eliminated in the East European region as women constitute half or more of the students at all levels of the educational system in all seven countries. However, it should be noted that, for the population as a whole, older women are generally not as well educated as men.

Education by occupational career is segregated along gender lines. At the secondary level, girls tend to study in secondary schools, which provide general knowledge, while boys mainly attend vocational schools, where they attain much narrower and, until the present, more lucrative skills. Girls are

---

[2] It seems that if a job vacancy specifies gender it is for a male, and there are very few posts advertised for women.

[3] In comparison, a study of displacement and job loss in 15 OECD countries in the 1980s revealed that men were less likely to lose their jobs than women and that it was women, unemployed as a result of redundancy, who had the greatest difficulty in finding a new job. In addition, the proportion who left the labour force rather than remain in the labour force unemployed was higher for women than for men. Overall, the study concluded that unskilled workers, women, and older workers were more likely to become long-term unemployed than other workers ('Displacement and Job Loss: The Workers Concerned', in OECD 1990).

directly excluded from some types of training; for example, in Hungary they are not permitted to enter some types of training for vehicle mechanics. There is also a gender specialization by subject (see Table 10.10). At the higher-education level, women predominate in teacher training, natural science and maths, health work, economics, business administration, services, trade, and the humanities. There are few women in technical sciences and engineering. This specialization also occurs at the secondary level; for example, in Hungary girls constitute 80–90 per cent of the students in trade, economic, and postal services at technical secondary schools. Thus, there is considerable matching between likely growth areas in the economy and the types of training that women have tended to dominate.

However, educational specialization cannot be treated as an exogenous variable, but rather as a factor that has been influenced by other components in the economy. In Eastern Europe, men have tended to undertake vocational educational courses that have led to the better-paying occupations. Changes in relative wages in the growth sectors of the economy during the reform process, as a result of the pressures of supply and demand, may lead to a change in occupational and educational choices of males. Men may move into

TABLE 10.10 Percentage of females in higher education in Eastern Europe, by subject

	Hungary 1987	Poland 1985	Yugoslavia 1989	Romania 1989/90	Albania 1988
All subjects	51.7		49.0	49.5	50.3
Engineering	15.3				30.2
Agriculture	31.2	45.2	39.1		47.8
Teacher training	73.4				61.1
Natural science and maths		61.5	62.1		
Maths and computer science					50.4
Technical sciences		19.8	29.6	41.7	
Medicine	54.4	62.3	62.1		
Health work	96.3			56.1	49.8
Veterinary medicine	19.5				
Economics	64.6	56.6		74.3	
Commercial and business administration					64.4
Transport and communications					47.8
Service trade					77.1
Law and public administration	57.3			65.3	33.2
Arts			56.6	42.1	34.8
Humanities		75.5	61.5		65.5
Physical education		35.8			

Sources: Central Statistical Office (1989) (Hun.); Mitter (1991) (all); Pesic (1991) (Yug.); Popescu (1991) (Rom.); World Bank (1991) (all).

formerly female-dominated occupations in growth sectors, and any current advantage women have in their training may quickly diminish.

Government regulations on hiring

In many countries in Eastern Europe, there are legal regulations prohibiting the employment of women in certain jobs on the grounds of health. For example, in Czechoslovakia women are banned from work involving physical strain, noise, vibrations, extreme temperatures, handling of chemical substances that can accumulate in the body, effects of electro-magnetic fields, work underground, ionizing radiation, metal-casting, and activities involving high mental stress. In Poland there are ninety types of jobs in eighteen branches of industry on the list of work banned to women, such as work underground and work demanding great physical effort, including driving tractors. In addition, laws prohibit the employment of pregnant women on night shifts and for overtime work. These regulations may hinder the re-employment of women, since they would allow 'men only' vacancies. However, it also appears that many of these types of regulations affect heavy industry rather than such areas as the service sector, and their impact on women's choice of employment may diminish in the future.

The real and perceived cost of female labour

Fairly extensive maternity and child-care leaves, return rights to employment after these, and company provision of crèches and kindergartens have facilitated the employment of women with small children in most East European countries. For Hungary, Adamik reports that mothers worked on the average 50 per cent of the standard working hours as a result of their legal concessions and leave taken for children's illnesses. The cost of such provisions to the company in terms of direct expenditures, as well as indirect costs of, say, keeping employment open during child-care leaves or work lost to care for sick children, were of minor significance to a state socialist enterprise. In post-reform conditions, however, such costs can no longer be borne by profit-maximizing enterprises, which will contract for the cheapest qualified labour. For women, the development of a government-run social insurance system is therefore one of the priorities on the reform agenda.

Although the child-related costs of female employment must be transferred from the firm to the government, the perception of women as less reliable workers may continue and may influence employers' demand for female labour. Despite their high participation in the labour force, women in Eastern Europe have remained responsible for the overwhelming majority of child care and household work. For example, in Hungary surveys have shown that women are responsible for 75 per cent of domestic labour (Mitter 1991).[4]

This unequal distribution of household obligations between the sexes inevitably has spill-over effects on the labour market. It is argued that women are less able to take employment far from their homes, to do overtime, or to undertake further training, because of housework and child care. They are perceived as unstable employees, who are compelled to take more time off work in order to care for children and, increasingly, elderly parents. Because of the policies of maternity leave, young women are perceived as 'imminent mothers' who are bound to be absent from the work-place for many years while government regulations require the employer to hold the original job open.

With a triple work burden, limited opportunities for promotion or higher income, and decreasing job satisfaction, such an attitude on the part of employers may well have been correct in the years preceding the reform. In a rapidly changing economy, increased unemployment, lower incomes, higher prices, and increased labour mobility by one or both spouses, neither an assured income nor the traditional family model of the two-parent household may continue to apply. A decline in the participation of women in the labour market may be seen as an opportunity for women to be full-time mothers, but few women will now be able to afford to do this. However, unless or until they change, previous attitudes on women's employment can have a tangible effect on the demand for female labour.

Self-employment

Beginning one's own business in the private sector is an alternative to seeking employment. The ease and ability of women to enter into self-employment is an important issue in restructuring, for it may shape the gender profile of a new class of business entrepreneurs in the region. The experience in more developed economies suggests, however, that the self-employed are unlikely to become a large portion of the labour force.

The level of entrepreneurial experience for men and for women is ambiguous. Traditionally, men have dominated in the higher-management levels of the economy, which may enhance their ability to enter new private-sector business, although management skills are not identical to those required to begin a new business. However, women have been competent traders in the second economies of many countries (Mitter 1991).

The evidence on the role that women have played in the new private

---

[4] The distinction between household work and child care may be significant. Fertility levels in Eastern Europe are below replacement level, with less than 2 children per woman. Over a life's work, therefore, child care is likely to take the smaller portion of a woman's non-working time, and housework the major share.

sectors is mixed. A recent survey in Hungary found that 32 per cent of the owners/managers/members of new small enterprises were women (Szalai, n.d.). Female participation in trading was 65 per cent and in new small co-operatives, 43 per cent. Moreover, the women regarded their previous market experience in their household economies or in other private/ semi-private spheres of production as the most decisive factor in their choice of occupation. In another survey in Hungary, in 1988, 36 per cent of men, and only 16 per cent of women expressed the wish to become entrepreneurs (Mitter 1991). In Poland, Kuratowska (1991) reports that, because of the quick process of privatization in trade and the public services, women are often becoming owners/managers of shops, restaurants, and drugstores. It is unlikely, however, that a significant proportion of the labour force will become entrepreneurs. The numbers will be extremely small; in Bulgaria, for example, women were owners of only 1.1 per cent of registered private companies in 1990 (Staikova-Alexandrova 1991).

Measures to aid the development of small private businesses have been introduced in Poland and Hungary and similar policies are proposed in other countries. These include 're-start loans' to the unemployed and other individuals, training and education programmes for small businesses, tax concessions, business premises at advantageous rates, and the creation of business advisory groups. In Poland, at the end of 1990 a very small portion, 2.4 per cent, of the registered unemployed had received loans to start enterprises. Although growth in the private sector in many of the countries has been buoyant, the impact on aggregate employment is very small at this time. Potential entrepreneurs, both male and female, face such difficulties as a serious lack of training in business-related skills, a shortage of business infrastructure such as communications, transport, and buildings, and a severe shortage of credit on affordable terms. As the reform process continues, the role of the private sector will clearly increase, and women's participation therein could grow in importance. This will depend not only on women's initiative and their ability to take risks, but also on their access to formal and informal sources of credit and to small-entrepreneurship training.

THE LABOUR SUPPLY OF WOMEN

Part of the reform packages in Eastern Europe involve the freeing of prices from previous constraints, with the result that prices are expected to rise. In combination with stabilization policies, real wages in the region have fallen; for example, in Poland real earnings fell by approximately 28 per cent in 1990, and in Hungary real wages are back to the level of the early 1970s (Economist Intelligence Unit 1991*b, c*).

The decline in real wages and the consequent need for households to maintain two incomes are expected to exert an extremely strong influence on the continued supply of female labour, despite unemployment benefits, early retirement age, and flexible hours. On the other hand, women in the prime child-bearing ages are especially susceptible to a decline in their incentives to work if provision of child-care facilities is reduced and maternity leave and child-care benefits are increased. In addition, many women may welcome the opportunity to withdraw temporarily from the labour force. These factors are likely to reinforce the second-class position of women in the labour force and to leave them economically vulnerable.

Unemployment benefits

Measures providing for the payment of unemployment compensation to the unemployed have been introduced throughout Eastern Europe. Such measures may affect men and women differently. First, eligibility require-ments may have differing effects on men and women. In most schemes, the unemployed must have a certain period of previous employment to be eligible. This requirement in most cases provides for a number of exceptions, for example on return from maternity leave, care of young children or training, and for individuals entering the labour force after completing their education. In Poland this regulation was not introduced until an amendment to the Employment Law in July 1990, when it became apparent that a proportion of the unemployed consisted of women who had entered the labour force in order to claim benefit without any intention of under-taking employment. This loophole now having been closed, unemployment compensation is likely to have little effect on the labour supply of women.

Second, the level of benefits paid may differ between men and women because of previous earnings. Benefit levels in most countries are currently calculated as a percentage of previous earnings, usually as a declining proportion as the period of unemployment lengthens and with a minimum benefit level. Because of their lower average wage, women receive lower benefit payments. However, the ratio of the previous earnings level to benefits (the replacement ratio), which has been shown to be most important, does not differ for men and women. If flat-rate benefits are introduced, as appears likely, this ratio will be relatively higher for women on average and they may be more willing than men to leave employment.

Maternity and child-care leave and benefits

Families in Eastern Europe have benefited from substantial maternity leave and child-care allowances.[5] While the payment of family allowances for

---

[5] For example, in Hungary 88.9% of those entitled to child-care allowance took it up in 1986 and 62.2% of children aged 0–3 were cared for by mothers on maternity leave or using the child-care grant in 1984 (Szalai, n.d.).

children, unrelated to the mother's employment position, will not have a major effect on the participation rate of women, the provision of paid or unpaid maternity leave or leave to care for children will affect the role of women in the labour market. It should be noted that, where either parent is entitled to such leave, it is extremely rare for men to leave employment for this reason.

Two major concerns have been expressed about the future of maternity and child-care leave. First, tight budget constraints may force governments to reduce their expenditure on maternity and child-care leave by cutting benefit levels and the period of entitlement. Such developments would encourage women to shorten their leave and increase the effective supply of labour. Second, because those on leave are considered still employed, they represent a form of 'hidden employment'. Encouraging women to take longer periods of leave by providing higher benefits or longer periods of entitlement would reduce the labour force and the number of formally unemployed.

Recent developments suggest that the second concern may be of greater significance. In Czechoslovakia, the Parental Allowance (Maternity Allowance until October 1990) is a flat-rate benefit paid to non-working parents caring for one or more children under the age of 3. As of October 1990, the benefit level was increased, eligibility was broadened from the mother to both parents, and the length of receipt was lengthened from one year to three in the case of one child. It is estimated that these improvements will increase the number of beneficiaries from 270,000 in 1989 to 320,000 in 1990 (Holzmann 1991). In Romania maternity leave has been extended from sixteen weeks to the whole first year of the child's life at 65 per cent of the previous wage. In Albania, Tarifa (1991) reports increasing political pressure for an extension of the period of maternity leave.

Provision of child-care facilities

Extensive child-care facilities operated by the state or enterprises at a low cost to parents have been developed in many East European countries because of the need to increase female labour-force participation. Their importance in enabling women to undertake full-time employment can be demonstrated by the enrolment rates. For example, in Hungary, in spite of the existence of the child-care allowance (paid maternity leave), 12 per cent of children under the age of 3 attended crèches and 90 per cent of children aged 3–6 attended kindergarten in 1988. In Romania, in 1989 about 31 per cent of children were enrolled in crèches and kindergartens. For Albania, Tarifa (1991) reports from survey data that 97 per cent of urban families and 50 per cent of rural families send their children to kindergartens.

Recent developments suggest that the provision of child-care facilities may not continue on a similar scale in the future, although evidence is very sparse.

For example, Adamik (1989) reports that more and more child-care institutions are being closed down in Hungary in response to preference for other solutions such as the child-care allowances and mothers giving up work. Lado (1991) reports that firm kindergartens are being closed because of the financial difficulties of the companies and constraints of the state budget for the state-run kindergartens. In Poland, Popowicz and Budziszewska (1991) report a falling number of children attending kindergartens because of rising fees and the closing of a number of kindergartens in 1990 and 1991. In addition, private child-care facilities in Eastern Europe, which are expensive and not yet well developed, provide only very limited solutions.

Old-age pensions

Sex differences in retirement age and the level of old-age pension will influence the relative participation rates in the labour force of the older cohorts of men and women. In Eastern Europe, the standard retirement age is 60 years for men and 55 years for women except for Poland, where men can retire at 65 and women at 60. Eligibility depends upon a minimum employment record of twenty to twenty-five years in different countries.

The effect of old-age pensions on labour supply does not have a clear-cut differential by sex. The younger retirement age for women obviously creates incentives for women to leave the labour force earlier than men; for example, 293,000 women in Hungary are potentially affected by the earlier retirement age at the current time (World Bank 1991c). However, because pension levels are a function of past earnings, women, on average, receive lower pension payments than men, which may make them less likely to retire than men. For example, in Czechoslovakia, survey data indicate that, even after reaching pensionable age, 58.7 per cent of women aged 55–59 remained economically active (Venerova 1991). The economic strain on many households in the course of the transition is likely to intensify this effect, and to increase the supply of workers by keeping older women workers in the labour force.

Flexible work hours and attitudes towards work

Under central planning labour markets were rigid, offering little flexibility in work hours and little opportunity to work part-time. This arose from the high demand for labour and the need for a full-time income to maintain household living standards. Opportunities for part-time work and other flexible employment options are now becoming more widespread, enhancing the ability of women to devote more time to domestic responsibilities and less to formal full-time employment.

In Czechoslovakia, until the reform period, uniform rules regulated the length of the working week and little use was made of regulations for women with children to work shorter hours. In 1986 only 7.6 per cent of female workers worked part-time, but this proportion had risen to 11.6 per cent in 1989. In Hungary the use of part-time work is increasing in the small-firm sector in particular. In Yugoslavia the possibilities for part-time work and fixed-term employment were increased in the 1988 Enterprise Law and the 1989 Labour Code (World Bank 1991i).

The opportunity for working flexible or shorter hours will encourage some women to remain in the labour force, but it will also allow some women currently working full-time to reduce their hours. Overall, which effect will be greater will depend also on other factors, such as the need for income. However, part-time employment frequently involves less skilled work and lower hierarchical positions, and part-time employees constitute one of the weaker groups in the labour market, with lower pay and lower pensions, and often are the first to be made redundant during recessions. A large-scale transfer to part-time employment, though attractive to women from the point of view of caring for the household, runs the risk of leaving substantial numbers of women in a much weakened position in the labour market, in the longer as well as in the shorter term.

Attitudes to work

The effect of reform on women's choices is unclear. The tenor of the emerging debate suggests that many women would accept unemployment for the time being, looking forward to the opportunity to be able to spend more time with their children or attend to domestic responsibilities. Staying at home is becoming 'fashionable', as women seek greater involvement in raising their children. However, a number of opinion polls suggest that the preference of women would be to continue to work if given the choice. For example, in 1986 in Hungary, 77 per cent of women questioned thought that they would keep their jobs even if they were in a position to stay at home, although the majority also expressed a preference to be able to work part-time or at home. About a third were in favour of work for material reasons, while the remainder justified their choice for reasons of interest in their work or to participate in the community (Central Statistical Office 1989). In the case of Bulgaria, only 20 per cent of working women showed an inclination to stay at home according to a study carried out in February 1991 (Staikova-Alexandrova 1991).

CONCLUSIONS

One of the objectives of the reform programmes in Eastern Europe is to reduce the role of government in the economy. Government involvement affecting the role of women in employment has been a source of inefficiency through gender-based regulations on employment, restrictions on the terms of employment, and gender differences in the effects of government social programmes in the labour market. The reduction of government involvement in these areas would enhance efficiency and the employment opportunities for women.

However, there are cases in market economies when government action is the optimal policy, and it is particularly important that the reform programmes recognize these areas when the role of government is being reduced. A major area where it is efficient for the government to play an active role is in the case of incomplete markets. Insufficient provision of child-care facilities in Eastern Europe and the lack of a well-developed service sector reduces the ability of women to participate in the labour force; government provision of such services, at least until they develop more fully in the private sector, would provide greater choice for women and enhance the availability of female labour resources. A second area is the lack of information about the value of women as employees. Government policy can promote an improved understanding and greater use of the potential female labour force by providing information on the skills that women have to offer, by reducing unjustified perceptions that women have less value as employees, and by encouraging women to take advantage of their talents through such measures as retraining and employment services.

Removal of current protective legislation on the employment of women

The analysis has highlighted a number of areas where pro-active measures may be desirable to support the position of women in the labour market during the period of transition. Some are specifically aimed at mitigating the potential adverse consequences of the reforms for women, while others seek to ensure that the female labour force is employed to its full potential in the longer term. One measure is to remove current regulations on employment for women, including restrictions on night-shift, overtime work, or work with health risks. Protective legislation should be extended to all workers, and not be limited to women.

Government programmes in the labour market

Another pro-active measure concerns government programmes in the labour market. The employment services providing job information, job search facilities, and career counselling should be developed to meet the particular needs of women, especially older women with poorer skill and education levels and women re-entering the labour force following maternity or child-care leave.

Flexible training programmes should be designed to meet the special training needs of women and the time constraints they face. Training strategies should apply to employer-provided training as well as to government-sponsored training, and women should be encouraged to participate in in-plant programmes, vocational, apprenticeship, and technical and managerial training schemes. Child care at reasonable cost and other supportive services, including transportation, necessary for women to take advantage of training opportunities should be provided.

Specialized counselling services, training, and credit facilities should be provided to enhance women's potential as entrepreneurs.

Part-time and informal sector work

In summary, governments should be encouraged to seek to ensure that, not only do women have equal access to these programmes, but their particular needs as a group are recognized and policies are designed to meet these needs. As a result, the ability of unemployed women to attain new work or to become self-employed could be greatly increased.

The structure of cash benefits should not discriminate between men and women. The earlier retirement age for women clearly reduced the incentive for older women to participate in the labour force, and retirement ages for men and women should be the same. The discussion has shown that women may be more likely than men to take advantage of the increasing opportunities to work shorter hours and the system of benefits and contributions should not discriminate against part-time work; for example, contributions should rise as smoothly as possible with individual earnings. Finally, it is likely that an informal sector will develop in the East European economies and women may be particularly attracted to this type of employment. It is important to ensure that the right to social benefits providing protection against poverty should be attached to the individual and not to a record of formal employment. Overall, these policies aim to provide women with equal rights to social benefits without distorting their incentive to work.

Child care

The analysis in the section 'Labour Demand for Women' shows that the ability of women to undertake employment in the future may be inhibited by the closing of state and enterprise child-care facilities, while private-sector alternatives are insufficiently provided and are too expensive for the average household. In addition, the discussion on the labour demand side indicates that employers cannot be expected to provide costly child-care facilities for their employees under the reform programme. The costs of raising children,

either in the form of reduced employment opportunities or in the direct cost
of private child care, should not be borne by households with children alone,
however. Therefore, governments need to provide good-quality child-care
facilities on a non-profit basis or should subsidize private provision. This will
involve the continuance of current state-run facilities and the transfer of
enterprise-run facilities either to state management or into the private sector.
The purpose of such measures is to remove any disincentive for employers
to employ women because of associated child-care costs and to ensure that
child-care costs do not prohibit women with children from participating in
the labour force.

Educational campaigns

The position of women in employment in Eastern Europe is partly a result
of certain cultural traditions and perceptions which have reduced the role
that women are able to play in the labour force. Two such areas have been
identified in this chapter. First, the division of domestic responsibilities
places a greater share of the burden of household chores and child care
on women than on men, diminishing the perceived value of women as
employees. Second, the educational choices of women and the occupational
segregation by sex reflects the stereotyping of particular types of employment
into 'male' and 'female' areas, narrowing the desirable options for both men
and women. Finally, the issue of women in employment has not been a
subject of discussion in Eastern Europe because of the view that high labour-
force participation rates for women and equal educational qualifications
demonstrates that equality has been achieved. This lack of discussion has
resulted in little recognition of the problems that women face in the labour
market, and solutions have not been developed.

The first two problems should be addressed through educational campaigns,
conducted either by governments or by women's groups within the countries.
Occupational-segregation career counselling should encourage women to
consider occupations that have traditionally been male-dominated. More
generally, the educational system and mass media campaigns should be used
to eliminate gender stereotypes and to attract public attention to the issues
of equality between men and women. Publicity should also be given to
measures designed to promote equality.

The lack of awareness should be addressed through the collection and
publication of information concerning the role of women either by women's
groups or by such international organizations as the World Bank, with the
aid of government data. The development of labour-force statistics collection
systems by the governments in Eastern Europe should provide data on
employment and unemployment disaggregated by sex and facilitate the
analysis of the changing role of women in employment in the region. In

addition, movements by sex in educational and skill specialization and relevant policy developments, such as those concerning child-care provision and maternity leave, should be monitored and published.

REFERENCES

ABRAHAM, KATHARINE, and VODOPIVEC, MILAN (1991), *Labor Market Dynamics during the Transition of a Socialist Economy* (Research Proposal). Washington, DC: World Bank (June).

ADAMIK, MARIA (1989), 'Women and Welfare State in Hungary' (ELITE University, Hungary), mimeo, World Bank.

Albania Statistical Book (1990), Tiranë.

BARR, NICHOLAS (1991), 'Consistency of Policy Advice on Cash Benefits', World Bank Office Memorandum, EM4HR (April).

BOUSE, VLADIMIR (1991), 'The Restructuring of Labour Markets in Czechoslovakia', mimeo, World Bank (March).

CELAC, MARIANA (1991) 'Romania', Regional Seminar, Vienna (April).

Central Statistical Office (GUS) (1989), *Women in Present-Day Hungarian Society.* Budapest: GUS.

—— (1991), *Statistical Bulletin.* Budapest: GUS.

CORICELLI, FABRIZIO, and REVENGA, ANA (1991), *Wages and Unemployment in Poland: Recent Developments and Policy Issues.* Washington, DC: World Bank.

DRAKULIĆ, SLAVENKA (1991), 'Women and the New Democracy in Yugoslavia', Regional Seminar, Vienna (April).

Economist Intelligence Unit. (1991*a*), *Czechoslovakia Country Report,* no. 2.

—— (1991*b*), *Hungary Country Report,* no. 2.

—— (1991*c*), *Poland Country Report,* no. 1.

—— (1991*d*), *Romania Country Report,* no. 1.

—— (1991*e*), *Yugoslavia Country Report,* no. 1.

ERNST & YOUNG (1991), 'Women in the Newly Emerging Democracies of Eastern Europe: Phase I', draft report prepared for the US Agency for International Development (May).

FRETWELL, DAVID, LOVELL, MALCOLM, and BEDNARZIK, ROBERT (1991), *Employment Dimensions of Economic Restructuring: A Review of Related Labor Policies and Programs in Industrialized Countries.* Washington, DC: World Bank (April).

GORA, MAREK, KOTOWSKA, IRENA, PANEK, TOMASZ, and PODGORSKI, JAROSLAV (1991), 'Labour Market Industrial Relations and Social Policy: A Report on Poland' (Warsaw School of Economics and London School of Economics), mimeo, World Bank.

HAGEMANN-WHITE, CAROL (1989), *Perspectives and Pitfalls in Improving the Qualification of the Female Labour Force.* Paris: OECD (October).

HOLZMANN, ROBERT (1991), *CSFR: Cash Benefits During Economic Transition— Background and Strategies for Reform.* Washington, DC: World Bank (March).

HUNGARIAN OBSERVER (1991), 'Unprepared for Unemployment', *Hungarian Observer,* 4/1991: 2–5.

International Labour Office (1990), *Yearbook of Labour Statistics, 1989–90*. Geneva: ILO.

—— (1991), *Bulletin of Labour Statistics, 1991*, nos. 1 and 2.

KURATOWSKA, ZOFIA (1991), 'Present Situation of Women in Poland', Regional Seminar, Vienna (April).

KWIATKOWSKI, EUGENIUSZ (1991), *Polish Unemployment During Economic Transition: Background, Tendencies and Interpretations*. University of Lodz, Poland (May).

LADO, MARIA (1991), 'Women in the Transition to a Market Economy: The Case of Hungary', Regional Seminar, Vienna (April).

LAMPLAND, MARTHA (1989), 'Biographies of Liberation: Testimonials to Labor in Socialist Hungary', in S. Roueks, R. Rapp, and M. Young (eds.), 'Promissory Notes', mimeo, World Bank.

LEHMANN, HARTMUT (1991), 'Economies in Transition, Unemployment and the Role of Labour Market Policies: The Case of Poland' (London School of Economics), mimeo, World Bank (May).

MITTER, SWASTI (1991), 'A Comparative Analysis of Women's Industrial Participation during the Transition from Centrally-Planned to Market Economies in East Central Europe', Regional Seminar, Vienna (April) (see United Nations Office at Vienna).

MOSER, CAROLINE (1991), 'Urban Poverty and Social Policy in the Context of Adjustment', Research Proposal, Urban Development Division, Infrastructure and Urban Department, World Bank (July).

NAGY, GYULA, and SZIRACZKI, GYORGY (1991), 'Labour Markets in Transition: Employment, Lay-Offs, Unemployment and Policy Responses in Hungary', mimeo, World Bank.

OECD. (1990), *Employment Outlook*. Paris: OECD.

O'FARRELL, BRIGID (1989), *Combining Work and Family Care: Employer Initiatives*. Paris: OECD.

OKRUHLICOVA, ANNA (1991), 'The Influence of Social and Economic Changes in the Czech and Slovak Federal Republic on the Position of Women', Regional Seminar, Vienna (April).

PASCOE, K. M. (n.d.), *World Bank: Structural Adjustment Loan Social Safety Net: Paper on Employment Services*. London: British Employment Service.

PESIC, VESNA (1991), 'The Impact of Reforms on the Status of Women in Yugoslavia', Regional Seminar, Vienna (April).

POPESCU, DUMITRA (1991), 'Present Situation and Trends Affecting Women in Romania', Regional Seminar, Vienna (April).

POPOWICZ, ANNA, and BUDZISZEWSKA, GRAZYNA (1991), Inter-Regional Meeting on Economic Distress, Structural Adjustment and Women, Office of the Plenipotentiary of the Government of the Republic of Poland for Women and Family Affairs, London, June 1991.

RIVEROS, LUIS A. (1991), *Wage and Employment Reforms in Czechoslovakia: A Policy Analysis*. Washington, DC: World Bank (April).

RUTKOWSKI, M. (1991) 'Is the Labour Market Adjustment in Poland Surprising?' *Review of Labour Economics and Industrial Relations*, 5 (3): 79–104.

SOPNIEWSKA, HALINA (n.d.), 'Some Economic Problems of Unemployment in

Poland in the Period of Transition towards Market Economy', mimeo, World Bank.

STAIKOVA-ALEXANDROVA, RAIA (1991), 'The Present Situation of the Women in Bulgaria', Regional Seminar, Vienna (April).

SZALAI, JULIA (n.d.), 'Some Aspects of the Changing Situation of Women in Hungary in the Process of Transition', mimeo, World Bank.

TARIFA, FATOS (1991), 'Albanian Women in a New Social Context', Regional Seminar, Vienna (April).

THOMPSON, ALAN (1991), *The Czechoslovakian Social Safety Net Benefit Provision*. Washington, DC: World Bank (January).

UNESCO (1990), *Statistical Yearbook, 1990*. Paris: UNESCO.

UN Office at Vienna, Division for the Advancement of Women (1991*a*), *Report* of Regional Seminar on the Impact of Economic and Political Reform on the Status of Women in Eastern Europe and the USSR: The Role of National Machinery, Vienna (8–12 April).

—— (1991*b*), 'Women's Role in Making Reform Work', Regional Seminar, Vienna (April).

VENEROVA, LUDMILA (1991), 'Brief Survey of the Situation of Czechoslovakian Women at the Beginning of the Transitional Period from Centrally-Planned to Market Economy', Regional Seminar, Vienna (April).

World Bank. (1991*a*), *Bulgaria: Crisis and Transition to a Market Economy*, no. 9046-BUL. Washington, DC: World Bank (January).

—— (1991*b*), *Hungary: The Transition to a Market Economy: Critical Human Resources Issue*, no. 8665-HU. Washington, DC: World Bank (April).

—— (1991*c*), *Staff Appraisal Report: Hungary Human Resources Project*, no. 9183-HU. Washington, DC: World Bank (March).

—— (1991*d*), *Staff Appraisal Report: Poland Employment Promotion and Services Project*, no. 9408-POL. Washington, DC: World Bank (May).

—— (1991*e*), *Poland: Income Support and the Social Safety Net: Policies for the Transition.* Washington, DC: World Bank (June).

—— (1991*f*), *Labor Markets in Bulgaria: Policies, Institutions and Results*. Washington, DC: World Bank.

—— (1991*g*), *Romania: Accelerating the Transition: Human Resource Strategies for the 1990s*, no. 9577-RO. Washington, DC: World Bank (May).

—— (1991*h*), *Social Sector Statistics for Central European Countries* (Data on Disk Files). Washington, DC: World Bank.

—— (1991*i*), *Yugoslavia: The Labor Market and the System of Cash Benefits*, no. 9607-YU. Washington, DC: World Bank (May).

11

The Changing Economic Status of Women in the Period of Transition to a Market Economy System: The Case of the Czech and Slovak Republics after 1989

Liba Paukert

INTRODUCTION

The integration of women in the economy was one of the characteristic features of the centrally planned economic system that prevailed in Central and Eastern Europe during the past four decades. The transition to a market economy system, embarked upon in all the countries of the region recently, is bound to cause profound changes in the employment structure and in labour market conditions. The question arises as to how these changes may affect the vulnerable groups of workers such as women, young people, older workers, the handicapped, and the ethnic minorities. Women in particular might have to bear a disproportionate share of the burden of economic reform in terms of a decline in employment and loss of income, and their hard-won economic status might deteriorate. Although in the long run they should have a great deal to win under the new system in terms of free choice of occupation, free choice of education and training, greater flexibility of working time, access to entrepreneurial status, and (ultimately) rising income and living standards, they might also lose—mainly in the short run—by becoming massively unemployed during the restructuring period. For many of them, this unemployment spell might lead to discouragement and to a final departure from the labour force. The degree to which female labour will be affected by the reforms is related to the former employment structure and to the size of the shifts in female labour caused by the newly developing market pressures. It will also depend on the depth and duration of the transition-related crisis and on the rapidity with which the current depression can be overcome. This in turn is at least partly related to international aid and to the inflow of foreign investment.

The impact of reform on employment, and especially on women's employment, differs from country to country, particularly because reform measures started to be applied at different points of time and their intensity and content have been different. In some countries women have been less affected by the reform than men. In Hungary, for example, women's unemployment rates have been lower than men's and women have been under-represented in unemployment in all occupational groups (see Lado *et al.* 1991). In most

TABLE 11.1 Unemployment rates by sex and region, Czech and Slovak Federal Republics, 30 June 1991–31 May 1992 (%)

	Total				Male				Female			
	30.06 1991	31.12 1991	31.01 1992	31.05 1992	30.06 1991	31.12 1991	31.01 1992	31.05 1992	30.06 1991	31.12 1991	31.01 1992	31.05 1992
CSFR	3.8	6.6	7.1	5.6	3.6	5.9	6.7	5.3	4.0	7.3	7.5	5.9
Czech Republic	2.6	4.1	4.4	2.8	2.4	3.5	3.9	2.4	2.8	4.8	4.9	3.3
Prague	1.4	1.2	1.1	0.4	1.2	0.9			1.6	1.4		
Central Czech Region	2.6	4.0	4.3	3.0	2.1	3.0			3.1	5.2		
Southern Czech Region	2.7	4.2	4.5	2.6	2.3	3.5			3.1	4.9		
Western Czech Region	1.9	2.8	3.0	2.0	1.6	2.2			2.2	3.5		
Northern Czech Region	2.5	4.2	4.5	3.2	2.5	3.5			2.5	4.8		
Eastern Czech Region	2.2	4.1	4.4	2.6	2.0	3.6			2.5	4.7		
Southern Moravian Region	2.9	4.8	5.1	3.4	2.8	4.2			3.0	5.2		
Northern Moravian Region	3.7	6.2	6.6	4.4	3.2	5.2			4.2	7.3		
Slovak Republic	6.3	11.8	12.7	11.3	6.1	11.0	12.6	11.2	6.5	12.6	12.8	11.4
Bratislava	3.4	6.5	7.3	6.7	2.9	5.3			3.9	7.8		
Western Slovak Region	6.8	13.3	14.3	12.5	6.2	12.2			7.5	14.5		
Central Slovak Region	6.2	11.8	12.5	10.8	6.0	10.7			6.4	12.8		
Eastern Slovak Region	7.1	12.5	13.6	12.5	7.5	12.3			6.7	10.3		

Source: direct communications of the Ministry of Labour and Social Affairs, Prague; Federal Statistical Office, *Statisticke Predhledy*, various issues, Prague.

TABLE 11.2 Unemployment numbers and unfilled vacancies, Czech and Slovak Federal Republic, by sex and region, 31 May 1991–31 May 1992

	No. of unemployed			Unfilled vacancies	Unemployment–vacancy ratios
	Total	Men	Women		
31 May 1991					
CSFR	255,635	128,981	126,654	43,386	5.9
Czech Republic	118,280	58,426	59,854	37,129	3.2
Prague	9,724	5,299	4,425	6,539	1.5
Central Czech Region	11,281	4,816	6,465	3,981	2.8
Southern Czech Region	7,960	3,748	4,212	1,950	4.1
Western Czech Region	7,160	3,136	4,024	3,923	1.8
Northern Czech Region	13,481	7,254	6,227	4,740	2.8
Eastern Czech Region	12,410	6,114	6,296	3,603	3.4
Southern Moravian Region	24,678	13,096	11,582	5,278	4.7
Northern Moravian Region	31,586	14,963	16,623	7,115	4.4
Slovak Republic	137,365	70,555	66,800	6,257	22.0
Bratislava	8,727	3.771	4,956	520	16.8
Western Slovak Region	43,955	22,283	21,672	1,544	47.9
Central Slovak Region	40,063	20,331	19,732	2,133	18.8
Eastern Slovak Region	44,610	24,170	20,440	2,060	21.7
31 December 1991					
CSFR	523,700	239,421	284,279	56,603	9.3
Czech Republic	221,749	94,553	127,196	48,402	4.6
Prague	8,325	3,191	5,134	11,141	0.7
Central Czech Region	21,248	8,035	13,213	5,713	3.7
Southern Czech Region	15,066	6,370	8,696	2,353	6.4
Western Czech Region	12,662	4,921	7,741	4,996	2.5
Northern Czech Region	25,701	10,755	14,946	6,212	4.1
Eastern Czech Region	26,965	11,795	15,170	4,824	5.6
Southern Moravian Region	49,518	22,377	27,141	5,560	8.9
Northern Moravian Region	62,264	27,109	35,155	7,603	8.2
Slovak Republic	301,951	144,868	157,083	8,201	36.8
Bratislava	19,512	7,978	11,534	2,273	8.6
Western Slovak Region	102,494	49,083	53,411	1,883	54.4
Central Slovak Region	92,656	43,304	49,352	1,808	51.2
Eastern Slovak Region	87,289	44,503	42,786	2,237	39.0
31 May 1992					
CSFR	433,026	207,646	225,380	90,839	4.8
Czech Republic	149,665	64,828	84,837	78,306	1.9
Prague	2,935	1,139	1,796	17,804	0.2
Central Czech Region	15,350	5,582	9,768	8,844	1.7
Southern Czech Region	8,907	3,640	5,267	4,914	1.8
Western Czech Region	8,662	3,566	5,096	8,211	1.1
Northern Czech Region	19,307	8,426	10,881	9,818	2.0
Eastern Czech Region	16,751	7,185	9,566	9,715	1.7
Southern Moravian Region	34,450	16,239	18,211	8,638	4.0
Northern Moravian Region	43,303	19,051	24,252	10,362	4.2
Slovak Republic	283,361	142,818	140,543	12,533	22.6
Bratislava	19,170	8,518	10,652	3,752	5.1

TABLE 11.2 Continued

	No. of unemployed			Unfilled vacancies	Unemployment– vacancy ratios
	Total	Men	Women		
Western Slovak Region	94,121	46,267	47,854	2,320	40.6
Central Slovak Region	83,382	41,752	41,630	2,786	29.9
Eastern Slovak Region	86,688	46,281	40,407	3,675	23.6

Source: data made available by the Federal Ministry of Labour and Social Affairs, Prague.

other countries of the East European region, on the contrary, the current restructuring has affected women more than men.

The Czech and Slovak Republics represent cases where women have been more adversely affected by the economic reform than men. When monthly data on unemployment rates started to be published in a gender breakdown, it soon became apparent that women's unemployment was growing faster than that of men. By summer 1991, women's unemployment rates exceeded male rates practically in all the regions of the country, and they have continued to be systematically higher since then (see Table 11.1). Given the high female participation rates, women's unemployment has been greater

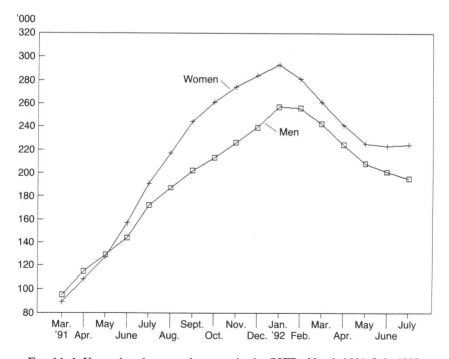

FIG 11.1 Unemployed men and women in the CSFR, March 1991–July 1992

than men's in absolute numbers, as illustrated in Table 11.2 and in Fig. 11.1. Country-wide, women represented 53 per cent of the unemployed: 58 per cent in the Czech Republic and 51 per cent in the Slovak Republic (data for end-July 1992).

In comparison with a number of OECD countries, women's unemployment rate is relatively low and the gap between the male and female rate is small. The unemployment rates for men and women in the Czech and Slovak Federal Republic as a whole correspond roughly to those of their neighbours, Austria and Germany. In the Czech Republic, however, the unemployment rates are similar to those in Switzerland, a country with a long-established record of low unemployment levels, whereas in the Slovak Republic they are nearer to those in Belgium or France.[1] The relatively narrow gap between the male and female unemployment rates in both the Czech and Slovak Republics is related to the fact that unemployment has started to grow only recently. As time goes on, however, the duration of female unemployment may be expected to increase, because unemployed women usually find it more difficult to get rehired than unemployed men, and the gap between male and female unemployment is likely to widen.

Women's unemployment represents a real social problem in the Czech and Slovak Federal Republic (CSFR), particularly in the Slovak Republic, because women's earnings are needed in addition to men's 'to feed the family'. This is due to the considerably lower average per capita income and to the higher share of food and other essentials in the average household expenditure in Czechoslovakia than in the industrial market economy countries. The structure of earnings that has developed during the past forty years is such that the average two-parent family needs two incomes in order to afford an 'average' pattern of consumption. In addition, an important proportion of women workers are heads of household as a result of the relatively high divorce rate. In their case, loss of employment creates a particularly serious problem.

The growth of unemployment, and particularly of female unemployment, observed after 1989 has been related to past developments and to the accumulation of structural problems resulting from the misallocation of resources, including labour resources, under the former command system. In order to analyse the present employment difficulties, it is necessary to provide a certain amount of background information on the labour structure and trends and on the role of women in the economy before 1989. This will be done in the first section of this chapter. The second section will be devoted to the analysis of women workers' situation, their attitudes to labour market involvement, and their prospects of finding employment in the newly developing private business sector.

[1] See ILO, *Bulletin of Labour Statistics* (various issues), Geneva.

This chapter contains some previously unpublished data on male and female employment and earnings which have become available in the CSFR since 1989, particularly the results of the earnings survey carried out in 1988.[2] It also uses the preliminary results of the Population Census of 3 March 1991. For this reason it contains a fairly large number of statistical tables, which can be of value to those interested in Eastern and Central European labour issues. The chapter also incorporates the main results of a survey on 'Women in the Labour Market' commissioned by the ILO from the Public Opinion Research Institute in Prague,[3] in the framework of the multi–bilateral technical co-operation project undertaken by the ILO on 'Women in the Labour Market in the CSFR' during the transition period to a market economy system, funded by the governments of the Netherlands and the United Kingdom.

THE TRENDS AND STRUCTURE OF EMPLOYMENT AND THE ROLE OF WOMEN IN THE CZECH ECONOMY, 1948–1991

Women's labour-force participation

During the four decades of central planning, women made a very significant contribution to economic development in Czechoslovakia. Their weight in the labour force increased spectacularly, both in quantitative and in qualitative terms. While in 1947 women represented 35 per cent of the labour force, and only 27 per cent of the non-agricultural labour force, the 1991 Population Census shows their share in the work-force to be 47 per cent, i.e. almost half

[2] The Special Sample Survey on earnings of the work-force in June 1988, carried out under the auspices of the Federal Ministry of Labour and Social Affairs in Prague, covered a sample of 768,700 workers and employees, corresponding to 12.4% of the labour force. It was carried out in 723 selected enterprises and organizations belonging to 38 sectors of activity (industries) in the Czech and Slovak Republics. The basic questionnaire included 56 items, ranging from personal data to the detailed structure of earnings, leave, taxes, etc. A considerable proportion (but not all) of the results have been published in a gender breakdown.

[3] The survey on 'Women in the Labour Market', commissioned by the ILO from the Public Opinion Research Institute (a subsidiary of the Federal Statistical Office) in Prague, was fielded first in February 1991 and a second round took place in February 1992. The final results became available in summer 1992. The survey enquired about women's attitudes to, and experience of, employment, unemployment, retraining, and the switch to a small private business activity. Concerning the method of the survey, two sets of questionnaires of about 120 items each, one for women and one for men, were prepared and used for personal interviews with a stratified sample of 2,050 women and a control group of 820 men. The survey covered the whole country and the questionnaires were issued in Czech, Slovak, and Hungarian. The second round of the survey provided a useful complement to information on the impact of the current policies and of the present economic and social developments on women's employment and attitudes to paid employment and to small private business, as well as on their involvement and success in the latter type of activities, following, in particular, the training programme carried out in the framework of the ILO technical co-operation project on 'Women in the Labour Market in the CSFR'.

TABLE 11.3 Women workers as a percentage of the total labour force, Czech and
Slovak Federal Republic, 1961–1991

Date of Population Census	CSFR	Czech Republic	Slovak Republic
1 March 1961	40.8	43.0	35.0
1 December 1970	44.6	45.9	41.3
1 November 1980	46.7	47.2	45.5
3 March 1991	47.0	47.1	46.8

Note: Includes women on regular maternity leave (6 months) and on extended maternity leave
(until the child's third birthday).

Source: *Scitani lidu, domu a bytu, 3.3.1991, Predbezné vysledky* (Census of Population, Housing
and Dwellings, 3 March 1991, Preliminary Results), Federal Statistical Office, Prague, June
1991.

(see Table 11.3), most of whom (90 per cent) are employed outside of
agriculture. If we compare these data with information available for OECD
countries during roughly the same period, we notice a generally lower share
of women in employment in the OECD area, but a slightly faster increase
of the share in terms of percentage points (see Table 11.4). In the OECD
countries, the massive influx of women into the labour force has been
considered as one of the salient features of labour market developments in
the last few decades. But it progressed more gradually than in Czechoslovakia
and the other East European countries, where a strong effort at integrating
women in the economy was made, particularly during the 1950s and the
1960s. The fast growth of female labour that occurred in Czechoslovakia in
the 1950s was associated with the strong industrialization drive that started
with the first Five-Year-Plan (1949–53). Women contributed well over half
of the employment increase required by the ambitious plan targets. While
in the OECD countries during the 1950s the increase in female labour
represented less than half of the total labour-force increment, in Czechoslovakia
women's contribution to the growth of the labour force amounted to 61 per
cent. A similar pattern could be observed also in the 1960s (see Table 11.5).
During the 1970s, a high growth of female labour took place both in
Czechoslovakia and in the OECD countries, where female labour continued
to grow during the recession period while male labour stagnated, particularly
in OECD Europe. In the 1980s however, the trends changed. The OECD
labour force continued to increase, women contributing 80 per cent of the
increment. In Czechoslovakia, on the other hand, the labour force (mainly
the male labour force but also the female) declined. As a result of these
developments, the gap between the female labour-force share in Czechoslovakia
and in the Western countries tended to close.

   The decline in the Czech and Slovak labour forces that occurred in the last
inter-censal period (see Tables 11.6 and 11.7) was not due to demographic
factors, i.e. to smaller age cohorts reaching the working age: on the contrary,

TABLE 11.4 Women workers as a percentage of the total labour force, OECD and Czechoslovakia, 1950–1991

	Total OECD	Czechoslovakia
1950	31.4	38.6
1980	38.7	46.7
1990	41.6[a]	47.0[b]
1950–90: difference in percentage points	10.2	8.4

[a] 1989.   [b] 1991.
Sources: as Table 11.2; OECD Labour Force Statistics, Paris; OECD Demographic Trends 1950–1990, Paris, 1979; OECD Economic Outlook: Historical Statistics, 1960–1989, Paris, 1991.

TABLE 11.5 Percentage changes in female labour and women's contribution to changes in the total labour force, OECD Europe and CSFR, 1950–1991

	1950–60		1960–70		1970–80		1980–90	
	A	B	A	B	A	B	A	B
OECD Europe	11.9	47.7	7.4	50.4	19.4[a]	96.4[a]	16.4[b]	79.9[b]
CSFR	17.1[c]	61.2[c]	18.4[d]	89.2[d]	17.7	63.6	–0.5[e]	–22.0[e]

A: percentage change in female labour force.
B: percentage contribution of women to total labour force change.
[a] 1970–81.
[b] 1981–89.
[c] 1950–61.
[d] 1961–70.
[e] 1980–91.
Sources: as Table 11.4.

the working-age population increased as a result of the post-1968 'baby boom'. But activity rates, which had been steadily increasing since 1950, went down (Table 11.6). The data on population and labour-force changes in Table 11.7 imply in fact quite a significant decline in male and female labour force for the population of working age (men aged 15–59 and women aged 15–54).

Detailed information on the decline in labour-force participation by age is lacking so far, as the preliminary results of 1991 Population Census do not provide an age breakdown for the labour force. It is generally assumed, however, that the decline in labour-force participation was due largely to a reduction in economic activity of post-retirement-age citizens and of young people who tended to stay longer in the educational system. It is not clear precisely when the decline in labour-force participation started, but a fall in the absolute numbers of labour was reported in 1989. Thus, the decline in labour-force participation started before the end-1989 change in the economic

TABLE 11.6 Population, labour force, and crude activity rates in the CSFR, 1950–1991

	Population ('000)			Labour force ('000)			Crude activity rates (%)		
	Total	Men	Women	Total	Men	Women	Total	Men	Women
Czech and Slovak Federal Republic									
1 March 1950	12,339	5,997	6,342	5,812	3,568	2,244	47.1	59.5	35.4
1 March 1961	13,746	6,705	7,041	6,439	3,811	2,628	46.8	56.8	37.3
1 December 1970	14,345	6,989	7,356	6,983	3,870	3,113	48.7	55.4	42.3
1 November 1980	15,283	7,441	7,842	7,849	4,185	3,664	51.4	56.2	46.7
3 March 1991	15,568	7,581	7,987	7,759	4,115	3,644	49.8	54.3	45.6
Czech Republic									
1 March 1961	9,572	4,641	4,931	4,695	2,677	2,018	49.0	57.7	40.9
1 December 1970	9,808	4,750	5,058	4,984	2,696	2,288	50.8	56.8	45.2
1 November 1980	10,292	4,988	5,304	5,364	2,830	2,534	52.1	56.7	47.8
3 March 1991	10,299	5,005	5,294	5,240	2,774	2,466	50.9	55.4	46.6
Slovak Republic									
1 March 1961	4,174	2,064	2,110	1,744	1,134	610	41.8	54.9	28.9
1 December 1970	4,537	2,239	2,298	1,999	1,174	825	44.1	52.4	35.9
1 November 1980	4,992	2,453	2,538	2,485	1,355	1,130	49.8	55.2	44.5
3 March 1991	5,269	2,575	2,694	2,519	1,341	1,178	47.8	52.1	43.7

Sources: ILO, *Yearbook of Labour Statistics, 1945–1989*, retrospective edn. on population censuses, ILO, Geneva, 1990; *Scitani lidu, domu a bytu, 3.3.1991, Predbezné vysledky* (Census of Population, Housing and Dwellings, 3 March 1991, Preliminary Results), Federal Statistical Office, Prague, June 1991.

TABLE 11.7 Changes in population and labour force in inter-censal periods, CSFR, by sex and age, 1950–1991 (%)

	Population			Total aged 0–14	Men aged 15–59	Women aged 15–54	Men aged 60+	Women aged 55+	Labour force		
	Total	Men	Women						Total	Men	Women
Czech and Slovak Federal Republic											
1950–61	11.4	11.8	11.0	19.4	5.9	0.6	25.7	33.9	11.9	6.8	17.1
1961–70	4.4	4.2	4.5	-11.5	6.6	6.0	29.9	20.4	8.4	1.5	18.4
1970–80	6.5	6.5	6.6	12.1	6.8	5.5	-4.6	3.5	12.4	8.1	17.7
1980–91	1.9	1.9	1.9	-3.3	2.9	4.7	7.3	0.9	-1.1	-1.7	-0.6
Czech Republic											
1961–70	2.5	2.3	2.6	-14.3	4.5	3.4	27.0	18.4	6.1	0.7	13.4
1970–80	4.9	5.0	4.9	15.9	4.0	2.7	-6.9	0.4	7.6	5.0	10.8
1980–91	0.1	0.3	-0.2	-7.3	2.3	4.0	5.4	-2.2	-2.3	-2.0	-2.7
Slovak Republic											
1961–70	8.7	8.5	8.9	-6.2	11.5	12.2	38.5	26.4	14.6	3.5	35.1
1970–80	10.0	9.6	10.4	5.6	13.1	11.7	1.5	12.5	24.3	15.4	37.0
1980–91	5.6	5.0	6.1	4.1	4.1	6.2	11.9	9.0	1.4	-1.0	4.2

Sources: ILO, *Yearbook of Labour Statistics, 1945–1989*, retrospective edn. on population censuses, ILO Geneva, 1990; *Scítaní lidu, domu a bytu, 3.3.1991, Predbezné vysledky* (Census of Population, Housing and Dwellings, 3 March 1991, Preliminary Results), Federal Statistical Office, Prague, June 1991.

system. The labour-force data published in the regular yearly statistical series differ in coverage from the Census data and cannot be used for calculating labour-force participation rates comparable with the Census data.

Table 11.6 shows that the initial differences in activity rates in the Czech and Slovak Republics narrowed during the four decades of planned development to a point where they most likely reflect mainly the differences in age structure, namely a different weight of the working-age population in the two republics. Women's activity rates increased particularly rapidly in the Slovak Republic between 1961 and 1980, rising by 16 percentage points, as compared with 7 percentage points in the Czech Republic. In the last intercensal period, i.e. between 1980 and 1991, the female activity rates declined less in the Slovak Republic than in the Czech Republic (while the female labour force increased in absolute numbers in Slovakia and declined in the Czech Republic). This further contributed to the narrowing of the difference in labour-force participation in the two republics.

Between 1950 and 1991 men's activity rates have had a declining trend, both country-wide and in the two republics, following the pattern observed also in OECD countries. The gap between the male and female activity rates has been closing. This also was true of the 1980s, when female labour declined less than male labour. However, the exact extent of this narrowing-down will be known only when the age-specific labour participation rates become available, i.e. when the final results of the 1991 Population Census are published, as the lower female crude activity rates shown in Table 11.6 are influenced by the longer female life expectancy.

As we have seen, in Czechoslovakia female labour underwent a period of rapid expansion in the 1950s, as a result of planned labour increases. The growth continued into the 1960s and 1970s before a decline started in the late 1980s. In the OECD countries similar high growth rates of female labour occurred from the 1970s, i.e. with a twenty-year gap, but there fast growth continued in the 1980s. The time differences may be related to the difference in factors determining the growth in Eastern and Western Europe. In Czechoslovakia, the spectacular rise in women's labour-force participation was caused by the requirements of the planned development and by the necessity for the planners to involve a maximum of the previously inactive labour resources in the process of heavy industrialization. It was also conditioned by the state socialist ideology, claiming women's equality to be attainable mainly through economic involvement. Moreover, the high growth of female labour was an integral part of the social policy based on a two-income model of family and the collective upbringing of children. This was reinforced by a planned low level of wages combined with price subsidies for food and other essentials as well as free health care and education (see Nesporova 1991). The high participation of women in the labour force decided by the planning authorities influenced in its turn the demography of the country, causing birth rates to fall. It also affected educational factors, giving women more incentives to study employment-oriented subjects to which they were channelled also by the administrative allocation of young people to various educational streams in function of the planned employment requirements. Finally, the integration of women in the labour force transformed the social environment; women's full-time life-long work became the established norm, to which the family and social life gradually adapted.

In the OECD countries, on the contrary, the inverse causal relationship seems to have prevailed. Demographic, educational, economic, and social changes were more the determinants of the rise in female labour-force participation than they were influenced by it. Demographic developments, namely the falling birth rates, the rise in the average age at first marriage, the concentration of birth between the ages of 25 and 30 (of the mother), etc., allowed women increasingly to take up paid employment and to develop a career, before and especially after their childbearing period. Women's educational levels have increased considerably, although a strictly 'employment-oriented' education has not become the norm, which may give women greater adaptability. The rising supply and quality of household appliances has freed women from many domestic chores, giving them time for outside activities. In the circumstances, rising labour-force participation rates appeared more as a consequence than a cause of the demographic and social changes, although the causal relationship has worked to some extent in both directions.

The convergence of women's labour-force participation trends in OECD countries and in Czechoslovakia may be taken as an indication that the introduction of the market economy system should not lead *per se* to a decline in women's labour participation, and that women's labour-force status should not be adversely affected by the change of system in Czechoslovakia, other things being equal. This, however, is a long-run consideration. In the short run, i.e. in the restructuring period, the rising level and duration of unemployment, and the difficulty of getting reinserted into employment in a situation where the labour market undergoes profound changes, might discourage many women workers, particularly those with family responsibilities, and lead them to withdraw from the labour force. Moreover, the quality of female labour is likely to deteriorate as occasional, short-term, seasonal, undeclared, and other 'precarious' employment increases. The phenomenon has been well known in OECD countries during recession periods. In the Czech and Slovak Republics it might be aggravated by the difficulties facing the newly starting private enterprises, many of which might have difficulties in surviving, and some of which might be undeclared and outside legal control.

It may be wondered whether the improvement in living standards and in per capita income expected to occur once the reform is successfully completed will render more women inactive, enjoying leisure in their homes. Available evidence tends to suggest that this is not likely to happen. At the present moment, both in the Czech and Slovak Republics and in Western countries, most women choose to work from economic necessity in spite of the large differences in GDP per capita. Various survey materials indicate, however, that the proportion of women who work purely for economic reasons is larger in the CSFR than the West. The ILO survey on 'Women in the Labour Market' has shown that 76 per cent of women worked for money or in order to ensure the basic needs of the family; only 7 per cent of women declared that they worked for reasons such as interest in the job, a sense of achievement, and the satisfaction of using their acquired qualifications, or the social side of the working environment. In an earlier survey carried out in five European Community countries (Belgium, France, Germany, Italy, and the Netherlands) 40 per cent of women of working age (20–54) quoted economic necessity as their main reason for working; about 20 per cent declared that they worked for non-economic reasons, such as the interest of the job or the status and independence it conferred (see Eurostat 1981).

It would be wrong to assume, however, that the economic necessity for women to work decreases with rising per capita income. In fact, a positive correlation exists between per capita GNP of OECD countries and female labour-force participation. Two main factors seem to explain this paradox. First, there is the subjective feeling of necessity linked to rising expectations as the wealth of society increases. But more importantly, there is the objective factor of the changing structure of the household expenditure with rising national income. Households try to maximize utility of both market-purchased and home-produced commodities. Many goods and services that under poorer economic conditions were produced in the household gradually become uneconomic to produce in that way because of the time it would take and so are purchased on the market. Female labour which was earlier directed at household production is being liberated by the substitution of market-produced goods and influenced to meet the cost of these goods by working outside the home for pay. This freeing of women from certain household duties is further accelerated by the growing availability of household appliances, which is also an income-related phenomenon. In addition, the rising level of female wages further increases the opportunity costs of not working outside the home (see Paukert 1984). This is a further reason why it is unlikely that, with rising prosperity in the Czech and Slovak Republics, female labour-force participation will decrease.

The professional activity of women has now become so much a part of the established social habits in the Czech and Slovak Republics that a change might be difficult to accept. While it is commonly said that women have to work because men's salaries are too low to keep a family, the ILO survey on 'Women in the Labour Market' has shown that only 28 per cent of married (or cohabiting) women would like to give up their job and stay at home if their husbands'/partners' salaries increased adequately. (However, 46 per cent of the husbands/partners would definitely like their companions to stay at home if they started to earn enough.) On the other hand, as many as 40 per cent of married (or cohabiting) women would definitely refuse to become housewives even if their husbands'/partners' salaries increased considerably. Thus, the Survey has confirmed the great attachment of women to the labour market and to a professional activity. How many Czech and Slovak women might get discouraged by a long spell of unemployment if the reform is slow to yield the expected results remains an open question.

Women's working conditions

During the period of development of the planned economy, considerable efforts were made and real success achieved in providing child-care facilities and health protection for working women (see Kroupova 1991). But as time went on, women's working conditions in Czechoslovakia started to lag behind those of the industrialized Western market economies in several other respects. In particular, part-time employment could rarely be arranged. Also, since high labour inputs were one of the intrinsic features of the centrally planned system, not only was there overemployment in terms of numbers, but working hours were also very long. In 1988, for example, Czechoslovakia had the longest weekly hours in the manufacturing sector of all the European countries reporting such data to the ILO, including Hungary and Poland.[4] A gender breakdown is not available on working hours for the CSFR; however, a careful comparison of the working hours in individual manu-facturing branches and of the share of women in these branches shows that many activities with a high share of female employment such as food processing had very long weekly hours, while some typically 'male' branches such as basic metals had much shorter hours (44.7 and 41.7 in 1988, respectively). In the retail trade sector, too, where women represent 75 per cent of the labour force, working hours were very long. Moreover, in the CSFR there were relatively shorter and fewer holidays in comparison with OECD countries; average working hours per worker and per year were higher in the CSFR by almost one-fifth. Apart from maternity leave and parental leave in the case of a sick child, women were not given free days for household chores, contrary to the practice in the GDR, for example.

Interestingly, the ILO survey on 'Women in the Labour Market' has shown that 82 per cent of women considered their working hours fully or generally satisfactory. The 18 per cent that did not consisted largely of mothers of young children, aged 18–29. But the survey has also shown that as many as 70 per cent of women could leave their work-place during working

---

[4] See ILO, *Yearbook of Labour Statistics 1991*, Geneva.

hours in order to attend to their own personal matters: 37 per cent could 'disappear' without much problem, 13 per cent of these 'any time' and 24 per cent 'from time to time', while another 33 per cent said they could do so exceptionally. This typical practice could, to a certain extent, be assimilated with the part-time or flexible-hour arrangements found in the industrial market economies. However, it contained many elements of arbitrariness and was particularly unfair to women doing assembly-line work and to those in small localities where such 'infringement of labour discipline' could be more easily discovered and possibly sanctioned. In all cases, it led to favouritism and its basic lack of fairness contributed to the often deplored deterioration of working morale. With the introduction of market conditions, this practice should gradually disappear, while working hours should be shortened, as has already started to happen. More part-time work should also become available, particularly for mothers of young children.

Distribution of female labour by sector and by industry

The industrialization drive and the process of deep economic restructuring that were launched after the introduction of the planned economy system in 1948 were destined to integrate the country's economy into the communist bloc and to adjust its export level and structure to the import requirements of the other members of the Council of Mutual Economic Assistance (CMEA, or COMECON). This required the channelling of vast labour resources, male and female, to industry, especially to heavy industry and heavy engineering, which soon became the country's main area of exports. By 1961, 54 per cent of the male work-force and 37 per cent of the female work-force were engaged in the secondary sector of the economy (manufacturing, mining, public utilities, and construction); in 1990 the respective shares of male and female industrial employment were 57 and 37 per cent, as illustrated in Table 11.8. The oversized industry gradually became a sort of 'trap' of the system, a problem for which it was difficult to find remedies even when it became obvious that there was a large industrial overemployment and that productivity was very low by Western industrialized countries' standards. The extent of industrial overemployment can be illustrated by an estimate made at the end of the 1980s that the non-utilization of working hours in industry amounted to 20–30 per cent (see Nesporova 1991). A major reason for the constant growth of employment in industry (which started to decline only in 1990, after the change in the economic system) was the incentive for enterprise managers to maximize their planned labour requirements, chiefly in order to increase their planned wage fund and hence the operating funds allocated to them by the central planning authorities. At any given level of funds allocation, the managers then had an incentive to hire, wherever possible, low-paid workers, which in the Czechoslovak context often meant

TABLE 11.8 Distribution of male and female labour by main economic sectors, CSFR, 1947–1990 (%)

	Both sexes				Men				Women			
	Total	Agriculture[a]	Industry[b]	Services	Total	Agriculture[a]	Industry[b]	Services	Total	Agriculture[a]	Industry[b]	Services
1947 Census	100	38[c]	37	25	100	30[c]	43	27	100	53[c]	27	20
1961 Census	100	25	47	28	100	21	54	25	100	30	37	33
1970 Census	100	17	48	35	100	17	55	28	100	16	40	43
1980 Census	100	13	50	37	100	15	57	28	100	12	40	48
1990 OE	100	11	48	41	100	13	57	30	100	9	37	54

Note: Owing to differences in coverage, data for 1990 are not strictly comparable with the Census data for 1947–80.
[a] Agriculture and forestry.
[b] Mining, quarrying, manufacturing, public utilities, and construction.
[c] Incl. quarrying.

Sources: ILO, *Yearbook of Labour Statistics, 1945–1989*, retrospective edn. on population censuses, ILO, Geneva, 1990; *Statistical Yearbook of Czechoslovakia*, various issues, Federal Statistical Office, Prague.

women. As a result, women were hired for industrial—largely administrative and service—jobs in numbers that were motivated more by 'fund allocation' or by 'enterprise growth' considerations than by productivity and industrial efficiency considerations. Few quantitative data are available so far on the occupational structure of women's employment in industry, but the existing evidence points to a serious overemployment of women in industrial white-collar jobs up to 1989. Many of these jobs were eliminated when the market system started to operate.

The policy of industrial overemployment and of cheap labour resulted not only in the wasting of labour resources but also in an insufficient level of capital investment. The slow modernization—particularly in the light, or 'women's', industries—was an important factor retarding the growth of productivity. Moreover, it led to poor working conditions (insufficient automation, high content of physical labour, high accident rates, lack of modern hygiene, etc.), which in turn were detrimental to labour morale. Large numbers of women workers have been employed in obsolete plants in the light industries using outdated technology. Under the new market economy conditions, the obsolete plants may either be closed, which will further add to the growth of female unemployment, or modernized and fitted with up-to-date (perhaps computerized) technology, in which case women workers will face the necessity of undergoing intensive retraining if they wish to keep their jobs. Their jobs might also become threatened by male competition as unemployment rises. The often observed phenomenon of unemployed men being more easily rehired than women in times of a depression can already be observed in the Czech and Slovak Republics.

However, some skilled women's blue-collar jobs in light industries, particularly in those with export prospects, provided they can be rapidly fitted with adequate technology, might be shielded or even advantaged by the new shifts in domestic and foreign demand. This is because production and exports of some well-designed, quality-competitive light industrial goods such as glass, china, ceramics, furniture, and wood products are likely to increase, while the engineering industries, which before 1989 employed 30 per cent of the male and 19 per cent of the female manufacturing work-force, have been facing serious sales problems, owing to the disintegration of the CMEA trade flows, to obsolete technology, and to the world-wide recession and low level of domestic and foreign demand.

Between 1948 and 1989, employment in the service sector developed at a relatively slow pace. As shown in Table 11.8, in 1990 only 30 per cent of the male work-force and 54 per cent of the female work-force were employed in service activities, compared with 43 and 70 per cent respectively in neighbouring Austria, for example. The larger difference between women's sectoral employment distribution and men's (in terms of percentage points) in Czechoslovakia and Austria suggests that more Czech and Slovak women than men may have to change jobs in the transition to a market economy system. The higher rate of job shift is likely to be an additional factor of higher female unemployment.

While for many years there has been a large unsatisfied demand for services, and their quality has been frequently sub-standard, the directive system of management tended to understaff the service sector both through direct allocation decisions and by fixing wages in the service sector at a low level. This applied even to highly educated professionals in the service activities such as doctors, who were considerably underpaid by Western standards. The insufficient development of the service sector adversely affected the country's living standards. It also contributed to the growth of the 'grey' economy, which was mostly concentrated in service activities. Services in the 'grey' economic sector were provided either on a monetary basis or on a barter, service-for-service, basis. The relatively wide development of the latter practice and the lack of information and control of prices in the former case tended to establish a climate of 'shady' or often doubtful dealing in private business transactions, which may adversely affect the development of a healthy small private business sector in the transition period. In the ILO survey on 'Women in the Labour Market', 49 per cent of men and 40 per cent of women agreed with the statement that most private businessmen want to cheat the customer. The overwhelming majority of respondents, however, were strongly in favour of the development of private business, which should 'help to improve the economy', provide 'better-quality products' (97 per cent of respondents) and 'lower prices' (85 per cent of respondents).

Even more important than the low standard of services to the population was the lagging behind of services for production and business, such as industrial design, management consulting, legal services, marketing, banking, insurance, and other commercial services. It is generally agreed that the insufficient development of these services has played quite an important role in the poor economic performance of the country and is also creating difficulties in the transition period. Table 11.9 shows that only 1.4 per cent of the total employment and 1.9 per cent of female employment was in banking, insurance, and business services in 1989. In order to reach the relative share of Austria at the time of the 1971 population census, i.e. 5 per cent, banking, insurance, and business service employment would have to be multiplied by 3; in order to reach the Austrian share of 1988, i.e. 6 per cent of total employment, it would have to be multiplied by 4. It may also be pointed out that the low standard of the banking services represents an obstacle to the development of foreign business relations. Their improvement, through programmes of training for employees in modern banking techniques, for instance, would represent a good investment that would help in the short run and pay off in the longer run, when the economy starts to grow.

TABLE 11.9 Employment by industry and sex, CSFR, 1989–1990[a]

	1989			1990			Share of women[b]		Percentage change 1990/1989[b]		
	Total ('000)	M ('000)	F ('000)	Total ('000)	M ('000)	F ('000)	1989 (%)	1990 (%)	Total	M	F
Total	7,937	4,309	3,628	7,843	4,369	3,474	45.7	44.3	-1.2	1.4	-4.2
Agriculture	812	496	316	777	483	294	38.9	37.8	-4.3	-2.6	-7.0
Forestry	98	73	25	106	77	29	25.5	27.6	8.1	5.5	16.6
Water management	45	32	13	45	32	13	29.6	28.9	0.3	1.3	-2.0
Manufacturing[c]	2,954	1,760	1,194	2,882	1,752	1,130	40.4	39.2	-2.4	-0.5	-5.4
Construction	704	608	96	766	674	92	13.6	12.0	8.7	10.9	-3.9
Geological prospecting	18	14	4	16	13	3	22.2	20.5	-14.6	-7.1	-21.0
Designing	86	46	40	74	40	34	46.9	45.8	-13.1	-13.0	-15.2
Printing and publishing	20	9	11	24	12	12	52.7	52.3	17.0	18.0	16.0
Transport	404	311	93	414	315	99	23.0	23.8	2.5	1.3	6.1
Communications	108	36	72	115	40	75	66.7	65.6	5.7	11.1	4.0
Domestic trade	728	179	549	667	163	504	75.4	75.6	-8.4	-8.9	-8.1
Foreign trade	24	8	16	24	8	16	64.9	65.0	-0.5	-0.8	-0.3
Material supplies	63	30	33	54	26	28	52.9	51.3	-13.7	-10.7	-16.4
Agricultural procurements	27	17	10	24	15	9	35.6	35.4	-10.6	-10.2	-11.2
Science, research and development	184	114	70	154	95	59	38.0	38.3	-16.1	-16.7	-15.4

Housing and dwelling services	105	62	43	101	59	42	41.2	41.7	-3.4	-4.8	-2.3
Accommodation services	58	17	41	53	16	37	70.5	70.2	-8.0	-7.2	-8.3
Tourism	8	3	5	9	3	6	66.1	66.1	13.3	13.1	13.3
Communal services	160	80	80	219	142	77	50.3	35.1[d]	36.8	77.5	-4.4
Education	488	140	348	470	129	341	71.3	72.5	-3.7	-7.9	-2.0
Culture	129	61	68	121	59	62	52.5	51.3	-6.5	-3.3	-8.6
Health	355	76	279	357	75	282	78.6	78.9	0.6	-1.3	1.1
Social care	57	6	51	53	5	48	88.6	88.6	-6.1	-5.7	-6.2
Business and technical services	73	35	38	66	32	34	52.2	51.4	-9.7	-8.6	-11.0
Banking	27	5	22	31	6	25	80.8	81.3	15.1	11.7	16.0
Insurance	9	3	6	10	3	7	66.7	68.3	15.1	9.7	17.8
Administration, justice, legal services	115	43	72	152	59	93	63.0	61.2	32.1	38.4	28.3
Civic organizations and other	78	45	33	59	36	23	42.2	39.7	-24.8	-21.5	-29.2

[a] Year-end data. Includes second-job-holders, in particular all registered private entrepreneurs (488,000 at end 1990) of whom 80% carried out their private business activities as a second job and some have not even started. Excludes women on maternity leave.
[b] Calculated from unrounded figures.
[c] Including mining, quarrying, gas, and electricity.
[d] The sharp decline in the share of women was due to the 77.5% increase of male workers in 'communal services', which was a branch where many small private businesses were registered, in 1990, mostly in the name of men.

The growth of the previously underdeveloped and understaffed service branches should provide new employment opportunities for women. But this growth is conditioned by a number of factors on both the demand and the supply side. The overall level of demand will have to increase and so will the supply of labour adequately qualified for the activities offering growth perspectives. Under the present conditions of recession and decline in output and in consumer demand, the development of services is held back, with the possible exception of tourist services and services financed with foreign participation.

The current recession and the decline in output and in consumer demand act as a 'trap' for women workers, who, if they become redundant in the formerly overstaffed industrial branches and activities, often have difficulties in getting rehired in the branches with obvious growth perspectives, as long as the decline in output continues. A set of selective support measures to the service activities with a growth potential, including consultancy and training, and to the small private business sector, would benefit female employment.

Women's earnings and male–female earnings differentials

With respect to money earnings, the planned economy system rewarded preferentially hard physical work, length of tenure, formal education, and heavy industrial activities. (This did not concern the 'Nomenklatura', however, whose positions within the Communist Party guaranteed them benefits in kind.) The system thus contained an in-built mechanism of gender discrimination, since women have been traditionally worse off than men on all counts just mentioned. In the highly 'feminized' branches of light industry and services, wages were set at a lower level than in the typically male-dominated activities such as mining or basic metal industries.

The earnings survey carried out in Czechoslovakia in June 1988 shows the overall male–female earnings differential for full-time workers and employees to be 29 per cent; i.e., women's average pay was 71 per cent of the average male pay (see Table 11.10). The wage preference accorded to heavy physical work explains the relatively large pay gap in the manual worker category, shown in the table. The largest earnings gap, however, existed in the administrative and managerial category, implying that far fewer women than men acceded to the top managerial posts. Table 11.11 shows the considerable bonus that a university education offered to women in terms of earning prospects. But even university-educated women have had a much lower average salary than university-educated men. In fact, the average university-educated women in 1988 earned Kcs3,580 per month, i.e. less than the average male vocational school graduate, who earned Kcs3,684, while the average male university graduate earned around Kcs4,543 (see Czechoslovak Federal Ministry of Labour and Social Affairs 1989).

TABLE 11.10 Earnings differentials between male and female workers in the CSFR by employment status, June 1988

	Average monthly full-time earnings		Women's earnings as % of men's earnings
	Men (Kcs)	Women (Kcs)	
All categories	3,917	2,778	70.9
Manual workers	3,786	2,571	67.9
Service workers	3,169	2,506	79.1
Technicians	4,236	2,993	70.7
Administrative and managerial staff	4,688	3,052	65.1
Other non-manual employees	4,368	3,307	75.7

Source: FMPSV (Federal Ministry of Labour and Social Affairs), *Jednorazove Statisticke Setreni o Mzdach Pracovniku za cerven 1988* (Sample Survey on Workforce Earnings, June 1988), Prague, 1989.

The male-female earnings gap in Czechoslovakia in 1988 was within the range observed in OECD countries. In the United Kingdom, for example, women earn on average 68 per cent of men's pay, while in Sweden they earn about 90 per cent (see UK Department of Employment 1990, and Sveriges Officiella Statistik 1992). However, in the OECD countries a considerable proportion of the earnings gap can be explained by women's shorter working careers, by a lower average age, and by the fact that women often retire from the labour market, or work part-time, during the childrearing period of their lives, as well as by receiving the (wrong) type of education and, last but not the least, by occupational segregation and occupational sex-typing. Available evidence indicates that women in Czechoslovakia (although being worse off than men in the above respects) have scored considerably better on these counts than women in Western countries. (1) The average age of women workers, their average length of work experience, and their average length of tenure have been higher than in most OECD countries. (2) Owing to the generous social security provisions concerning child care,[5] women have not been retiring from the labour market or going into part-time or other precarious work during the childrearing period of their lives. (3) Women's

---

[5] Paid maternity leave of 28 weeks (since 1987), 6 weeks of which are to be taken before confinement. Mothers acting as single parents or giving birth to more than one child have 37 weeks' leave. Maternity benefit amounts to 90% of net wage. After expiration of paid maternity leave, parental leave and a parental allowance may be claimed up to the third year of the child, to which either father or mother are entitled. The allowance is defined as a fixed sum (Kcs1200 in 1992) and the parent has the possibility of being employed for two hours a day (see Kroupova 1991). The employer has an obligation to keep the original job open until the end of the paid maternity leave.

TABLE 11.11 Earnings differentials between male and female workers in CSFR by educational attainment and employment status, June 1988 (Average monthly full-time earnings)

	Compulsory education			Vocational or incomplete secondary education			Secondary education with secondary school certificate			University education		
	M (Kcs)	F (Kcs)	F/M (%)	M (Kcs)	F (Kcs)	F/M (%)	M (Kcs)	F (Kcs)	F/M (%)	M (Kcs)	F (Kcs)	F/M (%)
All categories	3,476	2,509	72.2	3,847	2,666	69.3	3,987	2,911	73.0	4,735	3,835	81.0
Manual workers	3,542	2,539	71.7	3,877	2,645	68.2	3,773	2,592	68.7	3,560	2,479	69.6
Service workers	2,913	2,289	78.6	3,294	2,617	79.4	3,301	2,683	81.3	3,342	2,929	87.6
Technicians	4,028	2,708	67.2	4,124	2,830	68.6	4,135	2,953	71.4	4,569	3,623	79.3
Administrative and managerial staff	3,544	2,809	79.3	3,874	2,891	74.6	4,171	2,995	71.8	5,421	3,941	72.7
Other non-manual employees	3,053	2,491	81.6	3,556	2,464	69.3	3,786	2,953	78.0	4,533	3,860	85.2

Source: FMPSV (Federal Ministry of Labour and Social Affairs), *Jednorazove Statisticke Setreni o Mzdach Pracovniku za cerven 1988* (Sample Survey on Workforce Earnings, June 1988), Prague, 1989.

education has been more 'employment-oriented' than in the West because of the planned education policy. (4) Finally, occupational segregation has been less widespread in Czechoslovakia (and in the other planned-economy countries) than in the West. No recent data on employment in a detailed occupational classification and a gender breakdown are available for Czechoslovakia, but information provided in the 1970 Population Census indicates that in 1970 the degree of occupational segregation was markedly lower in Czechoslovakia than in the Western market economies. The coefficient of variation (standard deviation as a percentage of the arithmetic mean) calculated on the basis of women's employment shares in fifty occupations for twenty-five industrialized countries was significantly lower in Czechoslovakia than in Western Europe and North America, indicating a more even distribution of women across occupational categories than in the West. (A lower coefficient of variation, i.e. a more equal distribution of women by occupation, was found in 1970 only in the Soviet Union: (see UN/ECE 1980.) Since the main 'objective' determinants of the male–female earnings gap appear more favourable to women in Czechoslovakia than to women in the West, and since, in spite of this, the pay gap in Czechoslovakia is at the lower end of the range for Western European countries, the conclusion must be that the subjective, i.e. 'discrimination', factor has played a larger role in the fixing of women's wages in Czechoslovakia than in most Western countries.

The question arises as to how the introduction of the market economy system, and the emergence and fluctuation of unemployment, may affect relative women's earnings in the Czech and Slovak Republics. The fact that women's unemployment is higher than men's and that managers already hire men for certain jobs previously held by women is likely to depress women's wages. Previous experience of OECD countries shows, however, that in recession periods the male–female earnings gap need not necessarily widen, particularly in the public sector and in large enterprises, which predominate so far in the Czech and Slovak Republics. But it is true that earnings differentials are generally greater in the private than in the public sector. Thus, with the growth of the private sector, as privatization proceeds, the male–female earnings gap might display a tendency to increase. Female earnings suffer particularly in small enterprises, to which an important proportion of redundant women turn for 'precarious' employment. This may occur also in the Czech and Slovak Republics. Various malpractices on behalf of small private employers have already been reported and seem to be on the increase. Women are likely to suffer equally or more than men from these malpractices designed to bypass the minimum wage legislation and government 'social network' measures. Women workers' conditions could benefit considerably from the creation of a good labour inspection system, as well as from effective trade union policies on equal opportunities and equal treatment.

WOMEN WORKERS' SITUATION IN 1990–2

The legislation on economic reform began to be put in place during 1990, but, in the words of President Havel, 'economic reform started in earnest on 1 January 1991, twelve months after the victory of democratic forces' (*International Herald Tribune*, 15 July 1991). Since then, measures implementing the transition to a market system continued to be elaborated and adopted as the reform programme and the situation required it. In 1990 economic and employment changes were relatively limited, although unemployment started to appear, as a result of the decline in production caused by the disintegration of the CMEA, by the recession which had begun to take hold, and by the first privatization and restructuring steps. At the beginning of 1991, after the launching of the reform, unemployment started to grow relatively rapidly, particularly in the Slovak Republic, where it reached 11.8 per cent at the end of the year (it reached 4.1 per cent in the Czech Republic), as illustrated in Table 11.1 above. In June 1991 female unemployment started to rise considerably faster than male unemployment, and the gap between the two widened until the end of 1991 (Fig. 11.1). However, in February 1992 unemployment started to decline in both republics, and in the first quarter of 1992 the gap between male and female unemployment narrowed. The decrease in unemployment was due to several factors, including the shortening of the period of entitlement to unemployment benefits from twelve to six months and stricter controls on benefit entitlements. It was also due to a certain improvement in the economic situation in the first half of 1992. Although industrial output and employment continued to decline, output in construction started to grow, and 44 per cent of it originated in the new private sector. Consumer demand increased and the volume of retail sales went up in both the Czech and the Slovak Republics. In the Czech Republic it increased, in the first half of 1992, by as much as 20.5 per cent, without reaching, however, the level of 1990. New employment opportunities started to be created in 1992 and the unemployment–vacancy ratio improved, particularly in the Czech Republic, as illustrated in Table 11.2. In May 1992 there were six unfilled vacancies for one unemployed in Prague and about an equal number of unemployed and of vacancies in the Western Czech Region, which have been the two main poles of development in the country. In some other regions, such as the Northern Moravian Region and the Western Slovak Region, the situation looked grim, particularly for women, whose unemployment exceeded that of men considerably (see Table 11.2). However, in the Central Slovak Region female unemployment declined much more than male unemployment in the first half of 1992, becoming slightly lower in numbers. The analysis of the data in Tables 11.1 and 11.2 tends to suggest that unemployment is largely a regional problem, although it continues to give serious concern in the whole of the Slovak Republic because of its persistently high level. The better situation in the Czech Republic may be only temporary, as unemployment is expected to grow again, when the bankruptcy law, already approved by Parliament, comes into effect in early 1993.

The trends and structure of women's employment since the launching of the reform cannot be analysed, because at the time of the finalization of this chapter employment data in a gender breakdown are available only up to 1990. However, since the developments of the first post-revolutionary year, 1990, in many respects set the pattern for later trends, the changes in employment that took place in that year offer a certain interest. In 1990 total employment declined by 5 per cent, if one- or main-job-holders are counted; it declined by 0.4 per cent if second jobs are also included. Partly as a result of the rise in second jobs, male employment increased, in 1990, by 1.4 per cent; the employment of women, who generally find it more difficult to have a second job, declined by 4.2 per cent. In manufacturing both men's and women's employment declined, but women's employment declined by 5.4 per cent, while men's fell by only 0.4 per cent. The loss of 65,000 jobs by women in manufacturing (on a net basis) was not compensated by job creation in the newly developing service activities, such as communications, publishing, banking, insurance, tourism, and justice, mostly because of insufficient demand, but partly also because of a lack of supply of qualified workers, notably women workers (see Table 11.9). According to preliminary information published in the press, this pattern repeated itself in 1991, but took on more drastic proportions. Total industrial employment declined by 12 per cent, while industrial output declined by 21.2 per cent and labour productivity fell by 14.4 per cent. GDP decreased by 16 per cent and total employment in the national economy by 7.4 per cent. The situation of enterprises became particularly difficult in the second and third quarters of 1991, when most of the fall in output occurred. In spite of the credit squeeze, enterprises were slow to shed labour, preferring a situation of late payments, which gradually spread throughout most of the economy. When dismissing workers, enterprises tended to release women first, other things being equal, because they were considered either redundant under the new conditions, or easier to dismiss, because easier to replace or rehire. Qualified men were kept on the payroll, even at the cost of considerable financial difficulties. The reasons for this were, first, economic, as the existence of qualified teams of workers represents an asset for an enterprise in case of privatization or take-over by a foreign company, and, secondly, social, as public enterprise managers, in many cases elected by the staff, may have found it difficult to dismiss old colleagues and family breadwinners. It should be pointed out also that female employment was negatively affected by the fact that some industries employing largely women on the shop-floor, such as textiles and clothing, lost most of their East European markets after the disintegration of COMECON and either were closed down or had their activity scaled down considerably.

In the near future, employment prospects for women exist mainly in three areas: (1) in some of the light industries able to increase their export production; (2) in the tertiary sector, i.e. trade, banking, business services, tourism, legal services, communications, etc., particularly after the reform has advanced sufficiently and growth conditions have been re-established; (3) in small private businesses. The survey on 'Women in the Labour Market', commissioned by the ILO and carried out in 1991 and 1992, concentrated particularly on investigating the possibilities of women finding work in the small private business sector.

Private business activities were practically suppressed in Czechoslovakia during the four decades of the planned economy system. They started to develop timidly in the late 1980s after a first partial liberalization of the regulations. But the full legislation allowing a free development of private business activities was enacted only after the 1989 changes. The existing number of full-time private entrepreneurs and of their collaborators would have to be doubled to reach the lower end of the OECD countries' range for the small business employment share, although their number has been steadily increasing. The ILO survey on 'Women in the Labour Market' highlighted some of the obstacles to a faster take-off of small business activities. In spite of the population's resolutely favourable attitude to private business in general, 44 per cent of the respondents, men and women alike, considered that private business required experience that most people in the Czech and Slovak Republics do not have. Most respondents (59 per cent) also thought that an enterprise spirit could not be acquired by learning but had to be present at birth. A high proportion of the respondents (84 per cent of men and 81 per cent of women) feared that private business meant too much rush and stress. Moreover, 77 per cent of men and 69 per cent of women thought that private business was too risky as a main job. A considerable proportion of them, particularly many women (about 30 per cent), preferred in early 1991 to carry out private business activities only on a part-time basis together with a paid job in a (large) organization or enterprise. A year later, however, in early 1992, about 15 per cent of the total labour force and 12 per cent of the female labour force were in small private business, most of them (about two-thirds) on a full-time basis. In addition, a further 5 per cent of women stated in February 1992 that they had firmly decided to start a business in the near future and another 5 per cent replied that they might start in business during the next two years. Compared with the 3 per cent of women who were in small business in February 1991 and the 4 per cent who were then determined to start one, this appears to be a clearly positive development. In both 1991 and in 1992, the intention to start a business immediately or later was more frequent in the younger age groups, while people approaching retirement age or having reached it, particularly women, appeared strongly opposed to such an option. A significant proportion of women in business or wishing to start one expressed a preference for the status of 'family helper'.

In 1991, 44 per cent of female respondents and 45 per cent of the male respondents supported the opinion that entrepreneurship was mainly for men and that in a business venture women should only be helping. In general, a family business now seems to have better prospects for development than a business headed by a woman entrepreneur, among other things because it can cover a wider range of activities and it is easier to pool family resources.

About one-fifth of women in business or about to start one stated in 1991 that the reason for starting up was the loss of employment through the suppression of their former jobs and their inability to find new ones. The majority were attracted by the prospect of profit and also of personal independence and achievement. The survey has also indicated that, in the group of women who switched from employment to small private business, a larger share left on their own decision because they had a business idea and a smaller share were dismissed first and went into private business after-wards. Thus, unemployed women have not been the most dynamic group in small private business creation; however, among those who already lost their job, about one-third solved the problem of income replacement by going into small business. The government decision to offer the equivalent of twelve months (or more) of unemployment benefits as a loan to the unemployed wishing to start up a business has undoubtedly acted as an incentive, but the impact of this measure could have been better with a wider dissemination of information and less bureaucracy involved in obtaining such a loan.

The cautious attitude of many women to starting a small business, revealed by the ILO survey, may be explained by the prevailing circumstances. First of all, there has been a shortage of business premises, as the real property market has been slow to become fully operational, but prices and rents have been soaring, particularly in the capitals and larger cities. The ILO survey revealed that 24 per cent of the women who started a business activity carried it out in their own homes (in February 1992), while a further 20 per cent used other personally owned premises, often a garage or a cellar.

The second set of obstacles to small private business creation is related to economic conditions and economic policy. About 40 per cent of the survey respondents mentioned (in February 1992) tax reductions as the most efficient way for the government to support small business, while better administrative rules, less red tape, and better legislation were mentioned as the second most efficient practice. The availability of easier credit came third with only 8 per cent of replies, whereas in the 1991 round of the survey it ranked second with a much higher percentage of replies. This indicates that the efforts undertaken by public authorities and private institutions, during

1991, to improve the access to credit for small business owners have been relatively successful. On the other hand, the tax reductions for small businesses, decided by the government in 1991, were obviously not sufficient to satisfy the small business community. The 1992 round of the survey shows that 82 per cent of the women who had started a business financed the activity with their own savings, while 40 per cent had borrowed capital. The percentage of those who declared in 1992 to have borrowed capital was considerably lower than the percentage of those who declared a year earlier that they would do so. To what extent the prevailing credit conditions and the general situation of the credit squeeze have been responsible for this is difficult to judge.

SUMMARY AND CONCLUSIONS

The change in the economic system and the radical economic reform taking place in the Czech and Slovak Republics have had profound effects on the labour force, both positive and negative. While in the long run the advantages should outweigh the disadvantages, in the short run the costs are high in terms of unemployment, particularly in Slovakia, and of falling real wages and consumers' incomes in both republics. Women and the other vulnerable groups of workers tend to be more severely affected than adult men.

After the launching of the reform 'in earnest' on 1 January 1991, unemployment started to grow and women's unemployment grew faster than that of men. Although in the first half of 1992 unemployment declined and has been reduced to a low level in the Czech Republic, women's unemployment has continued to be higher than that of men in both republics. Female unemployment represents a social problem for a number of reasons, the main one being that a double income is necessary to guarantee an average living standard for the average family.

Since the 1950s, women have played a very important role in the economy. The share of women in the labour force kept growing throughout the last four decades. The 1991 Population Census has shown that women then represented 47 per cent, i.e. almost half, of the labour force. Women's labour-force attachment has become strong. This is confirmed by the results of the survey on 'Women in the Labour Market'. The introduction of the market economy system should not, by itself, lead to a decline in women's labour-force participation, since women's participation rates in Western industrialized countries have been growing and have become almost equally high as in Eastern Europe, the convergence having occurred particularly during the last two decades. It may happen, however, that the increase of the duration of women's unemployment will lead to worker discouragement, which the ILO survey has already indicated, although to a limited extent.

The insufficient allocation of resources to the service sector, and the overemployment of women in industrial white-collar jobs under the centrally planned economy system, has created a situation where more women than men may have to change jobs as market economy conditions are introduced. This is likely to lead to a higher labour turnover and greater unemployment for women. On the other hand, the previously undersized service sector has a considerable growth potential under market economic conditions and its development should offer new employment opportunities to women. However, the growth of the service sector will depend on the end of the present recession and an upturn in consumer and enterprise demand.

Average women's full-time earnings amounted to 71 per cent of the average men's earnings in 1988, the last year for which data are available. The male–female earnings gap was comparable to the one found in the industrialized market economy countries. As the process of privatization proceeds in the Czech and Slovak Republics, however, and the number of private enterprises increases, women's relative earnings might be adversely affected by the change, because in the private sector and in smaller enterprises the male–female earnings gap is known to be larger than in the large enterprises and in the public sector. Special attention should be paid to this problem in the future.

In the transition period, women's employment situation is likely to be affected differently in the two republics and in different regions of the countries. Existing evidence shows that unemployment, particularly female unemployment, has grown much more in the Slovak Republic than in the Czech Republic, where in mid-1992 it was lower than in most OECD countries. Available data also show unemployment to be higher in the regions with a high concentration of heavy industries, including the armaments industries, and considerably lower in the two capitals, particularly Prague.

The main areas where women could find new employment opportunities as the reform advances and market economy conditions prevail are: (1) the more dynamic, export-oriented light industries such as glass, china, and household fittings and fixtures; (2) banking, insurance, and business services; (3) the small private business sector, which has begun to grow quite rapidly, although starting from a low base: the 1991/2 ILO survey of 'Women in the Labour Market' has revealed that women's integration in private business activities has been relatively successful, even if men did take a more active part in small business creation and family business development seems to have better perspectives than the growth of small businesses owned by women; (4) tourist services, both large-scale and small-scale; these should offer good employment opportunities to women. Their advantage is that they are relatively little affected by the current recession and the dramatic fall in consumer demand, while they still benefit from the novelty of the opening up of the Central and Eastern European countries.

Within the framework of international aid offered to the Czech and Slovak Republics, in order to facilitate their transition to a market economy system, certain projects have been specifically targeted at women workers, while others, particularly those destined or able to assist small business creation, have also helped them. In November 1990 the ILO launched a technical co-operation project on *Women in the Labour Market in the CSFR* to study the plan of action for women during the transition to a market economy system. The project ended in the Czech Republic in March 1993, while at the time of writing it was continuing in the Slovak Republic. It covered a wide range of activities, from the specially commissioned survey on *Women in the Labour Market*, the main results of which have been presented in this chapter, to the dissemination of information through the mass media on the basic principles of the market mechanism and on private business activities, to consultancy services for women, particularly for those wishing to start a small business, and to country-wide training activities. This project has assisted a considerable number of women in coping with employment problems in the transition period, while gathering direct information and experience on the optimal plan of action for the future. This project provides an example of the types of initiatives that will be required in the future to help working women in the transition to a market economy.

REFERENCES

Czechoslovakia, Federalni ministerstvo prace a socialnich veci (Federal Ministry of Labour and Social Affairs) (1989), *Jednorazové Byberové Setreni o Mzdach Pracovniku za cerven 1988* (Special sample survey on earnings of workers and employees, June 1988). Prague.

—— Federalni statisticky urad (Federal Statistical Office) (1991), *Scitani lidu, domu a bytu, 3.3.1991, Predbezné vysledky* (Census of population, housing and dwellings, 3 March 1991, preliminary results). Prague.

Eurostat (1981), *The Economic and Social Position of Women in the Community*. Brussels: EC.

ILO (various issues), *Bulletin of Labour Statistics*. Geneva.

—— (various years), *Yearbook of Labour Statistics*. Geneva.

Kroupova, Alena (1991), 'The Promotion of Equality for Women in Central and Eastern Europe', case study prepared for the ILO Tripartite Subregional Seminar on Equality of Opportunity and Treatment in Employment in Central and Eastern Europe, held at the Czechoslovak Ministry of Labour and Social Affairs on 14–18 October 1991, mimeo, Prague.

Lado, Maria, Szalai, Julia, and Sziracki, Gyorgy (1991), 'Recent Labour Market Developments in Hungary', paper given at ILO/OECD–CCEET conference on 'Labour Market and Social Policy: Implications of Structural Change in Central and Eastern Europe', Paris, 11–13 September 1991.

Nesporova, Alena (1991), 'Recent Labour Market and Social Policy Developments in the Czech and Slovak Federal Republics', paper presented at ILO/OECD–CCEET conference on 'Labour Market and Social Policy: Implications of Structural Change in Central and Eastern Europe', Paris, 11–13 September 1991.

OECD, (various issues), *Labour Force Statistics*. Paris.

—— (1950–90), *Demographic Trends*. Paris.

—— (various issues), *Employment Outlook*. Paris.

—— (1960–89), *Historical Statistics*. Paris.

PAUKERT, LIBA (1984), *The Employment and Unemployment of Women in OECD Countries*. Paris: OECD.

SENGENBERGER, WERNER, LOVEMAN, GARRY W., and PIORE, MICHAEL J. (eds.) (1990), *The Re-emergence of Small Enterprises: Industrial Restructuring in Industrialised Countries*. Geneva: ILO.

Sveriges Officiella Statistik (1992), *Statistical Abstract of Sweden 1991*. Stockholm.

TOMES, JIRI (1991), 'Nezamestnanost u nas a v ES', in *Tydenik Hospodarskych Novin*, 40/91. Prague.

UK Department of Employment (1990), *New Earnings Survey 1989*. London: HMSO.

UN/ECE, Economic Commission for Europe (1980), *The Economic Role of Women in the ECE Region*. New York: United Nations.

12

Economic Reform and Women: A General Framework with Specific Reference to Hungary

Gordon Weil

INTRODUCTION

Although the literature on economic reform in Eastern Europe has grown rapidly, relatively little attention has been devoted to the impact of reform on women. This chapter hopes to fill that gap, at least in part, by providing an economic perspective on the way economic reform is affecting women in the context of the Hungarian economy.

Gender relations, including the socially and culturally accepted rights and responsibilities between men and women, underlie the economic structures and transformations in Hungary (or any nation) in both the public and private spheres. Gender relations are an important determinant of the types of careers men and women typically choose, the division of labour within the household, and therefore ultimately of the way in which reform affects women.[1]

In addition to gender relations, women's ability to earn secure incomes, i.e. their success in the productive sphere, is determined both by economic conditions and by economic policy. At the macroeconomic level, economic conditions influence the environment in which women seek and participate in work by determining, for instance, rates of inflation, unemployment, and economic growth. Microeconomic conditions, or the jobs that women tend to hold and their wages, directly determine women's incomes. Economic reform, the economic policy that is central to this chapter, includes stabilization policies which work mainly through macroeconomic channels, and ownership policies which operate at the microeconomic level. The impact of economic reform on women in the productive sphere is analysed in the following section by studying the consequences of the interaction of gender relations, economic conditions, and reform policies on women's earnings.[2]

---

[1] Economic change leads, over a long time, to changes in gender relations. This analysis, however, considers gender relations to be exogenous to economic reform. That allows me to focus on the ways that reform affects women in the current context of dominance and dependence between men and women in Hungary.

[2] Economic conditions and economic reforms have, at least, a two-way relation. First, one of the main factors that prompted reforms in the first place, and influenced their make-up, was

Economic success not only contributes to women's financial independence, an important element of full social equality, but also influences women's social independence. As John Stuart Mill put it more than one hundred years ago: 'the power of earning is essential to the dignity of women' (quoted in Ferge 1980).

Any full accounting of the effects of economic reform on women must consider women's multiple roles in both productive and reproductive spheres. Hence there follows a section on the reproductive sphere, which addresses women's roles as mother and housewife. In this sphere, too, gender relations combine with economic conditions (here, the set of policies that support women's reproductive chores) to determine the impact of reform policies on women.

Fig. 12.1 is a schematic representation of the relations just described. It shows that women's welfare is determined by their double burden of work and family responsibilities, and that economic success in the productive sphere is determined by the mix of reform policies, economic conditions, and gender relations. It also illustrates that in reproductive activities, too, gender relations, economic conditions, and economic reform policy interact to influence women's welfare.

The concluding section summarizes the main points of the chapter. It draws together the ways in which reform may work against women, and notes areas where potential opportunities arise. In the short run, reform promises very few benefits for women, with potential opportunities arising only after some time. It is important to use this time to strengthen women's voice in the public arena so that any potential benefits can be realized.

THE PRODUCTIVE SPHERE

Hungary has a dual economic structure. The primary sector (the state socialist sector) includes state-owned enterprises and co-operatives, while the 'second' economy includes legal and illegal private economic activities and several new forms of mixed public–private activities. Most work done in the 'second' economy is in addition to work done in the primary sector; these are the second jobs that so many Hungarians hold.

The state socialist sector encompasses the heart of Hungary's industrial

poor economic performance. Secondly, as reforms affect different segments of Hungarian society differently we can expect to find these segments trying to slow down or accelerate those reforms. Thus, economic conditions act both as a brake on reform movements, and as an impetus for them. Ultimately, the pace and pattern of economic reform, and hence its impact on women, are influenced largely by economic performance. Beyond these comments, the interaction between policy and economic conditions is a complex one which is beyond the scope of this chapter.

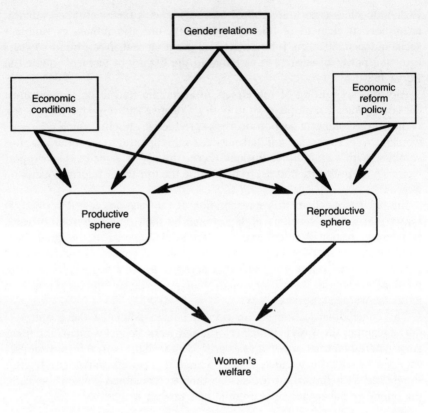

FIG 12.1 Framework for viewing the impacts of reform on women's welfare

structure. In 1988 it accounted for 94 per cent of gross domestic product (Boote and Somogyi 1991), and employed approximately 70 per cent of the labour force (*Economist* 1990). Reform measures have been aimed primarily at this sector. Co-operatives dominate the agricultural sector, accounting for some 75 per cent of agricultural employment in the mid-1980s.

All activities in the 'second' economy experienced rapid growth during the 1980s. Estimates of its contribution to national income vary, but one observer (Sziraczki 1990) put it at 20 per cent in 1985. This sector has relatively few women in it. One reason for this is a matter of time. Given the double burden of work and family chores that most women assume, they have little time to take on a second job.[3] Another reason is that many women do not have the

---

[3] Most of the jobs in the 'second' economy are indeed second jobs for their holders. Women tend to be more prevalent in secondary agricultural activities. One reason for this may be that farming is an activity that can be carried out in conjunction with many child-care responsibilities.

skills that are transferable to this sector, such as auto repair, construction, plumbing, etc.

The next two subsections focus on economic conditions: the current macroeconomic situation, and the gender-influenced microeconomic situation of women in the productive sphere.

Economic conditions

Macroeconomic conditions.   Hungary's external indebtedness has had a large influence on the direction and speed of economic reform. Stemming from its lack of adjustment to the oil price shock of 1973, Hungary's hard-currency accounts began to deteriorate, and, as in many Third World countries, its hard-currency debt began to escalate. In 1988 this external debt amounted to over \$17.5 billion, and required debt service payments of over 23 per cent of its export earnings, which was a reduction from 60 per cent in 1986 (Jeffries 1990). This ratio led the World Bank to classify Hungary as one of the world's seventeen 'severely indebted middle income countries'. Hungary's debt burden requires it to direct a substantial amount of resources to Western banks, rather than use them to support living standards and economic restructuring. The external debt also requires Hungary to restrain imports and promote exports to hard-currency markets, and is a motivating factor behind policies designed to make Hungary an attractive place for direct foreign investment.

In addition to hard-currency trade with Western nations, Hungary also trades with the Council for Mutual Economic Assistance (CMEA, or COMECON) countries. Its exports to CMEA nations, however, have declined from 41 per cent in 1989 to 32 per cent in 1990. In January 1991, trade with these nations began to be settled in hard currencies. This has produced a substantial terms-of-trade loss for Hungary as a result of rising energy and raw material prices, and has reduced income and government revenues (Boote and Somogyi 1991).

As Hungary entered the 1990s, its inflation was high but still manageable, in the 20–30 per cent per year range.[4] Nevertheless, government subsidies have kept the prices of some basic necessities such as food, water, milk, rents, and mortgage rates low. While transfer payments have partially protected incomes, rising inflation rates have reduced living standards for many.

Unlike other industrialized nations, unemployment has traditionally not been a significant problem in Hungary. Up to the middle of the 1980s,

---

[4] Many believe this severely understates the true inflation rate, because it does not include goods and services produced in the 'second' economy which has grown rapidly over the last five years, and has free-market prices.

Hungary was able to maintain full employment. During the second half of
the 1980s, however, labour redundancies began to occur, and for the first
time in three decades open unemployment now exists (Sziraczki 1990). Still,
unemployment has remained small; the official unemployment rate for 1990
is 1.7 per cent (US Council of Economic Advisers 1991). Rising levels of
open unemployment may reflect earlier levels of disguised unemployment,
which according to Hillman (1990) was perhaps as high as 10–20 per cent of
the labour force. As constraints on the dismissal of workers and subsidies to
state-owned enterprises are reduced, we will see less retention of redundant
workers.

The 1980s was largely a decade of stagnation. Following almost ten years
of relatively rapid growth in production and consumption (about 6 per cent
per year for each variable), GDP grew at an average annual rate of 1.6 per
cent from 1980 to 1988. Since 1988 GDP has declined or stagnated each year,
falling by 3 per cent in 1990 (*Economist* 1991), and in 1988 real wages were
about 15 per cent less than their 1978 level.

As might be expected, stagnating production and market reforms have led
to growing inequality and poverty. In 1980 the highest 10 per cent of wage-
earners in the state and co-operative sector earned 3.6 times as much as the
lowest paid 10 per cent, but by 1988 that gap had increased to 5.3 times
(Sziraczki 1990). Inequalities in living conditions grew as young couples found
it increasingly difficult to buy flats of their own (Revesz 1990). According to
one source, by 1990 some 40 per cent of the Hungarian population was living
at or below the official poverty line—defined in forints as Ft4,500 per person
per month (Volgyes 1990). Furthermore, a disproportionate number of the
elderly, and families with several children, are among the impoverished.
Beyond that, women in general are more often poverty-stricken than men.

Driven by a need to reduce its external debt, Hungary enforced austerity
measures in the early 1980s, and again under the aegis of the IMF in the late
1980s. The country's poor economic performance may well be a stimulus for
economic reform, but stagnation is not good news for women. As the
economy moves in the direction of greater reliance on markets under stagnant
economic conditions, women are likely to suffer disproportionately. Some
feel that this is because, compared with men, women have a more tenuous
connection to their jobs; others argue that women are expensive workers
when one includes their benefits such as paid maternity leaves.

Microeconomic conditions. The largest source of income for women in
Hungary today is wage earnings, primarily in the state sector.[5] To

[5] More generally, incomes accrue to citizens in their roles as labourers, entrepreneurs, lenders
of capital, landlords, and as transfer payments from the government. In communist Hungary
very little capital or land was privately owned, and although entrepreneurship is growing, it is
not growing rapidly for women. Transfer payments are covered in connection with the
reproductive sphere, hence the focus here is on wage incomes.

understand how reform affects women's productive lives, then, we must note their positions in the labour force.

An understanding of women's work patterns requires an examination of the training and education that men and women receive before they enter the labour force. Throughout the post-war period, the educational levels of the Hungarian population steadily improved, and with it the educational levels of women. By the mid-1980s women's educational accomplishments surpassed those of men in several areas. For instance, among active wage-earners, women tended to surpass men in the highest grade level achieved. On the other hand, the percentage of males finishing vocational training exceeded that of women, and men made up some 67 per cent of those in adult education (CSO 1989). Thus, women and men tend to receive very different training before entering the labour force.

Even when men and women train at similar institutions, they tend to specialize in different areas. In vocational schools in 1987, women made up at least two-thirds of the students in garments, services, leatherwork, and textiles. But very few women were found training for the machine industry, construction or telecommunications industries, and there are practically no women at all training to be vehicle mechanics or to work in tool manufacturing. Women and men also study different disciplines at the university level. Women make up more than 50 per cent of students in teacher training, medicine, health care, economics, and law; yet they make up much less than 50 per cent of students in engineering, veterinary medicine, and agriculture (CSO 1989). These patterns are similar to those found in many Western industrialized countries.

Although the vast majority of women work outside the home,[6] they have not contributed equally in all occupations. Compared with men, women are less well represented in physical (blue-collar) occupations than non-physical (white-collar) ones. In 1988 58 per cent of female workers were in physical occupations and 42 per cent in the non-physical ones (as compared with 78 and 22 per cent for men). Women in physical activities made up about 40 per cent of these workers (slightly below their proportion in the work-force in general). Of these, 25 per cent were unskilled, 50 per cent were semi-skilled, and 25 per cent were skilled workers. Some 60 per cent of male workers were skilled (CSO 1989). Furthermore, younger women tended to be skilled workers while older women dominated the semi- and unskilled jobs (Kulcsár 1985).

Gender segregation exists within physical occupations. Although the percentage of women employed in industry was roughly equal to their overall

---

[6] In 1988 roughly 82 per cent of all women between the ages of 15 and 55 were active wage-earners or on child-care leave, and they comprised about 46 per cent of all active wage-earners.

labour-force participation rate, they tended to be over-represented in light industry and under-represented in heavy industry (see CSO 1989 and Volgyes 1985). This difference is important because investment patterns have favoured heavy industry. Gender segregation can also be seen in specific occupations. Women play a decisive role in the food industry, trade, and services, but are barely visible in tool manufacturing or among vehicle mechanics (CSO 1989).[7]

Not surprisingly, gender segregation is also evident in non-physical occupations. In 1988 some 62 per cent of these workers were women. Throughout the 1980s, women worked in service occupations which have traditionally been female-dominated. For instance, in office work and administrative jobs women comprise over 90 per cent of workers. Women also dominate the occupations of teachers, nurses, librarians, chemists, and financial controllers. In technical occupations such as engineers, on the other hand, fewer than 25 per cent of employees are women. Even in the female-dominated occupations, women are not usually found in positions of authority. For instance, although women make up 88 per cent of elementary schoolteachers, they constitute less than 15 per cent of primary school heads. Similarly, women make up over two-thirds of nurses, and almost half of all physicians, but only 8 per cent of surgeons and obstetrics–gynaecology doctors, which are among the highest paid specialists (Berney 1990). Women have done best as business executives and financial managers; in 1980, 41 per cent of these jobs were held by women (Kulcsár 1985).

These data reveal the following patterns. The vast majority of women work outside the home. They tend to gravitate towards light rather than heavy industry, and to the service occupations in particular. There are fewer skilled women workers than skilled men, and the skilled women tend to be younger. Furthermore, women tend to be under-represented in authority positions in all occupations, but less so as business executives.

Given these differences, it is not surprising to find a gap between the earnings of women and men. Between 1982 and 1987, women's average wage as a percentage of men's average wage narrowed from 69 to 72 per cent (CSO 1989). This may reflect the growing number of women in the skilled labour category, for the gap between women's skilled and non-skilled wages increased in this period.[8] Another way to view the wage gap is by the extremes in the earnings in each occupation. Even in the trade branches (which are female-dominated), in 1980 over 40 per cent of the women earned

---

[7] Gender segregation exists in agriculture, too. In 1988 women made up over 60% of plant cultivation and horticulture workers, but less than 40% of stock breeders and livestock-minders. In the agricultural field in general, men have greater access to new technology than women.

[8] Of course, these are averages, so that the wage gap varied differently for different occupations between 1982 and 1987.

less than Ft3,000 per month but only 16 per cent of the men earned that little. At the other extreme, over 14 per cent of male employees earned over Ft6,000 per month, but less than 4 per cent of the women. This tendency is also found in other occupations (Barta *et al*. 1985).

There are many reasons for these wage differentials. The first is 'tracking', or 'streaming', which begins with schools. Women's education tends to steer them away from the higher-paid occupations. Some argue that this is because higher paying jobs require work that is too strenuous for women. This is not credible; women do hard work in agriculture and cotton mills. Nor is it clear that a machine operator really engages in such strenuous work. Other reasons for the gap include the fact that women often interrupt their careers to look after young children, and the official retirement age for women is five years earlier than for men (55 versus 60), which reduces their average relative wage.

As shown in Fig. 12.1, women's productive activity is also affected by economic reform policy. The impact of reform on women is analysed below in light of economic conditions and the gender segregation of work.

Economic reform policy

Hungary has more experience with economic reform than any other East European nation. Major reforms began in 1968 with the New Economic Mechanism (NEM), the most far-reaching reform seen anywhere at that time.[9] Since then Hungary has alternately pushed forward and backed off from economic reforms. Reforms will continue in the future, as the government elected in 1990 is committed to radical economic reform.

Economic reform is intended to transform the economy from one dominated by state-owned industry and direct bureacratic intervention to one featuring private ownership and markets. This requires two major institutional changes: a price structure that gives appropriate signals to producers and consumers, and an ownership structure, or set of rules, that encourages producers to respond productively to those signals. The policies to achieve these two broad goals have macroeconomic and microeconomic aspects. The formation of a rational price structure requires a price liberalization and stabilization programme built on several macroeconomic policies. The microeconomic issues surrounding ownership include policies to encourage the growth of the private sector, policies to improve the functioning of the state sector, and privatization (shifting the balance between the sectors).

---

[9] Even before the NEM, Hungary implemented reforms in agriculture and in light industry. Hungary's long experience with reform has led economists to label it a *gradual approach* to economic reform.

Macroeconomic aspects. Although Hungary's inflation rate is much lower than Poland's or Yugoslavia's, containing inflation is still an important aspect of its stabilization policies. Hungarian industry is very concentrated.[10] Under these conditions, attempts to liberalize prices must be accompanied by stabilization policies to combat monopoly prices, which add to inflationary pressures, distort resource allocation, and shift income away from labour.[11] Furthermore, inflation makes it difficult to generate a rational price structure, because increases in the general price level tend to hide or blurr relative price changes, which are at the heart of forming a rational price structure. In the Hungarian environment inflation is particularly problematic, as it makes it more difficult for government bureaucrats to resist growing enterprise demands for financial relief.[12]

This leads to a second part of the stabilization programme: the restoration of fiscal balance. One reason Hungary has run budget deficits has been its subsidies to inefficient industries. In 1988 some 15 per cent of GDP was redistributed via state subsidies (Abel 1990). Hare (1990) concludes that the main effect of Hungary's tax/subsidy system has been to prop up enterprises that long ago should have been forced to operate more competitively. Hungary has also heavily subsidized consumer goods. But as part of the stabilization programme, it plans to reduce consumer and producer subsidies to 7 per cent of GDP in 1991 (Boote and Somogyi 1991). These cuts have already led to price increases for agricultural and food products.

Alterations in the tax system have also contributed to fiscal balance. Recently Hungary introduced two new types of taxes: a VAT tax and a progressive personal income tax. To some extent they replace the system of non-uniform profit taxes on state enterprises and co-operatives, which in 1985 siphoned off some 85 per cent of gross enterprise profits (Hare 1990). Furthermore, these taxes had been tailored to each enterprise and were frequently adjusted as the outcome of bargaining between enterprises and the government. The new taxes are intended to raise revenue without causing the distortions in the price structure that the older individualized profits taxes caused. The income tax is also intended to capture some of the earnings from the 'second' economy, and in that way to help stem the growing disparity in incomes.

[10] To illustrate, in 1987 some 372 enterprises (out of 1,225) accounted for over 75% of industrial employment and over 80% of industrial sales; furthermore, of these, there were 45 that alone accounted for over 35% of industrial employment and over 60% of sales (Hare 1990).

[11] Another reason to be concerned with inflation, to which we return in our discussion of women's reproductive role, is that inflation may redistribute income in ways not consistent with society's sense of equity.

[12] All stabilization programmes also include the establishment of financial discipline. In Hungary financial discipline is maintained primarily through direct government control over credits, subsidies, and tax relief granted to state enterprises. The creation of a private banking system, discussed more fully below, will also help enforce financial discipline.

A final element of the stabilization package deals with foreign trade. In addition to a reduction in enterprise taxes and subsidies, efficiency has been encouraged through import liberalization. In 1991 the share of hard-currency imports free of quotas or licensing restrictions rose to 90 per cent. This exposes approximately 70 per cent of domestic production to foreign competition (Boote and Somogyi 1991). In light of its large debt service obligations, Hungary also needs to encourage hard-currency exports. However, with less government control over state enterprises, it is difficult to get them to shift to production for the West (Brada 1988). Furthermore, higher-quality standards found in the West make it difficult for enterprises to crack these markets. Nevertheless, devaluations of the forint have been used to encourage exports and discourage imports.

How do these policies affect women's productive activities? The primary impact of any stabilization programme is to reduce demand. Of course, the idea is that the savings generated from reduced spending can be directed into productive investment leading to higher consumption and income. Initially, however, stabilization reduces production and increases unemployment, and this directly hurts women.

Some industries, however, will be affected more than others. Although it is not clear exactly which industries will contract and which will expand as market prices rise, we can make some informed guesses. According to Kornai (1990), the mining industry is quite dependent on subsidies; as subsidies are reduced, therefore, we can expect to see this industry contract, eliminating many jobs. Similarly, the energy and heavy industrial sectors, e.g. metallurgy and chemicals, have received a good deal of support and will likely contract. Mining, energy, and heavy industry are the high-wage sectors of the economy, and, not coincidentally, are also sectors with low levels of efficiency. Women, who have been little represented here, may be shielded from this restructuring.

Some industries will expand. These most likely are the industries that currently bear heavy levels of indirect taxes. Hare (1990) suggests that electricity supply and engineering are two such industries. Engineering is another almost exclusively male-dominated sector. For women to benefit from this expansion, there will need to be a shift in their training.

As noted above, part of the stabilization package includes devaluations of the forint. Following currency devaluations, the tradable goods sector (including exports and import substitutes) expands relative to non-tradables. The service sector is part of the non-tradable sector, and is the major employer of women in Hungary today. Hence we can expect these women to be hurt by devaluations. On the other hand, attempts to shift trade from CMEA countries to the West may be to the advantage of women. Typically, the products traded with CMEA countries have not been ones in which Hungary holds a comparative advantage with the West. A shift towards

Western markets will expand trade in light industry such as clothing and textiles. These industries are more female-dominated than the heavy industrial goods traded with CMEA countries.

Women in the service sector may be affected in another way. Much of the funding for this sector comes from the central budget, especially for health care, education, and social care. This sector's growth depends upon political decisions about the state budget.[13] Since part of the stabilization programme's goal is to reduce central government spending, these women are at risk. Spending cuts on health and education will directly reduce women's employment. Furthermore, since women tend to work in the lower levels of these professions, they are particularly vulnerable. On the other hand, relative to other nations at the same level of development, Hungary's service sector is much smaller; hence over the longer term we might anticipate an expansion of this sector which at some point may benefit women.

In the past, the 'second' economy has provided a buffer through which living standards have been maintained when production in the state sector slows. As reforms seek to liberalize the private sector, we can expect this sector to grow. However, this is not a sector in which women traditionally have been very active. This is particularly true of those women living in towns (without substantial household plots to farm) and without capital equipment or transferable skills. Additionally, since women often have home, child-care, and even elderly care responsibilities, time constraints and reduced mobility prevent them from being very active in the 'second' economy. Thus, women are not able to enjoy the countercyclical benefits that men enjoy from that sector.

Stabilization and price liberalization policies have a complex and varying impact on women. In the short run, however, the major impacts are negative. It is only over a longer time period, as different sectors expand and contract under market prices, that women may gain.

Microeconomic aspects. The vast majority of reforms, beginning even before the NEM of 1968, have attempted to give state-owned enterprises greater autonomy. Although during the 1970s Hungary took many steps backwards, since 1979 reforms have steadily encouraged enterprise managers to act more and more in a market-oriented fashion.

An essential aspect of economic reform is price liberalization, which helps prevent large imbalances between demand and supply from arising. Since 1968 several attempts have been made to remove distortions in the price structure and move closer to competitive prices. By 1990 approximately 80 per cent of all producer and consumer goods were classified as free prices

---

[13] The number of women elected to Parliament, however, has declined since 1990.

(Boote and Somogyi 1991).[14] Although there remain distortions in Hungary's price structure, imbalances are not as severe as in other Eastern European nations largely because Hungary has a long history of reform in this area. Imbalances are still evident, however, in several sectors, including health services where women make up a large share of the labour force. In light industry, another area dominated by women, and agriculture, fewer distortions exist than in other sectors of the economy. In their role as producers, women in the health services can expect to feel the impact of future price reforms more than those employed in light industry. Yet generally, as a result of the gendered patterns of work, women will be affected less than men by price reform.

Wage and employment practices have also undergone many reforms since 1968. Although policies have not always leaned towards less bureaucratic influence, since the mid-1980s managers have gained greater autonomy. Managers have gained more authority to release redundant or inefficient workers, and direct control of wage rates has diminished. Nevertheless, wage and employment practices are an area in which central influence remains strong.[15] Liberalized wage and employment policies, combined with the stabilization programme implemented in the 1980s have led to an increase in the demand for skilled relative to unskilled and semi-skilled labour (Sziraczki 1990). Although the extent of this shift differs by geographic region, we can expect it to benefit men relative to women since a disproportionate share of skilled jobs are held by men. Furthermore a disproportionate number of skilled women workers are young women. Hence, wage and employment reforms combined with stabilization policies will tend to hurt women more than men, and older women workers most. A liberalized wage policy will also lead to more rapid wage increases for skilled labourers than for semi- or unskilled workers, and will work to the relative detriment of women. This is particularly troublesome since women are also so poorly represented in other high-wage jobs such as management.

Some of the most interesting reforms of state enterprises have come recently. Managerial reform began in 1985. Although this has not affected the largest enterprises (e.g. those in electricity generation, oil production, aluminium production, and transport), it has begun a new selection process for management in all other enterprises. These reforms created Enterprise Councils, which were given the responsibility of hiring, dismissing, and setting the salaries of management. The councils include representatives of workers and management. Such councils operated in over 80 per cent of state-owned enterprises by the end of 1987. Will these reforms, which put

---

[14] Price categories now include fixed, flexible, and free prices. But even 'free' prices are subject to the requirement that they cannot exceed the prices of comparable imports.

[15] For instance, the wages of blue-collar workers appear higher than consistent with free markets, and wages also exhibit less dispersion than we would find without intervention.

more authority for choosing enterprise leaders in the hands of workers, lead to greater representation of women in management? The evidence to date is discouraging. Most 'new' managers have had an engineering background, which is a male preserve. There is, however, one ground for optimism: there is a disproportionate number of women among those who are, and are training to become, economists, accountants, and financial managers. Certainly people with such training will become more important to enterprises operating in a market environment where political connections are less important.

Reform has also produced rapid change in the financial system. In 1987 the National Bank of Hungary was reorganized to separate the Central Bank from commercial banks' operations. These reforms attempt to steer lending more in the direction of risk and return considerations, and away from ministerial bargaining. Along with the growth of commercial banks has come the beginning of rudimentary stock and bond markets, but these remain highly regulated. Women with backgrounds in economics, accounting and finance should be valuable to the expanding banking and financial sector. This is one service area that does not depend heavily on government expenditure, and could become a source of jobs for women in the future. Although the financial sector is still in a rudimentary state, as reform continues it will become a growth sector.[16]

The private sector has also undergone several reforms, and its growth is evidence of the viability of Hungarian markets. Since 1968 this sector has grown as licences have become more readily available for activities such as craftsmen, construction contractors, shopkeepers, restauranteurs, etc.[17] Although the official private sector remains small in terms of total production, it is expanding rapidly. In the 1980s the government encouraged the growth of this sector by permitting new forms of business organization. Small co-operatives with less than 100 members can now get credit on generous terms, and have no upper limit on the income that they earn.

In 1988 a new Company Law was passed which permitted many new types of business organization. These include joint stock companies, joint income companies, limited liability companies, and joint ventures with foreigners. Foreign corporations are now allowed to be majority owners. This is meant to encourage transnational corporations to employ cheap Hungarian labour to produce goods for the domestic market and for export. It is also a way to earn additional foreign exchange, and to gain access to modern technology.

[16] There are several additional areas of reforms which I have not discussed. For instance, the roles of enterprise management and bureaucrats in the investment process has changed several times, as have trade practices both with CMEA nations and with nations of the West.
[17] Private activities have also been encouraged in the agricultural sector with two important changes. Restrictions have been reduced on the size of the household plots, and households were given the right to own and raise livestock.

To date, however, relatively few transnationals have shown interest. They view Hungary as a nation in transition and attach a substantial amount of risk to such ventures.

Although it might be premature to speculate on the impact on women of increased direct foreign investment, some of the lessons from Third World countries can be applied here. The main attraction for transnational corporations in Hungary is low-cost labour. In other parts of the world with similar attractions these corporations have tended to hire female workers, because they can be paid even lower wages and are a more docile labour force. It is not clear that women are well served by these jobs. Although they do provide paid employment, working conditions are often poor, job security is low, as are wages, and many argue that these jobs are more a form of exploitation than a boon.

New forms of mixed ownership have also emerged. The most important type is the 'enterprise business work partnership'.[18] These are created by employees in state-owned enterprises who rent equipment from the enterprise and carry out production after regular hours, but at a higher wage. Many simply carry on the regular work of the enterprise, but some enter into contracts with other enterprises for speciality work. Although these activities do help to use excess capacity and provide additional hours for those who want them, they also can create jealousy among workers who are not involved, and they may provide an incentive for workers not to work as hard during regular hours. Also, the development of these partnerships may not benefit men and women equally. The main reason for this is simply a matter of time. Given their reproductive responsibilities, women tend to participate less in second jobs than men do. As these opportunities and others like them in the private sector grow, income inequality by gender will increase. In some cases these work-teams are selected by enterprise management as a reward to good workers. Given past experience, it seems that, without more women in management positions, they will not be chosen equally with men.

Until recently, Hungarian reform has taken two parallel paths, although not without backsliding: steps to encourage state-owned enterprises to act more in a market-oriented fashion, and actions to encourage the growth of private production. Reform took a third approach recently with the privatization of state-owned enterprises. The government plans to privatize about 60 per cent of state-owned enterprises over a five-year period (Volgyes 1990). In 1990 the process of privatization began for twenty large state enterprises, and plans call for the privatization of 16,000 small firms over a two-year period (US Council of Economic Advisors 1991). There are many different techniques for privatizing industry and many concerns about their outcomes,

---

[18] Another mixed form includes agricultural co-operatives which rent equipment and expertise to households.

most specifically focusing on efficiency aspects (Borensztein and Kumar 1991). To date, privatization has provided a way for management to protect itself in the new uncertain economic environment found in Hungary (Hare 1990). No matter how the details of privatization work themselves out, they have the real potential to provide more opportunities for women at higher levels of management. So far things have not worked out that way, though.[19]

The policies of stabilization and reform in the context of Hungary's gendered work patterns will result in a complex pattern of potential gains and losses for women. It goes without saying that converting potential benefits into actual ones demands a strong voice for women in the government and in work spheres. Forming and strengthening women's organizations during this period of economic restructuring is a task with important economic implications.

THE REPRODUCTIVE SPHERE

From Fig. 12.1 the reproductive sphere of women's lives can also be analysed by examining the interaction of gender relations, economic conditions, and economic reform. Although communist ideology encouraged rapid increases in women's labour-force participation, it did little to change the gender relations that underlie the traditional division of labour in the household. According to one survey, in three out of four complete Hungarian families, 80–85 per cent of traditional family chores are done by wives (CSO 1989).[20] Recent time-budget studies indicate that, even though many more men than women have second jobs, women still have less free time than men (CSO 1989). This division of labour has led policy-makers (who are primarily men) to equate women's issues solely with reproductive responsibilities.

The equation of women's concerns with family responsibilities is one of the obstacles to their full emancipation. To attain political and economic equality with men, the close relationship between women's roles in the productive and reproductive spheres must be recognized and addressed. Because women have multiple and complex responsibilities, policy-makers must consider both the impact of policies implemented in the work-place on the family, and the impact of policies implemented at the family level on women's jobs. Policies that support women's reproductive responsibilities provide the economic conditions, or context, under which women carry out these tasks.

---

[19] Some privatization schemes call for the free distribution of vouchers (e.g. ownership shares of the enterprise). This approach has not materialized in Hungary. If it does, it is essential that women and men, and not families, have access to these shares.

[20] Obviously, in families with single mothers this ratio is much higher.

Economic Conditions

Hungary provides transfer payments, both in cash and in kind, to help support the living standards of its citizens. Two of the largest cash benefits include pensions, and family and child-support payments. Comparatively speaking, Hungary has a generous system of support for child care, and it comes in several forms. First, there is a twenty-four-week maternity leave during which mothers receive their full salary. At birth, if the mother has had at least four previous doctor's visits (and most have more than this), the mother receives a birth allowance of Ft6,000. Perhaps the best-known aspect of the system is the 'mother's wage'; this is a wage-adjusted child-care allowance, available to mothers only, up to the child's first birthday.[21] This same allowance is also available up to the child's second birthday, with the single difference that it is payable to either the mother or the father. It usually pays about 65–75 per cent of an individual's annual earnings, depending on the length of employment and earnings level. For the next year, until the child's third birthday, the mother receives a flat-rate monthly allowance scaled to the number of children she has, and an additional Ft930 per month (CSO 1989). The number of mothers who take advantage of these payments has steadily grown, and in 1988 reached almost 90 per cent of new mothers (CSO 1989). In addition, Hungary pays a 'family supplement'. This payment, indexed to the number of children in the family, covers at most 30 per cent of the costs of raising children.

Although this system does help support new mothers, it can have a negative affect on their productive activities. Ferge (1980) argues that it legitimizes the current division of labour within the household, and reinforces the notion that women's issues and main chores are in the reproductive area. Ferge also notes that the right to be only a mother can quickly turn into an obligation, with a negative impact on a woman's career. Thus, even as these policies help women in the reproductive sphere, at the same time they slow their full integration into the productive division of labour.

Additional child care is provided by state-supported institutions. After children reach the age of 3 institutional care becomes important to most families. Approximately 80 per cent of 5-year-olds are enrolled in kinder-gartens. Altogether, for complete families some 45 per cent of all children under 14 years of age are placed in either crêches, kindergartens, or day schools while their parents are at work; the figure exceeds 50 per cent for single mothers (CSO 1989). When these are high-quality services they support women in their roles as both mothers and wage-earners.

Hungary also provides 'free' health care for mothers and children. During pregnancy mothers must receive at least four medical check-ups to be eligible

---

[21] After the first 24 weeks mothers are also permitted to take on part-time work.

for the birth allowance. By the end of the 1980s, over 99 per cent of all babies were born in a hospital. Furthermore, the number of paediatric doctors has been steadily increasing over the past decade, and although this has led to a fall in infant mortality rates (to 17 per 1,000 live births) they remain high by European standards (CSO 1989).

Provisioning the family can be a time-consuming activity. Although Hungary is fortunate to have a vital agricultural sector which provides an adequate food supply, the same cannot be said of the availability of other consumer goods, services, and consumer durables. The relative neglect of light industry for several decades has led to shortages of many consumer goods. These shortages are common in Eastern European countries, and force women to spend more time and energy provisioning the household.

A shortage of housing is of particular concern. The most common living arrangement in towns is in flats or apartments in state-owned buildings, where rents are fixed at a low rate.[22] Since once a person gains access to these flats (and in Budapest the wait can be from four to ten years), they can have them for a lifetime, and because relatively little state money is spent to build new apartment buildings, there is a chronic housing shortage (Revesz 1990). The other side of this housing shortage is overcrowding. Overcrowding makes itself felt in many different ways. Lack of storage space means that women must shop more frequently, often daily. The housing shortage has also been a stimulus for the 'second' economy as a large percentage of new building is currently undertaken outside the state sector. These homes, however, are expensive, making it particularly difficult for young couples to find their own place.

Even as young people have a difficult time finding a suitable place to start a family, the elderly are finding living conditions in general more and more difficult. Because of their age, and sometimes their deteriorating health, they have little access to the supplementary income that comes from work in the 'second' economy.[23] Without a second source of income, most retirees rely on their pensions. The average women's pension is less than men's because women's salary is on average less than men's, and because women retire five years earlier. In 1988 about 70 per cent of elderly women who received pensions found that they were not enough to place them over the poverty line of Ft4,000 per month. Furthermore, individual pensions have not always kept up with inflation, leading to a reduction of real income as ageing proceeds.

[22] It is worth noting that the subsidy that state-owned flat-dwellers receive tends to redistribute income in a regressive fashion.
[23] The exception may be women who live in the country and have plots on which to grow food.

Economic reform policy

The major impact of economic reform on women's reproductive activities has come through stabilization policies. Spending cuts and the increase in inflation that follows price liberalization make the managing of household consumption a much more difficult task. On the expenditure side, reductions in subsidies drive upward the prices of food, milk, mortgage rates, and other consumer goods, forcing women to spend more time looking for bargains, or to cut back on purchases.[24] In addition, if child-care allowances and family supplements do not increase at least as rapidly as inflation, mothers will find it more difficult to stay home with their young children. If expenditure on crèches, kindergartens, and day schools is reduced, it will become more difficult for women to juggle work and family responsibilities. Families with several young children would be particularly hard hit.

The elderly could also be particularly vulnerable to expenditure cuts. Many older women depend on pensions that are already too small to keep them out of poverty. Cuts in government spending on pensions, or even increases below the rate of inflation, will further erode these women's already low standard of living. In short, the two most vulnerable groups in Hungary during this period of reform are the elderly and families with several young children (Andorka 1988). Given women's nurturing role, these cuts will have a powerful, if indirect, effect on most women.

The housing shortage too will be made worse by expenditure cuts. Government spending in this area is already low. Further reductions will make it even more difficult to find and afford new housing. A growing housing shortage will reduce the mobility of labour, which is especially problematic in an environment where labour demands are changing. In the same vein, any reduction in government subsidies on mortgage rates will further increase the cost of living for most urban families.

The change in Hungary's tax structure further tightens the squeeze on household consumption. Replacing taxes on profits with a VAT tax and income tax will reduce taxes on investment and increase them on consumption. Although a reduction in consumption demand may help to slow inflation, its main impact is to reduce household disposable income, and in that way it will make the lives of housewives more difficult.

There may be a brighter side to this. There is some hope that liberalized prices will spur an increase in the production of consumer goods and services and relieve shortages, and there is some evidence that this is occurring. Certainly spending less time queuing for goods, and finding improved access to prepared foods, laundries, etc., will make housewives' jobs easier. But it is unrealistic to think that this increased production will have a major impact

---

[24] Devaluations of the forint also tend to drive prices upward, further reducing housewives' purchasing power.

on most women. As the economy becomes more market-oriented and income inequality increases, there will be a stratum of relatively well-off women who will enjoy these new services, and the remainder who will not. In countries (e.g. Sweden) where these services are widely available, women receive a good deal of government support.

Stabilization, and rising unemployment rates, will also impinge upon women's reproductive activities. With high unemployment, women cannot easily reduce their productive activities since the income they bring home is crucial. Also, men will be more eager to take on second jobs. Together, this means that women will have less time or help at home.

Economic reforms will surely make the reproductive aspects of women's lives more difficult in the short run. For a few well-off women life will become easier as a result of an increased provision of consumer goods and possibly an expanded market for domestic help. The majority of women, however, will not benefit from such changes.

CONCLUSIONS

The analytical framework presented in this chapter is general enough to be applied to other nations. An assessment of the effects of reform, however, will depend on the specific economic conditions and gender patterns in each country, and of course on the actual reform policies that the countries implement. In Hungary economic reform will make some women's lives more difficult at the same time that it creates potential opportunities for others.

In the productive sphere, the major negative impact that Hungarian women will experience in the short run is rising levels of unemployment. It is no secret that in depressed economic times in the market-place women generally fare worse than men. Also, since sources of growth must come more and more from productivity increases rather than from additional resources, demands for skilled relative to unskilled or semi-skilled labour will rise. Compared with men, women have a disadvantage in this area. Hungary's strategy of opening up to foreign investment holds mixed blessings for women. Although more unskilled and semi-skilled jobs may be created there, neither the pay nor the working conditions are likely to be very rewarding. Women's dominant position in the service sector is hurt by the currency devaluations and fiscal stringency that are part of reform.

There are few areas where reform helps women in their reproductive roles. Price increases, as subsidies are reduced and the forint depreciates, will make provisioning the household more and more difficult. The change in tax policies will also lead to reductions in household income. Certainly real reductions in government spending on family support and pensions can only make life more difficult for women.

Potential benefits for women may materialize in the future. Shifting trade to Western markets may benefit women, given their distribution across occupations and the types of Hungarian goods demanded by the West. The potential for long-run growth in Hungary's service sector also holds out hope for additional employment opportunities for women. Women's strong background in economics and finance puts them in a particularly good position to benefit from the growth of the private financial sector, too. This same background provides hope for their greater representation in management positions as firms become more market-oriented.

Building on their strong economics and finance training, perhaps the greatest potential for women is to attain management positions in the financial sector. If more women can move into these positions, they may be more successful in providing financing and encouragement for other women to seek out opportunities to become private entrepreneurs, which could offer the best chance for securing independent sources of income.

To mitigate the harsh short-run impact on women of economic reform, the government must provide a safety-net for its female population. Although a few small steps have been taken in that direction (Sziraczki 1990), more needs to be done. Beyond that, there is a critical need for women to strengthen their organizations to ensure that they have a stronger voice in the work-place, and are able to gain access to resources in the new economic environment to be found in Hungary.

REFERENCES

ABEL, ISTVAN (1990), 'Subsidy Reduction in the Hungarian Economy', *European Economy*, 43: 21–34.

ADAM, JAN (1989), *Economic Reform in the Soviet Union and Eastern Europe since the 1960s*. New York: St Martin's Press.

ANDORKA, R. (1988), 'Economic Difficulties–Economic Reform: Social Effects and Preconditions', *Acta Oeconomica*, 39: 291–302.

BARTA, BARNABAS et al. (1985), 'Hungary', in Valentina Bodrova and Richard Anker (eds.), *Working Women in Socialist Countries*. Geneva: ILO WEP Study, 23–55.

BERNEY, LOUIS (1990), 'East of Equality', *Boston Globe Magazine*, 30 December: 12–33.

BLANCHARD, OLIVIER et al. (1991) *Reform in Eastern Europe*. Cambridge, Mass.: MIT Press.

BOOTE, ANTHONY R. and SOMOGYI, JANOS (1991), *Economic Reform in Hungary since 1968*, International Monetary Fund Occasional Paper no. 83. Washington, DC: IMF.

BORENSZTEIN, EDUARDO, and KUMAR, MONMOHAN S. (1991), 'Proposals for Privatization in Eastern Europe', *International Monetary Fund Staff Papers*, 38 (2): 300–26.

300   G. WEIL

BRADA, JOSEF C. (1988), 'Is Hungary the Future of Poland or is Poland the Future of Hungary?' *Eastern European Politics and Societies*, 2 (3): 466–76.

Central Statistical Office of Hungary (CSO) (1989), *Women's Position in Socialist Hungary*. Budapest: Hungarian News Service on behalf of Hungarian Women's Council.

DANIEL, ZSUZSA (1985), 'The Effect of Housing Allocation on Social Inequality in Hungary', *Journal of Comparative Economics*, 9: 391–409.

Economist (1990), 'Survey: Perestroika', *The Economist*, 28 April.

—— (1991), 'Hungary', *The Economist*, 7 September: 111.

FERGE, ZSUZSA (1976), 'The Relation between Paid and Unpaid Work of Women: A Source of Inequality—with Special Reference to Hungary', *Labor and Society*, 1–2: 37–52.

—— (1980), *Society in the Making: Hungarian Social and Societal Policy, 1945–1975*. White Plains, NY: M. E. Sharpe.

HARE, PAUL G. (1988), 'Industrial Development of Hungary since World War II', *Eastern European Politics and Societies*, 2(1): 115–51.

—— (1990), 'Reform of Enterprise Regulation in Hungary from Tutelage to Market', *European Economy*, 43: 37–56.

HILLMAN, ARYE L. (1990), 'Macroeconomic Policy in Hungary and its Micro-economic Implications', *European Economy*, 43: 57–65.

JEFFRIES, IAN (1990), *A Guide to the Socialist Economies*. London: Routledge.

KENEN, PETER B. (1991), 'Transitional Arrangements for Trade and Payments Among the CMEA Countries', *International Monetary Fund Staff Papers*, 38(2): 235–67.

KORNAI, JANOS (1986), 'The Hungarian Reform Process: Visions, Hopes, and Reality', *Journal of Economic Literature*, 24(4): 1687–1737.

—— (1990), *The Road to a Free Economy*. New York: W. W. Norton.

KULCSÁR, ROZSA (1985), 'The Socioeconomic Conditions of Women in Hungary', in Sharon L. Wolchik and Alfred Meyer (eds.), *Women, State and Party in Eastern Europe*. Durham, NC: Duke University Press, 195–213.

MARER, PAUL (1990), 'Hungary Joins the West', *Challenge*, September–October: 8–10.

McINTYRE, ROBERT J. (1985), 'Demographic Policy and Sexual Equality: Value Conflicts and Policy Appraisal in Hungary and Romania', in Sharon L. Wolchik and Alfred Meyer (eds.), *Women, State and Party in Eastern Europe*. Durham, NC: Duke University Press, 270–85.

REVESZ, GABOR (1990), *Perestroika in Eastern Europe: Hungary's Economic Transformation, 1945–1988*. Boulder, Colo.: Westview Press.

RICHET, XAVIER (1989), *The Hungarian Model: Markets and Planning in a Socialist Economy*. New York: Cambridge University Press.

SILK, LEONARD (1991), 'Trickle Down: At the Summit, A Chance to Set the Stage for Growth', *New York Times*, 14 July, sec. 4:1.

SZIRACZKI, GYORGY (1990), 'Employment Policy and Labour Market In Transition: From Labour Shortage to Unemployment', *Soviet Studies*, 42(4): 701–22.

US Council of Economic Advisors (1991), *Economic Report of the President: 1991*. Washington, DC: US Government Printing Office.

VOLGYES, IVAN (1985), 'Blue-Collar Working Women and Poverty in Hungary', in Sharon L. Wolchik and Alfred Meyer (eds.), *Women, State and Party in Eastern Europe*. Durham, NC: Duke University Press, 221–33.

—— (1990), 'For Want of Another Horse: Hungary in 1990', *Current History*, December: 421–35.

World Bank (1990), *World Development Report 1990*. New York: Oxford University Press.

13
Gender Aspects of Dismantling the Command Economy in Eastern Europe: The Case of Poland

Maria Ciechocinska

INTRODUCTION

In Poland, the policy of full employment combined with relatively low wages and a high share of non-pecuniary benefits pursued in the years 1945–88 resulted in a large proportion of women in overall employment. The taking up of jobs by women on a mass scale in the late 1940s and early 1950s was one of the elements of the communist revolution. One consequence of this was the decline of the importance of the family as an economic institution and as the basic unit of social life, with a concomitant weakening of the authority of parents, whose role was being taken over by state institutions. It also marked the collapse of the model of a multi-generation family living together and running a single household. The loss of authority and respect accorded to the eldest family members were other consequences of the system. A typical week consisted of gainful employment for 48 hours, in addition to the time needed for commuting, which quite often took up to two hours one way, and the obligation to attend various political events, such as rallies and meetings, or to do compulsory overtime. Cultural attractions, participation in programmes pursued by factory common rooms, theatre productions, film shows, festivals, and parades were a disincentive to returning home in a hurry, especially when factory canteens served meals and children could be left for a whole day or even a week in the care of a kindergarten. This contributed to a relaxation of family ties.

Taking up gainful employment automatically transported a woman to a different milieu, while her earnings gave her a sense of independence. This made the proposed departure from traditional patterns extremely attractive. The role of the man as head of the family became less marked. The model of family based on partnership became more appealing than the old authoritarian or paternalistic model.

The spectacular election victory of Solidarity on 4 June 1989 was a manifestation of the will to embark on a reform of this system, dictated by the overwhelmingly negative public appraisal of the situation that had developed. This marked the beginning of change, although no one realized at that time how much inertia there was in the old patterns and what a long and painful process their dismantling would be. We now know that the transition to a market economy will take longer and that its social consequences are being differentially experienced by various sectors of the population. This chapter focuses on the impact of the transition from a state socialist economy to a market economy on women's employment and access to child care. The purpose is to illustrate the gender dynamics of Polish employment and unemployment and the bias entailed in certain policy choices, such as the closing down or privatization of child-care facilities.

THE COLLECTIVIST-STYLE ORGANIZATION OF SOCIAL LIFE, AND GEOGRAPHICAL FACTORS

The authorities assumed the operation of a simplified scheme whereby the state took upon itself all the obligations related to the satisfaction of broadly conceived social needs, from education, health care, and welfare to culture, housing, sports, and recreation. The citizen's duty was to work. A clause in the Constitution stipulated that work was an honour and dignity of each able-bodied citizen. At the same time, the implementation of the principle of social justice, interpreted as 'to everyone according to his work', was to guarantee the efficient functioning of the society and the economy.

In reality, many Eastern European countries did not see the materialization of that Utopia, while the equality of social opportunities remained a political slogan. None the less, the work-place was turned into the main axis of organization of social life. It was the factories and institutions that distributed various goods and benefits, all the more valuable when there was no genuine market or currency. As a result, next to production, enterprises were preoccupied with all sorts of welfare activities and had special services that took care of running factory clinics, holiday homes, day centres, kindergartens, shops, etc.

In the old system, the factory was a factor in the differentiation of society, depending on its affluence and place on the prestige ladder. Other factors contributing to the differentiation were the plant's location (rural or urban area; if urban, the size of the town, and its status as the capital of the country or region). It should be emphasized that, next to inequalities generated by the system of authority and the economy, which were closely interrelated, important differences also arose out of the features of regional or local space, in other words the geographic environment.

Attempts had been made to set in motion some mechanisms that would reduce disparities and differences not approved by society, but they usually failed to produce the desired results because the totalitarian system of authority severely restricted social mobility owing to housing shortages and the citizen's ties to his or her place of work. One could say, ironically, that

the nineteenth-century patterns of capitalist paternalism were adopted by the
socialist state.

During the period in question, the scope of individual action or family
strategy remained limited. The declaration of equality of all citizens and
equal opportunities guaranteed jobs to women, but these were usually
inferior jobs, for which the women would typically get less pay than men.
The system also provided institutionalized assistance in child care. Another
factor responsible for differences was the place of residence and its distance
from the enterprise, which determined the practical availability of various
benefits provided by the employer at no or very little charge.

The model of the organization of social life, outlined briefly above,
generated the patterns of professional and social careers which relied on the
system of formal education, and of political careers, chiefly associated with
activity in the Communist Party, trade unions, youth associations, or, less
often, social activity. In the event of a promising political career, the gaps
in formal education could be filled through courses aimed at turning out
activists and staff of the political and economic apparatus.

The size and number of industrial enterprises determined the prosperity
of a region. A relatively high standard of living was guaranteed by heavy
industry and mining, which had a predominantly male work-force, whereas
the regions in which manufacturing prevailed and where women constituted
the majority of the work-force were characterized by the highest percentage
of people in active employment and the lowest wages. The farming regions
as a rule had a lower standard of living, although that depended to some
extent on natural conditions. There may have been private farm-owners
running specialized farms and earning a very high income, but that required
hard physical labour. As a result, young people, and especially girls, eagerly
migrated to towns and moved to non-agricultural trades. Given the absence
of fundamental technical and social infrastructure, life in the countryside was
considered unattractive. A similar attitude was observed in the north-western
regions, where huge and heavily subsidized state farms predominated. The
authorities took special care to guarantee greater availability of public
facilities, well-equipped dwellings, and cultural institutions in villages inhabited
by state farm employees, often at the expense of villages inhabited by private
farm-owners. However, the maintenance of relatively low produce procurement prices over whole decades slowed down the growth of prosperity of the
people involved in farming. Besides, with varying intensity, there was the
pressure to collectivize farming; this was successfully resisted by the Polish
farmer, deeply attached to his land, which he regarded as patrimony.

Nevertheless, as a result of these complex processes, the depopulation of
the countryside could be observed in various parts of Poland beginning in
the 1970s; there was also a shortage of women of marriageable age. In Polish
conditions, private farms are family farms, and the lack of wives for farmers

had diverse socio-economic consequences. At the same time, in other parts of Poland, especially in the south and the central regions, areas characterized by huge urban centres and much industry, many farmers worked also in industry, commuting over great distances. This phenomenon pertained to men with low professional skills, who did the heaviest menial jobs, often in conditions hazardous to health. Meanwhile, the women kept the farms running, and the occupation of farmer was feminized. It was only at harvest time or during other pressing fieldwork that the men took their holidays to help out with the necessary farmwork.

The gender disparities mentioned above had demographic, economic, and social consequences, including what we may call a certain feminization, to which we now turn.

FEMINIZATION AS THE DISTINCTIVE FEATURE OF
DEMOGRAPHIC AND TERRITORIAL STRUCTURES IN POLAND

According to the national census, in December 1988 women numbered 19,414,300 or 51.3 per cent of the country's population. Out of that number, 62.1 per cent lived in towns and 37.9 per cent in the countryside. By the end of 1989 the number of women rose to 19,497,900; according to the 1988 census, there were 950,000 more women than men. Since 1977, the sex ratio —that is, the number of women per 100 men—has stood at 105. (It should be noted that in 1946 the sex ratio amounted to 114 and in 1955 to 108, as a result of human losses sustained during the Second World War.) Among other factors affecting the male–female ratio, one should note the higher number of male births (51–49 per cent), the higher death rates of men (in recent years, the ratio has been 53 per cent men to 47 per cent women) and the lack of equilibrium among migrants, with women predominating in both domestic and international migrations.

The predominance of women among those migrating from the countryside to towns (in 1988, for example, 114,000 men and 120,000 women migrated) has contributed to the fact that in towns there are 108 women per 100 men while in the countryside the ratio has been 100–100. The migration of women from the countryside is responsible for the fact that, while in towns women account for the majority of the population aged 21 and over, in the countryside the female population exceeds the male population only over the age of 48.

The sex ratio has reached the highest level in the oldest population groups, as women live much longer than men in Poland. At the same time, there are large regional variations with regard to the sex ratio of urban and rural populations compared with the national average. The predominance of women was the highest in the towns of Lódz *voivodship* (116) and the lowest in Katowice *voivodship* (103). The disparities were smaller in rural areas: the highest index—103—was recorded in Warsaw, Krosno, Rzeszów, and Tarnów *voivodships* and the lowest—95—in Suwalki *voivodship*.[1]

It should be emphasized that there was a large deficit of women in the 15–39 age group in the rural areas of all *voivodships*. The situation was the worst in north-eastern Poland, where the deficit of women of marriageable age was the most acute. For example, in the 20–34 age group, the number of women per 100 men was 72 in Bialystok *voivodship*, 75 in Lomza *voivodship*, 78 in Ostroleka and Suwalki *voivodships*, and 80 in Biala Polaska and Siedlce *voivodships*. Another indicator of the acute shortage of women in rural areas with low population density in the north-eastern regions was the number of unwed women per 100 bachelors aged 18–29: it amounted to 37 in Lomza, 38 in Bialystok, 40 in Suwalki, and 42 in Ostroleka *voivodships*, which means that over half of the unmarried men had no chance of finding a wife in their immediate neighbourhoods.

As a result of changes in the political system and the transformations taking place in the economy, one should now expect the occurrence of new tendencies defining the directions of migration and the preferences of the population. It can be expected that ultimately the new mechanisms will introduce corrections to the present regional disparity of the sexes. However, this is a process that is bound to take time, and the first effects cannot be visible for several years to come. In addition to domestic factors, external ones will also become more pronounced as the trends present in the integrating Western Europe begin to affect the Central and East European countries. The opening of state frontiers and interregional co-operation in border regions will usher in situations and opportunities unknown in the forty-five years of state socialist development. There is a chance, therefore, that the areas now affected by depopulation and demographic, social, and economic degradation will in the long run become politically and economically more attractive and will witness accelerated growth.

THE PLACE OF WOMEN IN THE NATIONAL EMPLOYMENT PATTERNS

One of the indices characterizing the position of women is their percentage share of total employment in the national economy. Fig. 13.1 shows the general trend of employment growth in absolute figures in the years 1950–89.

The current shifts in the economic system affect in particular the public sector of the economy, which in 1989 accounted for 70.3 per cent of total employment in Poland and whose growth for decades determined the country's economic situation. Priorities awarded to it and enforced by

---

[1] *A voivodship* is a territorial unit roughly equivalent to a region.

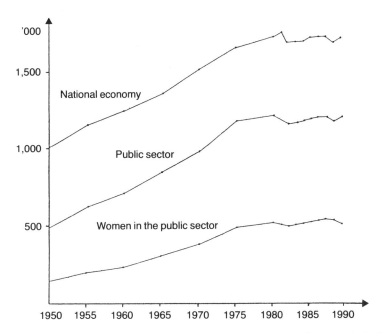

FIG 13.1 Employment in the national economy and in the public sector in Poland, 1950–1989

Source: author's own elaboration, based on Central Statistical Office (1990*a*: p. xxxii, table 1; 1990*b*: 316, table 1).

administrative means guaranteed its monopoly position. Nevertheless, the inefficiency of the command economy had become obvious as early as the mid-1970s, as is confirmed by the slower growth rate demonstrated in the graph. This was the time when the authorities timidly and on a very limited scale began to accept private enterprise; for example, loss-making shops owned by state enterprises could be leased to private persons.

Employment in the public sector stagnated in the latter half of the 1970s and began to fall in the early 1980s. In this context, it is worth emphasizing that the curve illustrating the employment of women, relating only to the public sector (because of the lack of data on private-sector employment), was characterized by smaller shifts and a steady growth. Twice in the period in question, in 1980–2 and 1987–8, the downward trend was milder with regard to women than for overall public-sector employment.

Fig. 13.1 points to a steady growth in the employment of women, whose share of the total work-force in the public sector amounted to 30.6 per cent in 1950 and 46.7 per cent in 1989. Paradoxically, as the sector concerned began to shrink as a whole, the share of women in the work-force increased.

To a larger extent than men, women hang on to their jobs regardless of the low pay, tax constraints, lack of promotion prospects, and the strong pressure for accelerated privatization, which brings with it the risk of bankruptcies and liquidation of enterprises. At the end of 1989 over 8 million women were employed in Poland's economy. Out of that number, 26 per cent worked in the private sector of farming. The public sector of the economy employed 5.5 million women, out of which only 4.7 per cent worked from home or as agents who could organize their work on their own.

Women in farming

According to the census, in 1988 women accounted for 49.6 per cent of people living in households connected with private farms. Owing to the specific nature of that milieu, the level of occupational activity was particularly high, i.e. 75.1 per cent of all such women over the age of 15. The vast majority of women working in private farms were married—74.7 per cent —with widows accounting for another 16.1 per cent of the total. Widows ran their private farms until a very advanced age; in 1988 there were 45,000 women aged 80 and over who ran their own farms! The need to do hard physical work, regardless of the size of the farm, was a huge burden for the elderly woman. Of the rural women over 15 years of age who were not gainfully employed, the majority had their own source of income, mainly old-age pensions (54.8 per cent) or disability pensions (30.2 per cent) earned by turning their farm over to the state.

Branches of the economy with a predominantly female work-force

Of the women employed in the public sector outside agriculture, almost half (48.1 per cent) worked in industry and 26 per cent worked in the trade/ distribution sector. At the start of the transition period, attempts were made to introduce reforms in these two branches, with the aim of a radical restructuring in industry and ownership transformations in trade. The aim of the moves was to break up monopolistic structures and the administrative apparatus of the communist system. This entailed the liquidation of many central management and planning agencies, in which women accounted for the bulk of the employees. Unfortunately, no definite data illustrating that process have been available so far.

The available figures for 1989 only made it possible to identify the most heavily feminized branches, such as distribution (69.7 per cent), communications (58.7 per cent), financial and insurance services (84.5 per cent), health care and welfare (80.5 per cent), education (76.5 per cent), the civil service and the judiciary (64.4 per cent), culture and the arts (61.0 per cent), and physical culture, tourism, and recreation (55.2 per cent).

The process of structural reforms has occurred with varying intensity in individual branches of the economy, professions, and regions. For example, in Warsaw public-sector shops were replaced by private shops, which employed predominantly young saleswomen. Older shop assistants from the formerly state-run shops had to look for other jobs or retire. This was the cause of many personal tragedies.

The transition from a state economy to a free market calls for a different kind of worker, with different skills and predispositions. For many older workers, in particular those with a low level of skills and little formal education, this is quite a shock, as their experience is no longer valued. On the other hand, as inflation has made a dent in the purchasing power of old-age pensions, many pensioners have decided to seek part-time jobs. This process actually began earlier; in 1989 the number of female pensioners holding a job was three times higher than in 1980. Almost 261,000 women began to supplement their pensions with job incomes during the period in question.

It is worth noting that the figures quoted at the outset of this section indicated the concentration of the female work-force in industry, which was typical of the state socialist economy, given its small service sector. The low level of employment in services is characteristic of all ex-communist countries. As certain symptoms of economic recovery appear, we can expect the emergence of new trends in the pattern of employment of women.

REGIONAL VARIATIONS IN THE GROWTH OF WOMEN'S SHARE
OF THE WORK-FORCE, 1980–1989

From 1980 to 1989, the share of women in the total work-force increased by 3.2 per cent, with considerable regional variations (see Fig. 13.2 and Table 13.1). The relationship between regional feminization coefficients and occupational activity of women was examined with a view to explaining the differences. It turned out that no relationship existed. For example, in Rzeszów *voivodship* the high feminization coefficient was accompanied by a low level of occupational activity of women, while in Siedlce *voivodship* it was the other way round. There were also areas in which both indices were low (Tarnobrzeg *voivodship*) or both high (Bielsko Biala). More detailed analysis revealed that the growth of employment of women was determined by shifts in the overall employment in a given region. A synthetic picture of the trends in the shifts taking place in Poland and the growth or decrease of the employment of women is presented in Table 13.2.

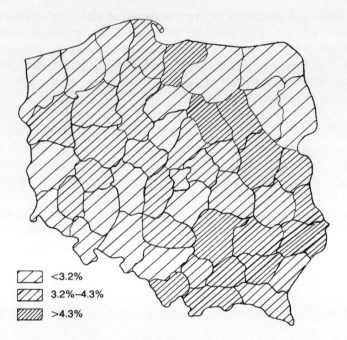

FIG 13.2 Shifts in women's employment in the public sector, by *voivodship*, 1980–1989 (1980 = 100)

Source: author's own elaboration, based on Central Statistical Office (1990c: 52, table 5).

It should be noted that the main shifts in the pattern of employment in Poland in the 1980s consisted in the movement from the productive sector, which experienced a stagnation or a recession, to the service sector in the broad sense, which is referred to in Poland as the non-trading sector. The latter encompasses housing, science and technology, education, culture and the arts, health care and welfare, sports, rest and recreation, the civil service, the judiciary, and finance and insurance. These were heavily feminized branches with relatively the highest employment growth, especially in education, health care and welfare, the civil service, and the judiciary and finance and insurance. By contrast, a marked drop in employment occurred in science.

Table 13.2 explains the logic of these shifts, revealing an almost 22 per cent growth of employment in the non-trading sector and the growth of the employment of women that went with it. The regional shifts were concentrated in *voivodships* with a predominantly agricultural or a mixed industrial and agricultural economy, with the biggest growth of the employment of women amounting to 4.3 per cent. If Poland were divided in half by a meridian axis, the thirteen (out of forty-nine) *voivodships* in which the

TABLE 13.1 *Voivodships* with the highest and lowest percentage of women's employment, 1980–1989

	1980			1989	
Voivodship	'000	%	*Voivodship*	'000	%
Voivodships with the highest percentage of women's employment					
Lódz	251.4	50.4	Lòdz	203.5	52.6
Skierniewice	48.6	48.4	Skierniewice	47.7	52.0
Warszawa	476.6	48.2	Bielsko Biala	129.4	51.9
Jelenia Góra	93.8	47.9	Warszawa	422.4	51.4
Bielsko Biala	136.4	47.5	Lomza	32.3	50.2
Lomza	30.0	47.2	Jelenia Góra	83.0	50.0
Walbrzych	131.6	46.5	Siedlce	61.7	50.0
Bialystock	89.1	46.1	Nowy Sacz	78.4	49.8
Wroclaw	197.3	46.0	Czestochowa	98.6	49.7
Zielona Góra	102.4	45.6	Elblag	63.7	49.7
Voivodships with the lowest percentage of women's employment					
Katowice	604.1	37.1	Katowice	583.8	40.0
Tarnobrzeg	60.8	38.5	Tarnobrzeg	67.3	43.0
Konin	42.3	39.7	Legnica	74.8	43.5
Legnica	70.0	39.9	Konin	50.4	43.7
Krosno	56.1	40.0	Przemysl	45.7	43.8
Przemysl	41.4	40.5	Krosno	62.7	44.1
Leszno	40.4	40.8	Pila	61.1	44.8
Pila	56.0	41.0	Piotrków Tryb.	80.2	44.8
Zamosc	42.5	41.5	Leszno	45.2	45.1
Chelm	26.8	41.7	Gdansk	194.6	45.7

Source: author's elaboration, based on Central Statistical Office (1981: 70; 1990: 98).

TABLE 13.2 Main trends in employment in the public sector in Poland, 1980–1989

Specification	1980	1985	1989
% of female employment in the productive sector[a]	37.1	37.0	37.0
of which: in industry	38.6	36.4	37.1
% of female employment in the non-trading sector	68.5	69.6	70.9
Employment dynamics in the productive sector (1980=100)	100.00	98.1	91.4
Employment dynamics in industry (1980=100)	100.00	90.4	83.9
Employment dynamics in the productive sector (1980=100)	100.00	116.5	121.8

[a] Consisting of industry, construction, agriculture, forestry, transportation, communications, municipal economy.

Source: author's elaboration based on the Central Statistical Office employment data.

growth was the highest would all be in the eastern half. Among them was the eastern part of the ring of agricultural areas surrounding Warsaw (Ciechanow, Ostroleka, and Siedlce *voivodships*) and the *voivodships* forming the old Polish industrial heartland (Kielce, Radom, Cracow, Rzeszow). Most of the *voivodships* were the so-called new ones, formed in 1975 out of the former bigger *voivodships*, and most have a low level of infrastructure. It should be emphasized that all these regions were situated on the peripheries of large urban agglomerations and industrial centres and were an integral part of their functional regions.

By contrast, the growth of the female work-force was the lowest in seventeen regions situated mainly along the northern and western border and in some centrally situated regions, notably Lódz, Wloclawek, Torun, Piotrkow Trybunalski, and Kalisz. The case of Lódz, Poland's second-largest city, is especially interesting. Being a centre of the textile industry, it has always had the highest proportion of women in its total work-force, with virtually non-existent possibilities of growth in this respect because of demographic and economic limitations. In 1989 the 203,000 women working in the town accounted for 52.6 per cent of the total employment. But in 1980 female employment had numbered 251,900, or 50.4 per cent of the total. This represented a decline in absolute terms by almost one-fifth, although there was a slight increase in the female percentage share. These figures demonstrate the depth of shifts in the local labour market and in the national economy as a whole.

Katowice *voivodship* was at the opposite end of the pole, although, in the light of Fig. 13.2, it belonged in the same group as Lódz. However, Katowice has traditionally been one of the regions with the lowest proportion of women in employment, as the patriarchal family model was persistently upheld in the numerous coal mining families, with the man as the central figure; besides, because of the risks involved, work in the mines was better rewarded. The closing down of some mines, the drop of coal output, and the relative fall in miners' incomes in the 1980s did not produce any major growth in the employment of women in this region; the proportion of women in the work-force rose from 37.1 per cent in 1980 to 40.0 per cent in 1989, while in absolute figures it slid from 604,100 to 583,800. It should be stressed that in absolute figures Katowice *voivodship* had the largest female work-force, followed by Warsaw, with Lódz only third (see Table 13.1).

It should be noted that the regions with the smallest growth of the proportion of women in total employment were for the most part the *voivodships* situated along the border, in areas with lower population density, a relatively high level of development of social infrastructure of a higher technological standard, and chiefly in the west and in the north, e.g. Szczecin, Koszalin, Slupsk, Olsztyn, Zielona Góra, Jelenia Góra, Walbrzych, Opel or Suwalki, and Bialystok. This was due to the fact that the state border and border crossings did not have the accelerated effect on local and regional economic development they should have had.

Despite official declarations and the advancing democratization and liberalization in Central and Eastern Europe, the legacy of the decades of pursuing a policy of sealed borders, dating back to the beginning of the Cold War, has so far failed to produce a stimulation of economic activity in the border regions and new job opportunities for women.

The figures quoted above fully bear out the thesis about a general growth in the share of women in overall employment, which is related to the diminishing share of the productive sector and the growing importance of services.

INSTITUTIONALIZED ASSISTANCE FOR CHILDREARING

Regional variations in use of child-care facilities

There are considerable local variations with regard to the satisfaction of elementary social needs, and the distribution of child-care facilities can serve as an illustration of this point. The study is limited to kindergartens, as empirical studies have shown a distinct correlation between the number of kindergartens and other child-care institutions in Poland.

Table 13.3 lists ten *voivodships* with the highest and lowest numbers of children going to kindergarten per 1,000 children in the 3–6 age group and of nurseries for children up to 3 years of age; that was compared with the proportion of mothers taking advantage of paid child-care leaves to the overall employment. This is an oversimplification, because the occupational activity of women is influenced by other factors, the cultural factor being one of the most important ones. None the less, in three of the ten *voivodships* with the ighest numbers (Lódz, Olsztyn, and Szczecin), there was a link between the large number of child-care institutions and the low number of mothers on child-care leave; in two more it is possible to trace a relationship between the large number of children in kindergartens (Warsaw) or in nurseries (Koszalin) and the low proportion of child-care leaves. Opole *voivodship* stands out only because of the large number of child-care institutions.

Of the ten *voivodships* with the lowest proportion of children in kindergarten or nursery, Przemysl, Zamosc, and Tarnów had the highest proportion of child-care leaves. In five more, the highest number of child-care leaves went hand in hand with the lowest proportion of children in kindergarten (Nowy Sacz, Lomza, Tarnobrzeg) or in nurseries (Biala Podlaska), with Konin *voivodship* having few kindergartens and also few nurseries.

The data contained in Table 13.3 shows that the proportion of people taking child-care leave was the lowest in heavily industrialized regions or

TABLE 13.3 *Voivodships* with the highest and lowest indices of children in kindergartens, nurseries, and people on paid child-care leave, 1989

Rank	*Voivodship*	No. of children in kindergardens per 1,000 children in 3–6 age groups	*Voivodship*	No. of children in nurseries per 1,000 children up to 3 years	*Voivodship*	People on paid child-care leave as % of total work-force
	Poland	487	Poland	44.3	Poland	6.5
1	Lódz	615	Walbrzych	126.7	Nowy Sacz	9.3
2	Zielona Góra	577	Lódz	107.8	Tarnów	9.3
3	Warszawa	562	Wroclaw	87.6	Rzeszów	8.5
4	Opole	534	Jelenia Góra	82.5	Biala Podlaska	8.4
5	Poznan	532	Koszalin	72.8	Siedlce	8.4
6	Gorzów	528	Legnica	72.1	Lomza	8.2
7	Olsztyn	525	Olsztyn	67.6	Tarnobrzeg	8.0
8	Jelenia Góra	524	Szczecin	66.7	Zamosc	7.8
9	Leszno	518	Opole	65.2	Przemysl	7.7
10	Szczecin	506	Slupsk	63.9	Radom	7.7
.						
.						
.						
40	Kielce	451	Zamosc	24.9	Warszawa	5.9
41	Konin	446	Konin	24.6	Pila	5.8
42	Tarnów	440	Sieradz	23.6	Wloclawek	5.7
43	Siedlce	437	Bielsko Biala	23.2	Szczecin	5.7
44	Zamosc	435	Tarnów	20.8	Olsztyn	5.7
45	Ostroleka	434	Przemysl	18.9	Koszalin	5.7
45	Nowy Sacz	431	Czestochowa	17.8	Lódz	5.5
47	Lomza	431	Biala Podlaska	14.3	Konin	5.5
48	Tarnobrzeg	427	Wloclawek	13.9	Katowice	5.4
49	Przemysl	426	Ostroleka	12.0	Plock	5.3

Source: author's elaboration based on Central Statistical Office (1990*a*: pp. lxvi and lvii, table III).

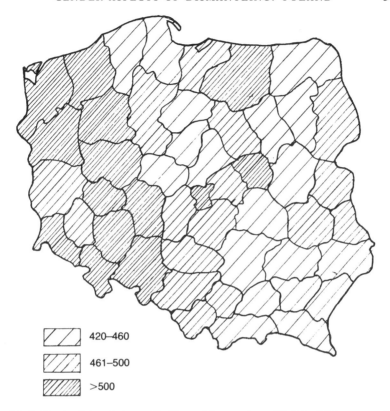

420–460

461–500

>500

FIG 13.3 Territorial variations of indices of the number of Polish children attending kindergartens per 1,000 children in the 3–6 age group, 1989

Source: author's own elaboration, based on Central Statistical Office (1990*a*: p. lxvi, table III).

those with huge state-owned industrial plants that could afford to provide child-care for their workers and had a long tradition of employing women. On the other hand, the ten *voivodships* with the lowest percentage of children in day-care centres were predominantly agricultural regions or ones with a mixed agricultural–industrial economy, in which women traditionally combined work in the family farm with jobs outside agriculture; hence the greater interest in paid child-care leave.

On this basis, it is also possible to formulate a hypothesis about different attitudes towards gainful employment on the part of women living and working on farms, for which a job is primarily a source of income. By contrast, women working in towns and industry centres perceive their jobs as careers, and the values that go with them are also important. Indeed, a woman's satisfaction and social position increasingly often depend on her career. However, this is a separate subject that will not be elaborated upon here.

Fig 13.3 complements the above observations, presenting regional differences in the proportion of children attending kindergarten in 1989. There is a marked division of the country into the eastern half, with the indices on the whole lower, and the western part, where the respective figures are higher. This is a reflection of historical processes, the degree of development and centuries-old division into affluent and poor regions. The importance of regional variations is attested to by the largest indices of growth in the share of women in employment (see Figs. 13.2 and 13.5), despite the low level of investment in the eastern part of the country.

Downward trends in the use of child-care institutions

The abandonment of the collectivist model of a welfare state adversely affects the material and social position of women, especially young mothers with low skills and earnings, who in many cases bring up their children on their own. In the transition period, incomes as a rule remain at the previous very low level, although prices and the costs of services become relatively expensive. At the same time, state-run institutions are either being liquidated or raising their fees to a level not warranted by the standard of service they provide. Some institutions try to maintain the old organizational pattern, with irrational overemployment. In any event, the dismantling of the collectivist model leaves a vacuum as no alternative network of facilities is yet available.

Factory-run nurseries are a very good case in point. The process of their liquidation is taking place gradually. First, a large percentage of mothers are giving up their services because of the increased fees. Depending on family situation, this often involves the discontinuation of active employment and a child-care leave. The factories also have financial problems, and as the fixed costs of running the nurseries go up and their capacity is not fully utilized, they are ultimately closed down. The impoverishment of society has created a situation in which it costs less to keep children at home than to avail oneself of specialized private or state-run institutions.

In the 1980s the number of factory-run nurseries decreased by a quarter, the number of places by a third, and the number of children in nurseries by almost half. The demand for places fell more slowly in generally accessible municipal nurseries than in factory-operated ones, which are deemed relics of old times now that the country's economic system is being reformed. Without going into the economic rationale of such decisions, it should be pointed out that the price for the changes was paid first and foremost by women. The falling number of children under 3 years in nurseries per 1,000 children is given in Table 13.4.

Fig. 13.4 illustrates the number of children in nurseries per 100 children and demonstrates the dramatic fall in demand. Given Polish conditions, there

TABLE 13.4 Child-care institutions in Poland, 1980–1989

	1980	1985	1986	1987	1988	1989
Nurseries						
Factory nurseries	434	344	335	325	315	305
Number of places	28,654	22,018	21,821	21,170	20,645	19,867
Total users	194,186	199,674	201,510	197,903	170,679	150,631
Municipal nurseries	142,597	159,770	162,097	160,419	139,509	123,399
Factory nurseries	51,589	39,904	39,413	37,484	31,170	27,232
Users per 1,000 children						
up to 3 years of age	52	51	54	55	45	44
Day care for young children						
Institution/homes	62	55	53	52	51	54
Beds	4,773	3,871	3,701	3,577	3,587	3,654
Users	6,645	5,451	5,510	5,068	4,578	4,319

Source: Central Statistical Office (1990*a*: 498, table 16/770).

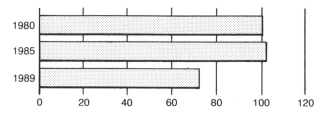

FIG 13.4 Number of Polish children in nurseries per 100 places, 1980–1989
Source: Central Statistical Office (1990*b*: 110).

was always a scarcity of places in nurseries compared with public needs. The withdrawal of subsidies and the calculation of charges on the basis of actual costs led to the appearance of vacancies for the first time in the history of these institutions and to a drop-off of interest in them. It should be emphasized that the main reasons for this state of affairs are financial, e.g. tight family budgets, and are not a result of demographic phenomena.

A similar situation can be observed in the case of kindergartens and children in the 3–6 age group. Fig. 13.5 shows the downward trend with regard to the number of children in kindergartens per 100 available places, a process that has occurred with greater intensity in towns than in the countryside. The relatively high share of rural children in kindergarten is the result of mandatory one year for 6-year-olds prior to going to school rather than of the mother's decision to take up gainful employment; had it not been for this mandatory one year, the drop would have been even bigger.

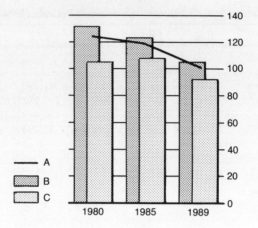

Fɪɢ 13.5 Number of Polish children in kindergartens per 100 places, 1980–1989
A: total; B: town; C: countryside
Source: Central Statistical Office (1990*a*: 494).

Previously, the pressure on the part of mothers to have their children admitted to kindergarten was such that most kindergartens were over-crowded; this coupled with the generally low standard of the premises, had adverse effects on the children's mental and physical development. In the post-communist transition, the problem of shortage of kindergarten space and the nightmare of securing a place in it has automatically disappeared.

Another aspect of the same process that places working women in an exceptionally difficult situation is the shrinking supply of organized holidays

Tᴀʙʟᴇ 13.5 Children's and youth's recreation and out-of-school education in
Poland, 1980–1989

Recreation forms and facilities	1980	1985	1988	1989
Users ('000)				
Total	6,892.1	4,757.0	5,639.2	5,181.2
Summer holiday camps	1,405.3	1,043.9	1,058.4	1,038.0
Camps	1,076.6	710.3	712.5	651.6
Picnics	178.4	57.3	68.3	69.3
Excursion centres for rural children	100.9	51.6	46.2	37.8
Facilities				
Total	750	682	669	645
Circles of out-of-school activities	350	356	322	305
Open-air kindergartens	108	73	58	57
Out-of-school sport centres	148	115	133	126

Source: author's elaboration, based on Central Statistical Office (1990*a*: 480, tables 31/726/ and 32/727).

for children and youths such as summer and winter camps, picnics, and, for rural children, excursions (see Table 13.5). At the same time, facilities providing out-of-school hobbies, sports, and similar activities are closing down because of a lack of sponsors. One cost-cutting measure being employed is the organization of recreation in the home locality in the form of attractive but costly trips.

Because of the disastrous environmental situation in the most densely populated heavily industrialized regions, such stop-gap measures do not contribute to an improvement of the state of health of children and youths. For years, it has been advocated that children from Upper Silesia be entitled to at least one month's stay away from home. This shows how the problems with offspring affect their mothers' situation. The poor health of children caused by environmental pollution forces many women to give up employment and to seek a way of helping their children recover on their own.

The transition period and the crises of traditional child-care institutions puts an especially heavy burden on the shoulders of single mothers. It was only quite recently that some public initiatives were launched with a view to filling the institutional vacuum. However, the lack of experience and of the ability to institutionalize social initiative and to organize and secure financial support and the necessary facilities means that, at a time when domestic capital is being formed and a market economy is being introduced, it is the poorest who pay the biggest price.

The conflict between career and childrearing

Under the command economy, the official view was that motherhood could not be an obstacle to gainful employment. Typically, women would return to their former place of work between six weeks and three months after childbirth. It was only in 1980 that Solidarity secured three-year paid child-care leaves, an opportunity taken up by very many women because the benefits paid during the period could guarantee a decent standard of living to the mother looking after her baby.

However, the disintegration of the command economy and the high inflation rate accompanying it have stripped the leaves of their attractiveness. The purchasing power of the child-care benefits plummeted and they no longer guarantee even a very modest standard of living. In 1989, 731,800 women were taking advantage of such leaves, which was 50.2 per cent more than in 1980 but 12.9 per cent less than in 1985. Nevertheless, a reappraisal of the role of a woman's career in the context of motherhood has been taking place in Polish society. Increasingly, the view is being voiced that the pursuit of a career should be suspended for some time. This translates into the acceptance of a lower standard of living and of reduced career opportunities in connection with motherhood.

This could be treated as a new phenomenon compared with the old model which proclaimed full equality of the sexes. This time no illusions are being cherished: motherhood requires sacrifice. The most recent Polish statistics have revealed a strong downward trend in occupational activity of women in the 25–34 age group. This is the age in which the clash between career and family aspirations is the strongest. The system of child-care leaves and benefits introduced a legal regulation of the problem of a temporary break in careers of young women.

On the other hand, occupational activity among women in the 35–49 age group, and in towns in the 35–54 age group, is up. It appears that, once the children are a little older, the women return to active employment. This observation follows from a comparison of employment statistics for the same generation of women in 1978 and 1988. For example, in 1978 in the 25–29 age group, 75.1 per cent of women held jobs; ten years later, the figure for the 35–39 age group was 83.0 per cent. Such changes were observed not only in towns but also in rural areas, despite the fact that fewer rural women took advantage of paid child-care leaves. It is beyond the scope of this chapter to study the effect of child-care leaves on the drop in incomes and the lower position on the career ladder in comparison with the women who did not take a break from work. But it is clear that there is a conscious forgoing of career opportunities in favour of maternal duties on the part of young mothers. It subsequently takes several years to regain the lost ground.

Out of the total number of women gainfully employed in the public sector of the economy, 13 per cent took advantage of child-care leaves. In individual branches of the public sector, the proportion varies from 18.8 per cent in distribution to 17.5 per cent in industry, 15.5 per cent in communications, 14.4 per cent in transport and construction, 11.4 per cent in municipal services, 9.6 per cent in the civil service and the judiciary, and 7.7 per cent in education. For those women employed in the private sector, there was less interest in taking child-care leave because the pay as a rule was higher. Therefore the women did not put their careers on hold but used commercial forms of child care more often because they could more easily afford it. This was also true for self-employed women.

In the present transition period, the standard of living of mothers tends to decrease, either because they give up employment or because they have to pay more for child care if they themselves continue to work. That decline would be obvious anywhere, but in Polish conditions it is relatively steep.

UNEMPLOYMENT AMONG WOMEN

In 1990 unemployment appeared in Poland for the first time in five decades. Initially it was thought to be a symptom of restructuring of the economy and a factor accelerating desirable transformation. It soon turned out, however, that overemployment in the command economy, where thousands of people could hold jobs regardless of the economic rationale behind it, was grossly underestimated. After a few months, it became evident that the inertia of the public sector of the economy was immense. This was compounded by the absence of efficient market mechanisms and of capital. The old habits associated with the command economy were also responsible for the inability of people more easily to find themselves a place in the nascent system. Therefore unemployment could not by itself accelerate the reform of the system, while it did add to public discontent, tension, and conflicts that could trigger destructive actions.

Fig. 13.6 shows that the steep growth in unemployment is accompanied by characteristic shifts in the proportion of men and women who are being dismissed. From August 1990, unemployment among women exceeded that among men. At the end of October 1990, the proportion of women among

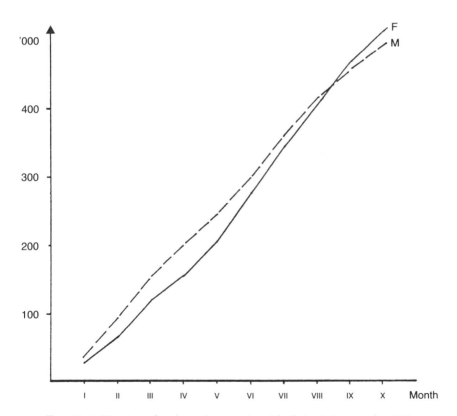

FIG 13.6 Number of registered unemployed in Poland, by month, 1990
Source: author's own elaboration, based on the working reports of the Central Statistical Office.

322   M. CIECHOCINSKA

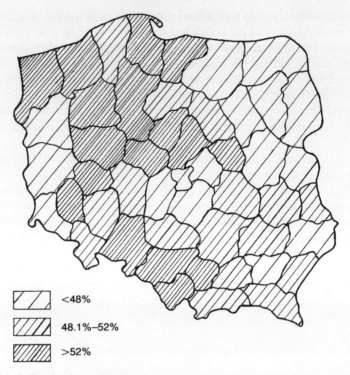

<48%

48.1%–52%

>52%

FIG. 13.7 Territorial variations of the percentage of women in Poland among the
unemployed, 30 October 1990

Source: author's own elaboration, based on the working reports of the Central Statistical Office.

the unemployed exceeded 51 per cent, with big regional variations (see Fig. 13.7). The biggest share of women among the unemployed, in excess of 52 per cent, was recorded chiefly in the western part of the country in the industrial and industrial–agricultural region with a predominant role of the public sector.

In the agricultural and agricultural–industrial regions of eastern and central Poland, in which the public sector consisted of smaller and more modern enterprises, the share of women among the unemployed was markedly lower. It should be recalled that it was precisely there that the biggest growth of the employment of women occurred in the 1980s (cf. Fig. 13.2). On this basis, it is impossible to formulate the hypothesis that the greatest growth of female unemployment occurred in the regions that had huge old industrial plants and a traditionally high proportion of women in the whole workforce. It can be assumed that the above features make up a syndrome conducive to high unemployment among women in the early stage of structural transformations. Detailed empirical studies in towns confirmed the existence of such a syndrome: for example, in April 1990 women accounted for 68.3 per cent of the total number of unemployed (those who had no jobs for over three months before registering as unemployed) in Lódz, 59.4 per cent in Walbrzych, 57.2 per cent in Gorzów, 55.5 per cent in Bielsko Biala, etc.

The biggest share of women among the unemployed occurred in urban agglomerations and the most affluent parts of the country. In absolute figures, Katowice *voivodship* topped the table with 36,200 women looking for jobs.

At the end of October 1990, unemployment reached 1,008,400, or 5.5 per cent of the total working population. There were 514,000 women among them, and their share was growing all the time (see Fig. 13.6). At the time it was estimated that by the end of 1990 unemployment would reach 1.2 million, and it was feared that this could double in 1991. Programmes of restructuring and reconstruction of Poland's economy even mentioned 3.5 million unemployed, while Western experts put the figure as high as 4.5 million in forecasts prepared in the first half of 1990. Official statistics for 31 December 1991 reveal a total number of registered unemployed of 2,155,660 of which 1,134,100 were women.

The predominance of women among the unemployed should be regarded as a feature that will remain for some time to come, because a larger proportion of women used to work in the public sector and their mobility on the labour market is lower. This is why they are paying a higher price for the transformations now taking place. Figs. 13.2 and 13.7 make it possible to predict the likely nature of the transformations. In general, this is going to be a modernization of the pattern of employment, the liquidation of monopolistic dinosaurs, and the development of services in neglected regions.

The development of services will first of all involve the growth of the employment of women in education, health care, and welfare. It is in this context that one should interpret the shifts illustrated in Figs. 13.2 and 13.7. On closer analysis, it can be seen that the shifts go in many conflicting directions and occasionally overlap one another. The employment of women is the subject of various transformations, the implementation of which has already begun. The changes will be easier to assess in perspective; besides, the authorities will have to come up with a policy of counteracting unemployment.

The large percentage of women among the unemployed can have dangerous consequences. Fig. 13.8 shows that the growth in the number of jobless is accompanied by a low number of vacancies. With regard to men, the number of unemployed per vacancy was stable, whereas the respective ratio for women showed a marked upward trend. At the end of October 1990, the number of female job-seekers per vacancy was four times as high as the corresponding figure for men. Not only were women being laid off at a faster

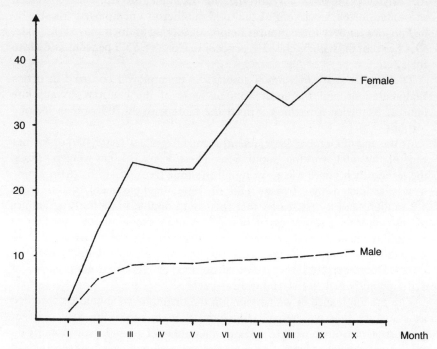

FIG 13.8 The number of female and male jobless in Poland per one vacancy, by
month, 1990
Source: author's own elaboration, based on the working reports of the Central Statistical Office.

rate, but their chances of finding another job were looking slimmer and
slimmer.

CONCLUSIONS

This chapter only touches upon some issues, pointing out that, in the period
of transformation from a command to a market economy, gender is an
important factor determining the chances of employment and promotion. In
the Polish situation, one's sex determines one's vulnerability to becoming
unemployed and one's prospects of finding another job.

    While on the one hand there has been a certain growth in the share of
women in employment in the public sector, the proportion of women among
the unemployed is rising fast. This shows that women are more strongly tied
to the low-paying jobs in the shrinking public sector. They make much
smaller use of the chances offered by the private sector. This is a result not

only of women's reluctance to change jobs, but also of the pronounced deterioration in the situation on the labour market, which is confirmed by the very small number of job offers, much smaller than in the case of male occupations. Furthermore, the shrinking availability of institutionalized child care leads to a drop in occupational activity of women in the 25–34 age group, which happens to be the age group preferred by private-sector employers.

All of this creates a syndrome of underprivilege for women on the labour market, with considerable regional variations. The inevitable and difficult transformation of the economic system turns out to be exacting a bigger toll on women than on men.

REFERENCES

ANDERSON, B. S., and ZINSSER, J. P. (1988), *A History of Their Own: Women in Europe from Prehistory to the Present*. New York: Harper and Row.

Central Statistical Office (1981) *Statistical Yearbook 1981 (Rocznik Statystyczny 1990)*. Warsaw: Głowny Urząd Statystyczny (GUS).

—— (1988), 'Issue Polska', Series *Materiaty i Opracowania Statystyczne NSP*. Warsaw: GUS.

—— (1990a) *Statistical Yearbook 1990*. Warsaw: GUS.

—— (1990b), *Concise Statistical Yearbook 1990 (Maty Rocznik Statystyczny 1990)*. Warsaw: GUS.

—— (1990c), *Women in Poland (Kobieta w Polsce)*. Warsaw: GUS.

—— (1990d), *Demographic and Socio-Vocational Structure of Population (Struktura demograficzna i spoleczno-zawodowa ludnosci)*. Warsaw: GUS.

COUTRAS, J., and FAGNANI, J. (1978), 'Femmes et transports en milieu urbain', *International Journal of Urban and Regional Research*, Women and the City, 2(3).

—— (1989), 'Espace, Population Societés', *Sexes et espaces*, no. 1: 11–14.

Die Frau (1987), 'Kleine Enzyklopaedie', *Die Frau*. Leipzig: Bibliographisches Institut.

EICHER, C., FAGNANI, J., GLOGAU, M., MORVILLE, M., and SHAW, G. (1982), 'Les Femmes face aux choix technologiques: un terrain vague de la recherche francaise', colloquium on 'Femmes, Feminisme et Recherches', Toulouse 17–19 December.

HOECKE-POERSGEN, B. (1982), *Konzepte der Emanzipation der Frau*. Bonn.

MCAULEY, A. (1981), *Women's Work and Wages in the Soviet Union*. London: George Allen & Unwin.

PIOTROWSKI, J. (1963), *Praca zawodowa kobiet a rodzina (Paid Work and Family)*. Warsaw: KiW.

PREISS-ZAJDOWA, A. (1967), *Zawód a praca kobiet (Profession and Women's Work)*. Warsaw: WZ CRZZ.

Proceedings of the All-Polish Conference (1990), 'A Woman in Contemporary Poland: Opportunities and Risks' (in Polish), mimeo, Warsaw, 15 December.

Proceedings of the Fourth International Conference of Women Engineers and Scientists (1975) Cracow, Poland (8–13 September). Warsaw: NOT.

SIEMIEŃSKA, R. (1986), 'Women and Social Movement in Poland', *Women in Politics*, 6(4): 5–35.

—— (1989), 'Women and Solidarity in Poland in the Early 1980s', in W. Cohen and Y. Cohen (eds.), *Women and Country Power*. Montreal/New York: Black Rose Books.

—— (1990), 'Kobiety w Solidarnosci, lata 1980–81: Wplyw kryzysu na ksztaltowanie swiadomosci i zachowan kobiet' ('Women in Solidarity in 1980–81: The Impact of Crisis on the Women's Consciousness and Behaviour'), *Kobieta*, Pismo Zwiazkowe, no. 1 (November).

SOKOLOWSKA, M. (1976), 'Women's Emancipation and Socialism: The Case of the People's Republic of Poland', *International Journal of Health Services*, 6(1): 35–51.

—— (1986), 'The Woman Image in the Awareness of Contemporary Polish Society', *Polish Sociological Bulletin*, no. 3: 41–50.

UNESCO (1975), *Women, Education, Equality: A Decade of Experiment*. Paris: UNESCO.

—— (1986), *Women's Concerns and Planning: A Methodological Approach for their Integration into Local, Regional and National Planning*. Paris: UNESCO.

14

Bringing the Third World In:
A Comparative Analysis of Gender and Restructuring

Valentine M. Moghadam

INTRODUCTION

This chapter examines two cases of restructuring and economic reform: industrializing countries in the Third World, and Eastern Europe and the Soviet Union. The main objective of the comparison is to discern similarities and differences in the two cases in order to assess the likely impact of restructuring on women and on gender relations in the transitional economies. Another objective is to establish restructuring as a global phenomenon and transformations in the former state socialist countries as part of world-systemic imperatives. Finally, the chapter illustrates the salience of gender in processes of economic and political change. The theoretical model that informs this study combines a modified world-system perspective associated with Wallerstein and his colleagues, and the production–reproduction scheme suggested by Engels in the first edition of *The Origin of the Family, Private Property and the State*.[1] Thus, restructuring is explained as a fundamental feature of the world economy and not just of individual national economies; at the same time, it is a process with class and gender dynamics.

According to Engels (1884), 'The determining factor in history is, in the last resort, the production and reproduction of immediate life'; that is, the production of the means of subsistence, and the production of human beings themselves. Engels goes on to state that social institutions in different historical periods are shaped by 'the development of labour and of the family'. Theoretically, this provides the basis for a class-gender analysis of historical development, stability, and change.[2] Gender and the status of women is especially salient in the process of reproduction, which contains biological, material, and symbolic/cultural aspects. The physiological fact of female reproductive capacity has been culturally translated into primary

For comments on the first draft of this chapter, I am grateful to: Terry Boswell, Christopher Chase-Dunn, Massoud Karshenas, David Lane, Dorothy Rosenberg, Guy Standing, Lynn Turgeon, and Gordon Weil. All deficiencies remain mine.

[1] The conceptual framework of production and social reproduction was also used by Marx in *Capital*. However, I shall be adapting Engels's use of the concepts to this chapter.

[2] For a further discussion of Engels's path-breaking analysis, see the essays in Rosaldo and Lamphere (1974), Reiter (1975), and Leacock (1981).

responsibility for socialization, family, culture, and tradition. Women's central role in reproduction includes their assigned responsibility for bearing and rearing 'the next generation', providing early socialization into the dominant ideology, and transmitting cultural values. Although historically and cross-culturally women have always had a role in production, that role has been largely unrecognized, devalued, or unremunerated.[3] And their role in social reproduction—housework, reproductive labour, childrearing, caring for elderly relatives, and other informal work contributing to the reproduction and survival of the household—is entirely unpaid. Over *la longue durée*, gender came to consist of a definition of 'male' as breadwinner and provider and 'female' as childbearer and domestic worker.[4]

As we near the twenty-first century, however, women's role in production has started to be acknowledged, and this has had an impact on gender definitions. Women's rights to employment are recognized, and in many countries women are no longer defined solely in terms of reproduction.[5] As national economies have become integrated into the world market, and as women have been increasingly drawn into production, labour markets, and public life, concepts of gender have changed. To put it simply, as women have become workers and citizens, they are no longer viewed solely in terms of their reproductive roles. Concomitantly, important demographic changes occur, such as rising educational attainment of women, declining fertility,

[3] Where women's labour power has been 'valued' in pre-capitalist settings—for example, for agricultural production or carpet-weaving (which in some cases may explain the male preference for polygamy)—women themselves have been denied status as producers, without property rights over land, animals, or the products of their labour (including very often their children). This is also noted by Engels (1884).

[4] This attachment of women to the sphere of reproduction underlies the analytic distinction of 'public–private' spheres, discussed by Rosaldo and Lamphere (1974), but earlier noted by Engels (1884). Although some feminists have argued that this is a West-centred notion (i.e. peculiar to the Victorian age and the early stage of industrial capitalism), the association of women with domesticity and the distinction between public and private spheres are characteristic also of Muslim and Hindu cultures in the Near East and South Asia, expressed in veiling, seclusion, segregation, and *purdah*. It would appear, therefore, that the public–private distinction and the family attachment of women is hardly an invention of modern industrial capitalism and of the Victorian era, but is embedded in the major patriarchal religions and many pre-capitalist social structures. The breakdown of the practice and ideology of domesticity occurs as industrialization and internationalization proceed.

[5] See Alice Kessler-Harris (1990). Her book begins by noting that a man's wage is constructed as a 'badge of honor', with 'incentives to individual achievement', while 'a woman's wage by contrast is a term of opprobrium', functioning to ensure her 'attachment to family' and as a 'warning . . . [for women] to follow the natural order' (pp. 3, 19, 20). Her analysis of a 1923 Supreme Court decision that struck down minimum wages for women and children at a time when protective legislation was identifying women as 'wards of the state' shows that women represented a contradiction for employers. On the one hand, they were relegated to the domestic sphere and needed protection from the harshness of public life. On the other hand, capitalists were fighting for the right to use *all* available labour as cheaply as possible. However, capitalists recognized that this free use might 'destroy the golden egg that produced cheap labour' (p. 39). In subsequent chapters Kessler-Harris shows how women who were providers gained acceptance as labour-market participants.

and lower population growth rates. But because women are uniquely endowed with reproductive capacity, and in the absence of a viable solution to the problem of social reproduction, there continues to be a tension between the two roles and responsibilities of women.

Access to and participation in formal employment is clearly an historic gain for women, and a step towards the larger goals of gender equity and women's empowerment. But there are negative entailments which lie at both the economic and cultural levels. Women are still a source of cheap (and in some countries, 'flexible') labour, and the sphere of reproduction is still regarded as a woman's (rather than a man's) responsibility. In many countries, the cultural and institutional support to enable women to exercise the right of employment is inadequate if they have children. Moreover, the recent experience of global restructuring has everywhere rendered precarious the economic position of women. This is as true of the United States as it is of developing countries undergoing structural adjustment and the former state socialist societies in transition from planned to market economies. Massive lay-offs of women and their re-attachment to the family could interrupt the trend towards greater autonomy, equity, and empowerment of women. Women's dual labour role (their 'double burden') makes them especially vulnerable during periods of economic crisis. Trends towards socializing domestic labour are likely to be arrested or reversed as the state reduces or redirects expenditure and part-time women workers become especially attractive to employers (Sokoloff 1980: 219).

In this chapter I hope to show that, as economic reorganization entails changes in production and social reproduction, gender is embedded in the process and women are profoundly affected by it. The gender effects of economic processes are variable, mainly by social class, but also by economic sector, and entail both setbacks and gains for women. Gender, however, plays an integral part in the course and outcome of economic processes, including restructuring. To illustrate this, I focus on the similarities and differences in the gender dynamics of restructuring between the newly industrializing countries of the Third World and the newly privatizing countries of the former Second World.[6] But because restructuring is a global phenomenon, I will begin with a discussion of restructuring within the world-system.

THE GLOBAL CONTEXT: INTERNATIONALIZATION, RESTRUCTURING, AND REDEFINITIONS OF GENDER

Restructuring is the most recent development in the post-Second World War process of what has been variously called the internationalization of capital,

---

[6] In this chapter I will also refer to these two regions as the two semi-peripheries, both as a kind of shorthand, and because it is a concept of the world-system perspective.

the new, or changing, international division of labour, global Fordism, and the golden age of capitalism (Palloix 1977; Frobel *et al.* 1980; Nash and Fernandez-Kelly 1985; Southall 1988; Lipietz 1982; Marglin and Schor 1990). Growth, employment, and foreign productive investment were elements of this golden age and of internationalization. In this regard, the transnational corporations (TNCs) were significant, as were national development plans and industrialization projects. Throughout the Third World, states were major agents of the development process, but especially strong roles were played by state managers in East Asia (Harris 1986; Amsden 1989; Gereffi 1990). Internationalization entailed the increased integration, rationalization, co-ordination, and interdependence of the world-system at the level of the political economy and interstate relations. Plant relocations from north to south in search of cheap labour and production costs, the spreading importance of decentralized production sites in both north and south, and the control and co-ordination by TNCs of these decentralized production units were salient features of internationalization.

In the world-system perspective, global restructuring refers to the emergence of the global assembly-line in which research and management are controlled by the core or developed countries while assembly-line work is relegated to semi-peripheral or peripheral countries that occupy less privileged positions in the global economy. Restructuring paradoxically concentrates control over increasingly dispersed sites and decentralized organizations through subcontracting and product differentiation. As one theorist explains,

The global assembly line approach to production is attractive to transnational corporations (TNCs) and to employers seeking greater access to markets, diffusion of political and economic costs, improved competitive abilities, and product diversity. Within developing countries, restructuring is marked by growth of the service sector and specialization in export industries such as electronics, garments, and pharmaceuticals as a development strategy. Restructuring is also marked by increasing use of female industrial workers in the informal sector.

(Ward 1990: 1–2)

In the advanced capitalist countries this process has taken the form of industrial restructuring and a shift from manufacturing to services (Bluestone and Harrison 1982; Harvey 1989).

The centrepiece of global restructuring is the growth in the number of informal-sector workers and women workers. In contrast to the formal sector, the pay and working conditions in the informal sector are unregulated by labour legislation. The existence of this sector is functional for capital inasmuch as it provides an alternative, and cheap, source of labour. By subcontracting industrial production to informal factories or home-based workers, employers can minimize competitive risks, wages, and the threat of unionization, while maximizing their flexibility in hiring, their overhead costs, and their production processes (Ward 1990: 2). In the United States, the growth of informalization has paralleled the increasing use of immigrant labour (Portes and Sassen-Koob 1987: 48), drawing especially large numbers of Hispanic women into formal and informal arrangements in the garment and electronics industries of New York and California (Sassen and Fernandez-Kelly 1992). Temporality, comparatively lower wages, and reduced member-ship in unions or other workers' organizations are additional characteristics of women's employment.[7]

Economic internationalization has led to what Susan Joekes (1987) calls the 'globalization' of female labour, and Guy Standing (1989) the 'feminiza-tion' of labour. An important feature of the global restructuring of employ-ment affecting women workers has been the relocation of labour-intensive industries from industrially developed to developing countries in search of cheap labour—mostly young, unmarried, and inexperienced women—to engage in industrial work (ILO/INSTRAW 1985: 21). Textiles and clothing were the first industries to be relocated, followed by food processing, elec-tronics, and in some cases pharmaceutical products. In this process, various forms of subcontracting arrangements were made to relocate production, or subsidiaries were set up with foreign or partly local capital.

This TNC relocation has affected women mainly in Latin America and the Caribbean and in South-east Asia. The most important areas of activity for foreign investors in the export manufacturing sector in developing countries has been the textiles and clothing and electronics industries. Five countries dominate in terms of the size of their export-processing zone (EPZ) opera-tions: Hong Kong, South Korea, Puerto Rico, Singapore, and Taiwan. Rather less important but still substantial are EPZs in Brazil, Haiti, Malaysia, and Mexico (Joekes and Moayedi 1987: 21). Over the years, a majority of jobs created in the export manufacturing sector has gone to women (Standing 1989). Indeed, Joekes and Moayedi note 'the disproportionate access that women have to export manufacturing employment and their overwhelming importance as suppliers for the export manufacturing sector'. Joekes (1987: 81) concludes that industrialization in the Third World has been as much female-led as export-led. This is especially so in the newly industrializing countries of South-east Asia, or what are now called the

---

[7] Data from the Women's Bureau of the US Department of Labor (1991) show that 26 per cent of women workers in the USA held part-time jobs in 1989. Median earnings for women who worked year-round, full-time in 1988 was $17,606, while the comparable figure for men was $26,656. Regarding unionization, US workers have never been highly unionized compared with their counterparts in most West European countries. But between 1970 and 1985 the unionized share of the work-force plummeted in the USA, while growing or remaining stable in most other Western countries (*Dollars and Sense*, Sept. 1988: 22). On the other hand, public-sector unionization has been increasing in the USA (Freeman 1988), and women workers have made their greatest progress, particularly in the areas of pay equity, sexual harassment, and fair-employment practices, in the public sector (*WIN News*, 1991: 72).

Dynamic Asian Economies. These countries have experienced growth in large part because they have integrated women so massively in industrial production—as did the former state socialist countries.

Increased trade, multinational investment, and cross-regional flows of capital and labour have increasingly drawn women into the process of economic internationalization and restructuring. This has had the dual effect of undermining notions of the exclusively domestic role of women *and* of utilizing them as cheap and flexible labour in the Third World.

It may be useful to specify the major developments worldwide which have contributed to redefinitions of gender. Four appear to be the most significant: (1) the expanded utilization of female labour in national economies, first in the Soviet Union, then, in the post-war period, throughout Europe (East and West), North America, and modernizing countries in Asia and Latin America; (2) the efforts of international bodies, particularly agencies of the United Nations system,[8] to render more visible women's involvement in national development and to improve women's legal status; (3) the activities of women's movements and feminist researchers in countries throughout the world; (4) the remarkable progress of women in the Nordic countries of Finland, Norway, and Sweden, where women's share of the labour force and of political institutions is nearly equitable with that of men (see Haavio-Mannila *et al.* 1985; Skjele 1991). The combined and cumulative effect of these developments has been growing worldwide recognition of women as workers and citizens, as economic and political actors, and as participants in (if not always beneficiaries of) development. Internationalization seems to be undermining the most egregious aspects of patriarchal ideologies and practices (such as restrictions on women's mobility, access to education and employment, choice of spouse, and control over fertility), although gender inequality persists everywhere.

But social change is uneven and nonlinear. Thus, the expanded role of women in production and their visibility in public life has encountered a backlash in a number of countries. It appears that the men of certain social classes—such as the conservative lower middle class and among the economically insecure—find the expanded role of women in public life to be threatening. And for some women, the decline of the ideology of men as family providers and women as childrearers is·a source of anxiety. These fears follow from the decline of the 'family wage', from increased unemployment of men, from inflation and depreciating incomes, and from women's having to seek employment to meet household needs out of dire economic necessity rather than choice. In the United States, such people gravitate towards

[8] Especially the International Labour Office (Geneva), the Division for the Advancement of Women (Vienna), the UN Statistical Office (New York), and the UN Training and Research Institute for the Advancement of Women (INSTRAW).

the anti-abortion movement and other right-wing movements. In the Middle East they are drawn to Islamist movements (Moghadam 1991; 1993: 139). In both cases, conservatives call for the return of women to domestic life and traditional values. Thus, the trend I have described above should not be seen as unilinear; the process of internationalization, global integration, and socio-economic development entails gains and setbacks for women and for the goal of gender equity.

Since the 1970s, and especially during the 1980s, global restructuring has been characterized by the shift from import-substitution industrialization to export-led growth, from state ownership to privatization, from government regulation of prices and trade to liberalization, from a stable and organized work-force to 'flexible' labour, from formal employment to the proliferation and expansion of informal sectors. This process is likely to continue through the 1990s. During the 1980s, the worldwide economic crisis, and the requirements of structural adjustment programmes, contributed to these shifts in developing countries (see Standing and Tokman 1991). In the United States and Britain, international competition and declining profits in manufacturing led to a more combative stance on the part of capital, breaking the social pact with labour. In Britain 'flexible workers' increased by 16 per cent to 8.1 million between 1981 and 1985, while permanent jobs decreased by 6 per cent to 15.6 million. Over roughly the same period, nearly one-third of the 10 million new jobs created in the United States were thought to be in the 'temporary' category (Harvey 1989: 152). Now, 'flexibility' is the *sine qua non* of international economics.[9] Some celebrate 'flexible specialization' as an advance for women, at least in the case of Tokyo (Fujita 1991). I am inclined to agree with Harvey's assessment that,

Not only do the new labour market structures make it much easier to exploit the labour power of women on a part-time basis, and so to substitute lower-paid female labour for that of more highly paid and less laid-off core male workers, but the revival of sub-contracting and domestic and family labour systems permits a resurgence of patriarchal practices and homeworking.

(Harvey 1989: 153)

Standing is also critical of global feminization through flexible labour in that it coincides with the decline of organized labour and offers exploitative and unstable employment for women.

And now, restructuring has encompassed the former state socialist countries as well. The process invariably affects the position of women in production

---

[9] In the language of another school of thought—that of the French Regulation School,—restructuring represents the shift from Fordism (mass production) to post-Fordism ('flexible accumulation') in the advanced capitalist countries, and a combination of flexible accumulation (very often familial-type work arrangements) and 'peripheral Fordism' in industrializing countries. For an elaboration, see Harvey (1989: part II); see also Boyer (1989) and Lipietz (1991).

and reproduction. But before examining the gender dynamics of restructuring in the two semi-peripheries, let us address the question of why these changes should have occurred at all in Eastern Europe and the Soviet Union.

Explaining restructuring

The basic premiss of world-system theory is that there exists a capitalist world-economy which has integrated a geographically vast set of production processes. The economic organization of the world-system consists of a single, worldwide division of labour that unifies the multiple cultural systems of the world's people into a single, integrated economic system. The economic zones of the world-system are the 'core', 'periphery', and 'semi-periphery'. In the contemporary world-economy, the core countries are the OECD countries; the periphery consists of the least developed countries; the semi-periphery consists of newly-industrializing countries such as South Korea, Brazil, India, Israel, South Africa, Iran, Mexico, and some of the former state socialist countries. The political framework within which this division of labour has grown up has been that of an interstate system. The driving force of this world-system is global accumulation. The capitalist world-economy functions by means of a pattern of cyclical rhythms, a seemingly regular process of expansion and contraction of the world-economy as a whole. Sometimes called 'long waves' and sometimes Kondratieff cycles (after the man who first used the term in 1926), these are extended periods (about forty to sixty years) of economic expansion and stagnation occurring over the history of the world capitalist system at least since the industrial revolution. As Wallerstein (1982, 1990) explains it, over a period of some four hundred years, successive expansions have transformed the capitalist world-economy from a system located primarily in Europe to one that covers the entire globe. Chase-Dunn, another world-system theorist, has also argued that the simultaneity and broad similarities between Reagan/Thatcher deregulation and attack on the welfare state, the policies of austerity and privatization in Brazil, Mexico, Argentina, and Chile, austerity socialism in much of Europe, and marketization in the former communist states 'are all related to the B-phase downturn of the Kondratieff wave'. He states: 'The way in which the pressures of a stagnating world economy impact upon national policies certainly varies from country to country, but the ability of any single national society to construct collective rationality is limited by its interaction within the larger system' (Chase-Dunn 1990: 5).

It follows from this perspective that the state socialist societies did not constitute a separate socio-economic system with its own dynamic, but were rather 'an interactive part of the larger capitalist world-economy, albeit with some internal socialist features' (Chase-Dunn 1982a: 15). The strength of world capitalism, especially as it operates in the interstate system, pushed these states in the direction of reintegration. Writing in the early 1980s, Chase-Dunn explained that the crisis of the capitalist world-economy is transmitted to the national economy of the state socialist countries in a number of ways:

To the extent that they purchase anything on the world market, changes in world market prices will affect their internal pricing. In the present period of 'stagflation', the economies of the Eastern European countries have experienced inflation of somewhat smaller amplitude after a time lag following the inflation of prices in the larger world-economy. . . . To the extent to which these national economies produce commodities for profit on the world market, their internal pricing systems will tend to reflect the most 'economic' distribution for rewarding and encouraging profitable production, just as 'prices' within a capitalist firm come to reflect larger market prices. . . .

Extensive borrowing from the West [by Poland] was used to develop industrial production for export on the bet that world demand would be sufficient and Western markets would remain open to Polish export. The downturn of the long wave (Kondratieff wave) spoiled this Poland plan and contributed to the disappointment of rising expectations for material improvement among Polish workers. This, combined with the old grievances against the regime and anti-Soviet nationalism, led to the growth of . . . Solidarity . . .

Even when socialist states do not engage in commodity production for the world market, their national economies are affected by the larger world contraction . . . [A consequence of the downturn is that] individual core nations become more aggressive and begin increasing their armaments. In response, the socialist nations must increase military expenditures . . .

(Chase-Dunn 1982b: 46–7)

In a more recent paper, Chase-Dunn (1992) has argued that 'the history and developmental trajectory of the socialist states can be explained as socialist movements in the semi-periphery which attempted to transform the basic logic of capitalism, but which ended up using socialist ideology to mobilize industrialization in order to try to catch up with core capitalism'.

In their explanation of the political revolts and economic restructuring in Eastern Europe, Boswell and Peters (1990) note that the growing and innovative economic sector in the core has been changing from low-skill mass assembly run by military-type bureaucracies to more flexible, high-skill batch production with decentralized control. This ongoing 'industrial divide' in the world economy, they explain, is forcing all developed countries to either match the innovations in accumulation or to fall into the periphery and be satisfied with the low technology cast off by the core. Boswell and Peters place the concept of industrial divides in the more general theory of economic long waves. Economic divides are the critical turning-points during the transition from stagnation to expansion when firms, industries, and states must develop extensive socio-political accumulation innovations to foster renewed economic growth and development. 'Those that fail to adopt the accumulation innovations are left stagnating and eventually reduced to dependence on the innovators' (Boswell and Peters 1990: 3). This 'long wave approach' explains why a Stalinist bureaucratic organization of mass production was successful at industrial development in the past and why 'it is now being deconstructed'.

This explanation brings to mind another, earlier, observation about the power of the capitalist mode of production:[10]

The bourgeoisie, by the rapid improvement of all instruments of production, by the immensely facilitated means of communication, draws all, even the most barbarian, nations into civilization. The cheap prices of its commodities are the heavy artillery with which it batters down all Chinese walls, with which it forces the barbarians' intensely obstinate hatred of foreigners to capitulate. It compels all nations, on pain of extinction, to adopt the bourgeois mode of production . . . In one word, it creates a world after its own image.

(Marx and Engels 1848)

GENDER AND RESTRUCTURING IN THE THIRD WORLD

In the 1980s, restructuring took the form of stabilization, price and trade liberalization, and privatization, partly to service the enormous debt accrued by deficit-financing states and partly to adhere to World Bank and IMF conditionality for further loans, such as the Structural Adjustment Loans or Sectoral Adjustment Loans. There is consensus that stabilization and structural adjustment have had an intensely adverse effect upon the livelihoods and standards of living of masses of people throughout the Third World (Cornia et al. 1987; Commonwealth Secretariat 1989). In a recent paper, Frances Stewart compares macroeconomic indicators for sub-Saharan Africa and Latin America and the Caribbean for the period before and during structural adjustment. While noting that there are considerable variations, with some countries (e.g. Indonesia, Burkino Faso, and Mauritius) experiencing improvements while others (Zambia and Argentina) experienced massive deteriorations, Stewart concludes that on balance the experience in the 1980s as a whole was negative for both regions. Structural adjustment has not succeeded in restoring economic growth; and falling investment rates will make growth even more difficult to secure in the 1990s (cited in Elson 1991).

A recent study focusing on the impact of the economic crisis and adjustment process on the living standards of the Mexican population between 1982 and 1985 concludes that Mexico was left with a relatively

---

[10] The language, of course, is less than salubrious, but the point about the compelling nature of world capitalism is remarkably prescient. See also Harvey (1989: 180–8) for a discussion of the continuing relevance of Marx's *Capital*.

impoverished middle class and rising poverty (Lustig 1990). A study of Turkey's recovery from its debt crisis (Aricanli and Rodrik 1990) shows that, although price and trade liberalization and structural adjustment resulted in a remarkable growth in exports, income distribution deteriorated.[11]

A WIDER study of IMF- and World Bank-directed stabilization experiences in eighteen developing countries concludes that 'programmes of the Fund/ Bank type are optimal for neither stabilization nor growth and income redistribution in the Third World' (Taylor 1988: 3). Even the World Bank Development Report for 1990 conceded that poverty had increased during what some have called the 'lost development decade'—the result of austerity measures to tackle debts and deficits. According to the UN *1989 World Survey on the Role of Women in Development* (United Nations 1989), the latter half of the 1980s was characterized by 'uneven economic growth that has often aggravated the differences between regions'. The report elaborates:

[I]n most developing regions, Africa and Latin America and the Caribbean, economic stagnation or negative growth, continued population increase and the prolonged international debt crisis and adjustment policies designed to deal with this have shaped and constrained the activities of women as individuals, as carers and providers for families and households, and as participants in the practical development of their countries. The problems of recession and economic restructuring in the face of external debt have led Governments to focus on these, often to the neglect of longer-term issues that have direct bearing on the advancement of women. At the same time, pre-existing conditions of inequality—in health and nutrition, levels of literacy and training, in access to education and economic opportunity, and in participation in decision-making at all levels—between women and men have sometimes been exacerbated both by the crises themselves and by the policies adopted to cope with them.

(United Nations 1989: 7)

The now-classic UNICEF study showed that the poverty-inducing aspect of adjustment results in downward social mobility for middle-class women and an even more serious decline in the standard of living for poor women and their children (Cornia *et al.* 1987). Constraints on government expenditure serve to reduce programmes and services designed to integrate women into development and increase their employment and income opportunities. Poor women have become poorer, more women are poor, and women are now poorer in relation to men, as even the World Bank recognizes. In its *World Development Report 1990*, which focuses on poverty, it is stated: 'The plight

---

[11] The authors also point out that internal resource mobilization failed to materialize, and that 'successful growth in exports was only partly influenced by economic policies such as subsidies, which fell outside the "liberal" category'. This suggests that privatization and liberalization require more rather than less state management and investment. Or, as Chase-Dunn (1990: 6) notes, 'The typical capitalist state is not *laissez faire* but is rather *interventionist*, and the trend toward "state capitalism" has long been a secularly increasing tendency, not a wholly new departure.'

of poor women is troubling in itself. It is even more troubling because the health and education of mothers greatly influence the well-being and future of their children' (World Bank 1990: from the Foreword by Barber Conable, p. iii).

The gender dynamics of structural adjustment have been addressed in a number of studies (Commonwealth Secretariat 1989; Standing 1989; Beneria 1991; Elson 1991; Palmer 1991; Vickers 1991; Afshar and Dennis 1992). Reviewing the literature, Elson (1991) reports consensus that the burdens borne by women, especially poor women, during the course of adjustment have had not much of a pay-off for the national economy; neither have they paved the way for a sustainable growth in the 1990s. Gender bias, usually present in development projects, is exacerbated by structural adjustment. Structural adjustment exacerbates gender bias by overlooking, if not denying, women's access to and consumption of the type of productive resources and services, such as extension, credit, and input subsidies, that are targeted to export production. In so far as this limits women's productivity, adjustment policies are sabotaging their very goals of stable long-term growth (Joekes 1989: 25; Commonwealth Secretariat 1989: 4).

The gender impact of government expenditure is especially discernible in four areas: public employment, capital versus current expenditures, subsidies, and services and other government-sponsored programmes (Joekes 1989). In many developing countries, and of course in the former state socialist countries, the public or state sector is the major employer of women and minorities. The public sector is in many cases much less biased against women in its wage, recruitment, and promotions policy than is the private sector, although public-sector women employees remain concentrated in the lower-grade positions. Around the world, the trend towards greater participation of women is noticeable in every public service, especially education and health, though at lower skill levels (van Ginneken 1990: 446). Often the shorter working hours in the public sector make it a preferred employer to women with family responsibility (Joekes 1989: 10; Standing 1989). In Iran, census data reveal that all the women in the public sector are salaried and beneficiaries of social security, while women workers in the private sector are predominantly unwaged and without benefits (Moghadam 1993: 191–5). In Algeria, too, the small percentage of women who are salaried are government employees (Moghadam 1993: 60). Cutbacks in the public-sector wage bill under macroeconomic policy programmes of the sort favoured by the IMF and World Bank are therefore obviously damaging to women's labour market position. Indeed, a recent summary of evidence on changes in the structure of wage employment for women in developing countries suggests that, not only have some kinds of wage and salary employment opportunity diminished (notably in the public sector) while others have increased (notably in export-oriented manufacturing), but also this has been widely accompanied by a deterioration in conditions of employment (Standing 1989; Elson 1991).

In developing countries, rural women have been the most adversely affected by structural adjustment policies and the least positively affected by economic internationalization. A recent study of the impact of technical change on gender relations in Turkish agriculture concludes that 'structural adjustment policies, by adding to the pressures of small farms in the accumulation and survival process have contributed to the worsening of women's position' (Morvaridi 1992). Many policies implemented by states and by international agencies actually work to perpetuate the sexual division of labour and especially rural women's responsibility for domestic work. Attempts to increase rural women's productivity in the absence of parallel efforts to reduce their reproductive work merely result either in intolerable workloads, or in a redistribution of such tasks among women of different age groups within the same household (Kandiyoti 1990). A recent study of women in the economies of sub-Saharan Africa concludes that the interactions of population growth, environmental deterioration, and some technological advances have tended to increase women's workloads; these women are likely to remain overburdened until men start to assume more of the reproductive chores (Weil 1992). Moreover, as long as women are economic dependants of male kin rather than owners of productive assets in their own right, women will continue to be relegated to the sphere of reproduction and their productive work will continue to be devalued.

An analysis of development projects by Buvinic (1984) found that many rural WID programmes attempt to organize women into social groups, or to provide training in stereotypical female skills such as sewing, cooking, knitting, and gardening, and involve group activities through which women attempt to apply the skills they have learned to income-generation activities. Kandiyoti has argued that what is being called for in some WID rural projects is not simply an increase in women's labour productivity but an intensification and elaboration of their mothering and nurturing roles as well. For example, the so-called participatory strategies for health provision are predicated upon women's willingness as mothers to adopt, administer, and ultimately finance the GOBI technologies which have a decisive impact on child survival—growth monitoring, oral rehydration therapy, breastfeeding and improved weaning practices, and immunization. Given the increasingly restricted availability of public funds in the health sector, the onus is on women to extend their traditional responsibilities as the feeders and healers of their families to include the provision of basic health care—even though it is candidly acknowledged that this will make new demands on their time and financial resources (Kandiyoti 1990: 17). Clearly, such policies do nothing to eliminate gender hierarchy, transform traditional sex roles, improve women's social positions, or bring about qualitative and meaningful social change. These kinds of policies in fact reinforce women's reproductive and domestic roles, deliberately avoid the upsetting of the public–private distinction, and generally do not serve the goals of equity and empowerment of women.

Thus, one cannot escape the conclusion that, although economic internationalization has drawn more and more women into production and public life, structural adjustment has worked to the disadvantage of women. In countries undergoing structural adjustment, working women have lost jobs or seen their incomes fall. The quality of public services has deteriorated.[12] Poor women have had to assume more responsibilities for their households, and to devise all manner of survival strategies. For Eastern Europe and the former Soviet Union, there were important lessons to be learned from developing countries' experience with restructuring.

RESTRUCTURING AND GENDER IN EASTERN EUROPE AND THE USSR/CIS

Restructuring in Eastern Europe and the Soviet Union encompasses more than stabilization, price liberalization, and privatization. The scope of restructuring even exceeds the entire economy, as it entails political, juridical, and ideological changes.[13] The task is even more daunting in what was the Soviet Union. The future of restructuring of the former centrally planned economies is unclear, in part because considerable uncertainty exists as to the amount of saving that will emerge under the new economic conditions. There is also uncertainty about the role and extent of foreign saving and foreign investment. In the words of the authors of a recent WIDER study, 'despite the attractive low labour costs in Eastern Europe, foreign firms are likely to want to keep their options open and wait until the political and economic uncertainty has been reduced' (Blanchard *et al.* 1991: p. xvii). Notwithstanding the application of 'shock therapy' urged by Western orthodox economists, Poland has attracted very little investment

---

[12] Van Ginneken (1990) reports that high budget deficits have led all governments to reduce outlays on two main items: social security, subsidies, and other transfers on the one hand, and public investments (capital expenditure) on the other. In many countries, subsidies both to consumers (food, rent, etc.) and to public enterprises were cut as part of the stabilization policies (p. 444). The share of social security also declined, particularly in Latin America and the Middle East. In Tanzania, rural health-care expenditure was reduced in the early 1980s by cutting spending on drugs, bandages, and other items while preserving employment. The result was a drastic deterioration in the quality of care provided (p. 446). For a detailed analysis of countries, see the UNICEF study (Cornia *et al.* 1987).

[13] Considering the sweeping nature of the changes, the term 'revolution' is more apt, but what kind of revolution has occurred or is occurring requires more time to analyse. In particular, the role of intellectual and technocratic élites in effecting the economic, political, and ideological changes, and their international connections, deserves special attention.

capital. Private shops are booming, but output and growth continue to fall. Economic reorganization requires not only capital but also labour mobility, of the kind characteristic of Third World industrializing countries and the United States. This has wide-ranging social implications. For example, Blanchard *et al.* point out that in the former state socialist countries labour mobility depends in part on a housing market 'that provides the correct incentives for workers to move and for housing to be built where most needed'. They note that the current structure of the housing market, with its largely state-owned apartments, subsidized rents, and non-price allocation, makes it difficult if not impossible for workers to move. Also, it does not provide the right incentives for housing investment. Rapid marketization, therefore, will include the ending of all manner of subsidies and controls —as has happened in Poland and is occurring in the former Soviet Union. For these and other reasons, Blanchard and associates conclude that 'the process of adjustment that would emerge from the unfettered market process would likely involve too little job creation, too much job destruction, and too high a level of unemployment'.

Mass and long-term unemployment is indeed the spectre that is haunting Eastern Europe. In early 1992, experts expected that by the end of the year one-fifth of the active population in Poland and Bulgaria would be jobless, with figures of 13–14 per cent for Hungary and 12 per cent for Romania and Czechoslovakia. According to official figures, there were 2.1 million unemployed Poles, or 11 per cent of the population, along with 523,000 Czechoslovaks (6.6 per cent), 500,000 Bulgarians (10 per cent), 400,000 Hungarians (8.3 per cent), and 300,000 Romanians (4.4 per cent). Unemployment is likely to increase during 1993. The reasons for this accelerating joblessness are: a constant fall in internal demand and real wages, the collapse of trade with the former Soviet Union, the closure of big state enterprises, and the sacking of thousands of civil servants. In Hungary, despite cautious and gradual privatization of the economy and the injection of foreign capital, unemployment increased fivefold in one year, from 80,000 to 400,000. In all of Eastern Europe, young people are among the hardest hit, often at a time when they are seeking their first paid employment, as are women. In Poland, people aged 19–24 comprise 34.2 per cent of the jobless, and among the jobless more than half are women.[14] Income inequalities are growing, with the sharpest differences along class, gender, and generational lines. Lance Taylor argues that the process of restructuring, as defined by the conventional adjustment wisdom of the Bretton Woods institutions, widens an imbalance between aggregate supply and aggregate demand by plunging adjusting economies into unnecessary recession in the attempt to

[14] 'Unemployment—The Spectre Haunting Eastern Europe', *Tehran Times*, 28 January 1992: 13.

eliminate excess aggregate demand (Taylor 1992). The extent of the region's recession is neatly summarized by *The Economist*: 'economies shrinking by around 10 % in most countries last year, and by 20 % in Bulgaria; inflation in 1991 ranging from 40% in Hungary to 400% in Bulgaria; unemployment rising from next to nothing to 10% or more' (*The Economist*, 16 May 1992: 29).

According to an ILO study of restructuring in the Soviet Union, in 1991 'the extent of poverty is alarming' (Standing 1991). Some estimates suggest that 80 million people, or more than a quarter of the entire population, have fallen into a state of bare subsistence, living on less than the official poverty level of Rb80 per month. As noted by Standing,

National income fell by between 2 percent and 7 percent in 1990, the country's trade deficit trebled, even though the volume of trade actually declined, and an inflation rate of over 30 percent has threatened to drift upwards to levels usually characterized as hyperinflation, leaving those on fixed incomes in dire circumstances . . . Meanwhile, open unemployment has become an increasingly serious phenomenon, in circumstances in which the means of social protection are scarcely effective.

(Standing 1991: 1)

In 1992, an ILO survey of the Russian labour market found that more than 15 million workers were likely to become unemployed in the former Soviet Union, and that another 30 million in state-sector jobs could be pushed into unemployment 'because they are chronically unemployed'. The ILO said that 'unemployed workers will bear an excessive burden of the change to a market economy', in part because the new system of unemployment benefits for laid off workers 'rarely reaches any of the unemployed' (ILO 1992).

The restructuring of agriculture to achieve more effective labour mobility coincides with the radical redirection of social and labour policy, which includes more flexible wage determination processes, the abandonment of guaranteed employment, and the recognition of unemployment as a 'regret-table reality' (Standing 1991: 5). In 1991, Standing observed that 'unemployment has already become a particularly severe prospect for women workers and for ethnic minorities in the various parts of the country' (Standing 1991: 10). In Moscow in 1992, fully 80 per cent of the unemployed were females (Novikova, in Weir 1992).

The gender dimension of restructuring in the former state socialist countries lies most obviously in the changes to women's status as workers, as many of the chapters in this book show. In a region of the world that once enjoyed the distinction of the highest rates of female labour force participation and—most significantly—the largest female share of paid employment, women now face unemployment, marginalization from the productive process, and loss of previous benefits and forms of social security. Women's losses in the areas of employment and social provisions, such as maternity leaves and child-care facilities, have been well documented in many of the chapters of this book. According to Malgorzata Tarasiewicz, formerly head of Solidarity's Women's Division in Poland, women's situation is likely to worsen with the restructuring of those branches of industry, such as textiles, that employ mainly women. She is quoted as saying: 'At the moment, employment in some textile industries is kept stable, but in order to avoid mass reductions, women are sent on unpaid leaves or work only two days a week earning [a wage] that is far below the poverty line' (quoted in Baker 1991: 12). In the former German Democratic Republic women's employment was facilitated by state provision of child-care and maternity leave, and by a policy of positive discrimination. Prior to unification and restructuring, more than 90 per cent of GDR women had a secure job; 92 per cent had had at least one child by the time she turned 23 (Mussall 1991: 22). Infants were cared for in state nurseries until the age of 3; every child aged 4 and older had a guaranteed place in a state school or kindergarten. Parents had up to ten weeks of paid leave to care for sick children. Now, female employees are dismissed before male employees are; by May 1992, women accounted for 67 per cent of the unemployed (Tomforde 1992: 19). In the unprofitable companies, child care is the first benefit to be cut. According to one source, 'Many mothers have no choice but to accept termination and stay at home' (Mussall 1991: 22).

If the costs of providing the social benefits for women workers once borne by the state or the state socialist enterprise are now to be assumed by private employers, this will likely have the effect of reducing the demand for female labour, limiting women's access to full-time employment and reducing their earnings in the formal sector. Why? From a market point of view, female labour in Eastern Europe is more expensive than male labour —notwithstanding an earnings gap between men and women similar to that in Western countries—because of the costs involved in maternity and child-care provisions usually borne by enterprises. Certainly one's impression is that female labour in the state socialist countries was of a different order from the 'cheap and expendable female labour' of Third World industrializing countries, with their lax or non-existent labour codes (see Standing 1989). This economic rationale, as well as gender bias, explains what appears to be a concerted effort to remove women from the labour market in the context of economic restructuring and privatization. Although this may be profitable to employers, for women the consequences are dire. Withdrawal of state support for working mothers in the former state socialist countries is likely to diminish the identification of women as both workers and reproducers and replace it with an exclusive ideology of reproduction (Pearson 1990). In this way, not only are women among the principal losers in the restructuring process in the short term, but the longer-term impact may be a strengthening of patriarchal concepts concerning men's and women's roles.

As described by Posadskaya and by Bodrova in this volume, patriarchal sentiments are rather strong in the former Soviet Union, and seem to be intensifying with restructuring. One essential feature of restructuring in the Soviet Union is the planned transfer of labour out of agriculture and into the tertiary sector. This is considered 'necessary' because at present, one in every five of the Soviet Union's work-force is apparently occupied in farming, compared with one in fifteen in a country such as France.[15] Clearly, workers will need to be released from agriculture in order to be made available for work in services, particularly consumer services, which in the past was a very small sector by international standards and which is expected to grow (Standing 1991: 4). But this could have profound social and gender implications. It should be noted that in China the return to household farming, while boosting agricultural output, created 200 million redundant farmers. Even with a smaller rural population and lower birth rates in the former Soviet Union, rural privatization would put considerable strain on the labour market, not to mention the urban infrastructure. Furthermore, studies have shown that the retreat from collective farming to the family farm in China has resulted in a resurgence of patriarchy in the countryside and a diminished status for women (Davin 1987; Kelkar 1988). In the former Soviet Union, an end to collective farming (which paid salaries to women agricultural workers), and a return to family production could result in new gender inequalities, especially in the less developed republics.

A British trade union study of Central and Eastern Europe reports that in February 1991 a women's delegation from the International Federation of Chemical, Energy and General Workers' Unions (ICEF) visited Hungary and Czechoslovakia. In Hungary women members of the ICEF-affiliated chemical workers' union said that one of the main concerns of women workers in Hungary is future job security. Another is high inflation, 'which means that it is becoming more and more expensive to raise children' (NALGO 1991). The report goes on to say that, within the trade union movement in Central and Eastern Europe, women are under-represented in positions of authority. In Solidarity, for example, 'it was reported in March 1990 that there were no women representatives on the National Executive Commission, even though women made up some 30–40 per cent of the union's membership' (NALGO 1991: 158).

It is in the context of growing unemployment, higher prices, and falling investment, growth, and output in Eastern Europe and the former Soviet Union that the non-orthodox case for restructuring is gaining credibility among economists. Blanchard and associates (1991) conclude that governments must play an active role to minimize the social costs of adjustment. Standing (1991) makes a case for 'social adjustments', echoing the concerns

[15] The percentage share of workers in manufacturing is not too much out of line with industrialized market economies, but the share involved in services, particularly consumer services, is, according to Standing, remarkably small by international standards.

of Cornia *et al.* (1987) regarding the unacceptable social costs of structural adjustment in developing countries. Prowse (1992) has sharply criticized the application of 'shock therapy' for its macroeconomic and social effects. Taylor (1992) makes a strong case for state intervention during restructuring, in part to boost growth and output, in part to guarantee social needs. The argument of this chapter is that strategic intervention is also required to reduce the adverse effects of restructuring on women.

In both newly industrializing countries of the Third World and the newly privatizing countries of Eastern Europe, efficiency, productivity, and flexibility are key concepts in restructuring. In both regions this is to be accomplished through price reform, devalued currencies, foreign investments, and export promotion—that is, integration into the world market. But, whereas in the NICs integration into the world market has meant increased employment opportunities for women (because it coincided with accelerated industrialization and growth), in the latter, integration is being translated into redundancy for women workers, at least in the short run. This is a key difference in the two cases. In both cases, however, restructuring means a deterioration of terms of employment. Moreover, restructuring is everywhere leading to the growth of the informal sector (Portes *et al.* 1989).[16] In the wake of structural adjustment, women in developing countries have been devising strategies of survival that are casual and informal in nature, such as the expansion of small enterprises. In developing countries the lifespan of small enterprises may be short, and while they last they entail long working hours with minimal returns. In Eastern Europe and the Soviet Union, a possible outcome of restructuring may very well be the expansion of an informal labour market and informal services sector—especially if governments are unwilling or unable to provide credits and tax breaks for small businesses, and of course in the context of employment contraction rather than employment generation.

Turning from production to the material and symbolic aspects of reproduction, another important difference suggests itself. An essential difference between the two regions (and of course also between the advanced capitalist countries and the former state socialist countries) is that, at a time when the cult of domesticity and the ideology of family attachment of women is on the decline—the result of the massive economic incorporation of women, but also, especially in Western countries, the result of the feminist revolution— the ideology of domesticity appears to be growing in Eastern Europe and the former Soviet Union, as documented by many of the previous chapters. In

---

[16] Portes and Sassen-Koob (1987: 31) define the informal sector as 'all work situations characterized by the absence of (1) a clear separation between capital and labor; (2) a contractual relationship between both; and (3) a labor force that is paid wages and whose conditions of work and pay are legally regulated . . . the informal sector is structurally heterogeneous and comprises such activities as direct subsistence, small-scale production and trade, and subcontracting to semiclandestine enterprises and homeworkers.'

these newly privatizing countries, this (re)turn to domesticity may serve the function of legitimating economic reorganization and unemployment. The emergence of the discourse of domesticity and family attachment of women after years of female employment and public visibility also suggests the importance of a purposive feminist intervention—along with economic integration and political–juridical changes. That is to say, although the mass education and employment of women are the prerequisites of gender equity and women's empowerment (see Moghadam 1990), the advancement of women is crucially effected through a conscious women's movement and feminist activism. A related point is that the transformation of what has been called in the state socialist tradition 'the Woman Question' cannot come about solely through participation in the sphere of production: it must be addressed in the sphere of reproduction as well. Because of the lack of a proper resolution to problems and needs in the sphere of reproduction, and because of the lack of a feminist movement and discourse, a post-communist backlash has become possible.

SUMMARY AND CONCLUSIONS

In this chapter I have endeavoured to show that restructuring is a global phenomenon, that gender is a useful concept in the analysis of changes in the spheres of production and reproduction, and that economic inter-nationalization and restructuring have profoundly affected women. In the 1980s and into the 1990s, restructuring entails flexible production processes and the increased utilization of female labour in flexible labour markets. 'Flexibility' may be the new buzzword in international economics, but it is without a doubt biased towards capital and against labour.

In this chapter I have also compared two semi-peripheral regions in terms of their experience with restructuring and its impact on women and gender. Successful industrialization in the NICs and in the former state socialist countries was accomplished in large measure through concerted state action, planning, and the incorporation of women in employment and in production processes generally. But there have been important differences in gender dynamics between 'capitalist industrialization' and 'state socialist industrialization'. In the NICs the export-led development strategy has relied heavily on low-cost female labour. Organized labour is weak or non-existent, and the employment in the export-led sectors is often temporary, unstable, and without benefits such as entitlements for working mothers. Capitalist industrialization in the NICs has also increased the informalization and casualization of labour. In contrast, state socialist industrialization in the Soviet Union and Eastern Europe provided wages and benefits to all women workers. Because there was effectively no informal sector or private sector, jobs were secure and labour protection codes strong. This meant that social policies to assist working mothers were present—although in varying degrees of quality and generosity—across the state socialist countries. In this sense, female labour was 'expensive' in Eastern Europe and the Soviet Union, in contrast to the NICs, where female labour has been 'cheap'. Restructuring in Eastern Europe and the former Soviet Union means bringing labour, especially female labour, to the level of labour in the NICs.

At a global level, the integration of women into economic and political life —and feminist activism—has radically altered definitions of gender, leading to a decline of the patriarchal ideology which historically associated women with family and reproduction. Throughout the world, women's involvement in higher education, formal employment, and political institutions is both a reflection and a continuation of this trend. (Women's role in culture and the arts also helps to shape the new images of women and of gender.) But the process of social change is uneven, and setbacks are inevitable. Setbacks to women's equity and empowerment have emerged during the process of economic restructuring.

I will end by summarizing the similarities and differences in restructuring between the two semi-peripheries. Similarities entail the following: (1) austerity measures and the reduction of demand through stabilization programmes and debt servicing; (2) creation or increase of poverty and social inequalities; this is exacerbated by the lack of an effective taxation system and a reduction of public spending; (3) reduction of the public-sector wage bill, in terms of both public-sector employment and reduced expenditure in health and education; (4) mobility of capital and labour migration; growing unemployment of both men and women; (5) decline of unions and the social power of labour; the formation of a 'flexible' labour force; (6) deterioration of household budgets, requiring economic activity of its members in the informal sector; (7) growth of an informal sector (which is especially active in Hungary among the former state socialist countries).

The major differences in terms of gender and restructuring between the two regions are as follows. First, integration of Third World (especially South-east Asian) economies in the world-economy has led to increased levels of female employment, whereas integration of the former state socialist societies, which coincides with restructuring, will have the effect of reducing female employment. Secondly, restructuring is a far more radical process in the former state socialist countries than in the Third World or in the advanced capitalist countries. The shock to the working population may be greater, although its impact on labour, including female labour, may be variable by sector. Thirdly, the 'public sector' in state socialist countries is a far greater employer of labour than is the case in developing countries and therefore will have to 'release' a far larger proportion of the total labour force during restructuring. Fourthly, whereas the United States is a destination

for Hispanic labour (principally from Mexico and Central America), it is not
clear that Western Europe will welcome migrant labour from Eastern
Europe, especially as it still has its own 'periphery' of Turkey, Greece, Spain,
and Portugal. Fifthly, whereas the NICs benefited from transnational
investment, it is not clear that this will be forthcoming in sufficient volume
for the newly privatizing countries. Finally, continuing unemployment in the
transitional economies may intensify the discourse of domesticity and family
attachment of women. In the absence of a strong feminist movement,
women's economic status and social positions are in decline.

It remains to be seen how working women will respond to these changes
and prospects.

REFERENCES

AFSHAR, HALEH, and DENNIS, CAROLYNE (eds.) (1982). *Women and Adjustment Policies in the Third World*. London: Macmillan.

AMSDEN, ALICE (1989), *Asia's Next Giant: South Korea and Late Industrialization*. New York: Oxford University Press.

ARICANLI, TOSUN, and RODRIK, DANI (1990), 'An Overview of Turkey's Experience with Economic Liberalization and Structural Adjustment', *World Development*, 18(10): 1343–50.

BAKER, STEPHANIE (1991), 'Second Sex Takes Second Place in E. Europe', *The Guardian* (New York), 3 July.

BENERIA, LOURDES (1991), 'Structural Adjustment, the Labour Market and the Household: The Case of Mexico', pp. 161–84 in Guy Standing and Victor Tokman (eds.), *Towards Structural Adjustment*. Geneva: ILO.

BLANCHARD, OLIVIER, DORNBUSCH, RUDIGER, KRUGMAN, PAUL, LAYARD, RICHARD, and SUMMERS, LAWRENCE (1991), *Reform in Eastern Europe*. Cambridge, Mass.: MIT Press.

BLUESTONE, BARRY, and HARRISON, BENNETT (1982), *The Deindustrialization of America: Plant Closings, Community Abandonment, and the Dismantling of Basic Industry*. New York: Basic Books.

BOSWELL, TERRY, and PETERS, RALPH (1990), 'Rebellions in Poland and China', *Critical Sociology*, 17(1): 3–34.

BOYER, ROBERT, (1989), 'The Capital–Labor Relations in OECD Countries: From the Fordist "Golden Age" to Contrasted National Trajectories', CEPREMAC, CNRS, Working Paper no. 9020, Paris.

BUVINIC, MAYRA (1984), 'Projects for Women in the Third World: Explaining Their Misbehavior', International Center for Research on Women, Washington, DC.

CHASE-DUNN, CHRISTOPHER (1982a), 'Introduction', pp. 9–18 in C. Chase-Dunn (ed.), *Socialist States in the World-System*. Beverly Hills: Sage.

—— (1982b), 'Socialist States in the Capitalist World-Economy', pp. 21–55 in C. Chase-Dunn (ed.), *Socialist States in the World-System*. Beverly Hills: Sage.

—— (1990), 'Marxism and the Global Political Economy', paper presented at the annual meetings of the American Sociological Association, Washington, DC, August.

—— (1992), 'The Spiral of Capitalism and Socialism', in Louis F. Kriesberg (ed.), *Research in Social Movements, Conflicts and Change*, 14. Greenwich, Conn.: JAI Press, 165–87.

Commonwealth Secretariat (1989), *Engendering Adjustment for the 1990s*, ed. Mary Chinery Hesse *et al*. London: Commonwealth Secretariat.

CORNIA, GIOVANNI, JOLLY, RICHARD, and STEWART, FRANCES (eds.) (1987), *Adjustment with a Human Face: A UNICEF Study* (2 vols). Oxford: Clarendon Press.

DAVIN, DALIA (1987), 'The New Inheritance Law and the Peasant Household', *Journal of Communist Studies*, 3 (December)

ELSON, DIANE (1991), 'Gender and Adjustment in the 1990s: An Update on Evidence and Strategies', paper prepared for Inter-Regional Meeting on 'Economic Distress, Structural Adjustment, and Women', Commonwealth Secretariat, London, June 13–14.

ENGELS, FRIEDRICH (1884), *The Origin of the Family, Private Property, and the State*, in *Karl Marx and Frederick Engels, Selected Works*, iii. Moscow: Progress Publishers, 1970.

FREEMAN, ROBERT (1988), 'Contraction and Expansion: The Divergence of Private Sector and Public Sector Unionism in the United States', *Journal of Economic Perspectives*, 2(2): 63–88.

FROBEL, FOLKER, HEINRICHS, JURGEN, and KREYE, OTTO (1980), *The New International Division of Labour*. Cambridge University Press.

FUJITA, KUNIKO (1991), 'Women Workers and Flexible Specialization: The Case of Tokyo', *Economy and Society*, 20(3): 260–82.

GEREFFI, GARY (1990), 'Paths of Industrialization: An Overview', pp. 3–31 in Gary Gereffi and Donald L. Wyman (eds.), *Manufacturing Miracles: Paths of Industrialization in Latin America and East Asia*. Princeton, NJ: Princeton University Press.

HAAVIO-MANNILA, ELINA *et al* (eds.) (1985), *Unfinished Democracy: Women in Nordic Politics*. Oxford: Pergamon Press.

HARRIS, NIGEL (1986), *The End of the Third World: Newly Industrializing Countries and the Decline of an Ideology*. Harmondsworth, Middx: Penguin.

HARVEY, DAVID (1989), *The Condition of Postmodernity: An Enquiry into the Origins of Cultural Change*. Oxford: Basil Blackwell.

ILO/INSTRAW (1985), *Women in Economic Activity: A Global Statistical Survey 1950–2000*. Geneva: ILO and Santo Domingo: UN Training and Research Institute for the Advancement of Women.

ILO (1992), 'ILO Survey Findings: Unemployment Rising Sharply in Former Soviet Union', *ILO Washington Focus* (Washington, DC), 5(2).

JOEKES, SUSAN (1987), *Women in the World Economy: An INSTRAW Study*. New York: Oxford University Press.

—— (1989), 'Gender and Macro-Economic Policy', Association for Women in Development, occasional paper no. 4, Washington, DC.

—— with MOAYEDI, ROXANNA (1987), 'Women and Export Manufacturing: A Review of the Issues and AID Policy', ICRW (July), Washington, DC.

KANDIYOTI, DENIZ (1990), 'Women and Rural Development Policies: The Changing Agenda', *Development and Change*, 21(1): 5–22.

KELKAR, GIOVIND (1988), '. . . Two Steps Back? New Agricultural Policies in Rural China and the Woman Question', pp. 121–50 in Bina Agarwal (ed.), *Structures of Patriarchy: The State, the Community, and the Household*. London: Zed.

KESSLER-HARRIS, ALICE (1990), *A Woman's Wage: Historical Meanings and Social Consequences*. Lexington: University Press of Kentucky.

LEACOCK, ELEANOR BURKE (1981), *Myths of Male Dominance: Collected Articles on Women Cross-Culturally*. New York: Monthly Review Press.

LIPIETZ, ALAIN (1982), 'Towards Global Fordism?' *New Left Review*, 132: 33–47.

—— (1991), 'Idées fausses et questions ouvertes sur l'Aprés-Fordisme', CEPREMAC, CNRS, Working Paper no. 9103, Paris.

LUSTIG, NORA (1990), 'Economic Crisis: Adjustment and Living Standards in Mexico, 1982–85', *World Development*, 18(10): 1325–42.

MARGLIN, STEPHEN, and SCHOR, JULIET (eds.) (1990), *The Golden Age of Capitalism: Reinterpreting the Postwar Experience*. Oxford: Clarendon Press.

MARX, KARL, and ENGELS, FRIEDRICH (1848), *The Communist Manifesto*, in David McLellan (ed.), *Marxism: Essential Writings*. Oxford University Press, 1988.

MOGHADAM, V. M. (1990), *Gender, Development and Policy: Toward Equity and Empowerment*. Helsinki: WIDER Research for Action Monograph Series (November).

—— (1991), 'Islamist Movements and Women's Responses in the Middle East', *Gender and History*, 3(3): 268–84.

—— (1992), 'Women, Employment and Social Change in the Middle East and North Africa', in Hilda Kahne and Janet Giele (eds.), *Women's Work, Women's Lives: The Continuing Struggle Worldwide*. Boulder, Colo.: Westview Press.

—— (1993), *Modernizing Women: Gender and Social Change in the Middle East*. Boulder, Colo.: Lynn Reinner.

MORVARIDI, BEHROOZ (1992), 'Gender Relations in Agriculture: Women in Turkey', *Economic Development and Cultural Change*, 40(3): 567–86.

MUSSALL, BETTINA (1991), 'Women Are Hurt the Most', *Der Spiegel* (Hamburg); reprinted in *World Press Review*, June.

NALGO (1991), *Central and Eastern Europe: A NALGO Report*. London: NALGO.

NASH, JUNE, and FERNANDEZ-KELLY, M. P. (eds.) (1985), *Women, Men, and the International Division of Labor*. Albany, NY: SUNY Press.

PALMER, INGRID (1991), *Gender and Population in the Adjustment of African Economics: Planning for Change*. Geneva: ILO.

PALLOIX, CHRISTIAN (1977), *L'Internationalisation du capital*. Paris: Maspero.

PEARSON, RUTH (1990), 'Questioning Perestroika: A Socialist–Feminist Interrogation', *Feminist Review*, no. 39: 91–6.

PORTES, ALEJANDRO, and SASSEN-KOOB, SASKIA (1987), 'Making It Underground: Comparative Material on the Informal Sector in Western Market Economies', *American Journal of Sociology*, 93(1): 30–61.

—— CASTELLS, MANUEL, and BENTON, LAUREN (1989), *The Informal Economy: Studies in Advanced and Less Developed Countries*. Baltimore: Johns Hopkins University Press.

PROWSE, MICHAEL (1992), 'The Drawbacks of Shock Therapy', *Financial Times*, 2 March.

REITER, RAYNA R. (ed.) (1975), *Toward an Anthropology of Women*. New York: Monthly Review Press.

ROSALDO, MICHELLE ZIMBALIST, and LAMPHERE, LOUISE (eds.) (1974), *Woman, Culture, and Society*. Stanford, Calif.: Stanford University Press.

SASSEN, SASKIA, and KELLY, PATRICIA FERNANDEZ (1992), 'Recasting Women in the Global Economy: Internationalization and Changing Definitions of Gender', in E. Acosta-Belen and C. Bose (eds.), *Women and Development in the Third World*. Newbury Park, Calif.: Sage.

SKJEIE, HEGE (1991), 'The Uneven Advance of Norwegian Women', *New Left Review*, no. 187: 79–102.

SOKOLOFF, NATALIE (1980), *Between Money and Love: The Dialectics of Women's Home and Market Work*. New York: Praeger.

SOUTHALL, ROGER (ed.) (1988), *Trade Unions and the New Industrialisation in the Third World*. London: Zed.

STANDING, GUY (1989), 'Global Feminisation Through Flexible Labour', Working Paper no. 31, Labour Market Analysis and Employment Planning, WEP, ILO, Geneva.

—— (ed.) (1991), *The New Soviet Labour Market: In Search of Flexibility*. Geneva: ILO.

—— and TOKMAN, VICTOR (eds.) (1991), *Towards Social Adjustment: Labour Market Issues in Structural Adjustment*. Geneva: ILO.

TAYLOR, LANCE (1988), *Varieties of Stabilization Experience*. Oxford: Clarendon Press.

—— (1992), 'The Post-Socialist Transition from a Development Economics Point of View', paper prepared for the conference on 'Transformation from a System of Central Planning to a Market Economy', Government of Finland and UNU/WIDER, Helsinki, 6–7 February.

TOMFORDE, ANNA (1992), 'United They Fall', The *Guardian*, 6 May: 19.

United Nations (1989), *1989 World Survey on the Role of Women in Development*. New York: United Nations.

US Department of Labor (1991), *Handbook on Women Workers*. Washington, DC: US Department of Labor, Office of the Secretary, Women's Bureau.

VAN GINNEKEN, WOUTER (1990), 'Labour Adjustment in the Public Sector: Policy Issues for Developing Countries', *International Labour Review*, 129(4): 441–57.

VICKERS, JEANNE (1991), *Women and the World Economy*. London: Zed.

WALLERSTEIN, IMMANUEL (1982), 'Crisis as Transition', pp. 11–54 in Samir Amin *et al.* (eds.), *Dynamics of Global Crisis*. New York: Monthly Review Press.

—— (1990), 'Culture as the Ideological Battleground of the Modern World-System', pp. 31–55 in Mike Featherstone (ed.), *Global Culture: Nationalism, Globalization and Modernity*. London: Sage.

WARD, KATHRYN (ed.) (1990), *Women Workers and Global Restructuring*. Ithaca, NY: ILR Press.

WEIL, GORDON (1992), 'Women in the Economies of Sub-Saharan Africa', in Hilda Kahne and Janet Giele (eds.), *Women's Work, Women's Lives: The Continuing Struggle Worldwide*. Boulder, Colo.: Westview Press.

352   V. M. MOGHADAM

WEIR, FRED (1992), 'Russian Working Woman a Public Enemy', interview with
  Elvira Novikova, *The Guardian* (NY), 15 April: 12–13.
World Bank (1990), *World Development Report 1990*. New York: Oxford University
  Press.

Afterword

Lynn Turgeon

Despite the broad and generally thorough coverage of issues affecting women in Eastern Europe, only a few of the papers presented in this volume consider 'affirmative action', either in the descriptions of what transpired during the period of state socialism, or as a relevant policy for the future. The latter is particularly puzzling, since there is, in general, uncritical acceptance of other institutions (stock and commodity markets, credit cards, etc.) to be borrowed from the US model of a market economy. Is the acceptance of the nineteenth-century supply-side model of the market system, as expounded by Milton Friedman or Ludwig Von Mises, an appropriate response to the current problems of Eastern Europe? Or would the late twentieth-century model of the welfare state, including such institutions as affirmative action, be more appropriate?

As I have tried to explain elsewhere (Turgeon 1989), the global origins of affirmative action—or 'tilting' towards the less powerful—are found in the early Leninist years following the Russian revolution.[1] Lenin, in his criticism of capitalism, claimed that uneven development tended to occur as a result of market forces: the rich would get richer and the poor would become poorer. After the revolution, socialism would supposedly reverse this process and the altruistic rich would be expected to assist the poor, resulting in an levelling out of development. Within the nascent USSR, the rich Russia would be expected to assist the poorer non-white Central Asian republics.[2]

This same principle was applied to sexual inequality. Women were to be liberated from above by such institutions as universal suffrage (with legislation actually passed during the early months of the Kerensky regime), equal access to higher education, legalized abortion, easy no-fault divorce, earlier retirement than men, equal pay for equal work, and child care for mothers, whether married or unmarried. The *intentions* of the new social planners following the Bolshevik Revolution were to be at least in line with modern liberated women's demands.

---

[1] Vice President Richard Nixon appears to have been the first practitioner of affirmative action in the Eisenhower years.

[2] The mechanism for the subsidization of Central Asia was the higher agricultural procurement prices for cotton and the retention of turnover tax collections on consumer goods within the less developed republics. After the Second World War, the Baltic Republics and the Moldavian Republic tended to receive still greater subsidies in an attempt to reduce anti-Russian sentiment in these newly acquired territories.

Wherever the non-capitalist system spread after the Second World War, more or less the same policies, with one exception, were introduced under the guise of 'family policy' or 'women's policy'. Legalized abortion, which had been suspended by the USSR for two decades (1936–56), was only later introduced in most East European countries, following the Soviet lead, after 1956. The former GDR postponed a similar policy change until 1972, and Romania reverted to illegalizing abortions (leading to higher infant mortality rates) in 1967, in a draconian attempt to reverse its sharp decline in fertility rates. Throughout Eastern Europe, pro-natalist policies were pursued simultaneously, with Special Maternity Allowances allowing women the option of being paid to stay home and take care of their young infants, modelled to varying degrees after the Hungarian innovation in 1968.

As a result of government incentives and a seller's market for labour, female labour-force participation rates were considerably higher than those that have prevailed under capitalism, with the possible exception of Sweden, where support systems similar to those of the USSR have developed. The experience of the United States and Canada also shows a positive correlation between women's liberation and higher female labour-force participation rates, despite their much poorer provisions for child care.

The discrimination gap—the average wage of women as a percentage of the average wage for men—still amounted to about 70–75 per cent in Eastern Europe, primarily because of the continued sexual segregation of certain occupations: men in coal mining (the highest paid profession) and heavy industry on the one hand, and women in light industry and food processing, education, culture and public health, where average wages were significantly lower. Nevertheless, this percentage of 'discrimination gap' is more impressive than a similar percentage in a capitalist country by virtue of the much higher female participation rates. It can be assumed that, generally speaking, only the more qualified women tend to enter the labour force in the capitalist world, while virtually all women in the non-capitalist world did so.[3] The earlier retirement ages (60 for men and 55 for women) tended to reduce the lifetime discrimination gap since pensions were frequently paid, in addition to their wages, when older women chose to continue working.

In the non-capitalist passive legislatures, women (particularly those with humble occupations such as milkmaids) were more highly represented than would have been the case were there to have been democratic elections. This point has been illustrated by the sharp drop in the percentage of women in all of the post-communist parliaments.

The development of child-care facilities in the non-capitalist system, especially for married women, was particularly revolutionary. Capitalist

---

[3] This phenomenon can be illustrated by US experience in the 1960s, when large numbers of unskilled women crowded into the labour market with the encouragement of the women's liberation movement, thereby sharply increasing the discrimination gap.

countries have traditionally expected unmarried single women to work and in wartime have even provided child care for working mothers. But the state support systems for mothers, married or unmarried, were more impressive in the non-capitalist world. The disadvantages of single motherhood were significantly neutralized by state support policies. This was particularly true for the former GDR, where unmarried mothers (labelled 'mini-families') were provided with additional benefits. An unintended effect of supporting women and children, regardless of marital status, was a very high proportion of babies being born to unmarried women (one-third, according to Rueschemeyer).

Divorce rates were noticeably higher in the non-capitalist world, partly because of work opportunities and state child support, reducing the economic penalties of divorce for women. The Soviet divorce rate was second only to that of the United States, even including the Central Asian Muslim women who seldom divorced. Cuban women likewise had extremely high divorce rates. In addition to the lower divorce rates for Muslim women under the non-capitalist system, Poland had comparatively low divorce rates, presumably because of the influence of the Catholic Church.

WOMEN AFTER PERESTROIKA

Having examined what the non-capitalist system attempted to accomplish for women, it is now somewhat easier to see what has been happening and what can be expected to happen in the newly market-oriented countries of Eastern Europe.

As under capitalism, the market is particularly friendly to white talented males, who will tend to obtain jobs even when there is significant unemployment. In the post-communist transition period, unemployment has been rising to Western levels and beyond. This is particularly true for the five *Länder* or states formerly constituting the GDR, where ultra shock therapy was provided by the sudden unification of the two Germanies. Within a short period of time, the labour-short GDR economy was transformed into an economic basket-case, with double-digit unemployment. Women were especially adversely affected. By the third quarter of 1991, female unemployment reached 14.3 per cent compared with 9.1 per cent for men (see Rudolph 1992: 10).[4]

This same pattern of higher female unemployment rates holds true for all

---

[4] In the meantime, the West German unemployment rates have dropped from over 8% to about 6% as their economy benefited from the post-unification net flow of goods and services from west to east. By 1991, more than 5% of the former FRG gross domestic product represented public transfers from western to eastern Germany, according to Helmut Schlesinger, president of the German Bundesbank. See Silk (1992).

of the formerly state socialist countries with the exception of Hungary (see Chapters 1, 2, and 11). This is especially surprising since it is primarily the military and heavy industry, where women were seldom employed, that have been cut back in the post-communist economies. Women have apparently been reassigned to their more traditional roles as a 'reserve army of unemployed'.

The Hungarian exception to the rule deserves some comment. In my view, it is a reflection of the fact that the Hungarians have taken a more evolutionary approach to a market economy beginning in 1968 with the introduction of the New Economic Mechanism (see Turgeon 1992). As a result, they have developed a more extensive service sector in relationship to other Eastern European countries, one that can absorb women who lose their jobs in the goods-producing industries. This cushion tends to minimize the female unemployment rates, despite the fact that many of these jobs in the service sector (e.g. Amway salespersons) are poorly paid. The continuation of the Special Maternity Allowances will also tend to cushion the impact of unemployment on women's income. Thus, we would expect a widening discrimination gap in Hungary despite its relatively lower female unemployment rates.

With the relative drying up of employment opportunities for women, there are some who would try to make a virtue out of a necessity. Some women in Eastern Europe are supposedly anxious to return to their more traditional roles as homemakers and mothers. The threats to outlaw abortion in Poland and Hungary tend to be complementary to this move back to pre-communist values. Politics is presented as a 'dirty business', something that women should be thankful to be liberated from.

Women are supposedly more adverse to taking risks, which puts them at a disadvantage in the rapidly growing private sector. Because of this gender difference, they are also less prone to committing crimes, at a time when criminal activity has been growing rapidly in the post-communist transition years.

Some have argued that the current transition difficulties are only ephemeral and that in the long run women will be better off in a market system. The problem with this optimism is that it overlooks the positive role that unemployment is supposed to play under a market system. This was emphasized by Czech economists in 1968 during the period of the Dubcek 'Prague Spring'. And it was also the position of many Hungarian state socialists as they abandoned a planned economy. This emphasis on the need for microeconomic 'efficiency' and to become 'more competitive in world markets', as well as the role of unemployment in disciplining the labour force —something that capitalists would insist upon—was recognized as early as 1944 by Michal Kalecki.

By assuming that only increased unemployment can bring inflation under control—as posited by the Phillips curve—'bastard' Keynesian policy has fulfilled Schumpeter's prediction that it would be possible to stabilize the system with the Keynesian paradigm, but that it would also make the system less dynamic.

The breakup of the former Soviet Union and the moves towards the de-collectivization of agriculture will simply worsen the position of farm women and females in the less developed former Soviet Republics. Although this is not generally recognized by Russian feminists, the collectivization of agriculture played an important role in liberating farm women from their autocratic husbands on the former family farms.

Generally speaking, the model for women in former command economies is one that also applied to women in capitalist economies before the Cold War and women's liberation. Feminism, which got short shrift under communism (supposedly because it weakened the class struggle), is also under attack in post-communist Eastern Europe. Distaste for feminism is about the only thing on which there is great continuity between communism and capitalism.

REFERENCES

RUDOLPH, HEDWIG (1992), 'The Status of Women in a Changing Economy: East Germany', paper presented at the annual meetings of the Allied Social Sciences Association, New Orleans, 4 January.

SILK, LEONARD (1992), 'Conservative Plea to Aid Ex-Soviets', *New York Times*, 24 January.

TURGEON, LYNN (1989), *State and Discrimination*. Armonk, NY: M. E. Sharpe.

—— (1992), 'The Changing Status of Hungarian Women', paper presented at the annual meetings of the Allied Social Sciences Association, New Orleans, 4 January.

INDEX

N.B. All references are to the concerns of women, except where otherwise indicated. 'Transition' indicates the move from communist to market economy. Page references to charts and tables are set in italic.

abortion 4, 63–8
  Bulgaria 96, 97
  legalized 354
  Poland 66–7, 68
  Soviet Union 165
  state socialist countries 51
  West Germany 77, 89
adult education 98, 127
Africa 339, 340 n.
Albania 112, 219, 234, 239
  child-care 239
  maternal leave 239
  Statistical Book (1990) 219, 221
  unemployment 223, 226
  workers and employees 219, 220–1, 223
allowances, see benefits and allowances
apprenticeship trades, East Germany 81

Balcerowicz, Polish finance minister 120
banks 292
Bebel, A. 50
benefits and allowances:
  former Soviet Union 168–9, 176, 190–4
  Hungary 238, 295–6
Beyer, M. 55
Bialecki, I. 14–16, 52, 113 n., 127 n.
births:
  Bulgaria 96, 97
  Soviet Union 147
Blum, Norbert 75 n.
Bodrova, V. 10, 17, 18, 19
Bretton Woods institutions, see IMF; World Bank
Brezhnev, L. I. 17, 20, 138, 147
  policy dilemmas and options under, 150–3
Bukharin, N. 138
Bulgaria 11, 16–17, 92–108
  abortion 96, 97
  births 96, 97
  earnings 98, 99
  education 95, 98, 112
  equality, sexual 93–7
  families 92–3, 95, 103
  Labour Law (1986) 94, 105
  managers 105–6
  National Labour Bureau (1991) 101
  National Statistics 96, 97, 98, 99, 102, 105, 107

organizations and movements 106
  pensions 96
  politics 106–7, 107
  population 96
  self-employment 237
  State Gazette 102, 104
  Statistics 97
  transition (1989–91) 38, 100–4
  unemployment 101–3, 101, 104, 226
  work, attitudes to 240–1
  work, women at? 103
  workers and employees 97–100, 97, 98, 219, 220–1
Buxakowski 67

Cahen, C. 5 n.
Canada 354
capitalism:
  mode of production 336
  and world economy 334–5
careers, vis-à-vis child-rearing 319–20
Catholic Church:
  and abortion 66–7
  Poland 62–3
Central Europe:
  rights of women 48–72
  transitional politics 29–45
change, gender as dimension of social 2–5
child-care 61, 238–40, 243–4, 354
  Albania 239
  benefit 238
  East Germany 78–9
  Hungary 238, 239, 240
  Poland 10, 240
  state socialist 51–2
  West Germany 78
child-care, Poland 313–19, 314, 315, 317, 318
children:
  development 94–5
  families with 170–1
  Hungary 295–6
  organized holidays 318–19, 318
  Poland 314
  rearing, institutionalized assistance for 313, 315–16; see also maternity leave; parents
  rearing, vis-à-vis careers 319–20
  support 295–6

Children (*cont.*):
  see also abortion; births; child-care;
    education
China 344
Ciechocinska, M. 10
CIS, see Soviet Union, former
Civic Forum 37, 56
CMEA, see COMECON
coal-mining 312
collectivist-style social life 303–5
COMECON (CMEA) 100, 262, 264, 272,
  273–4, 283, 289–90
Commonwealth Secretariat (1989) 336, 338
communism, see Marx, K.; state socialism
Company Law 292
Conable, B. 338
contraception 63, 69
core countries 334
cross-cultural differences, division of labour
  and 198–200
CSFR, see Czechoslovakia
Czech Republic 258
  labour *254*, 272–6
  transition 248–78
  unemployment *249, 250*, 252
Czechoslovakia (CSFR):
  Civic Forum 37, 56
  crude activity rates *256, 257*
  earnings 227, *228, 229*, 268–9, *269, 270*, 271
  education *112*
  Federal Statistical Office (1991) 249, 254,
    256, 257, 263
  flexible working hours 240–1
  hiring 235
  labour 253–68, *254, 255, 256, 257, 263,*
    266–7
  labour distribution 262–5, 268
  maternity leave 269 n.
  men and women compared *254, 255, 256,*
    257, 258, 263, 266–7
  Ministry of Labour and Social Affairs 251,
    268, 269, 270
  organizations and movements 69, 70
  parental allowance 239
  pensions 240
  politics 56
  population *256, 257*
  transition 37–8
  unemployment 223–4, 231, *249, 250–1,*
    251–2, *251*, 272
  workers and employees *220–1*, 222, 223,
    254, 255, 261–2
  see also Czech Republic; Slovak Republic

democratization, and politics 5–9, 54–8
demographic structures, feminization
  and 305–6

Denmark 198–207 *passim*
division of labour, sexual 6, 198–200, 285–6
divorce 59, 146, 355
doctors 199–200, 207–9, *208*
Domanski, H. 113 n.
Drakulić, S. 5
Dubček, A. 356

earnings 50, 209–10, 226–7, *228, 229*, 354
  Bulgaria 98, *99*
  Czechoslovakia 268–9, *269, 270*, 271
  East Germany 50
  Eastern Europe 227, *228, 229*
  Hungary 227, *228*, 286–7
  Poland 227, *228, 229*
  Soviet Union *142*, 143–6, *143*, 170
East Germany (GDR) 75–90
  apprenticeship trades *81*
  child-care 78–9
  earnings 50
  education *112*
  families 51, 58
  leadership, occupational *80*, 81–2
  organizations and movements, women's 7,
    69, 70, 79
  in transition 82–5
  unemployment 7, 355
  welfare state 75
  West Germany, compared with 76–82, *81*
  work-force 78, *83*, 343
Eastern Europe:
  child-care 239–40
  in decline 341–2
  earnings 227, *228, 229*
  education 233–4, *234*
  employment, female 218–30
  labour supply 237
  maternity leave 239
  restructuring and gender 340–6
  rights, women's 48–72
  transitional politics 29–45
  unemployment 223–6, 230–2, 238, 341
  women's economic status in restructuring
    of 217–45
  workers and employees 218, *219*, 235–6,
    237
ECE (Economic Commission for Europe) 271
Economist Intelligence Unit 224, 225, 226,
  231, 237
economy, reform of, and employment 9–13
education:
  adult *98*, 127
  Albania *234*
  Bulgaria 95, *98*
  campaigns recommended 244
  Eastern Europe *112*, 233–4, *234*, 244
  equality of opportunity 127–30

feminized 113–19
  further/higher *112*, 114, 116–17, *234*
  Hungary 234, *234*, 285
  linkages with employment 13–17
  Poland 14–16, 110–32, *234*
  private schools 123–7
  professional schools *118*
  secondary 113–14, 115–16, *130*
  sports 126
  state socialist 52
  vocational 114–15, 121–3
egalitarianism, *see* equality, sexual
Einhorn, B. 5, 6, 7–8, 10
elections 30, 31, 36–7, 38
Elections (1990) 31
emancipation, women's 94, 176
employees, *see* workers and employees
Engelen-Kefer, U. 86
Engels, F. 50
engineers 17–18, 199, *202, 203, 207*
entrepreneurs 274–5
EPZ (export-processing zone) 331
equality, sexual 50
  Bulgaria 93–7
  defined 175
  in education 127–30
  former Soviet Union 185–9
  from patriarchy to 196
  West Germany 77
  'woman question' 174–7
Estonia 198–207 *passim*
ethnic conflicts 39
Europe, labour force participation rates *219*
executive careers *189*

families:
  benefits and allowances 168–9
  Bulgaria 92–3, 95, 103
  East Germany 51, 58
  female workers and 146–9
  Hungary 59
  importance of, to women? 182–5
  Poland 61
  socialist ideology and 58–63
  Soviet Union 138, 146–9, 165–71, 182–5
  and work roles 146–50
  see also 'Women in the Family' poll
farming 308, 357
feminism 34, 40, 177
  and 'woman question' 174–7
  see also organizations and movements
feminization:
  and demographic/territorial
    structures 305–6
  of education 113–19
  Poland 116–19, *118*
Finland 198–208 *passim*

Firestone, S. 174
flexible working hours 240–1
Fong, M. 9, 10, 14
Fordism 330, 333 n.
foreign trade 289
former Soviet Union, *see* Soviet Union, former
FRG 77
Friedman, M. 353

GDR, *see* East Germany
Gemeinschaft and *Gesellschaft*, 62
gender:
  and dismantling of command economy
    302–25
  divisions under state socialism 49–54
  ideologies 3
  and inequality/social change 2–5
  redefinition, global view 329–36
  relations and policies, former Soviet
    Union 162–78
  and restructuring 18, 137–57, 163–5,
    180–2, 194–5, 340–6
  role changes 32–3, 198
  Third World 336–40
  see also men and women
'genocide', abortion as 64
Germany:
  abortion 64–6, 68
  apprenticeships *81*
  Draft Laws 65
  unification and restructuring 85–90, 355
  see also East Germany; West Germany
Gianoplus, P. 127
glasnost 153–4
  and the 'woman question' 180–96
  see also Gorbachev, M. S.
'glass ceiling' 204
Glemp, Cardinal 64
global view of restructuring 329–36
Gorbachev, M. S. 21, 137, 143, 153, 162
Gordon, L. A., and Rimashevskaia, N. M. 148
government expenditure 338, 340 n.
grandmothers 10, 11
GUS, *see* Hungary, Central Statistical Office

harassment, sexual 205–6
Hasselfeld 88 n.
Havel, President 272
Havlová, D. 35
Heyns, B. 14–16, 52, 127 n.
Hildebrandt, R. 88 n.
Hillman, A. L. (1990) 284
hiring and new employment 232–5
Höffner, Cardinal J. 64
home, women at 60–1
housework 147–8, 189–90, 193, 201
housing 296, 297

Hungary 11–12, 38
  allowances and benefits 238, 295–6
  Central Statistical Office (CSO/GUS)
    (1989) 228, 234, 241, 285, 286, 294, 295,
    296
  children 238, 239, 240, 295–6
  earnings 227, *228*, 286–7
  economic reform 280–99
  education *112*, 234, *234*, 285
  families 59
  female employment 9, *222*
  flexible working hours 241
  foreign trade 289
  hiring 233
  housing 296, 297
  job losses 231, 232
  macroeconomics 283–4, 288–90
  microeconomics 284–7, 290–4
  organizations, women's 69, 70
  pensions 240
  politics 56
  poverty 284
  productive sphere 281–94
  self-employment 237
  tax 288
  unemployment 223, 224, 283–4, 341, 356
  workers and employees 218, *219*, *220–1*,
    222, *222*, 223, 235–6, 237, 241

ILO (International Labour Organization) 23,
  252, 260
IMF (International Monetary Fund) 12, 336,
  337, 338, 341
inequality, gender and 2–5
inflation 19, 289, 335
informal sector 243, 330–1
INSTRAW 331, 332 n.
internationalization 329–34
investment capital, Poland 340–1
Iran 4, 341 n.

Janicka, K. 113 n.
Jeziorna, A. 125
job losses, *see* unemployment
John Paul II, Pope 64

Kadar, J. 59
Kalecky, M. 356
KAMAZ (Soviet truck factory) 173, 204, 210
Katowice 312
Kauppinen-Toropainen, K. 16, 17, 18
Kerensky, A. F. 353
Keynes, J. M. 357
kindergartens 239–40
  Poland 313, *314*, *315*, 316–18, *318*
Klaus, V. 35, 37
Klimova, R. 40

Kohl, Chancellor H. 88 n., 89
Kollontai, A. 50
Kondratieff cycles 334, 335
Konstantinova, V. 177

labour, *see* workers and employees
labour, sexual division of 6, 198–200, 285–6
'Labour Activity of Women' poll (1990) 17–
  21, 181, 183, 184, 186–8, *187*, *188*, 191–2
Labour Law, Bulgaria 94, 105
Labuda, B. 57, 66
Lane, D. 19–21
Lapidus, G. W. 17
leadership, *see* 'Women at Work and in
  Management' poll
leadership, occupational *80*, 81–2
legal systems 3
legislation for women 50–4
Lenin, V. I. 175, 353
Licht, S. 55
life satisfaction 206–9, *208*
Lodz 312
'long waves' 334, 335

Mach, B. 113 n.
managers 53, 105–6
  see also leadership; 'Women at Work and in
    Management' poll
marriage 146, 165
Marx, K., and Marxism 19 n., 50, 175
maternal roles 34–5, 138, 355
maternity leave 354
  Albania 239
  and benefits 169–70, 238–9
  Czechoslovakia 269 n.
  Eastern Europe 239
  Hungary 295
  Poland 319
  state socialist 51–2
  West Germany 77
'maths anxiety' 199
medical profession 199–200, 207–9, *208*
men:
  activity rates, Czechoslovakia 258
  apprenticeships, Germany *81*
  and housework 189–90, 193, 201
  labour force participation rates *219*
  poll of, in Soviet Union 195–6
men and women:
  compared 198–200, *254*, *255*, *256*, *257*,
    263, *266–7*
  interaction at work 202–6
  see also division of labour; earnings
Merkel, A. 65, 66, 88 n., 89 n.
Mexico 336–7
Meyer, J. 112
migration, urban 305

Moscow 197–212 *passim* 208
Moserová, Dr J. 56, 70
'Mummy Policies' 54

NALGO (1991) 344
nationalism 164
Nickel, H. 86
NICs (newly independent countries) 345,
    346–7, 348
Nixon, President R. 353 n.
Nordic Council of Ministers (1988) 198, 199
Nordic countries, *see* Scandinavia
Nordic Statistical Secretariat (1989) 198, 210
Norway 198
Novikova, E. 342
nurseries, Poland *314*, 316, *317*

OECD (Organization for Economic
    Co-operation and Development) 254,
    255, 258, 259, 260, 269, 334
  women workers *255*
old-age pensions 96, 240
opinion polls 18–19, 181–96, 200–1
organizations and movements, women's 30,
    43, 48–72, 68–71, 79
  Bulgaria 106
  Czechoslovakia 69, 70
  East Germany 7, 69, 70, 79
  Hungary 69, 70
  Poland 69, 70
  Soviet Union 154

parents and parental leave 52, 79, 169–70,
    239, 269 n.
  see also maternity; paternity
part-time work 243
paternity benefits 176
patriarchy 61, 343–4
  and egalitarianism 196
  and 'woman question' 172–4
Paukert, L. 8
Paull, G. 9, 14
pensions 96, 240
perestroika (restructuring, Soviet Union), and
    gender issues 18, 137–57, 163–5, 180–2,
    194–5, 340–6
peripheral and semi-peripheral countries 334,
    347–8
Poland 4, 233, 235
  abortion 66–7, 68
  adult education 127
  Central Statistical Office 233, 307, 310,
    311, 314, 315, 317, 318, 321, 322, 324
  child-care 10, 240, 313–19, *314*, *315*, *317*,
    318
  churches 62–3
  command economy dismantled 302–25

earnings 227, *228*, *229*
education 14–16, 110–32, *112*, *234*
employment pattern 306–9, *307*
families 61
feminization 116–19, *118*
Institute of Philosophy and
    Sociology 113 n.
investment capital 340–1
kindergartens 313, *314*, *315*, 316–18, *318*
maternity leave 319
nurseries *314*, 316, *317*
occupational structure *118*
organizations and movements 69, 70
pensions 240
politics 56–7
population 305–6
public sector *311*
religion 62–3
self-employment 237
'shock therapy' 9, 120 n.
Solidarity 4, 37, 319, 343
STO (Social Education Association) 123–7
unemployment 223, 224–5, *225*, 232, 238,
    320–4, *321*, *322*, *324*
workers and employees *219*, *220–1*, 222,
    222, 223, 237, 306–9, *307*, 308–13;
    regional variations 309–10, *310*, *311*,
    312–13
politics 31–2, 33, 35–6
  Bulgaria 106–7, *107*
  Czechoslovakia 56
  and democratization 54–8
  the future? 41–5
  Hungary 56
  participation in, and democratization 5–9
  Poland 56–7
  reasons why women less involved? 56
  Soviet Union 154–5
  transition and 36–41
polls, *see* opinion polls
Popowicz, A. 54–5
populations:
  Bulgaria 96
  Czechoslovakia *256*, *257*
  Poland 305–6
Posadskaya, A. 5, 17, 18, 19, 22, 154, 177,
    343
poverty 284
  measures to prevent 170–1
  'Povyshat' politicheskuiu
    proizvodstvennuiu' (1975) 145
private schools 120–1, 123–7
pro-natalist policies, *see* maternity leave;
    parents
promotion prospects, Soviet Union *187*, *188*,
    189
protective legislation 242

public issues, women's interest in 33–4
public sector, Poland *311*
public/private boundary, state socialism
  and 58–63

religion 164
Catholic church 62–3, 66–7
reproductive sphere 12, 63–8, 294–8
restructuring:
  Eastern Europe 340–6
  global view 329–36
  Soviet Union, *see* perestroika
  Third World 336–40
  women after 355–7
rights, women's:
  Central and Eastern Europe 48–72
  reproductive 63–8, 294–8
  under state socialism 49–54
Romania:
  abortion 4 n.
  child-care 239
  education *112, 234*
  maternal leave 239
  unemployment 226, 231
  workers and employees *219, 220–1, 222*
Rönsch, H. 88 n.
Rosenberg, D. 8
Rueschemeyer, M. 5, 7, 8, 355
Russia, *see* Soviet Union; Soviet Union,
  former

salaries, *see* earnings
Scandinavia 197–212 *passim*
Scandinavia, *see* Denmark; Norway; Sweden
Schlesinger, H. 355 n.
Schumpeter, E. 357
Schwätzer, I. A. 88 n.
secondary-level students, Warsaw *130*
sector and industry, distribution of labour by
  (Czechoslovakia) 262–5, 268
segregation, sexual, *see* division of labour
self-employment 236–7
self-esteem 206–7
sex ratios, population 305–6
'shock therapy', Poland 9, 120 n.
Sikorska, J. 113 n.
single motherhood 355
Slomczynski, K. M. 113 n.
Slovak Republic 224, 233, 258
  transition 248–78
  unemployment *249, 250, 251,* 252, 272–3
  workers and employees *254,* 272–6
Smeltz, D. 127 n.
Solidarity 4, 37, 319, 343
Soviet Union, former (CIS; Russian
  Federation) 17–21, 187
  assistance, candidates for 190–4

equality, sexual 185–9
families 165–71
gender relations and policies 162–78
labour, female, restrictions 167–8
laws 165–71
men 195–6
opinion polls 17–21, 181–96, *187, 188,*
  195–6
restructuring, women and 155–7
'woman question' 171–7
workers and employees 197, 199
see also 'Labour Activity of Women' poll
Soviet Union (USSR):
  abortion 165
  births 147
  divorce 146
  earnings *142,* 143–6, *143,* 170
  economy, female labour in 139–41
  education *112*
  families 138, 146–9
  gender and restructuring 340–6
  glasnost and the 'woman question' 180–96
  housework 147–8
  marriage 146, 165
  men *142,* 195–6
  opinion polls (1989–90) 18–19, 181–96
  organizations and movements,
    women's 154
  political roles 154–5
  promotion prospects, job *187, 188, 189*
  restructuring, *see* perestroika
  sex-roles, traditional 210
  taboos 153–4
  workers and employees 138–53, *140*
  workers and employees, female *140,* 141–3
  see also 'woman question'
Spiegel, Der 63, 64, 65, 66, 75, 84
sports 126
'stagflation' 335
Stalin, J., and Stalinism 138–9, 165, 336
state socialism:
  collapse of 5, 29–32, 302–25
  education feminized 113–19
  and the family 58–63
  gender divisions and women's rights
    under 49–54
  legacy of 32–6
Stewart, F. 336
STO, *see* Poland
structural adjustment 338, 339
Suessmuth, R. 89
supervisors 204
Sweden 176–7, 298, 354
  work satisfaction 198–207
Szczucki, Jan 121 n.

taboos, Soviet Union 153–4

Tarasiewicz, M. 343
taxes 288
Tehran Times 341 n.
Teorin, M. B. 176
territorial structures, feminization and 305–6
Thatcherism 62, 334
Third World 327–48
  gender questions, restructuring and 336–40
TNCs (transnational corporations) 330, 331
Tönnies, F. 62
'tracking', effects 287
trade unions 344
transition:
  Bulgaria 100–4
  East Germany 82–5
TsSu SSSR 140, 142, 143, 144
Turkey 337, 339

UN (United Nations):
  and legislation for women 50–1
  UNESCO 112
  UNICEF (1987) 337, 340 n.
  World Survey on the Role of Women in Development (1989) 337
UN (United Nations)/ECE (Economic Commission for Europe) 271
unemployment 230–2, 231, 320–4, 356
  benefit payments 238
  Bulgaria 101, 101–3, *101*, 104, 226
  Czechoslovakia 223–4, 231, *249*, *250–1*, 251–2, 272
  East Germany 7, 355
  Eastern Europe 223–6, 230–2, 238, 341
  Hungary 223, 224, 231, 232, 283–4, 341, 356
  Poland 223, 224–5, *225*, 232, 238, 320–4, *321*, *322*, *324*
  Slovak Republic *249*, *250*, *251*, 252, 272–3
  Western Europe *227*
United Nations (1989) 337
USA (United States of America) 354
  Council of Economic Advisors (1991) 284, 293
  Department of Labor (1991) 23, 331 n.
  informal sector 331
  work satisfaction 197–207 *passim*
USSR, *see* Soviet Union

Von Mises, L. 353

wages, *see* earnings
Waigel, K. (German Finance Minister) 65
Wallerstein, I. 327
Warsaw 119, 122, 126 n., 127 n., 130, *130*, 309
  secondary students *130*
Weil, G. 11–12
welfare, women's *282*

welfare states 75
West Germany:
  abortion 77, 89
  child-care 78
  and East Germany 75–90, *81*
  egalitarianism 77
  maternity leave 77
Western Europe:
  education *112*
  unemployment *227*
WID (woman-in-development) 1, 2, 339
WIDER (World Institute for Development Economics Research) 1, 337, 340
WIN News (1991) 331 n.
Wolchik, S. L. 5–7
'woman question':
  'double burden' 189–90
  and employment 182
  and feminism 174–7
  former Soviet Union 171–7
  glasnost and 180–96
'Women at Work and in Management' poll (1989) 181, 182–3, 184, 186, 188–9, 189, *189*, 194–5
'Women in the Family' poll (1989) 185, 186, 190–1, 192, 193–4
women's movements and groups, *see* organizations and movements
work:
  attitudes to 240–1
  conditions 261–2
  cross-gender interaction at 202–6
  and family 146–50
  flexible hours 240–1
  importance of, to women 182–5
  quality 206–9
  satisfaction and commitment 197–212
  segregation at 53
workers and employees 197–8, 354
  Albania *219*
  Bulgaria 97–100, *97*, *219*, *220–1*
  commitment of 197–212
  Czechoslovakia *220–1*, 222, 223, 253–68, *253–76*, *254*, *255*, *256*, *257*
  East Germany 78, *83*
  Eastern Europe 218–30, *219*, *220–1*, 222, 235–6, 237
  and economic reform 9–13
  education of *98*
  and the family 146–9
  government programmes recommended regarding 242–3
  Hungary 9, 218, *219*, *220–1*, 222, *222*, 223, 235–7
  men *142*, 198–200
  participation rates, Europe *219*

workers and employees (*cont.*):
  Poland *219, 220–1*, 222, *222*, 223, 237,
    306–9, *307*, 308–13; regional
    variations 309–10, *310, 311*,
    312–13
  protective legislation removed 242
  real and perceived costs 235–6
  satisfaction of 197–212
  Soviet Union 138–53, *140, 142*, 167–8,
    195–6, 197, 199
workers and employees, female:
  Bulgaria *103*
  compared with men 198–200
  Czechoslovakia *254, 255*
  demand for 230–7
  Poland 308–9
  supply 237–41
  see also division of labour; earnings;

'Labour Activity of Women'
  poll
World Bank 244, 336, 337, 338, 341
world-system 334

Yeltsin, B. 21, 155
Yugoslavia:
  earnings 227, *228, 229*
  education *112, 234*
  flexible hours 241
  job losses 231
  unemployment 223, 225
  workers and employees 218, *219, 220–1*,
    222, 223

Zaborowski, W. 113 n.
Zakharova, N. K. 177
Zhivkov, T. 93